Releasing this volume at the same time as the data book was pretty rough. I'm hoping it'll make it more interesting if you read them both together. Here's *World Trigger* volume 14.

—Daisuke Ashihara, 2016

Daisuke Ashihara began his manga career at the age of 27 when his manga *Room 303* won second place in the 75th Tezuka Awards. His first series, *Super Dog Rilienthal*, began serialization in *Weekly Shonen Jump* in 2009. *World Trigger* is his second serialized work in *Weekly Shonen Jump*. He is also the author of several shorter works, including the one-shots *Super Dog Rilienthal*, *Trigger Keeper* and *Elite Agent Jin*.

WORLD TRIGGER VOL. 14
SHONEN JUMP Manga Edition

STORY AND ART BY DAISUKE ASHIHARA

Translation/Lillian Olsen
Touch-Up Art & Lettering/Annaliese Christman
Design/Sam Elzway
Editor/Marlene First

WORLD TRIGGER © 2013 by Daisuke Ashihara/SHUEISHA Inc.
All rights reserved.
First published in Japan in 2013 by SHUEISHA Inc., Tokyo.
English translation rights arranged by SHUEISHA Inc.

The stories, characters and incidents mentioned
in this publication are entirely fictional.

Printed in the U.S.A.

Published by VIZ Media, LLC
P.O. Box 77010
San Francisco, CA 94107

10 9 8 7 6 5 4 3 2 1
First printing, January 2017

www.viz.com

RATED
FOR TEEN

PARENTAL ADVISORY
WORLD TRIGGER is rated T for Teen and is
recommended for ages 13 and up. This volume
contains fantasy violence.
ratings.viz.com

THE WORLD'S MOST POPULAR MANGA
SHONEN JUMP
www.shonenjump.com

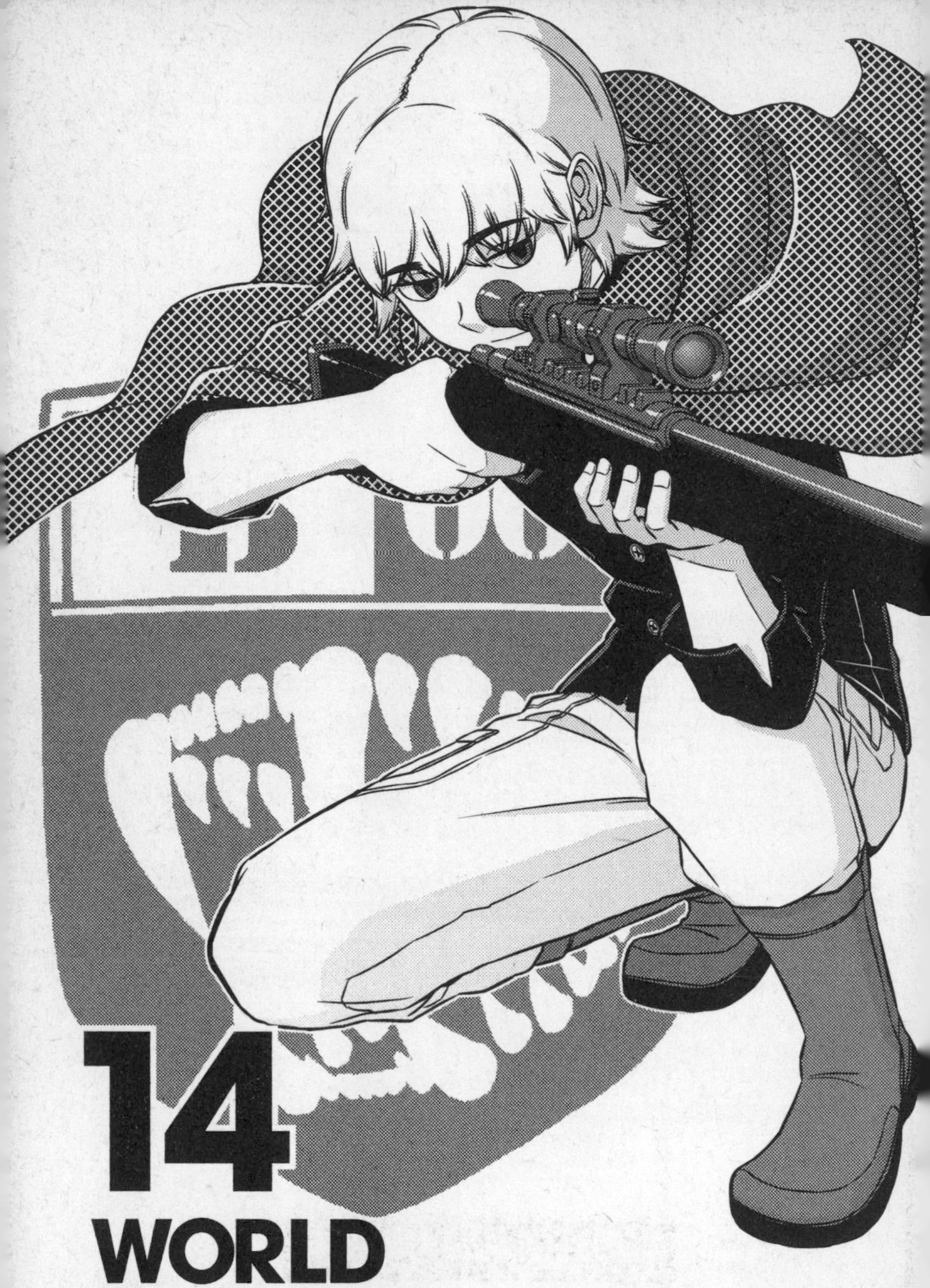

14

WORLD TRIGGER

DAISUKE ASHIHARA

SHONEN JUMP MANGA EDITION

WORLD TRIGGER DATA BASE

BORDER

An agency founded to protect the city's peace from Neighbors.

S-Rank Black Trigger Users (i.e. Tsukihiko Amo)

A-Rank (Elite) — Away teams selected from here (Arashiyama, Miwa squads)

Promoted in Rank Wars

B-Rank (Main force) — Agents on defense duty must be at least B-Rank (Tamakoma-2)

Promoted at 4,000 solo points

C-Rank (Trainees) — Use trainee Triggers only in emergencies (Izuho Natsume)

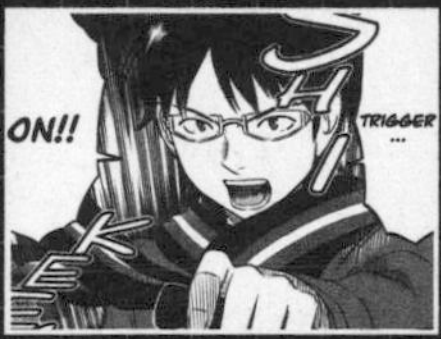
TRIGGER...
ON!!

TRIGGER

A technology created by Neighbors to manipulate Trion. Used mainly as weapons, Triggers come in various types.

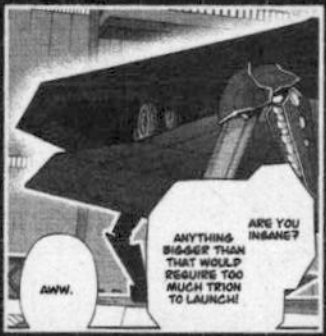
ARE YOU INSANE?
ANYTHING BIGGER THAN THAT WOULD REQUIRE TOO MUCH TRION TO LAUNCH!
AWW.

◀ Away mission ships also run on Trion.

POSITIONS

Border classifies them into three groups: Attacker, Gunner and Sniper.

Attacker

Close-range attacks. Weapons include: close-range Scorpions that are good for surprise attacks, the balanced Kogetsu sword, and the defense-heavy Raygust.

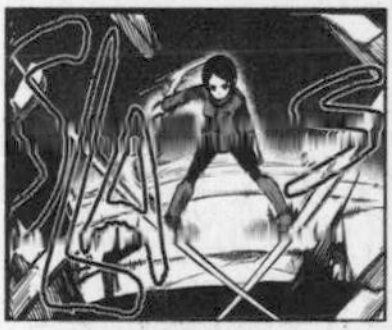

Gunner

Shoots from mid-range. There are several types of bullets, including multipurpose Asteroids, twisting Vipers, exploding Meteors, and tracking Hounds. People who don't use gun-shaped Triggers are called Shooters.

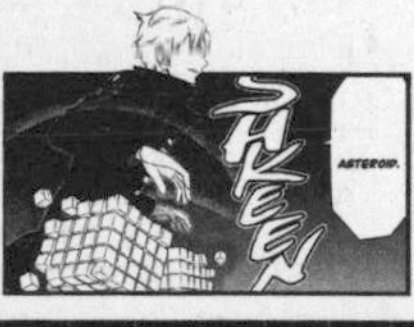
ASTEROID.

◀ Osamu and Izumi are Shooters.

Sniper

Fires from a long distance. There are three sniping rifles: the well-balanced Egret, the light and easy Lightning, and the powerful but unwieldy Ibis.

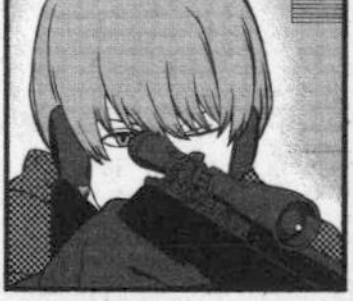

Operator

Supports combatants by relaying information such as enemy positions and abilities.

RANK WARS

Practice matches between Border agents. Promotions in Border are based on good results in the Rank Wars and defense duty achievements.

A-Rank

Top two B-Rank squads get to challenge A-Rank.

B-Rank

B-Rank agents are split into top, middle, and bottom groups. Three to four teams fight in a melee battle. Defeating an opposing squad member earns you one point and surviving to the end nets two points. Top teams from the previous season get a bonus.

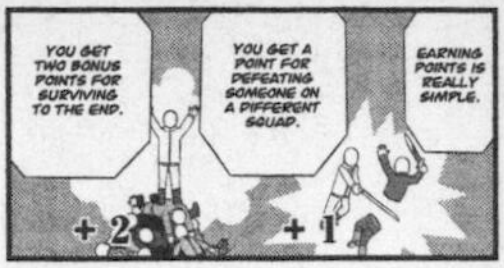

EARNING POINTS IS REALLY SIMPLE.
YOU GET A POINT FOR DEFEATING SOMEONE ON A DIFFERENT SQUAD.
YOU GET TWO BONUS POINTS FOR SURVIVING TO THE END.
+2
+1

B-Rank middle groups have set strategies. Top groups all have an A-Rank level ace.

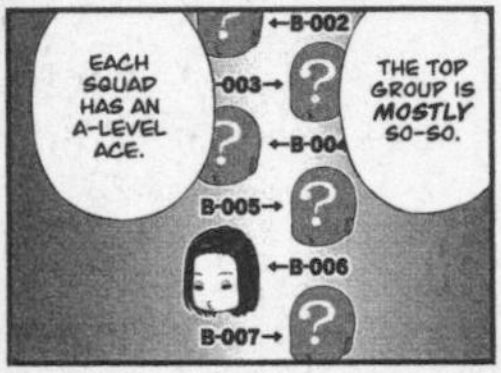

THE TOP GROUP IS MOSTLY SO-SO.
EACH SQUAD HAS AN A-LEVEL ACE.
B-002
003
B-004
B-005
B-006
B-007

The lowest-ranked team in each match gets to pick the stage.

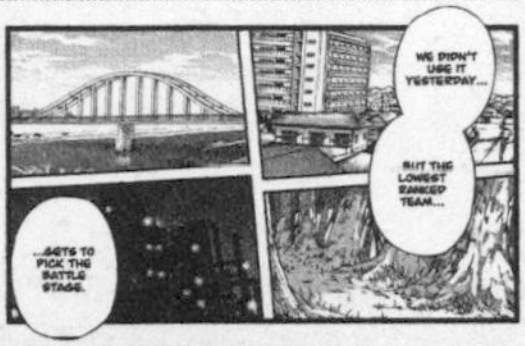

WE DIDN'T USE IT YESTERDAY...
BUT THE LOWEST RANKED TEAM...
...GETS TO PICK THE BATTLE STAGE.

C-Rank

Agents (B-Rank and above) can't fight trainees (C-Rank) for points.

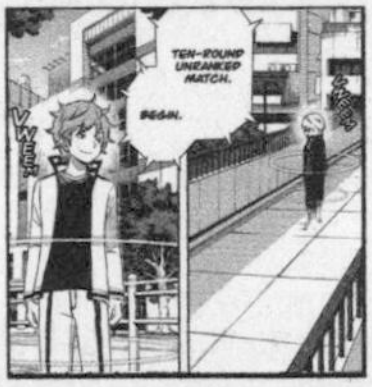

TEN-ROUND UNRANKED MATCH.
BEGIN.

C-Rank Wars are fought through solo matches. Beating someone with more points than you gets you a lot of points. On the other hand, beating someone with fewer points doesn't get you as many.

STORY

About four years ago, a Gate connecting to another dimension opened in Mikado City, leading to the appearance of invaders called Neighbors. After the establishment of the Border Defence Agency, people were able to return to their normal lives.

Osamu Mikumo is a junior high student who meets Yuma Kuga, a Neighbor. Yuma is targeted for capture by Border, but Tamakoma branch agent Yuichi Jin steps in to help. He convinces Yuma to join Border instead, then gives his Black Trigger to HQ in exchange for Yuma's enlistment. Now Osamu, Yuma and Osamu's friend Chika work towards making A-Rank together.

Aftokrator, the largest military nation in the Neighborhood, begins another large-scale invasion!! Border succeeds in driving them back, but over thirty C-Rank trainees are kidnapped in the process. Border implements more plans for away missions to retrieve the missing Agents.

Osamu's squad, Tamakoma-2, enters the Rank Wars for a chance to be chosen for away missions. They win a fierce battle in the third round against Suzunari-1 and Nasu Squads, but Osamu becomes painfully aware of his lack of skill. Before the fourth match against the top B-Rank squads, Ninomiya and Kageura squads, he goes to consult with A-Rank Shooter specialists. In the actual match, he is taken out early on by Azuma and his squad loses. For his next move to improve his squad's dynamic, he asks Jin to join Tamakoma-2!

WORLD TRIGGER CHARACTERS

TAMAKOMA BRANCH

Understanding toward Neighbors. Considered divergent from Border's main philosophy.

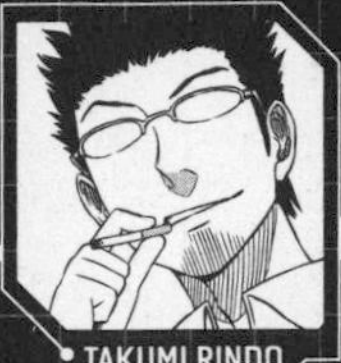

TAKUMI RINDO

Tamakoma Branch Director.

TAMAKOMA-2

Tamakoma's B-Rank squad, aiming to get promoted to A-Rank.

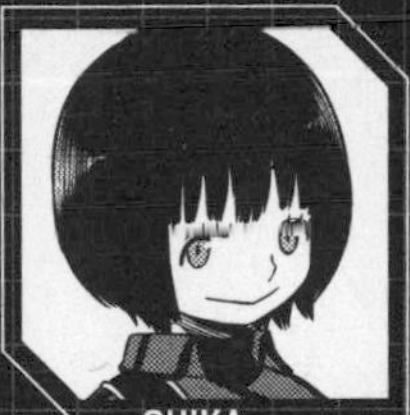

CHIKA AMATORI

Osamu's childhood friend. She has high Trion levels.

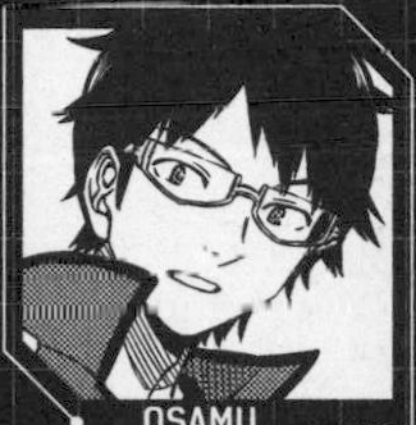

OSAMU MIKUMO

Ninth-grader who's compelled to help those in trouble. Captain of Tamakoma-2 (Mikumo squad).

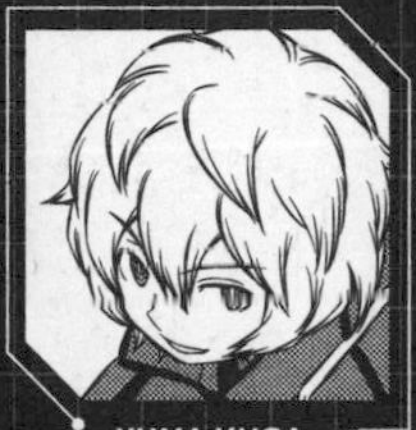

YUMA KUGA

A Neighbor who carries a Black Trigger.

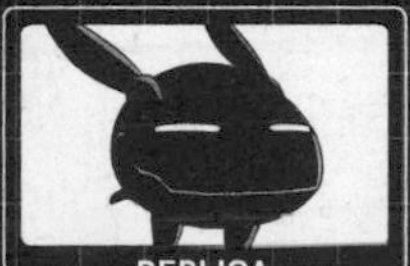

REPLICA

Yuma's chaperone. Missing after recent invasion.

TAMAKOMA-1

Tamakoma's A-Rank squad.

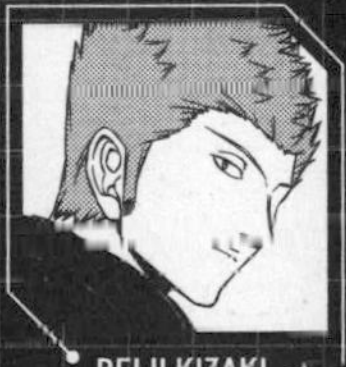

REIJI KIZAKI

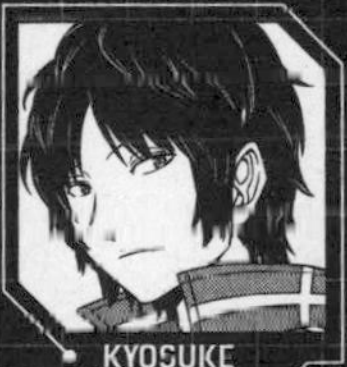

KYOSUKE KARASUMA

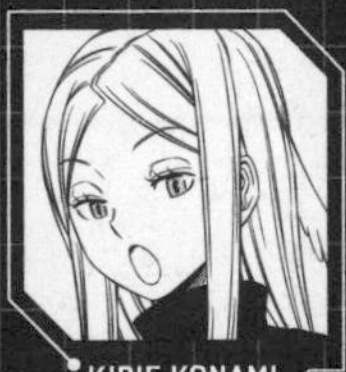

KIRIE KONAMI

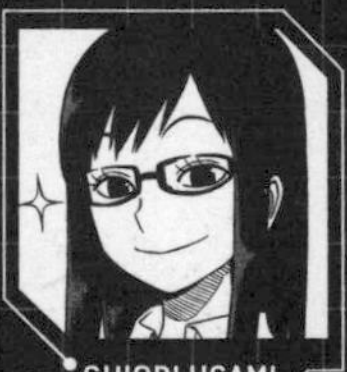

SHIORI USAMI

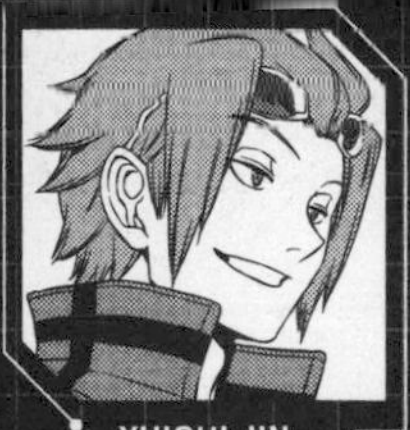

YUICHI JIN

Former S-Rank Black Trigger user. His Side Effect lets him see the future.

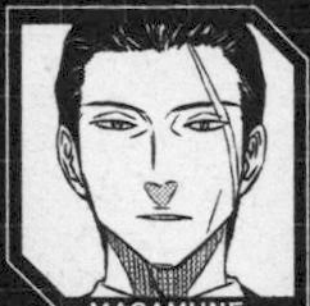

MASAMUNE KIDO

HQ Commander

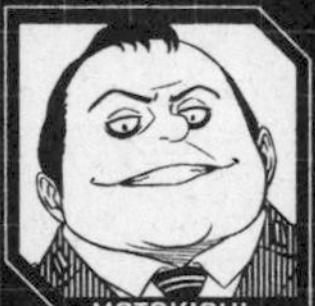

MOTOKICHI KINUTA

R&D Director

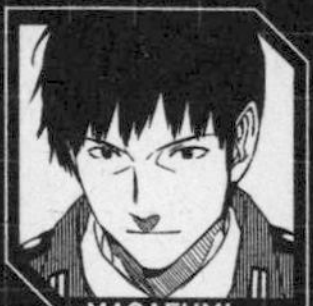

MASAFUMI SHINODA

HQ Director and Defense commander.

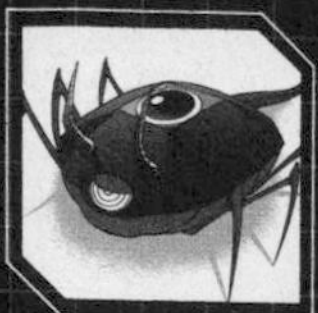

ENEDORA

Neighbor from Aftokrator killed during the invasion. Only his personality remains.

A-RANK AGENTS

ARASHIYAMA SQUAD

Border HQ A-Rank #5 squad.

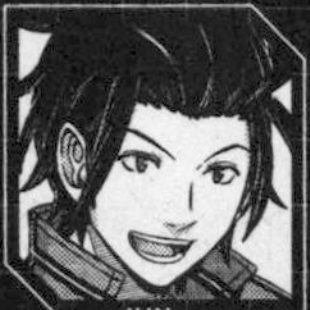

JUN ARASHIYAMA

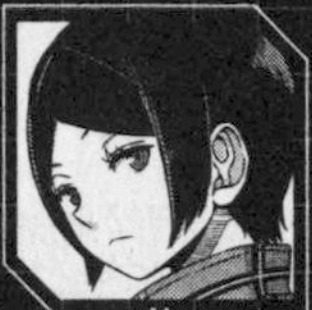

AI KITORA

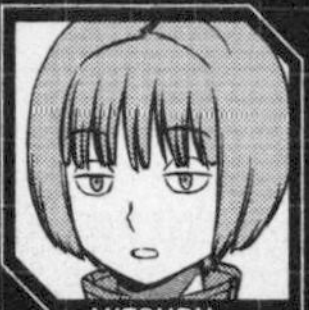

MITSURU TOKIEDA

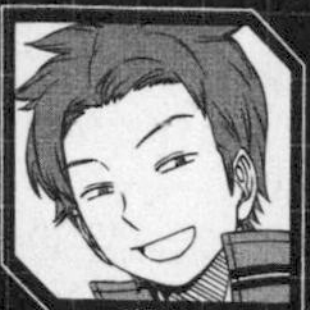

KEN SATORI

TACHIKAWA SQUAD

Border HQ A-Rank #1 squad.

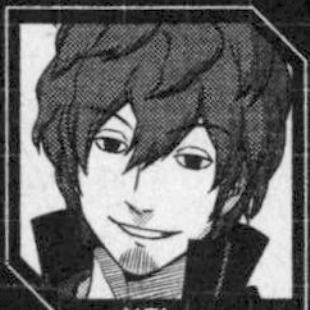

KEI TACHIKAWA

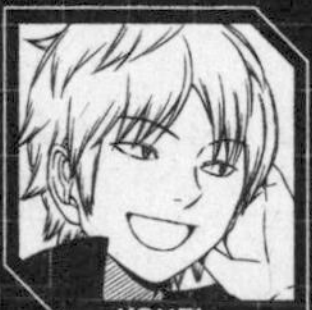

KOHEI IZUMI

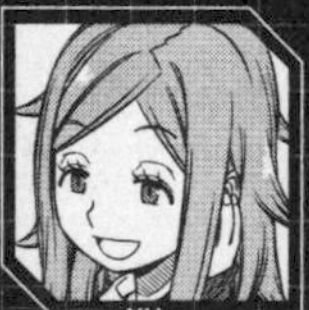

YU KUNICHIKA

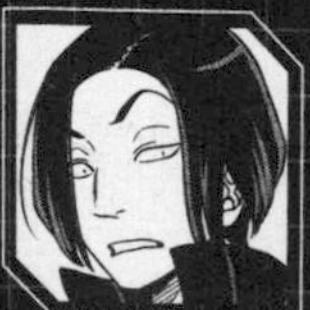

MASATAKA NINOMIYA

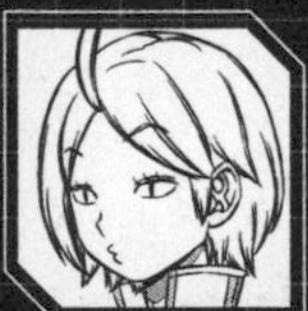

IZUHO NATSUME

Rookie Sniper and Chika's friend.

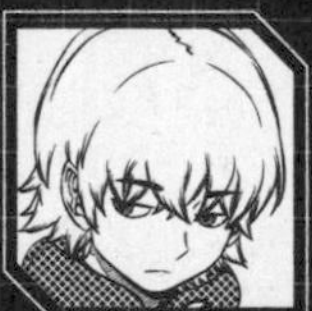

YUZURU EMA

B-Rank # 2 Kageura squad Sniper.

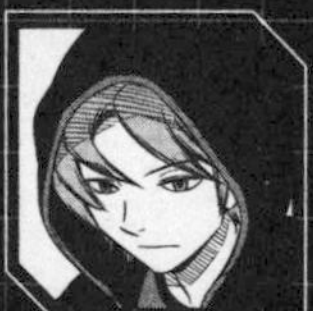

HYUSE

Neighbor from Aftokrator left behind in the invasion.

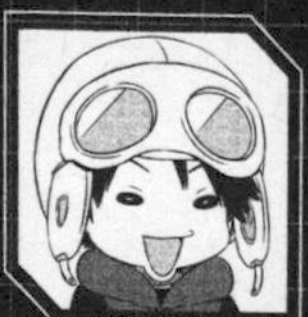

YOTARO RINDO

Tamakoma Branch kid.

WORLD TRIGGER
CONTENTS

Chapter 116: Yuichi Jin: Part 9 ● 9

Chapter 117: Yotaro Rindo ● 29

Chapter 118: Chika Amatori: Part 5 ● 49

Chapter 119: Aftokrator: Part 5 ● 69

Chapter 120: Aftokrator: Part 6 ● 89

Chapter 121: Galopoula ● 109

Chapter 122: Ai Kitora: Part 5 ● 129

Chapter 123: Galopoula: Part 2 ● 149

Chapter 124: Galopoula: Part 3 ● 169

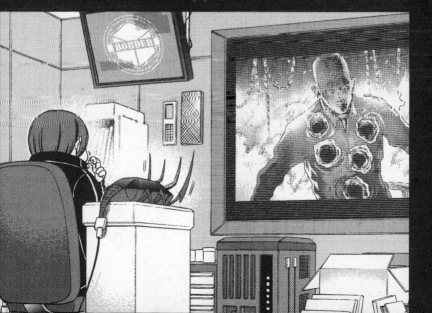

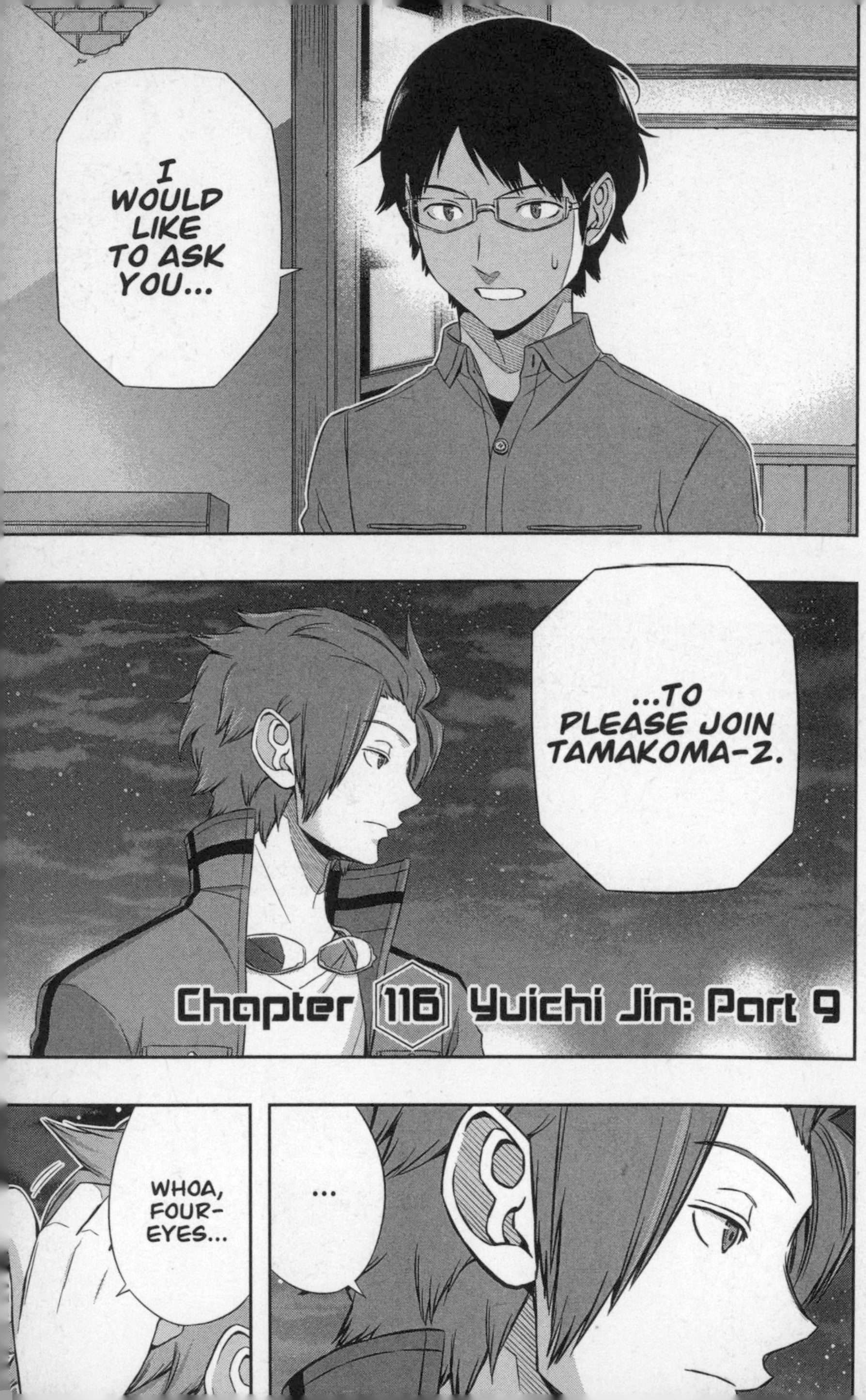
I WOULD LIKE TO ASK YOU...
...TO PLEASE JOIN TAMAKOMA-2.
Chapter 116 Yuichi Jin: Part 9
...
WHOA, FOUR-EYES...

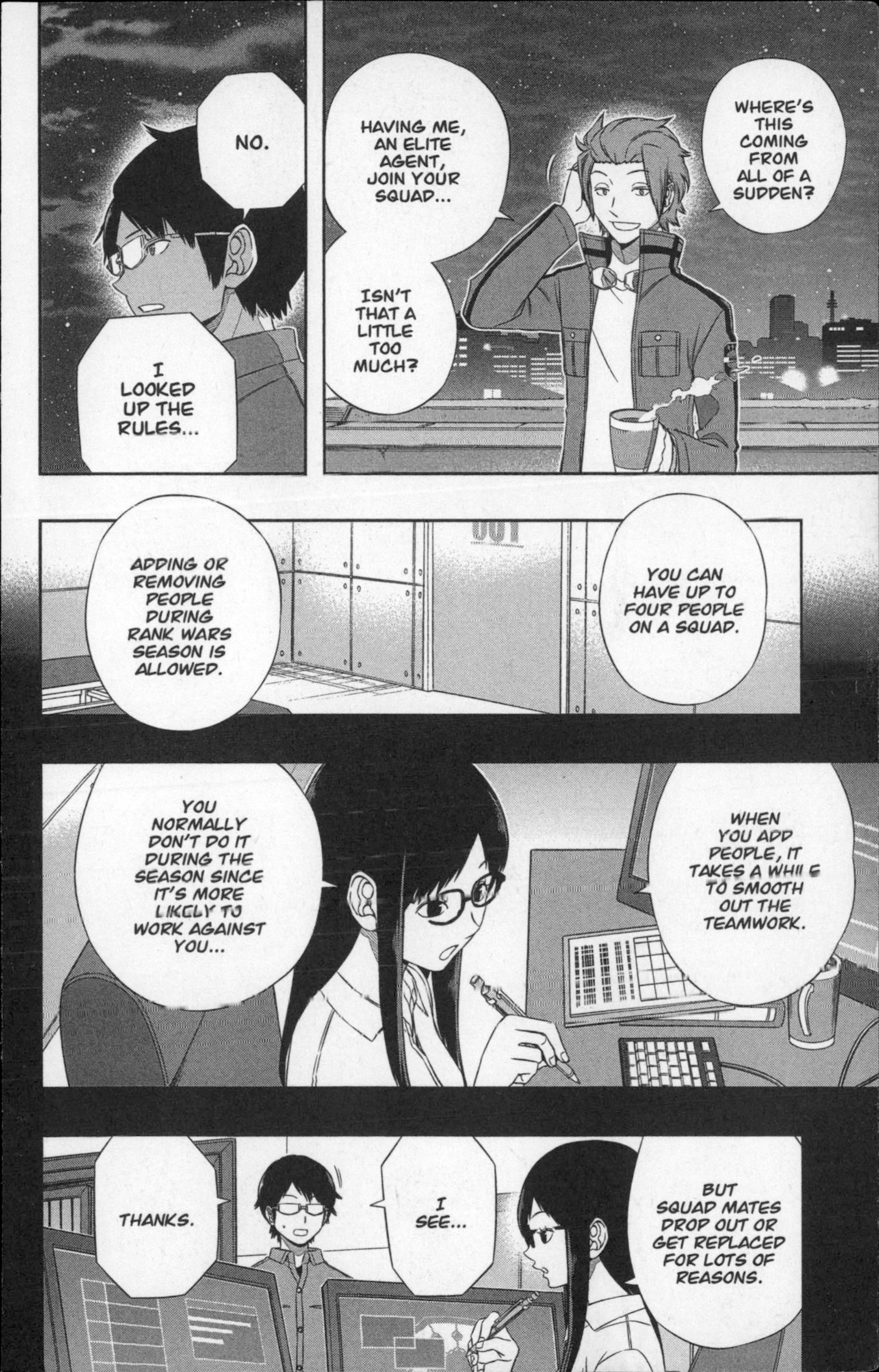
WHERE'S THIS COMING FROM ALL OF A SUDDEN?
HAVING ME, AN ELITE AGENT, JOIN YOUR SQUAD...
ISN'T THAT A LITTLE TOO MUCH?
NO.
I LOOKED UP THE RULES...
YOU CAN HAVE UP TO FOUR PEOPLE ON A SQUAD.
ADDING OR REMOVING PEOPLE DURING RANK WARS SEASON IS ALLOWED.
WHEN YOU ADD PEOPLE, IT TAKES A WHILE TO SMOOTH OUT THE TEAMWORK.
YOU NORMALLY DON'T DO IT DURING THE SEASON SINCE IT'S MORE LIKELY TO WORK AGAINST YOU...
BUT SQUAD MATES DROP OUT OR GET REPLACED FOR LOTS OF REASONS.
I SEE...
THANKS.

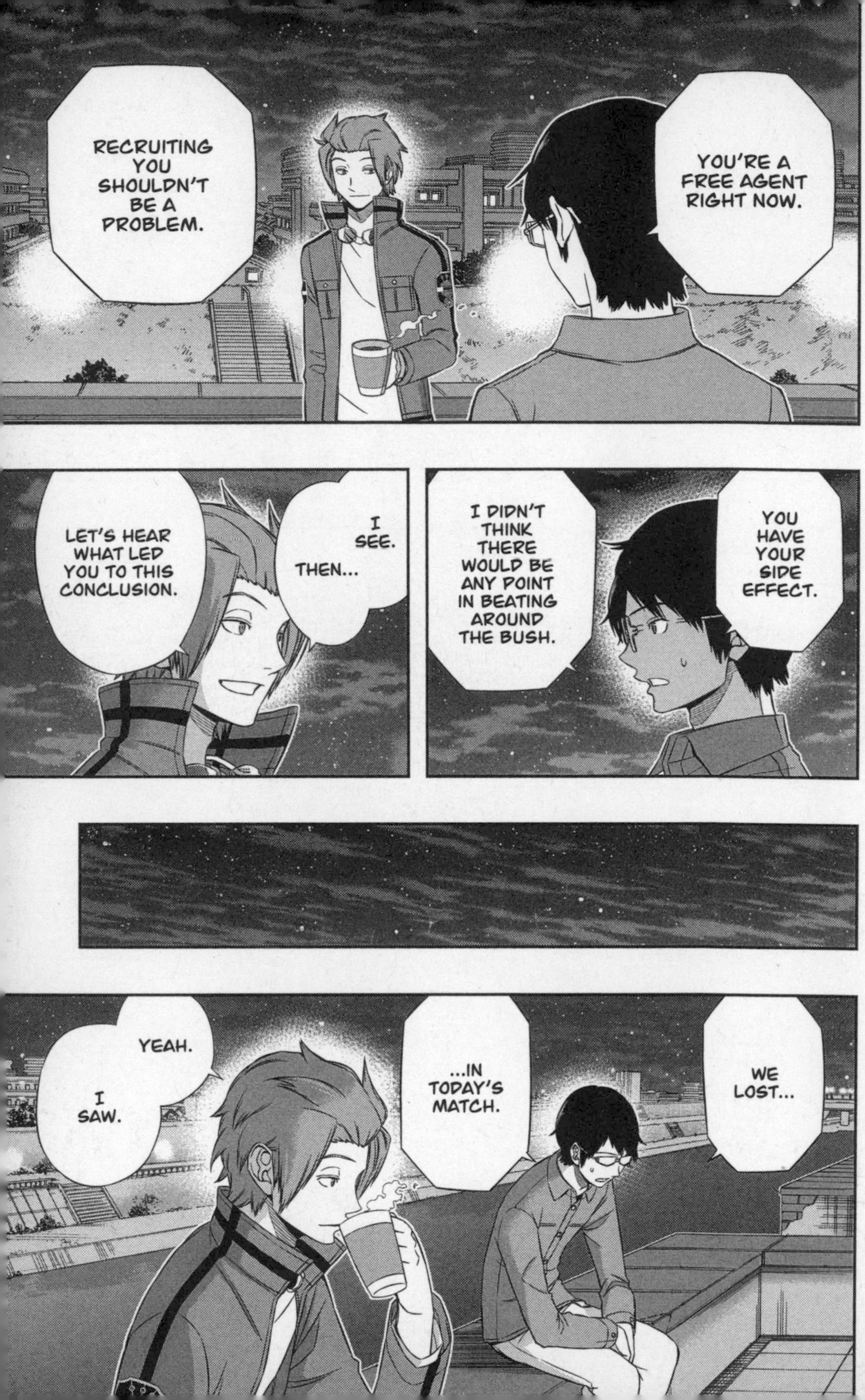
YOU'RE A FREE AGENT RIGHT NOW.
RECRUITING YOU SHOULDN'T BE A PROBLEM.
YOU HAVE YOUR SIDE EFFECT.
I DIDN'T THINK THERE WOULD BE ANY POINT IN BEATING AROUND THE BUSH.
I SEE. THEN...
LET'S HEAR WHAT LED YOU TO THIS CONCLUSION.
WE LOST...
...IN TODAY'S MATCH.
YEAH. I SAW.

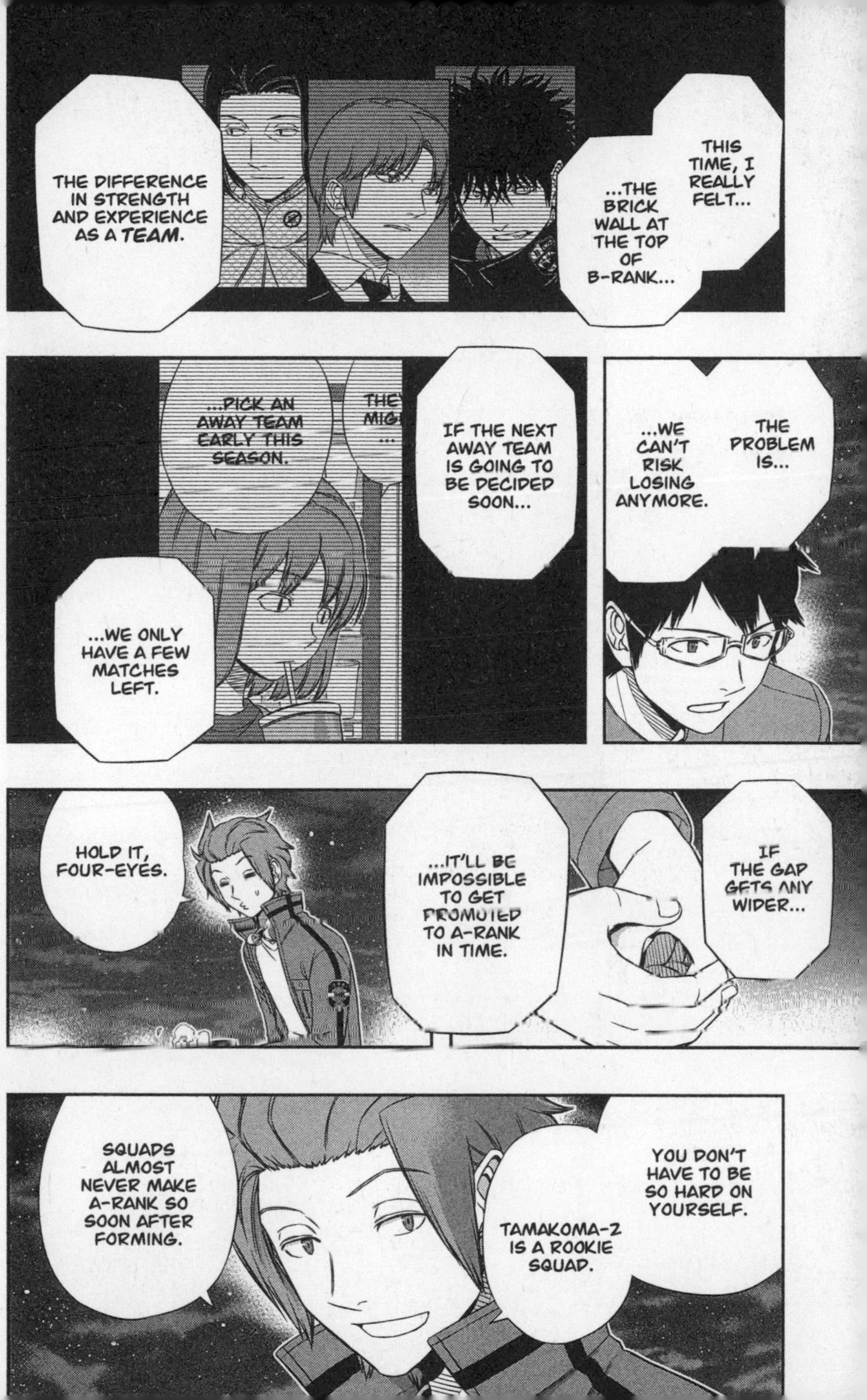
THIS TIME, I REALLY FELT...
...THE BRICK WALL AT THE TOP OF B-RANK...
THE DIFFERENCE IN STRENGTH AND EXPERIENCE AS A *TEAM*.
THE PROBLEM IS...
...WE CAN'T RISK LOSING ANYMORE.
IF THE NEXT AWAY TEAM IS GOING TO BE DECIDED SOON...
...PICK AN AWAY TEAM EARLY THIS SEASON.
...WE ONLY HAVE A FEW MATCHES LEFT.
IF THE GAP GETS ANY WIDER...
...IT'LL BE IMPOSSIBLE TO GET PROMOTED TO A-RANK IN TIME.
HOLD IT, FOUR-EYES.
YOU DON'T HAVE TO BE SO HARD ON YOURSELF.
TAMAKOMA-2 IS A ROOKIE SQUAD.
SQUADS ALMOST NEVER MAKE A-RANK SO SOON AFTER FORMING.

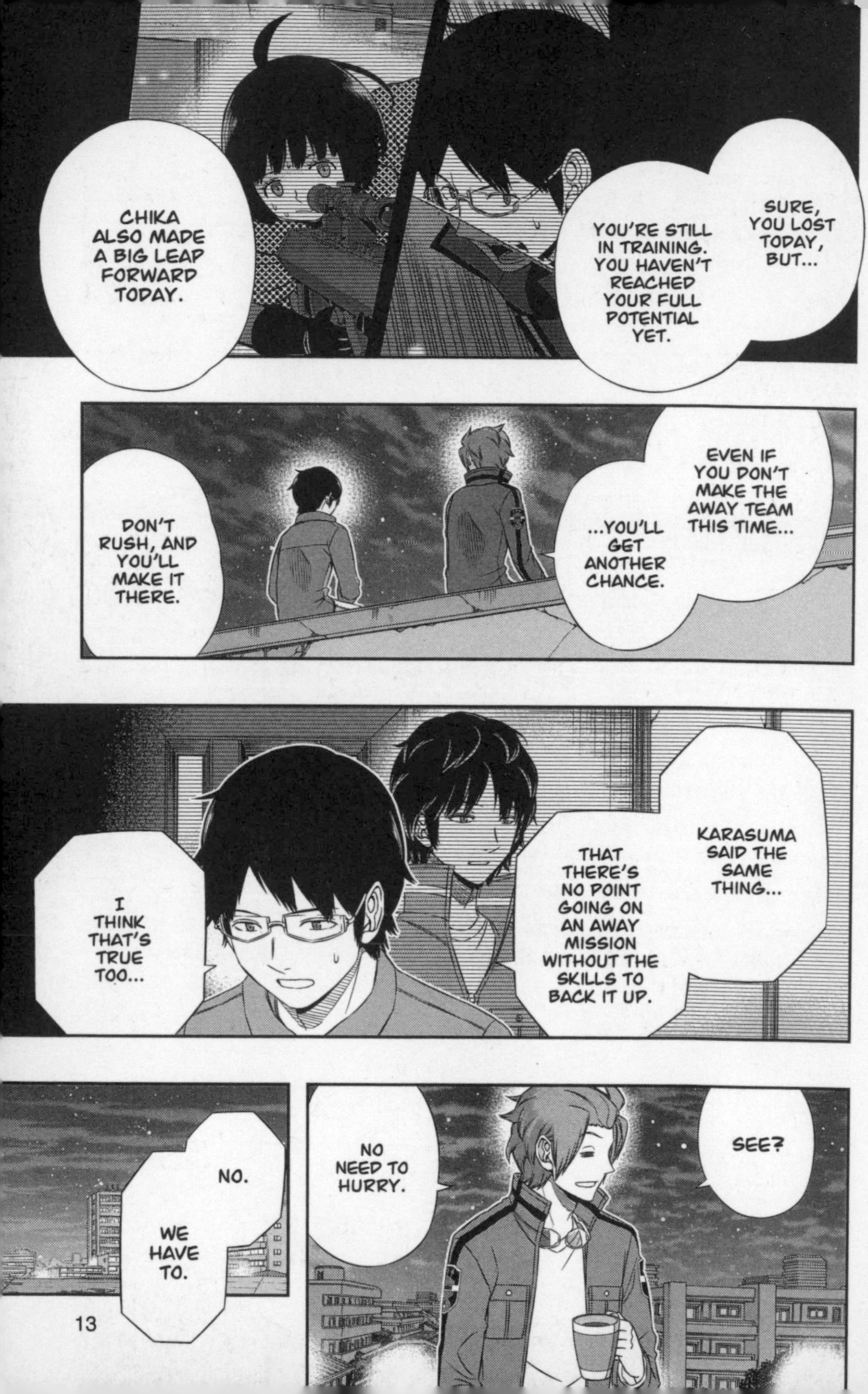
SURE, YOU LOST TODAY, BUT...
YOU'RE STILL IN TRAINING. YOU HAVEN'T REACHED YOUR FULL POTENTIAL YET.
CHIKA ALSO MADE A BIG LEAP FORWARD TODAY.
EVEN IF YOU DON'T MAKE THE AWAY TEAM THIS TIME...
...YOU'LL GET ANOTHER CHANCE.
DON'T RUSH, AND YOU'LL MAKE IT THERE.
KARASUMA SAID THE SAME THING...
THAT THERE'S NO POINT GOING ON AN AWAY MISSION WITHOUT THE SKILLS TO BACK IT UP.
I THINK THAT'S TRUE TOO...
SEE?
NO NEED TO HURRY.
NO.
WE HAVE TO.

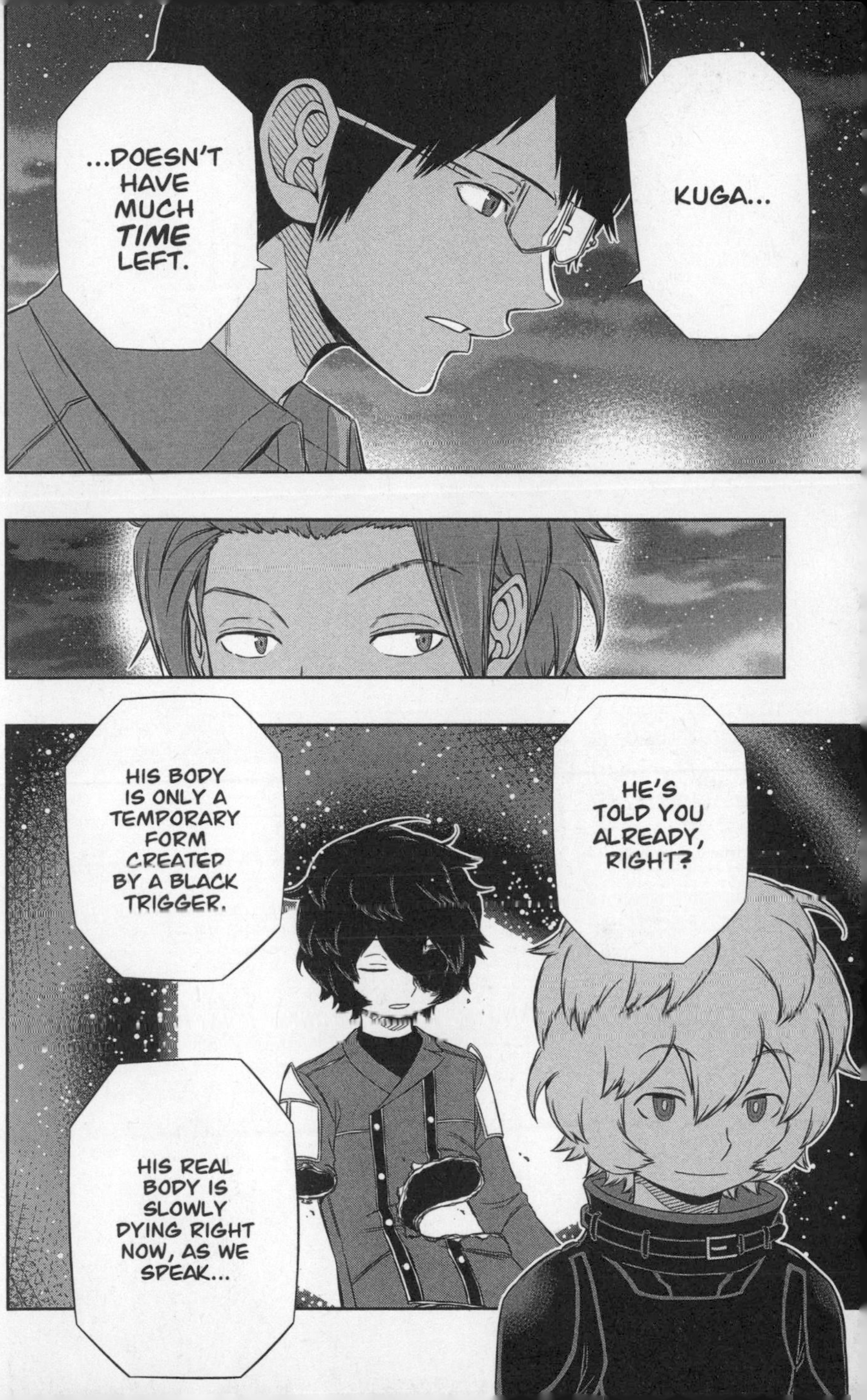
KUGA...
...DOESN'T HAVE MUCH TIME LEFT.
HE'S TOLD YOU ALREADY, RIGHT?
HIS BODY IS ONLY A TEMPORARY FORM CREATED BY A BLACK TRIGGER.
HIS REAL BODY IS SLOWLY DYING RIGHT NOW, AS WE SPEAK...

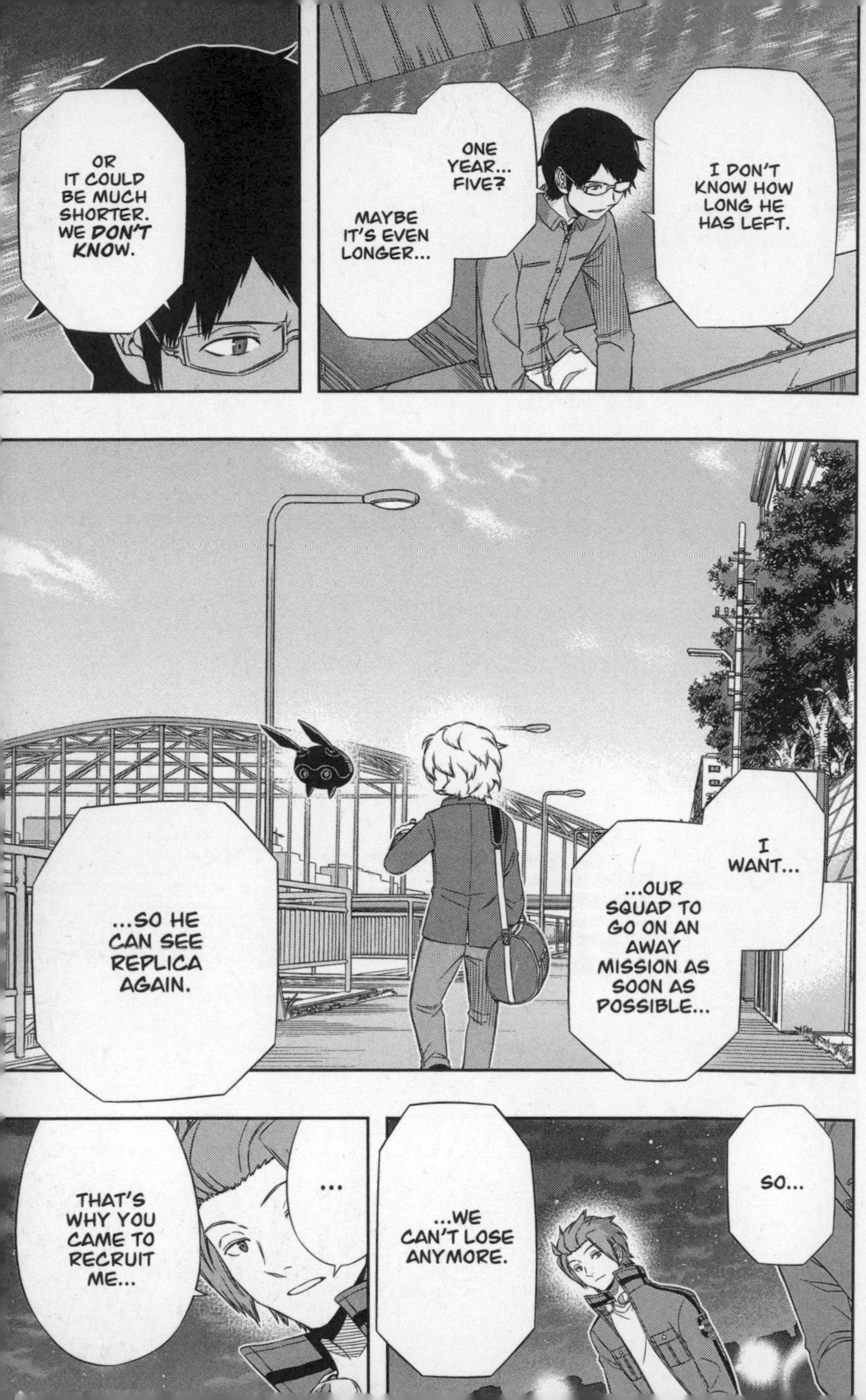
I DON'T KNOW HOW LONG HE HAS LEFT.
ONE YEAR... FIVE?
MAYBE IT'S EVEN LONGER...
OR IT COULD BE MUCH SHORTER. WE **DON'T KNOW**.
I WANT...
...OUR SQUAD TO GO ON AN AWAY MISSION AS SOON AS POSSIBLE...
...SO HE CAN SEE REPLICA AGAIN.
SO...
...WE CAN'T LOSE ANYMORE.
...
THAT'S WHY YOU CAME TO RECRUIT ME...

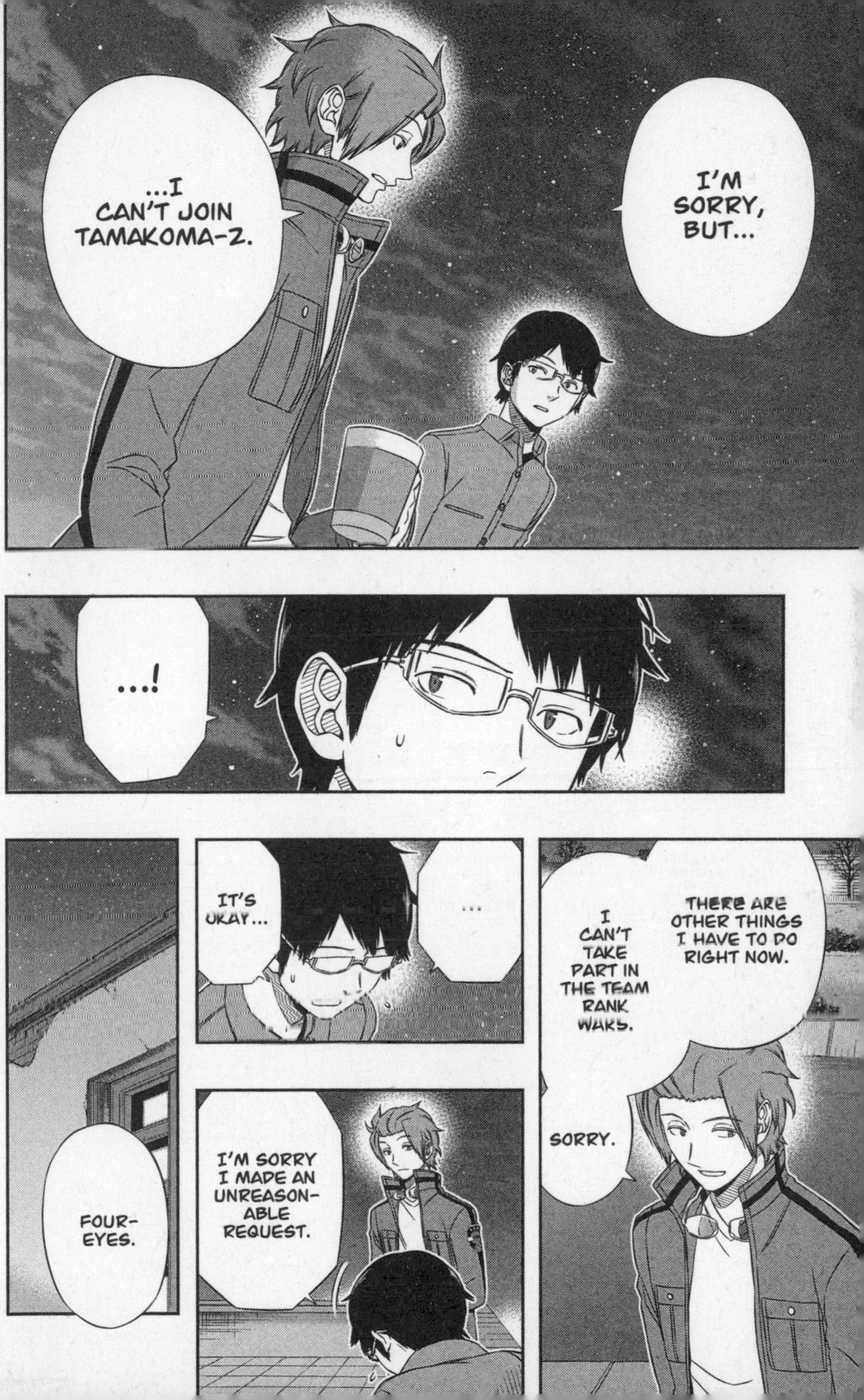
I'M SORRY, BUT...
...I CAN'T JOIN TAMAKOMA-2.
...!
THERE ARE OTHER THINGS I HAVE TO DO RIGHT NOW.
I CAN'T TAKE PART IN THE TEAM RANK WARS.
SORRY.
...
IT'S OKAY...
I'M SORRY I MADE AN UNREASON-ABLE REQUEST.
FOUR-EYES.

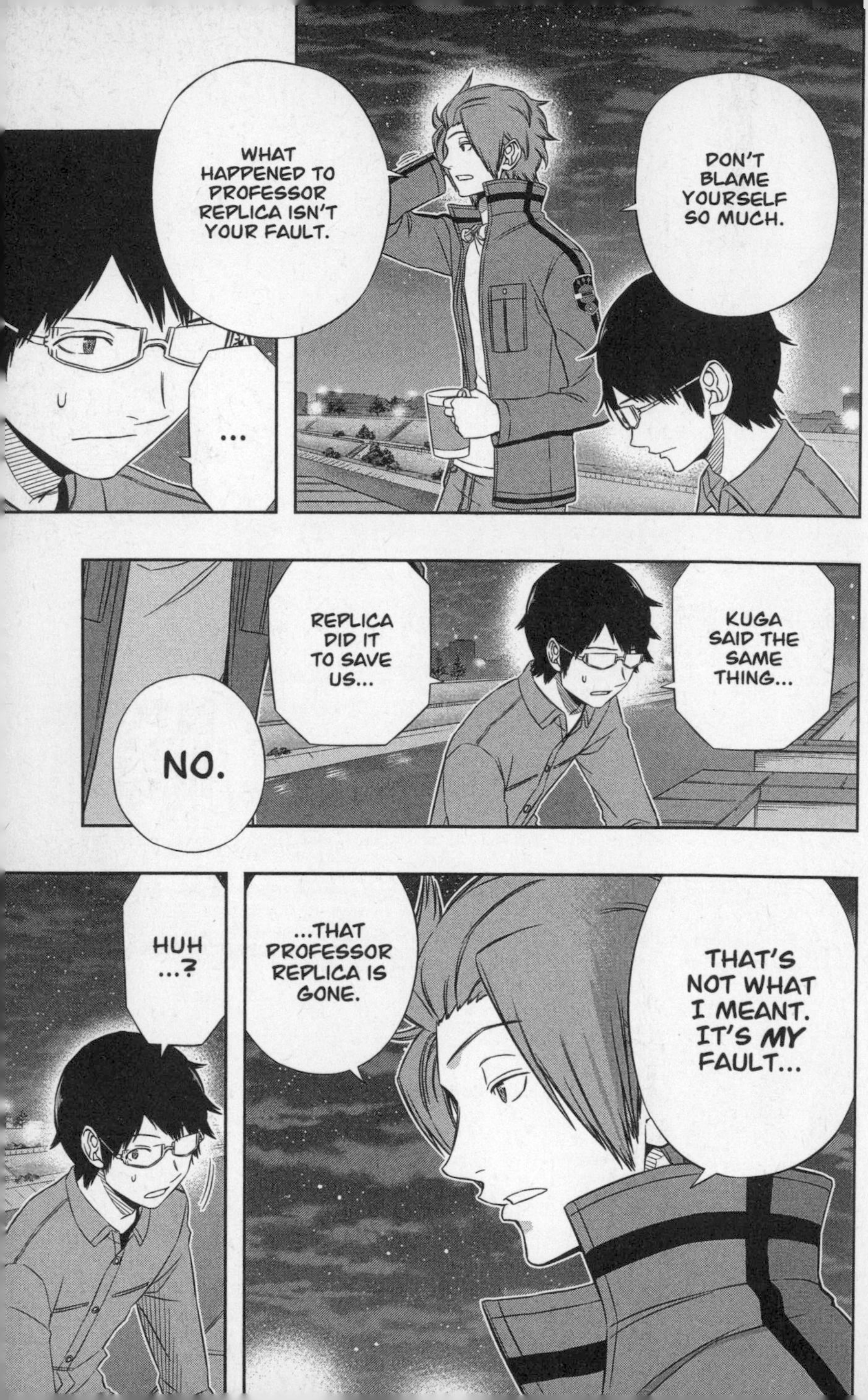
DON'T BLAME YOURSELF SO MUCH.
WHAT HAPPENED TO PROFESSOR REPLICA ISN'T YOUR FAULT.
...
KUGA SAID THE SAME THING...
REPLICA DID IT TO SAVE US...
NO.
THAT'S NOT WHAT I MEANT. IT'S *MY* FAULT...
...THAT PROFESSOR REPLICA IS GONE.
HUH ...?

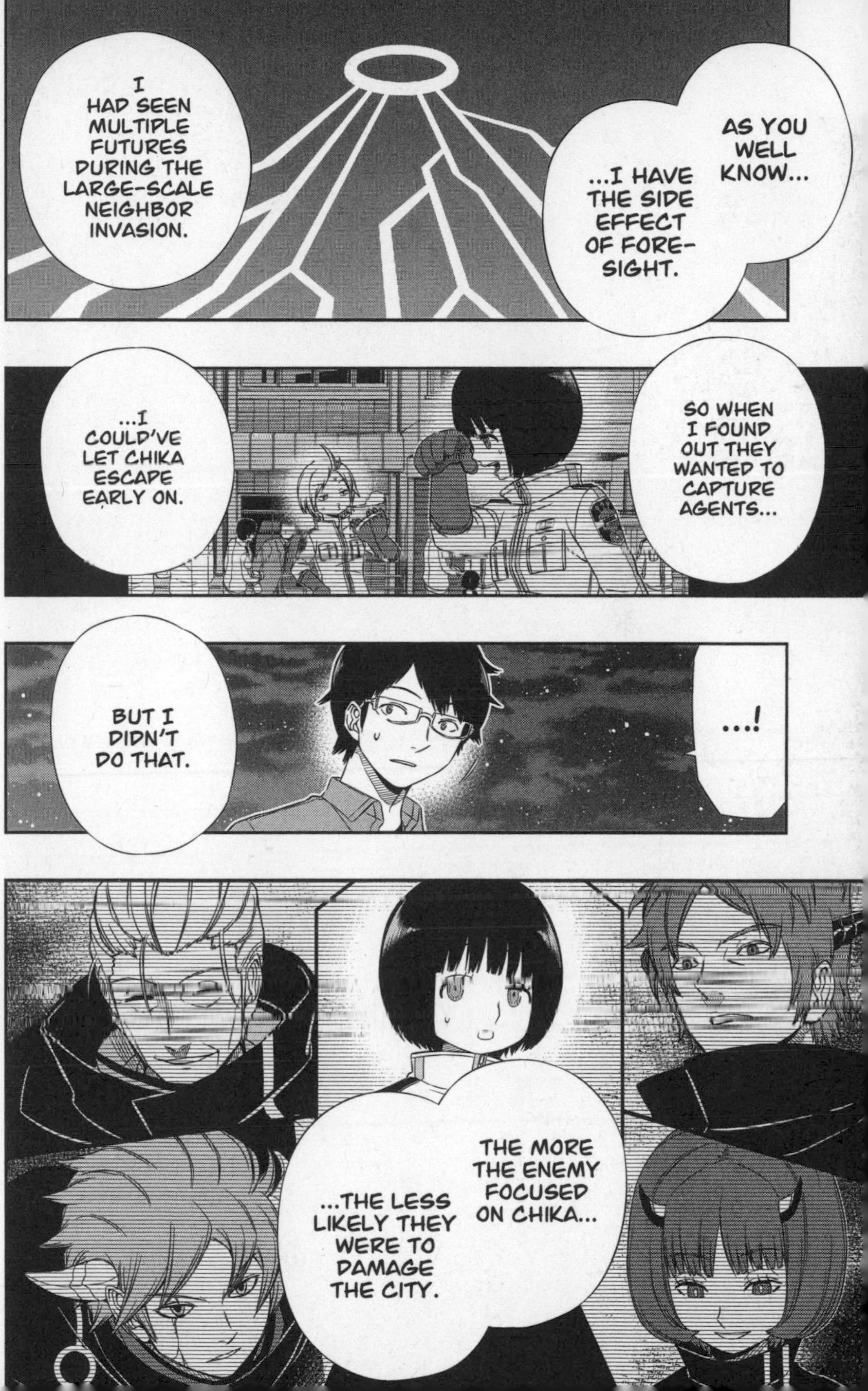
AS YOU WELL KNOW...
...I HAVE THE SIDE EFFECT OF FORE-SIGHT.
I HAD SEEN MULTIPLE FUTURES DURING THE LARGE-SCALE NEIGHBOR INVASION.
SO WHEN I FOUND OUT THEY WANTED TO CAPTURE AGENTS...
...I COULD'VE LET CHIKA ESCAPE EARLY ON.
...!
BUT I DIDN'T DO THAT.
THE MORE THE ENEMY FOCUSED ON CHIKA...
...THE LESS LIKELY THEY WERE TO DAMAGE THE CITY.

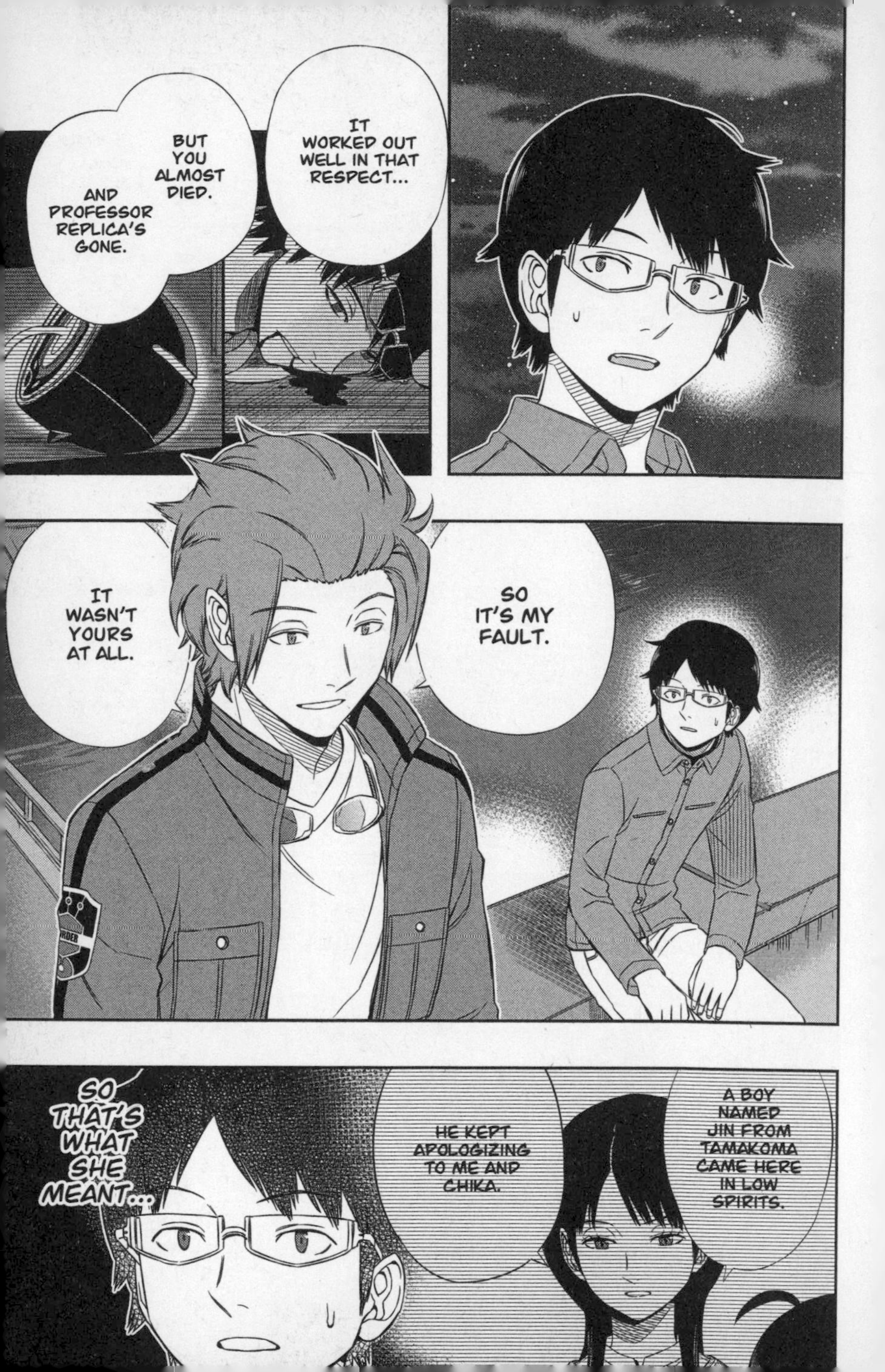
IT WORKED OUT WELL IN THAT RESPECT...
BUT YOU ALMOST DIED.
AND PROFESSOR REPLICA'S GONE.
SO IT'S MY FAULT.
IT WASN'T YOURS AT ALL.
A BOY NAMED JIN FROM TAMAKOMA CAME HERE IN LOW SPIRITS.
HE KEPT APOLOGIZING TO ME AND CHIKA.
SO THAT'S WHAT SHE MEANT...

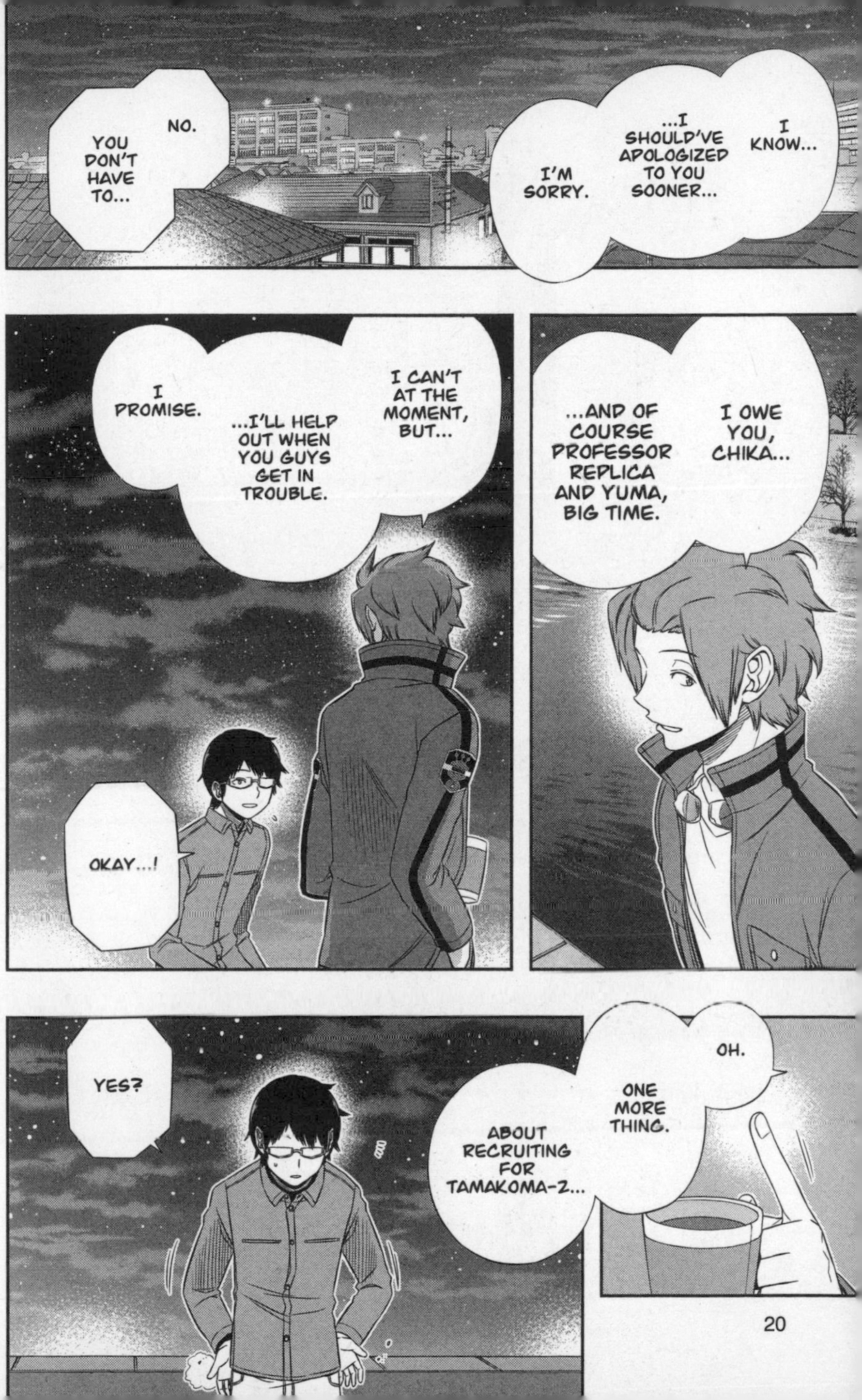
I KNOW...
...I SHOULD'VE APOLOGIZED TO YOU SOONER...
I'M SORRY.
NO.
YOU DON'T HAVE TO...
I OWE YOU, CHIKA...
...AND OF COURSE PROFESSOR REPLICA AND YUMA, BIG TIME.
I CAN'T AT THE MOMENT, BUT...
...I'LL HELP OUT WHEN YOU GUYS GET IN TROUBLE.
I PROMISE.
OKAY...!
OH.
ONE MORE THING.
ABOUT RECRUITING FOR TAMAKOMA-2...
YES?

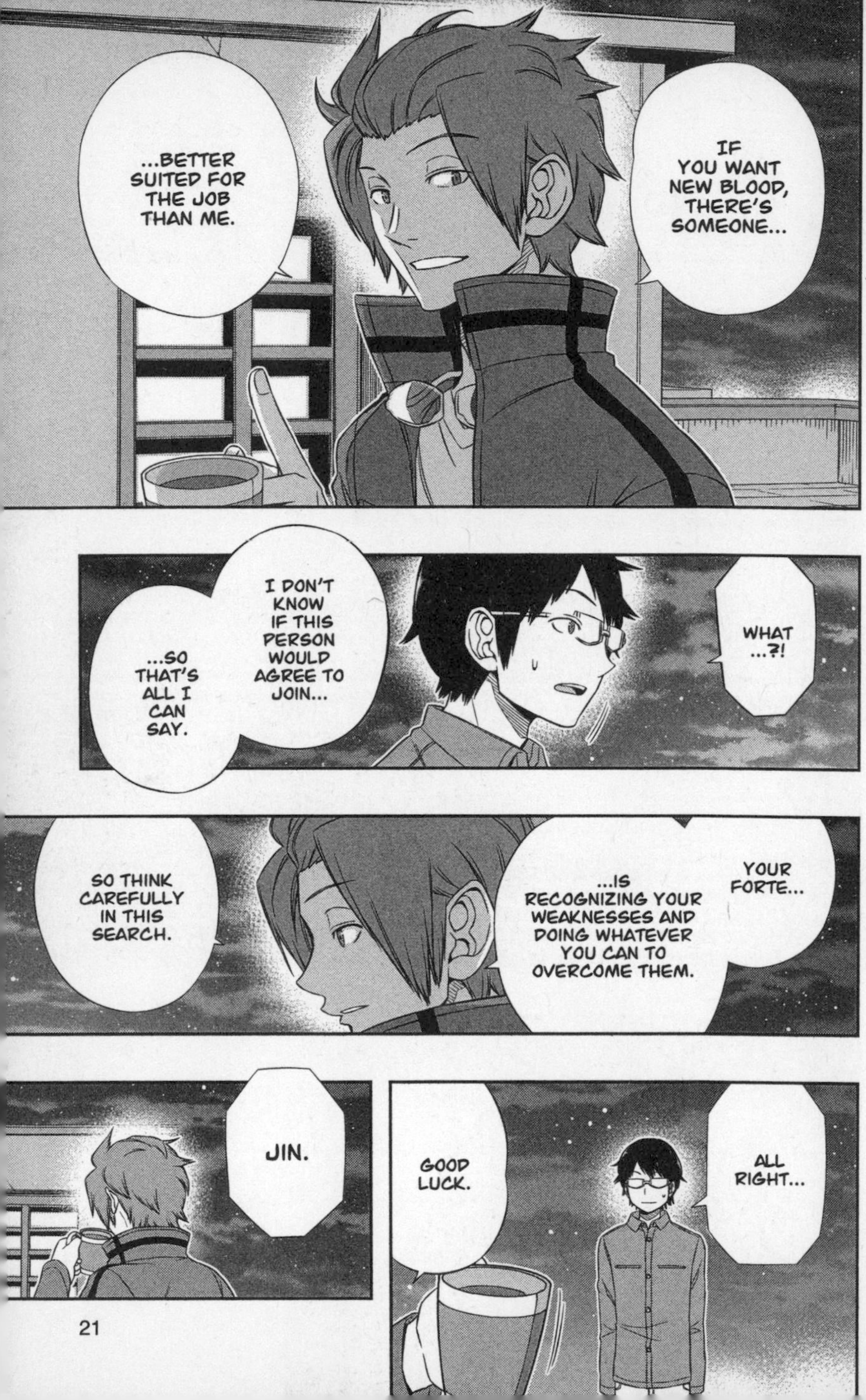
IF YOU WANT NEW BLOOD, THERE'S SOMEONE...
...BETTER SUITED FOR THE JOB THAN ME.
WHAT ...?!
I DON'T KNOW IF THIS PERSON WOULD AGREE TO JOIN...
...SO THAT'S ALL I CAN SAY.
YOUR FORTE...
...IS RECOGNIZING YOUR WEAKNESSES AND DOING WHATEVER YOU CAN TO OVERCOME THEM.
SO THINK CAREFULLY IN THIS SEARCH.
ALL RIGHT...
GOOD LUCK.
JIN.

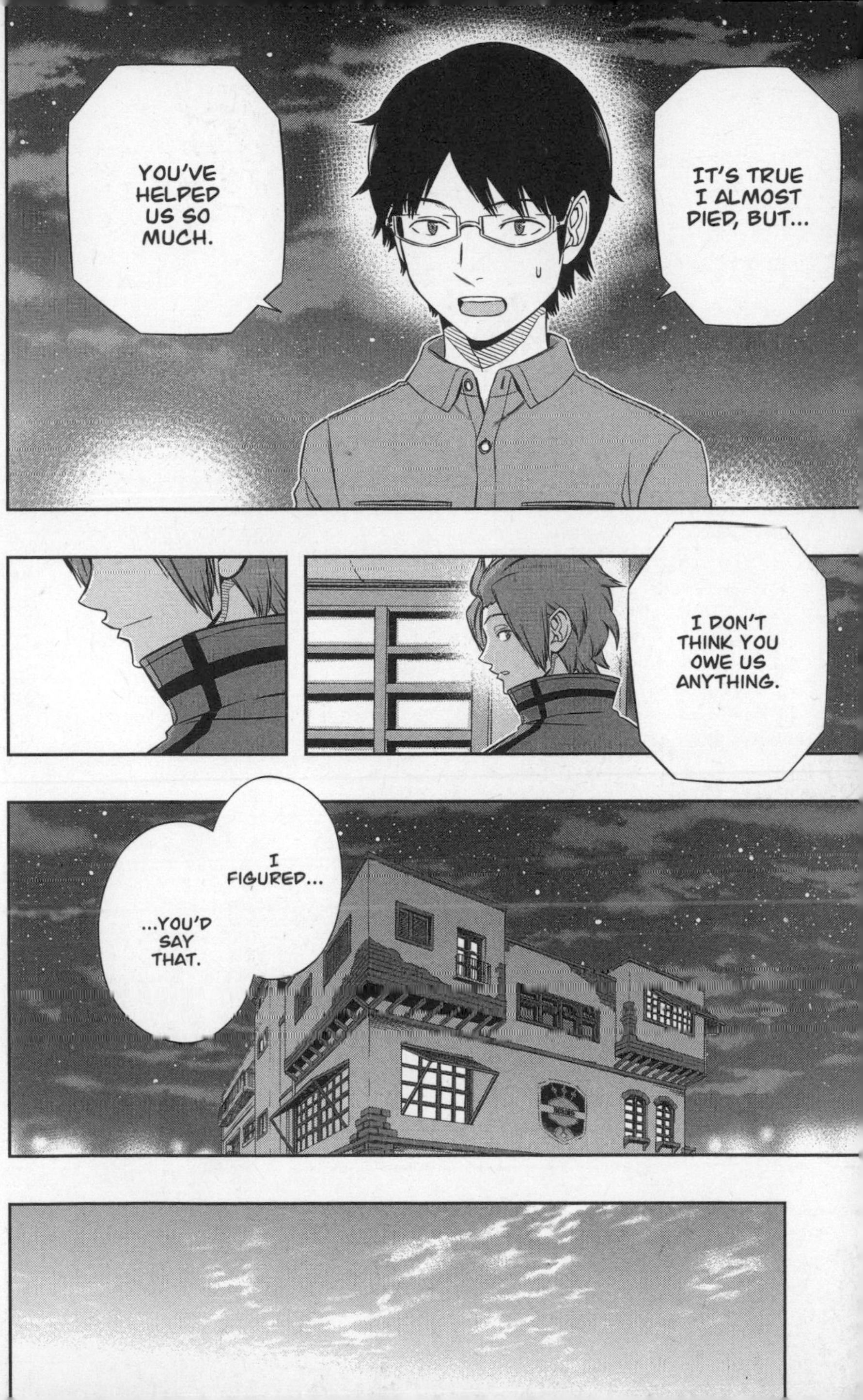
IT'S TRUE I ALMOST DIED, BUT...
YOU'VE HELPED US SO MUCH.
I DON'T THINK YOU OWE US ANYTHING.
I FIGURED...
...YOU'D SAY THAT.

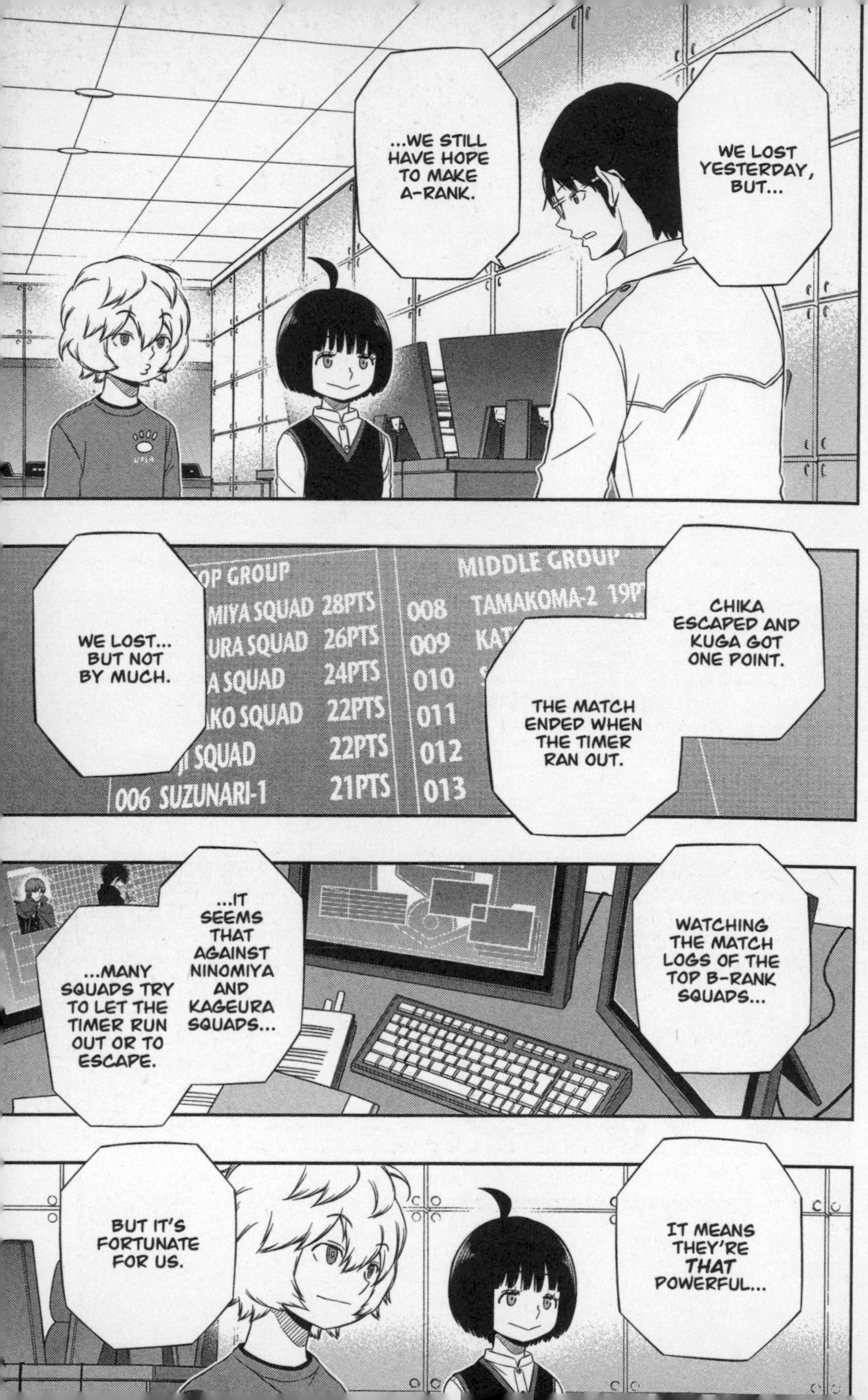
WE LOST YESTERDAY, BUT...
...WE STILL HAVE HOPE TO MAKE A-RANK.
CHIKA ESCAPED AND KUGA GOT ONE POINT.
THE MATCH ENDED WHEN THE TIMER RAN OUT.
MIDDLE GROUP
008 TAMAKOMA-2
006 SUZUNARI-1 21PTS
WE LOST... BUT NOT BY MUCH.
WATCHING THE MATCH LOGS OF THE TOP B-RANK SQUADS...
...IT SEEMS THAT AGAINST NINOMIYA AND KAGEURA SQUADS...
...MANY SQUADS TRY TO LET THE TIMER RUN OUT OR TO ESCAPE.
IT MEANS THEY'RE *THAT* POWERFUL...
BUT IT'S FORTUNATE FOR US.

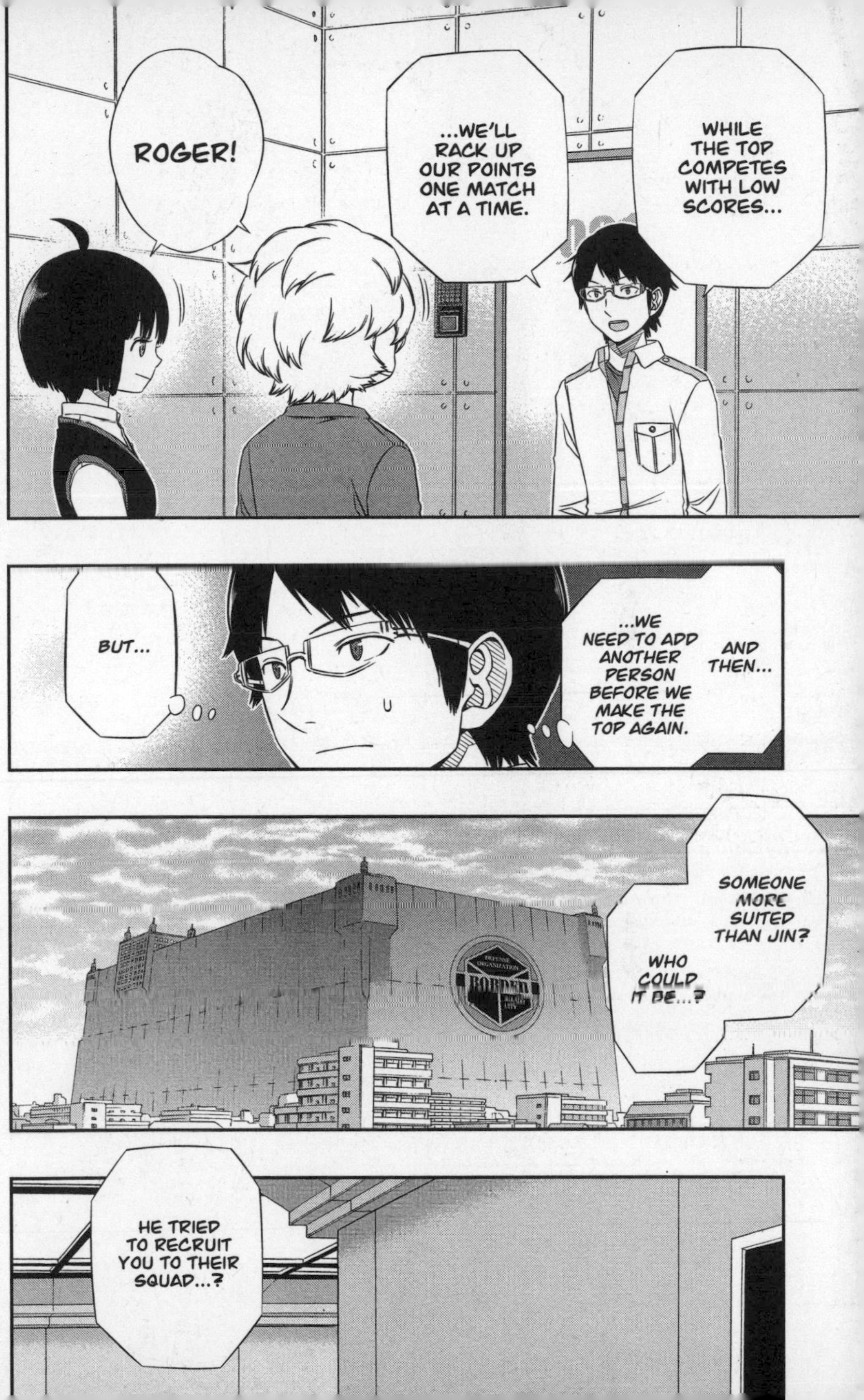
WHILE THE TOP COMPETES WITH LOW SCORES...
...WE'LL RACK UP OUR POINTS ONE MATCH AT A TIME.
ROGER!
AND THEN...
...WE NEED TO ADD ANOTHER PERSON BEFORE WE MAKE THE TOP AGAIN.
BUT...
SOMEONE MORE SUITED THAN JIN?
WHO COULD IT BE...?
HE TRIED TO RECRUIT YOU TO THEIR SQUAD...?

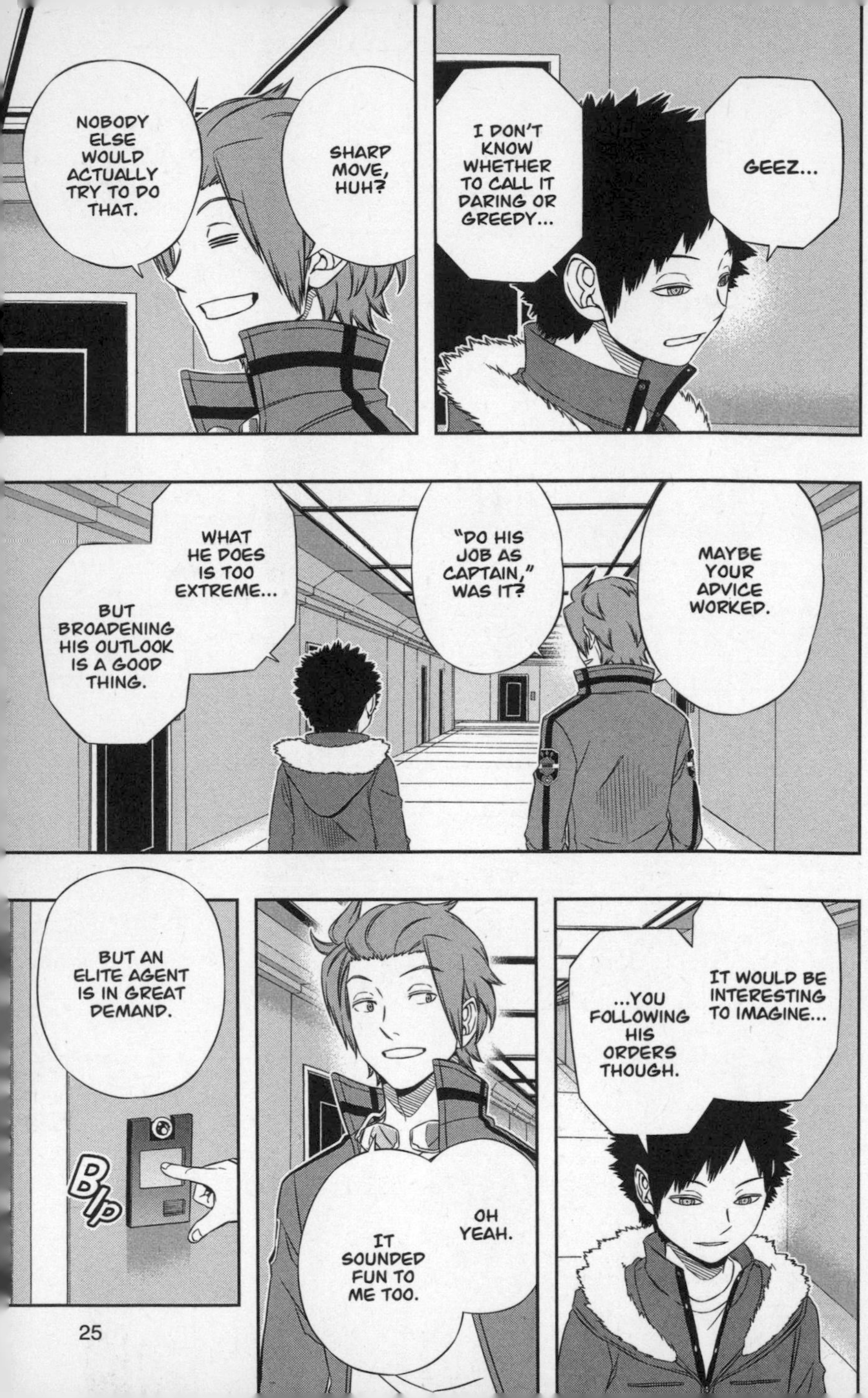
GEEZ...
I DON'T KNOW WHETHER TO CALL IT DARING OR GREEDY...
SHARP MOVE, HUH?
NOBODY ELSE WOULD ACTUALLY TRY TO DO THAT.
MAYBE YOUR ADVICE WORKED.
"DO HIS JOB AS CAPTAIN," WAS IT?
WHAT HE DOES IS TOO EXTREME...
BUT BROADENING HIS OUTLOOK IS A GOOD THING.
IT WOULD BE INTERESTING TO IMAGINE...
...YOU FOLLOWING HIS ORDERS THOUGH.
OH YEAH.
IT SOUNDED FUN TO ME TOO.
BUT AN ELITE AGENT IS IN GREAT DEMAND.
BIP

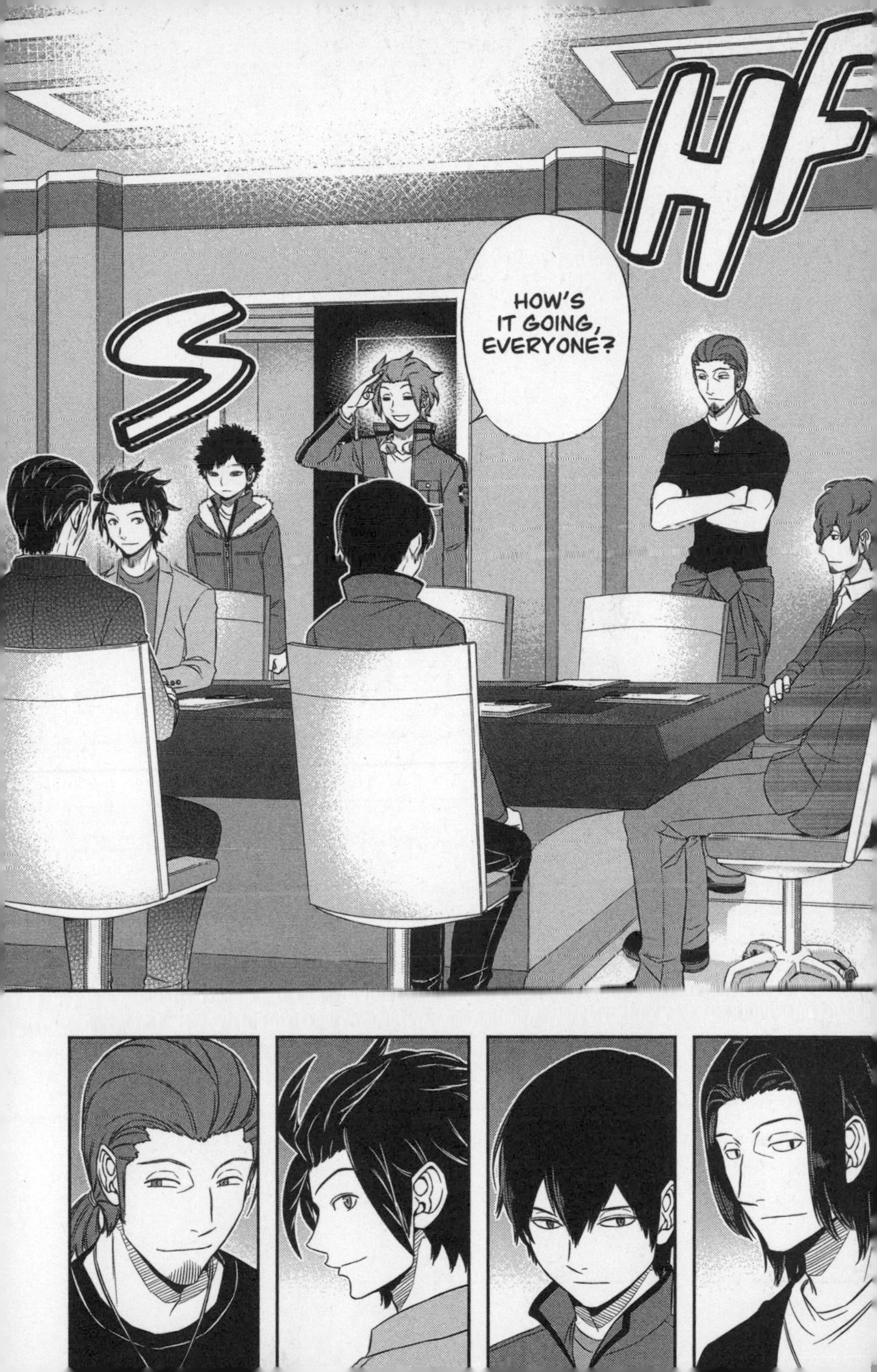
HF
HOW'S IT GOING, EVERYONE?
S

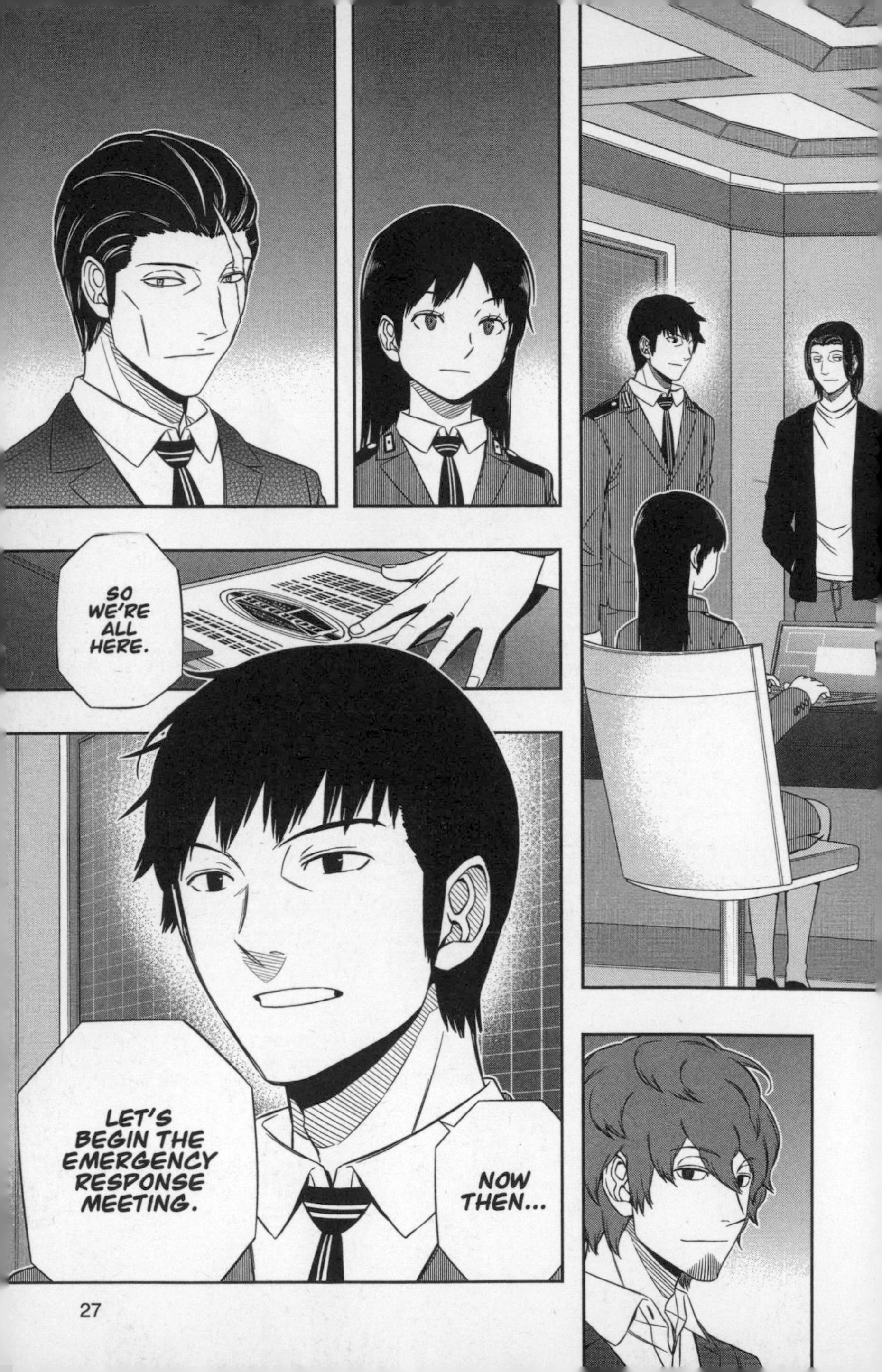
SO WE'RE ALL HERE.
NOW THEN...
LET'S BEGIN THE EMERGENCY RESPONSE MEETING.

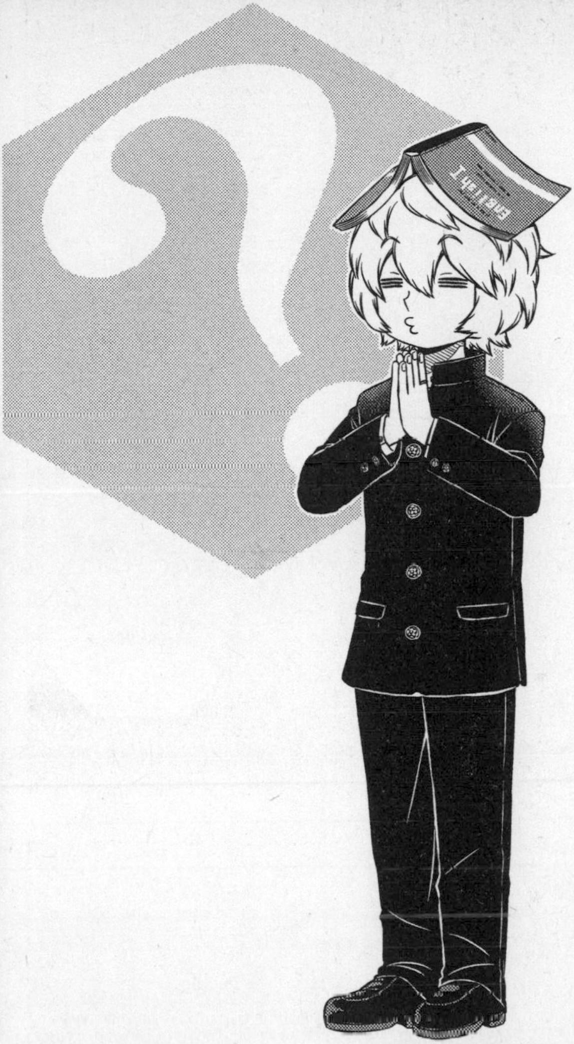

■ 2016 *Weekly Shonen Jump* 5-6 combined issue cover illustration

I drew this for the 5-6 combined issue cover of *Weekly Shonen Jump*. The characters were supposed to be praying to the academic gods. I messed up which side the cover of the workbook on his head was on, so he amusingly ended up being the only character with his back to the altar. This is the first time Yuma's worn a traditional school uniform.

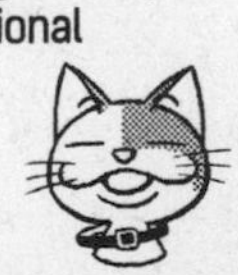

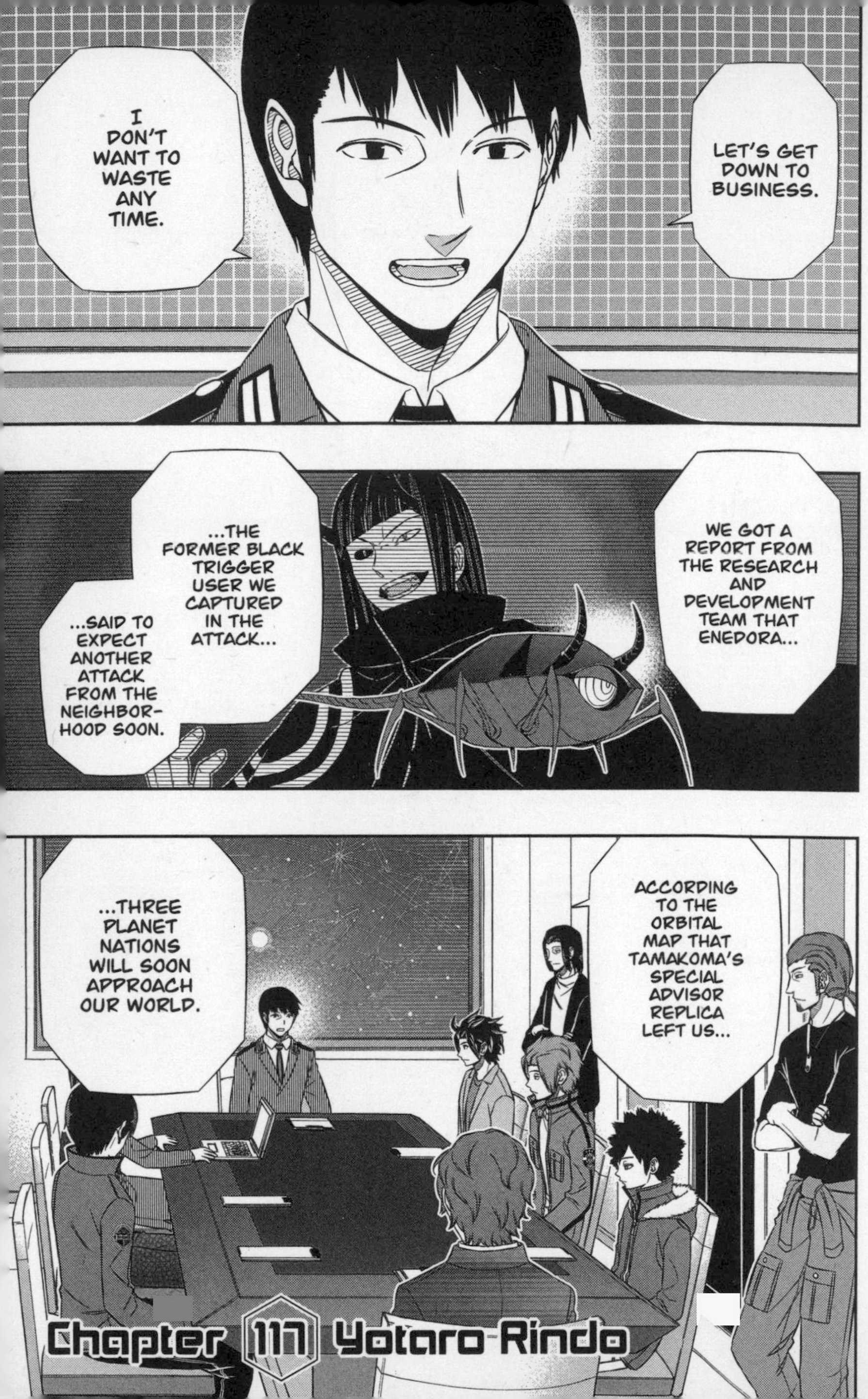
LET'S GET DOWN TO BUSINESS.
I DON'T WANT TO WASTE ANY TIME.
WE GOT A REPORT FROM THE RESEARCH AND DEVELOPMENT TEAM THAT ENEDORA...
...THE FORMER BLACK TRIGGER USER WE CAPTURED IN THE ATTACK...
...SAID TO EXPECT ANOTHER ATTACK FROM THE NEIGHBOR-HOOD SOON.
ACCORDING TO THE ORBITAL MAP THAT TAMAKOMA'S SPECIAL ADVISOR REPLICA LEFT US...
...THREE PLANET NATIONS WILL SOON APPROACH OUR WORLD.
Chapter 117 Yotaro Rindo

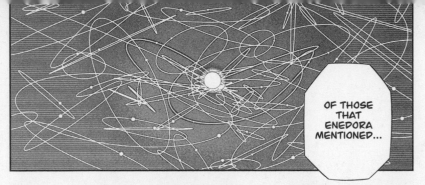

OF THOSE THAT ENEDORA MENTIONED...

...AND RHODO-KRHOUN...

...GALO-POULA...

...ARE TWO WORLDS...

...THAT ARE APPARENTLY VASSAL STATES OF AFTOKRATOR.

SO THEY'RE MINIONS OF THOSE GUYS WHO CAME HERE.

VASSAL STATES...?

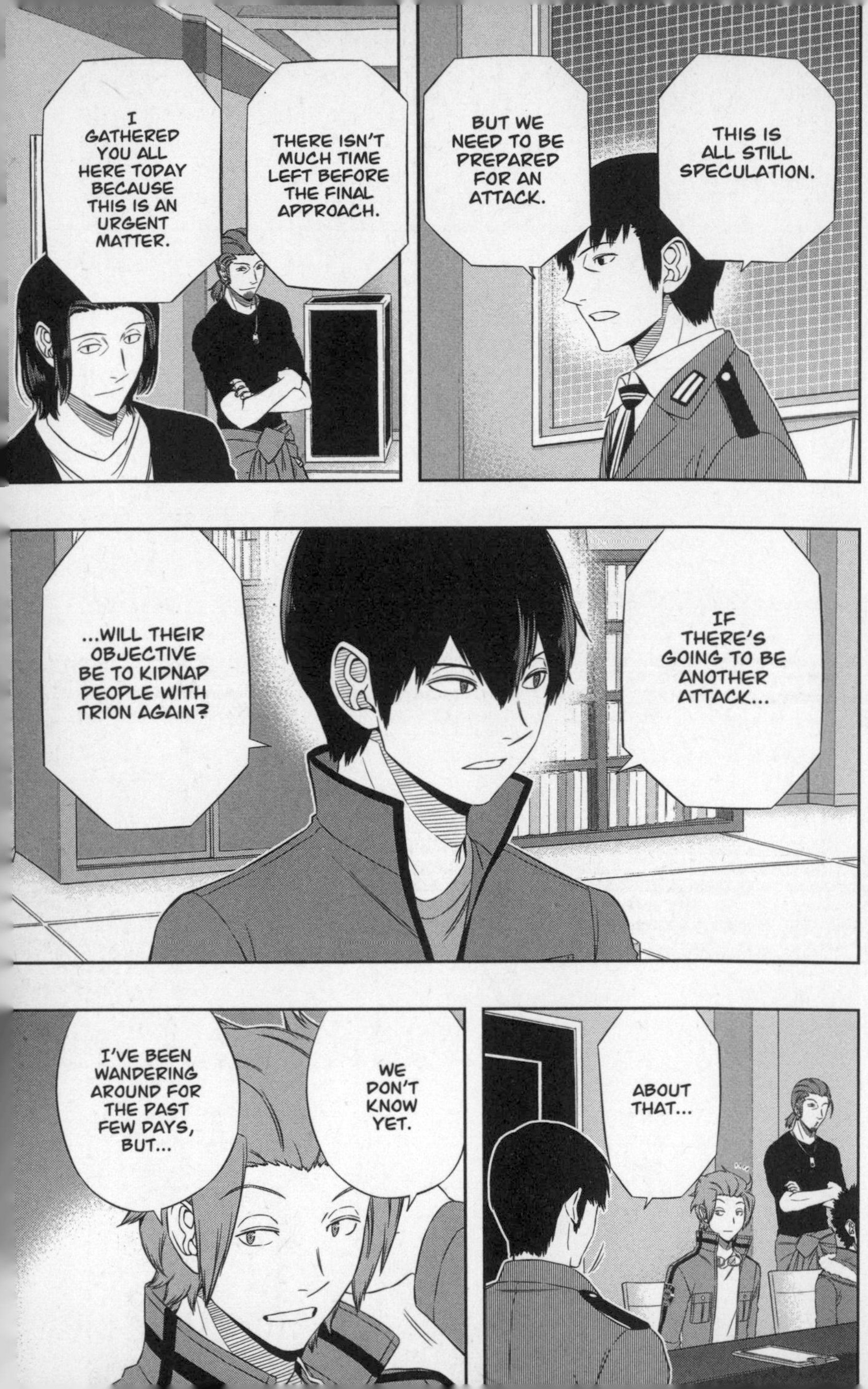
THIS IS ALL STILL SPECULATION.
BUT WE NEED TO BE PREPARED FOR AN ATTACK.
THERE ISN'T MUCH TIME LEFT BEFORE THE FINAL APPROACH.
I GATHERED YOU ALL HERE TODAY BECAUSE THIS IS AN URGENT MATTER.
IF THERE'S GOING TO BE ANOTHER ATTACK...
...WILL THEIR OBJECTIVE BE TO KIDNAP PEOPLE WITH TRION AGAIN?
ABOUT THAT...
WE DON'T KNOW YET.
I'VE BEEN WANDERING AROUND FOR THE PAST FEW DAYS, BUT...

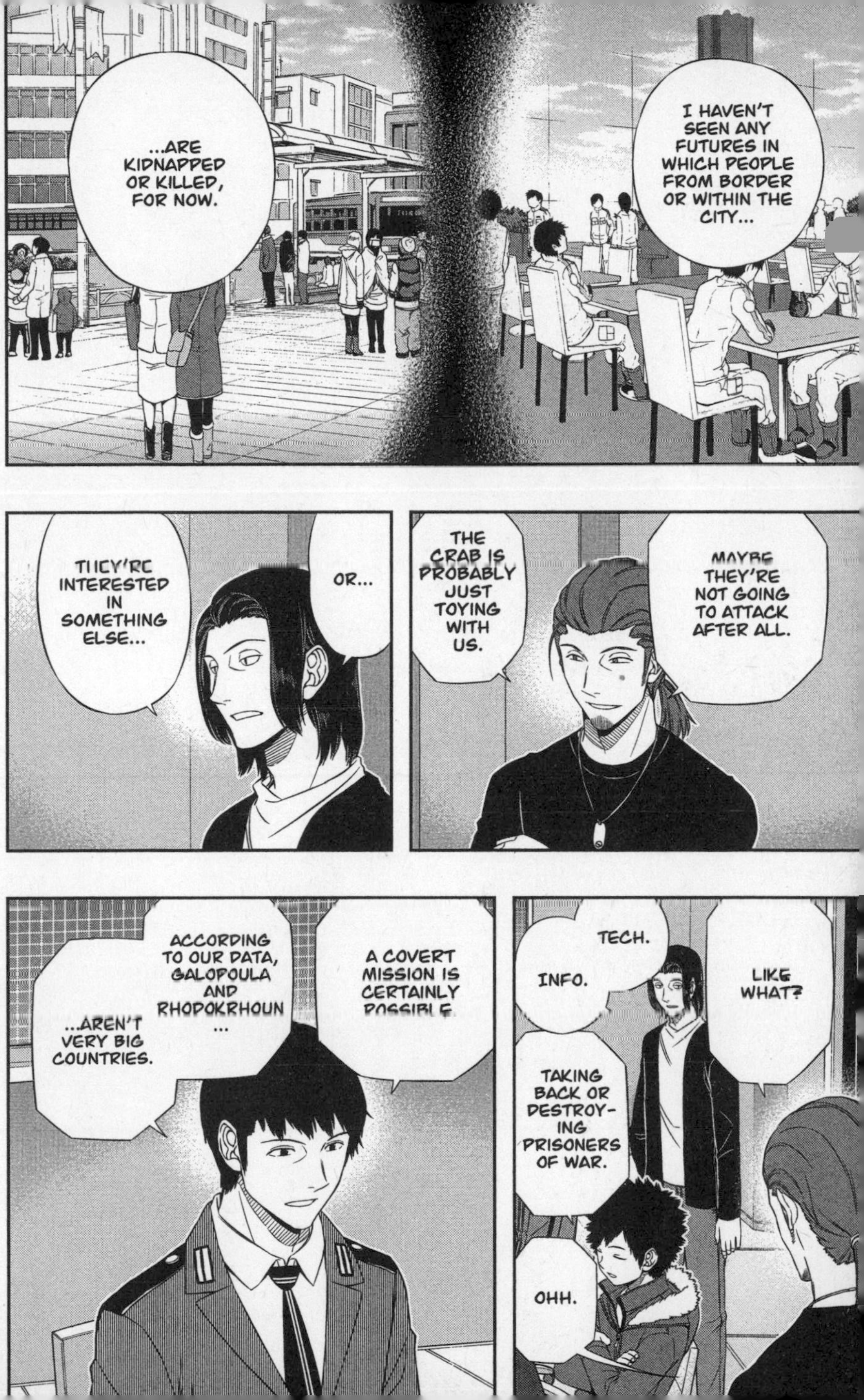
I HAVEN'T SEEN ANY FUTURES IN WHICH PEOPLE FROM BORDER OR WITHIN THE CITY...
...ARE KIDNAPPED OR KILLED, FOR NOW.
MAYBE THEY'RE NOT GOING TO ATTACK AFTER ALL.
THE CRAB IS PROBABLY JUST TOYING WITH US.
OR...
THEY'RE INTERESTED IN SOMETHING ELSE...
LIKE WHAT?
TECH.
INFO.
TAKING BACK OR DESTROY-ING PRISONERS OF WAR.
OHH.
A COVERT MISSION IS CERTAINLY POSSIBLE.
ACCORDING TO OUR DATA, GALOPOULA AND RHODOKRHOUN ...
...AREN'T VERY BIG COUNTRIES.

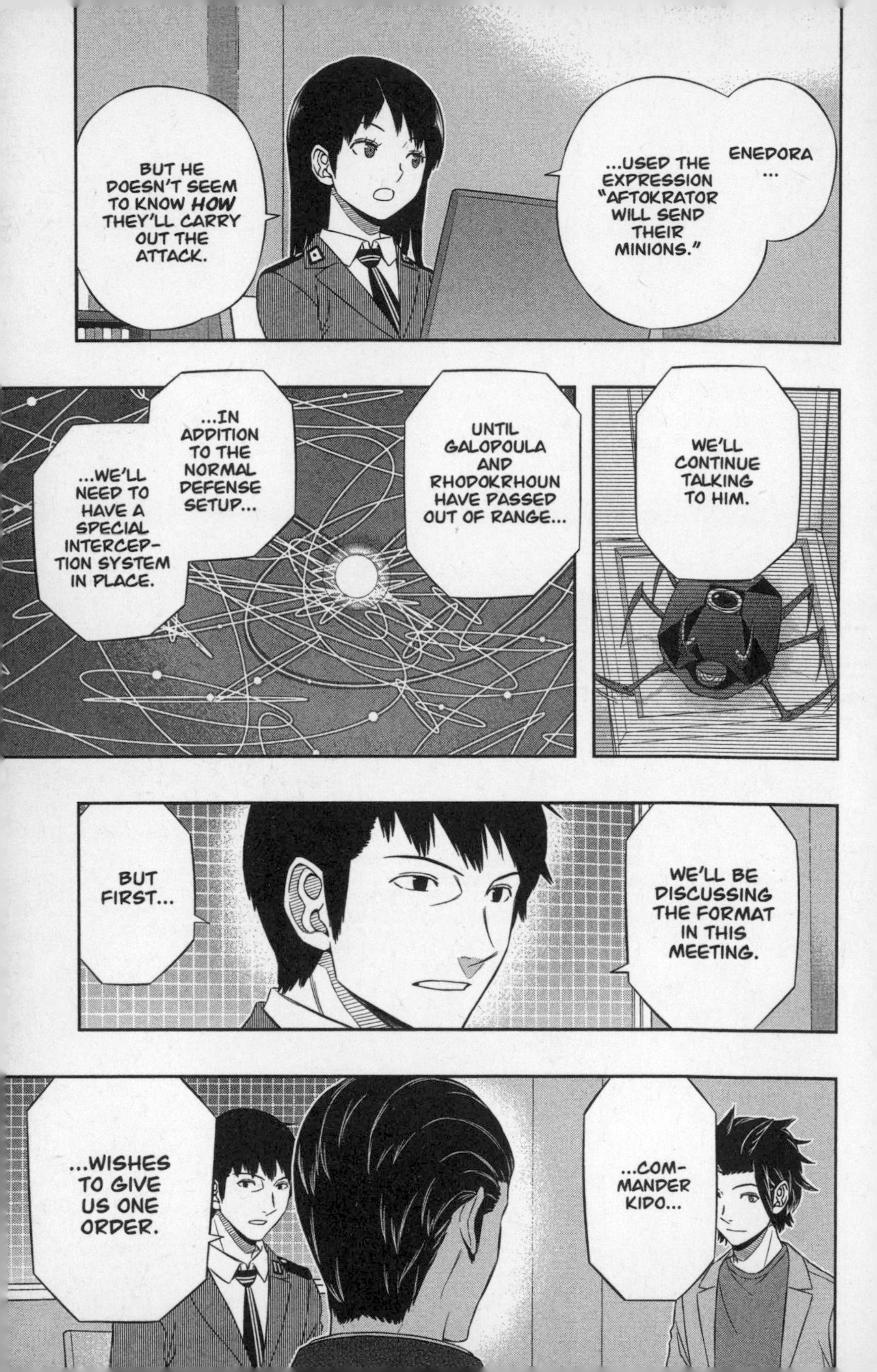
ENEDORA...
...USED THE EXPRESSION "AFTOKRATOR WILL SEND THEIR MINIONS."
BUT HE DOESN'T SEEM TO KNOW *HOW* THEY'LL CARRY OUT THE ATTACK.
WE'LL CONTINUE TALKING TO HIM.
UNTIL GALOPOULA AND RHODOKRHOUN HAVE PASSED OUT OF RANGE...
...IN ADDITION TO THE NORMAL DEFENSE SETUP...
...WE'LL NEED TO HAVE A SPECIAL INTERCEPTION SYSTEM IN PLACE.
WE'LL BE DISCUSSING THE FORMAT IN THIS MEETING.
BUT FIRST...
...COMMANDER KIDO...
...WISHES TO GIVE US ONE ORDER.

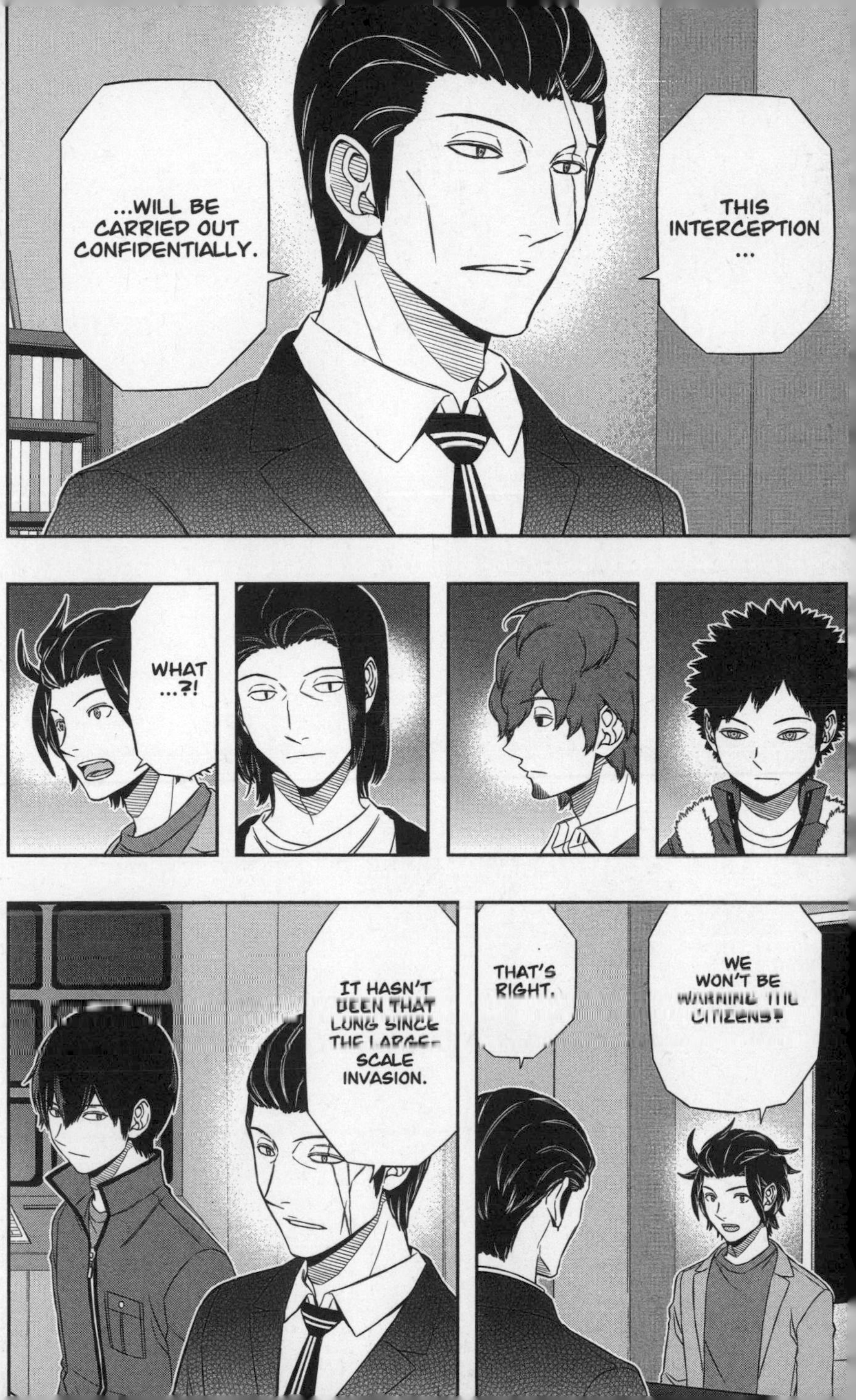
THIS INTERCEPTION ...
...WILL BE CARRIED OUT CONFIDENTIALLY.
WHAT ...?!
WE WON'T BE WARNING THE CITIZENS?
THAT'S RIGHT.
IT HASN'T BEEN THAT LONG SINCE THE LARGE-SCALE INVASION.

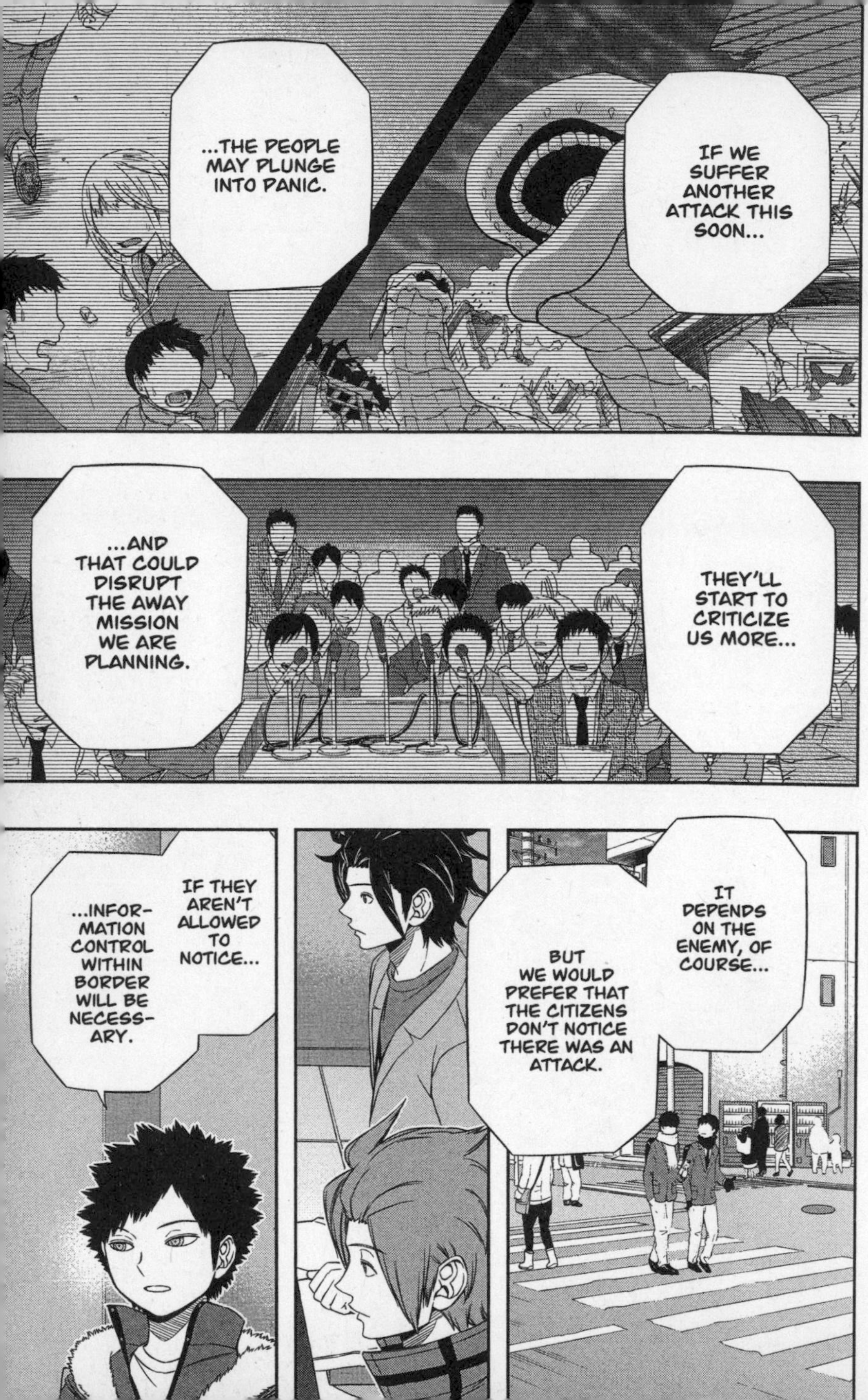
IF WE SUFFER ANOTHER ATTACK THIS SOON...
...THE PEOPLE MAY PLUNGE INTO PANIC.
THEY'LL START TO CRITICIZE US MORE...
...AND THAT COULD DISRUPT THE AWAY MISSION WE ARE PLANNING.
IT DEPENDS ON THE ENEMY, OF COURSE...
BUT WE WOULD PREFER THAT THE CITIZENS DON'T NOTICE THERE WAS AN ATTACK.
IF THEY AREN'T ALLOWED TO NOTICE...
...INFOR-MATION CONTROL WITHIN BORDER WILL BE NECESS-ARY.

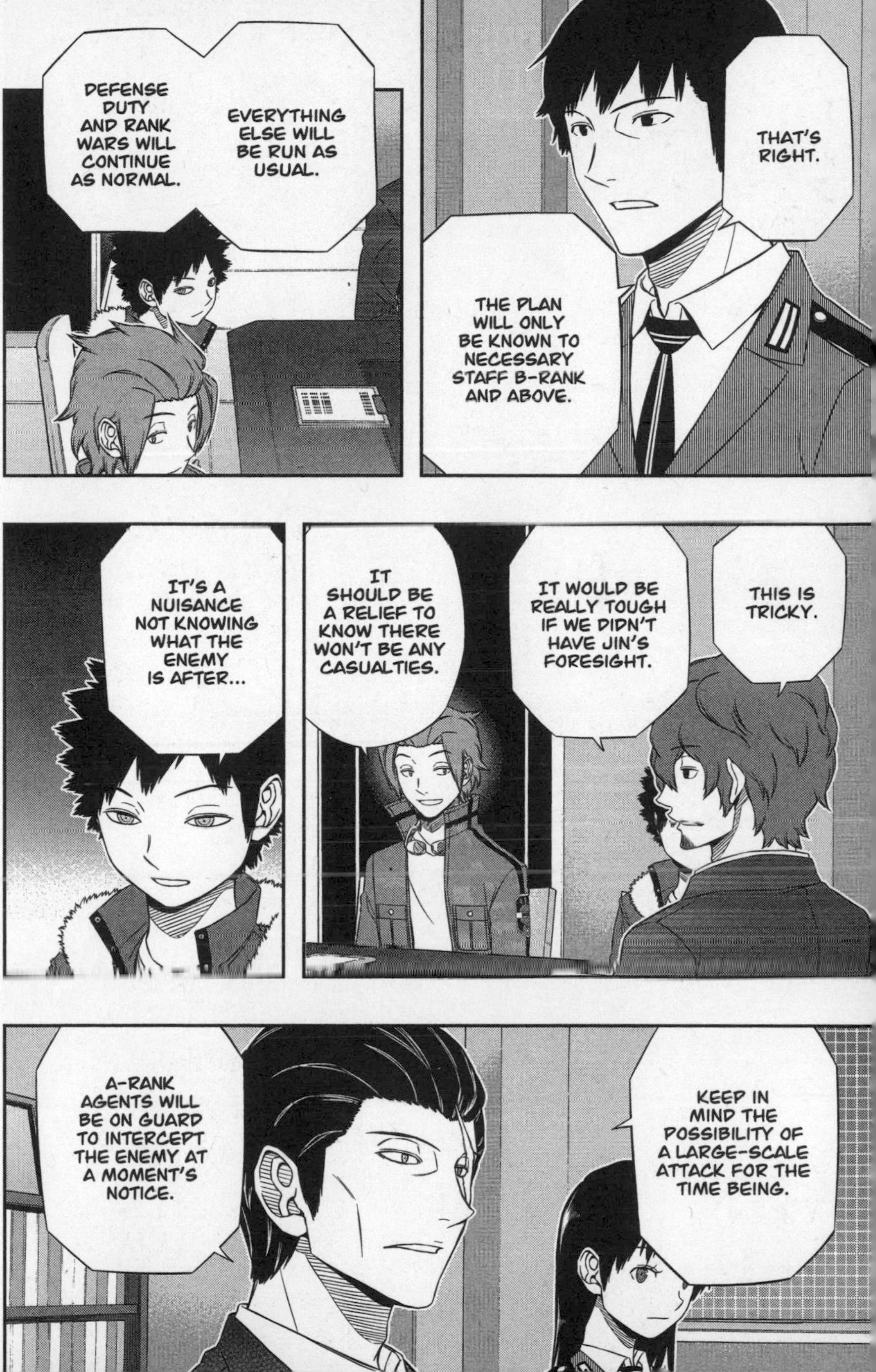
THAT'S RIGHT.
THE PLAN WILL ONLY BE KNOWN TO NECESSARY STAFF B-RANK AND ABOVE.
EVERYTHING ELSE WILL BE RUN AS USUAL.
DEFENSE DUTY AND RANK WARS WILL CONTINUE AS NORMAL.
THIS IS TRICKY.
IT WOULD BE REALLY TOUGH IF WE DIDN'T HAVE JIN'S FORESIGHT.
IT SHOULD BE A RELIEF TO KNOW THERE WON'T BE ANY CASUALTIES.
IT'S A NUISANCE NOT KNOWING WHAT THE ENEMY IS AFTER...
KEEP IN MIND THE POSSIBILITY OF A LARGE-SCALE ATTACK FOR THE TIME BEING.
A-RANK AGENTS WILL BE ON GUARD TO INTERCEPT THE ENEMY AT A MOMENT'S NOTICE.

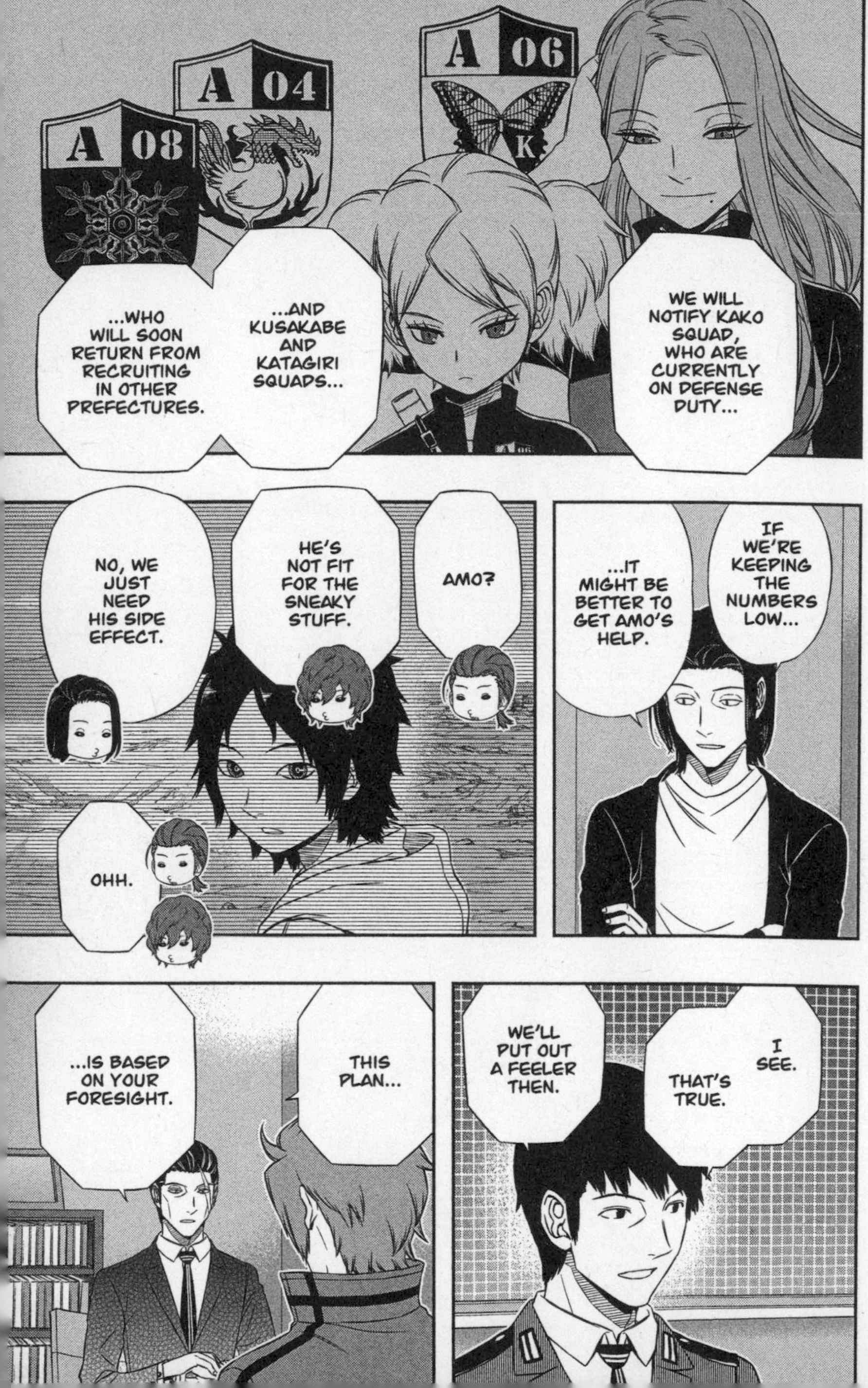
A 06
K
A 04
A 08
WE WILL NOTIFY KAKO SQUAD, WHO ARE CURRENTLY ON DEFENSE DUTY...
...AND KUSAKABE AND KATAGIRI SQUADS...
...WHO WILL SOON RETURN FROM RECRUITING IN OTHER PREFECTURES.
IF WE'RE KEEPING THE NUMBERS LOW...
...IT MIGHT BE BETTER TO GET AMO'S HELP.
AMO?
HE'S NOT FIT FOR THE SNEAKY STUFF.
NO, WE JUST NEED HIS SIDE EFFECT.
OHH.
I SEE.
THAT'S TRUE.
WE'LL PUT OUT A FEELER THEN.
THIS PLAN...
...IS BASED ON YOUR FORESIGHT.

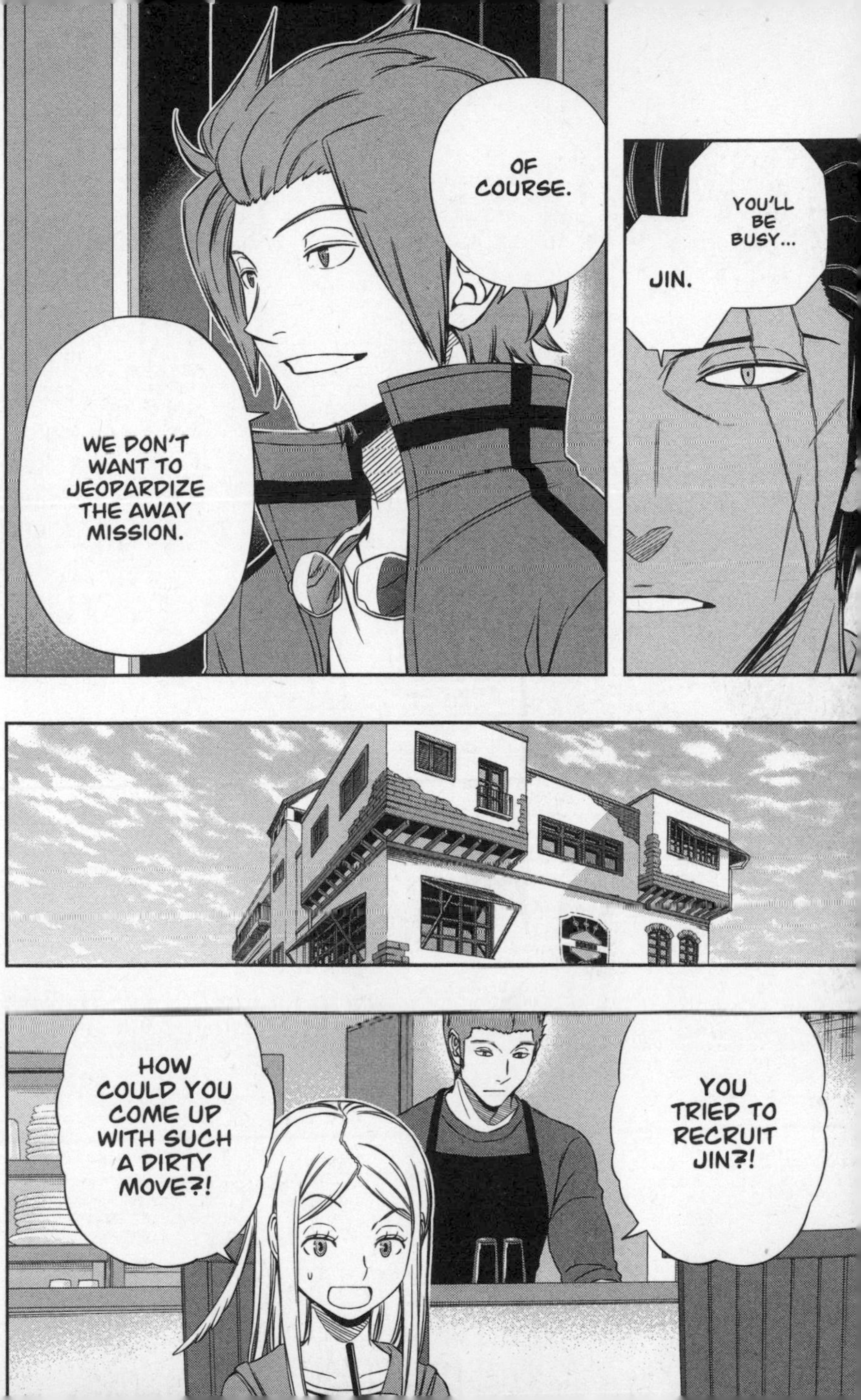
YOU'LL BE BUSY...
JIN.
OF COURSE.
WE DON'T WANT TO JEOPARDIZE THE AWAY MISSION.
YOU TRIED TO RECRUIT JIN?!
HOW COULD YOU COME UP WITH SUCH A DIRTY MOVE?!

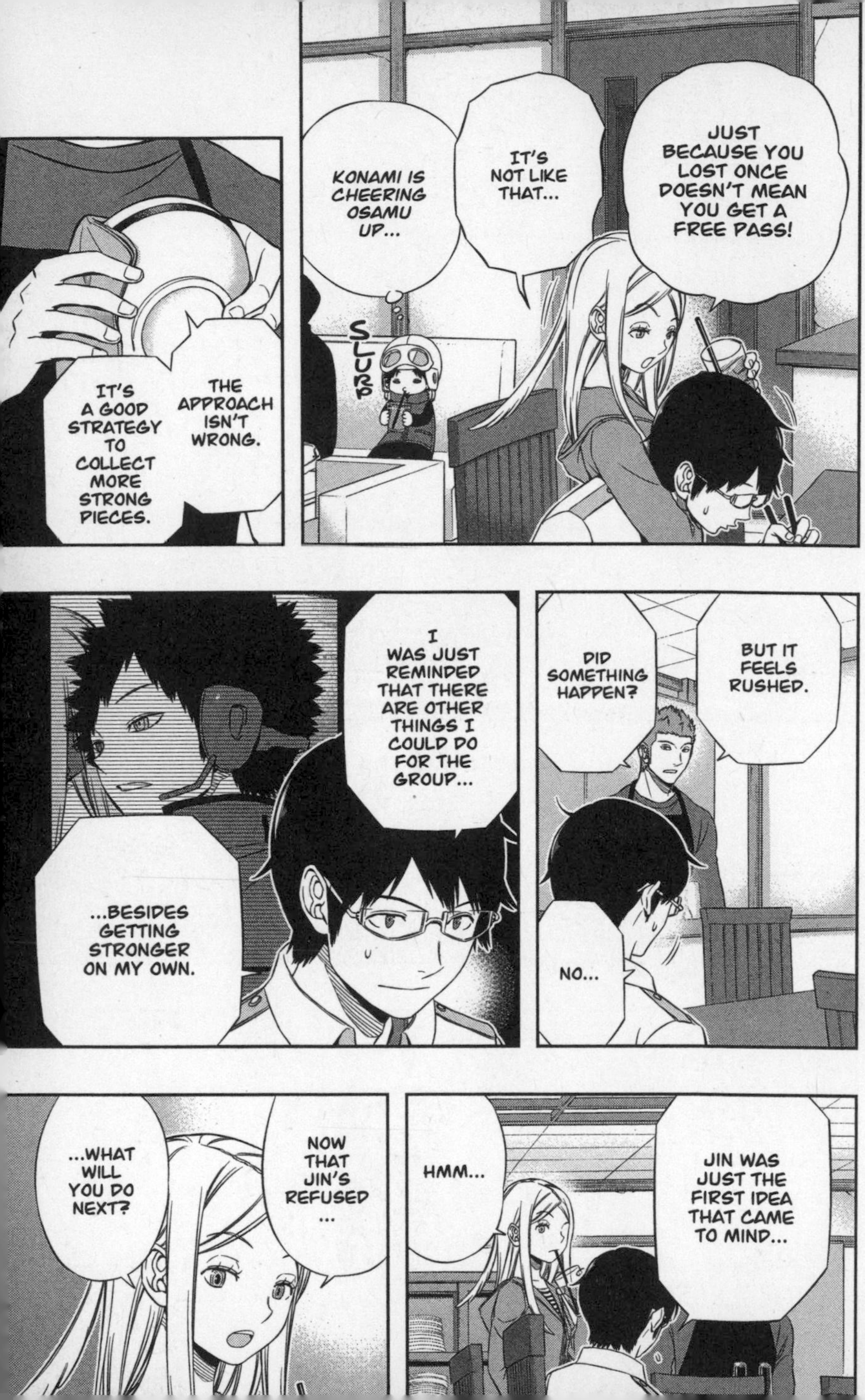
JUST BECAUSE YOU LOST ONCE DOESN'T MEAN YOU GET A FREE PASS!
IT'S NOT LIKE THAT...
KONAMI IS CHEERING OSAMU UP...
SLURP
THE APPROACH ISN'T WRONG.
IT'S A GOOD STRATEGY TO COLLECT MORE STRONG PIECES.
BUT IT FEELS RUSHED.
DID SOMETHING HAPPEN?
NO...
I WAS JUST REMINDED THAT THERE ARE OTHER THINGS I COULD DO FOR THE GROUP...
...BESIDES GETTING STRONGER ON MY OWN.
JIN WAS JUST THE FIRST IDEA THAT CAME TO MIND...
HMM...
NOW THAT JIN'S REFUSED ...
...WHAT WILL YOU DO NEXT?

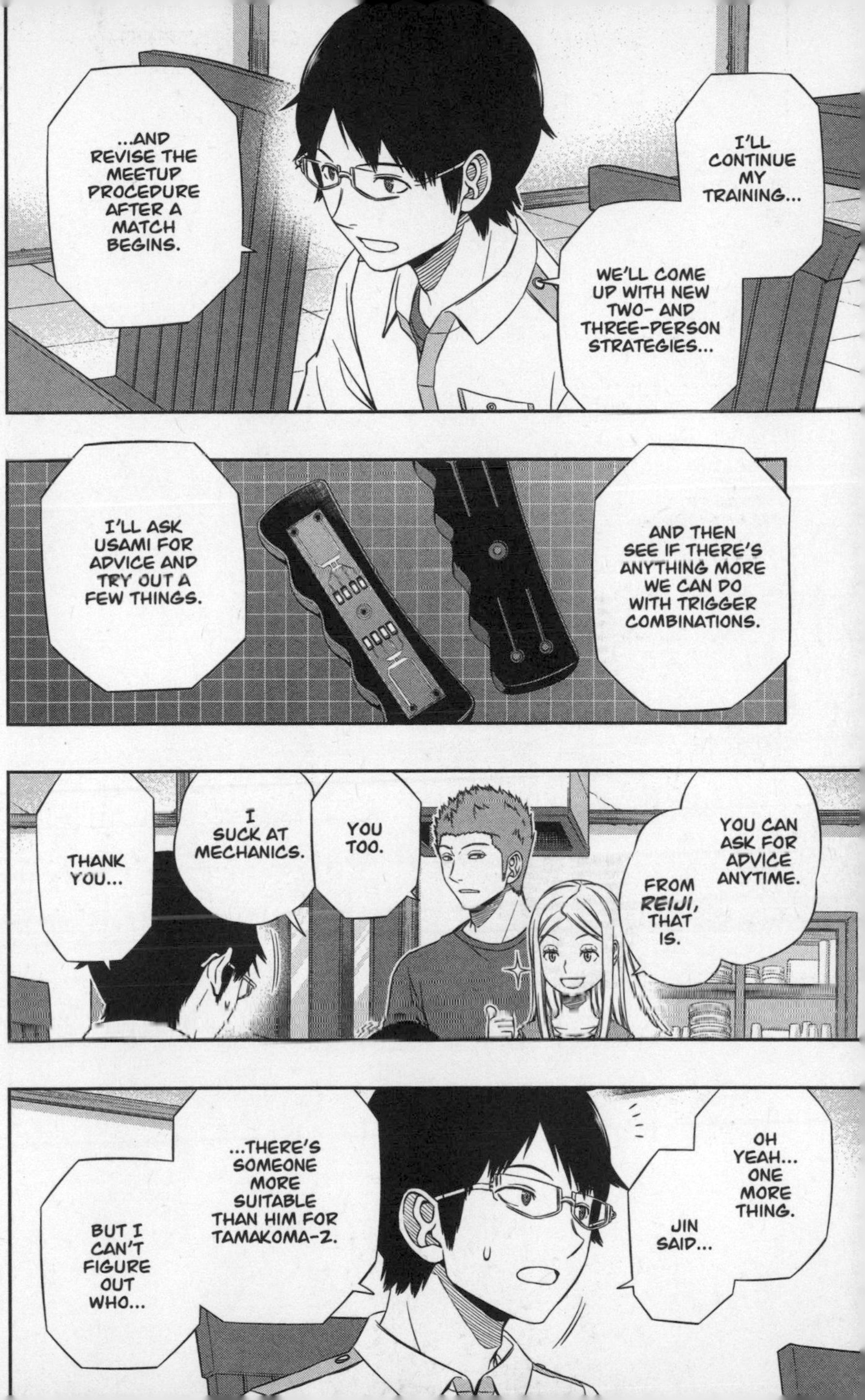
I'LL CONTINUE MY TRAINING...
WE'LL COME UP WITH NEW TWO- AND THREE-PERSON STRATEGIES...
...AND REVISE THE MEETUP PROCEDURE AFTER A MATCH BEGINS.
AND THEN SEE IF THERE'S ANYTHING MORE WE CAN DO WITH TRIGGER COMBINATIONS.
I'LL ASK USAMI FOR ADVICE AND TRY OUT A FEW THINGS.
YOU CAN ASK FOR ADVICE ANYTIME.
FROM REIJI, THAT IS.
YOU TOO.
I SUCK AT MECHANICS.
THANK YOU...
OH YEAH... ONE MORE THING.
JIN SAID...
...THERE'S SOMEONE MORE SUITABLE THAN HIM FOR TAMAKOMA-2.
BUT I CAN'T FIGURE OUT WHO...

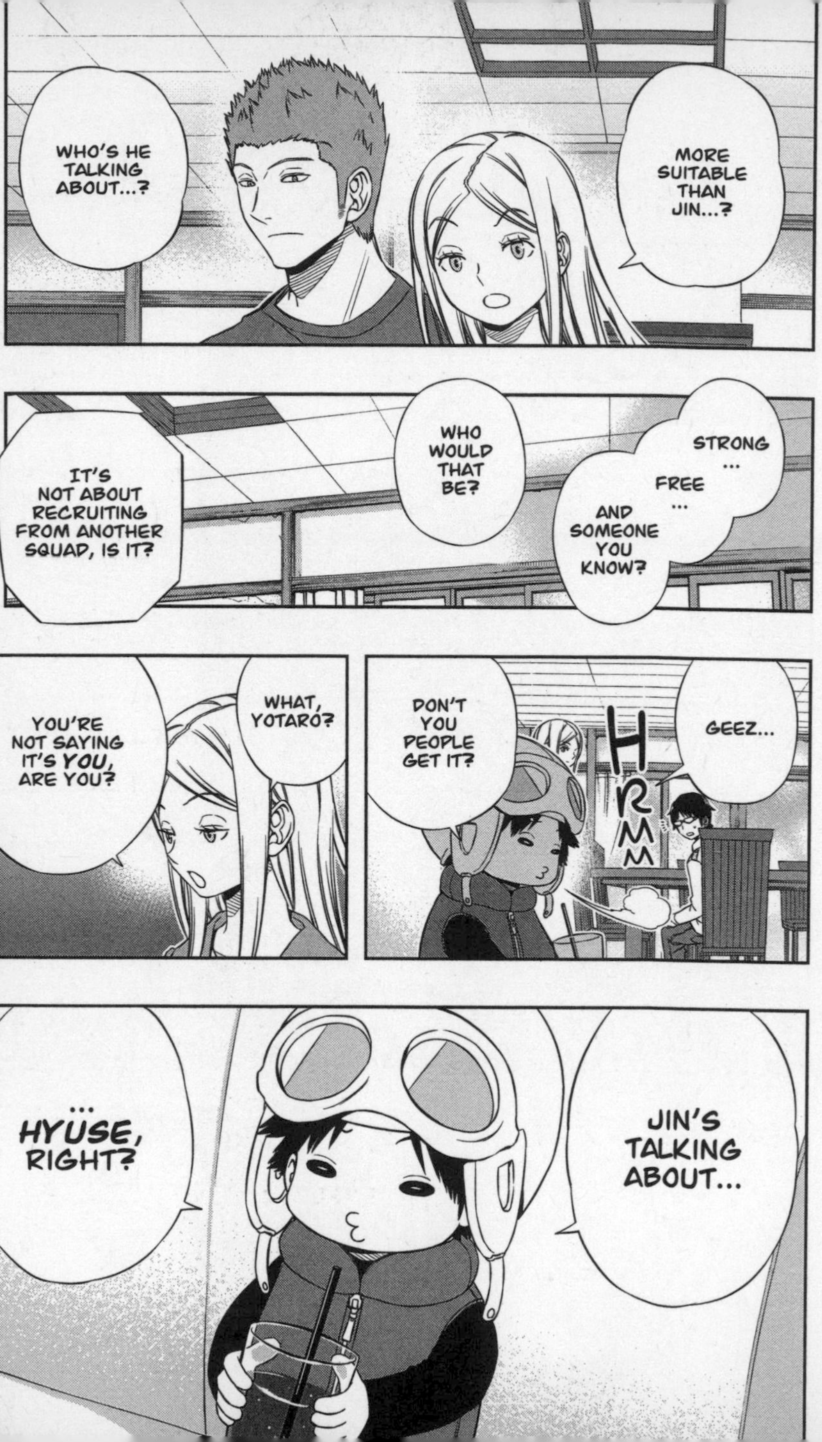
MORE SUITABLE THAN JIN...?
WHO'S HE TALKING ABOUT...?
STRONG... FREE... AND SOMEONE YOU KNOW?
WHO WOULD THAT BE?
IT'S NOT ABOUT RECRUITING FROM ANOTHER SQUAD, IS IT?
GEEZ...
HRMM
DON'T YOU PEOPLE GET IT?
WHAT, YOTARO?
YOU'RE NOT SAYING IT'S *YOU*, ARE YOU?
JIN'S TALKING ABOUT...
... *HYÜSE*, RIGHT?

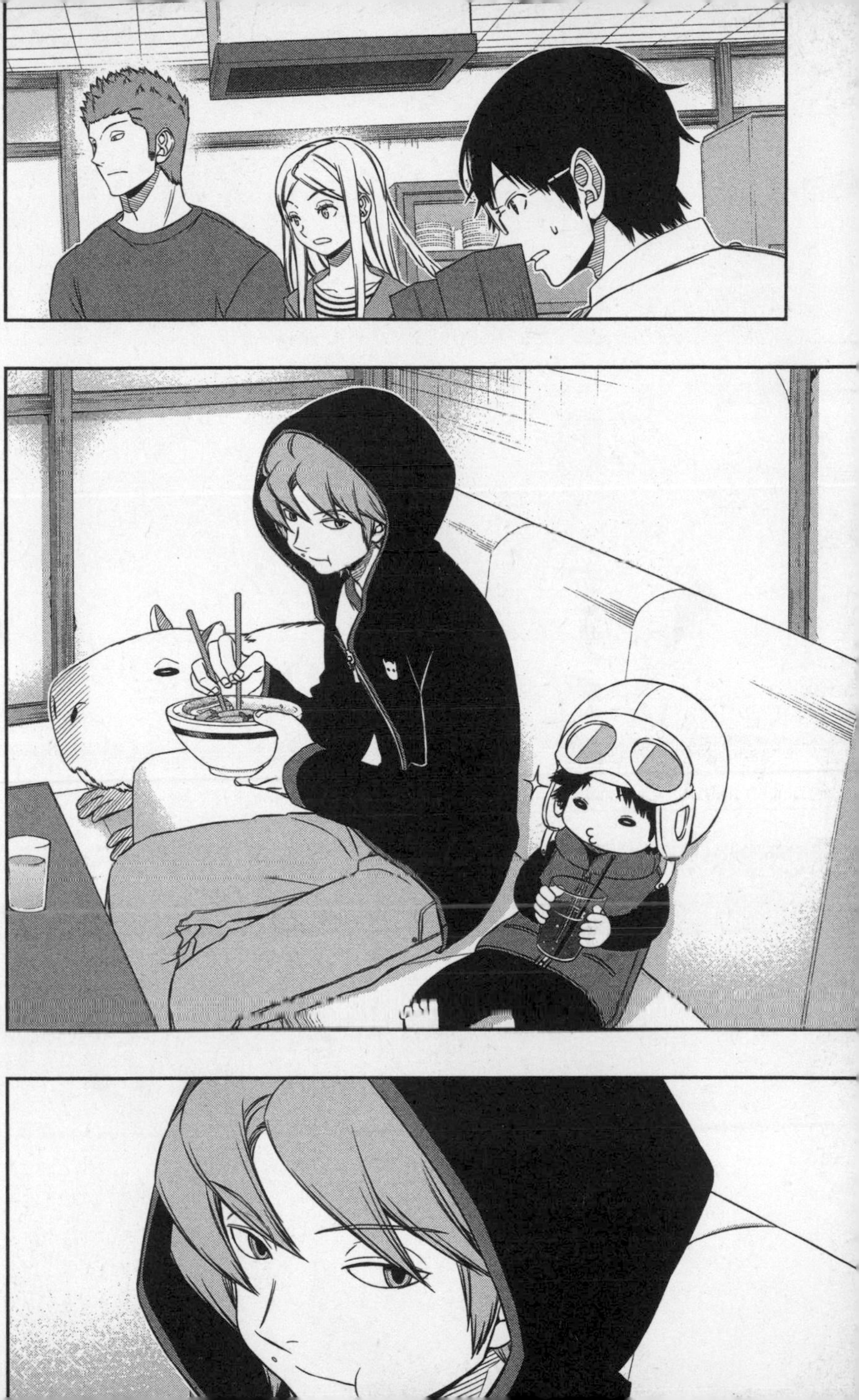

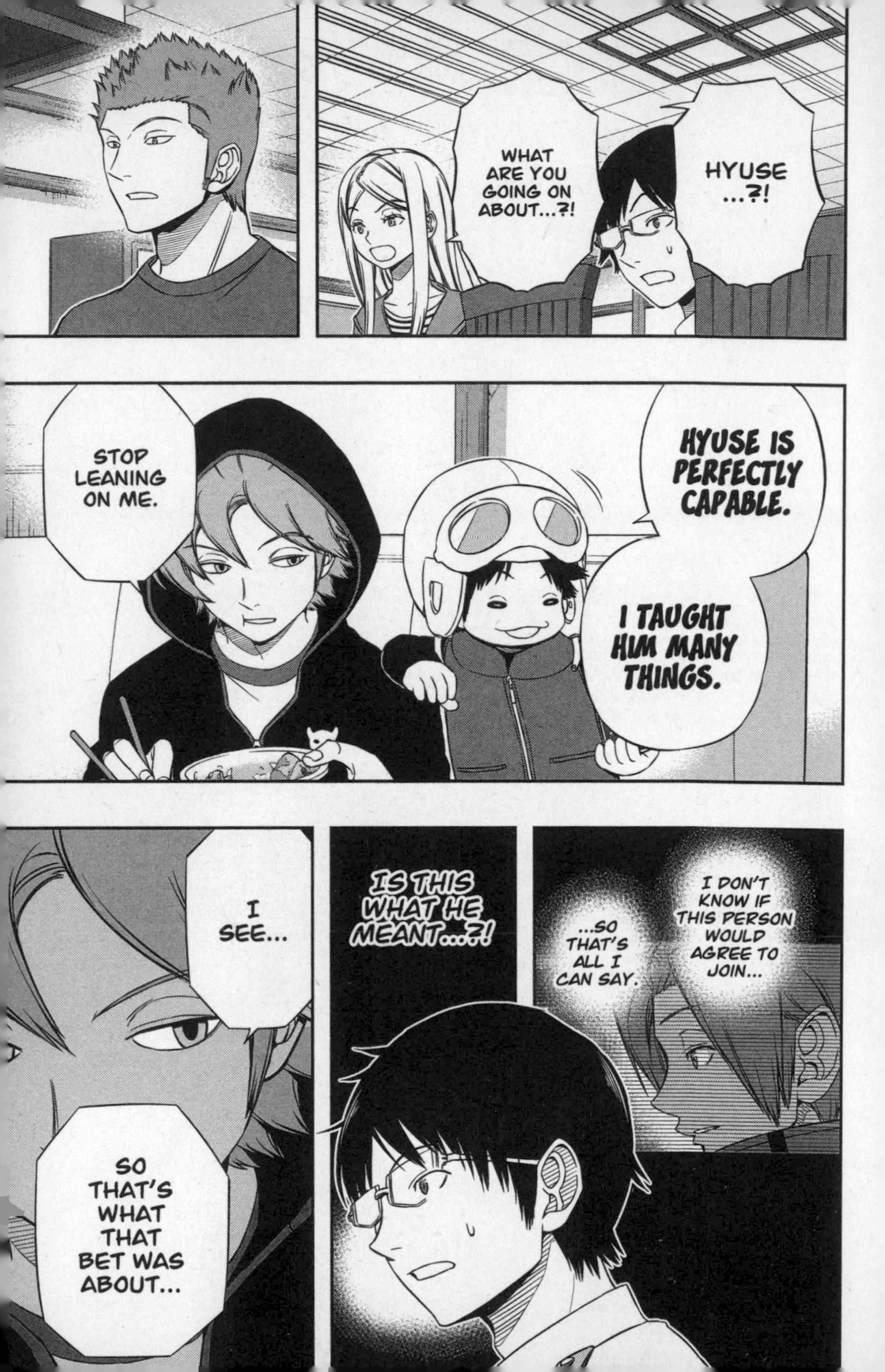
HYUSE ...?!
WHAT ARE YOU GOING ON ABOUT...?!
HYUSE IS PERFECTLY CAPABLE.
I TAUGHT HIM MANY THINGS.
STOP LEANING ON ME.
I DON'T KNOW IF THIS PERSON WOULD AGREE TO JOIN...
...SO THAT'S ALL I CAN SAY.
IS THIS WHAT HE MEANT...?!
I SEE...
SO THAT'S WHAT THAT BET WAS ABOUT...

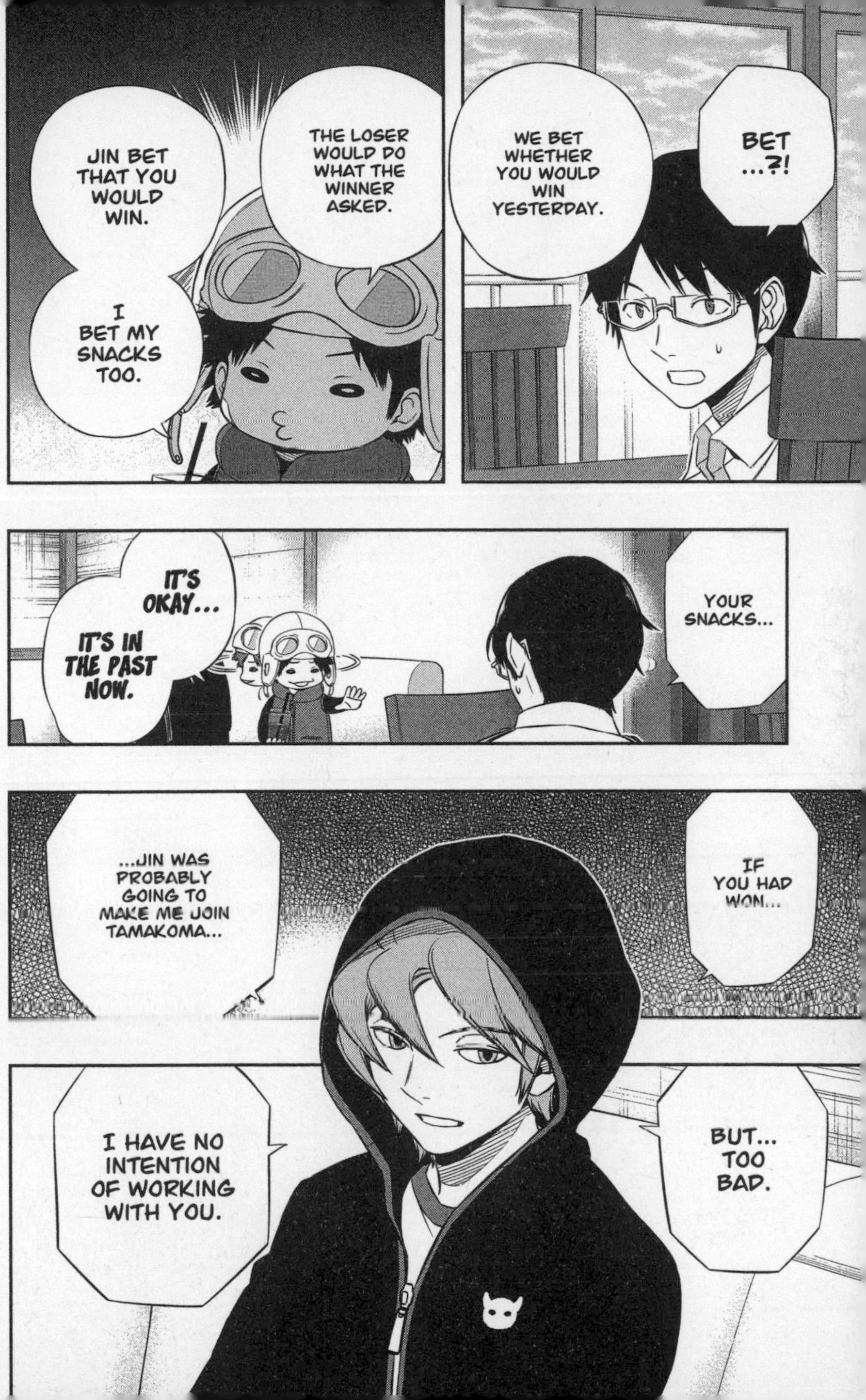
BET ...?!
WE BET WHETHER YOU WOULD WIN YESTERDAY.
THE LOSER WOULD DO WHAT THE WINNER ASKED.
JIN BET THAT YOU WOULD WIN.
I BET MY SNACKS TOO.
YOUR SNACKS...
IT'S OKAY...
IT'S IN THE PAST NOW.
IF YOU HAD WON...
...JIN WAS PROBABLY GOING TO MAKE ME JOIN TAMAKOMA...
BUT... TOO BAD.
I HAVE NO INTENTION OF WORKING WITH YOU.

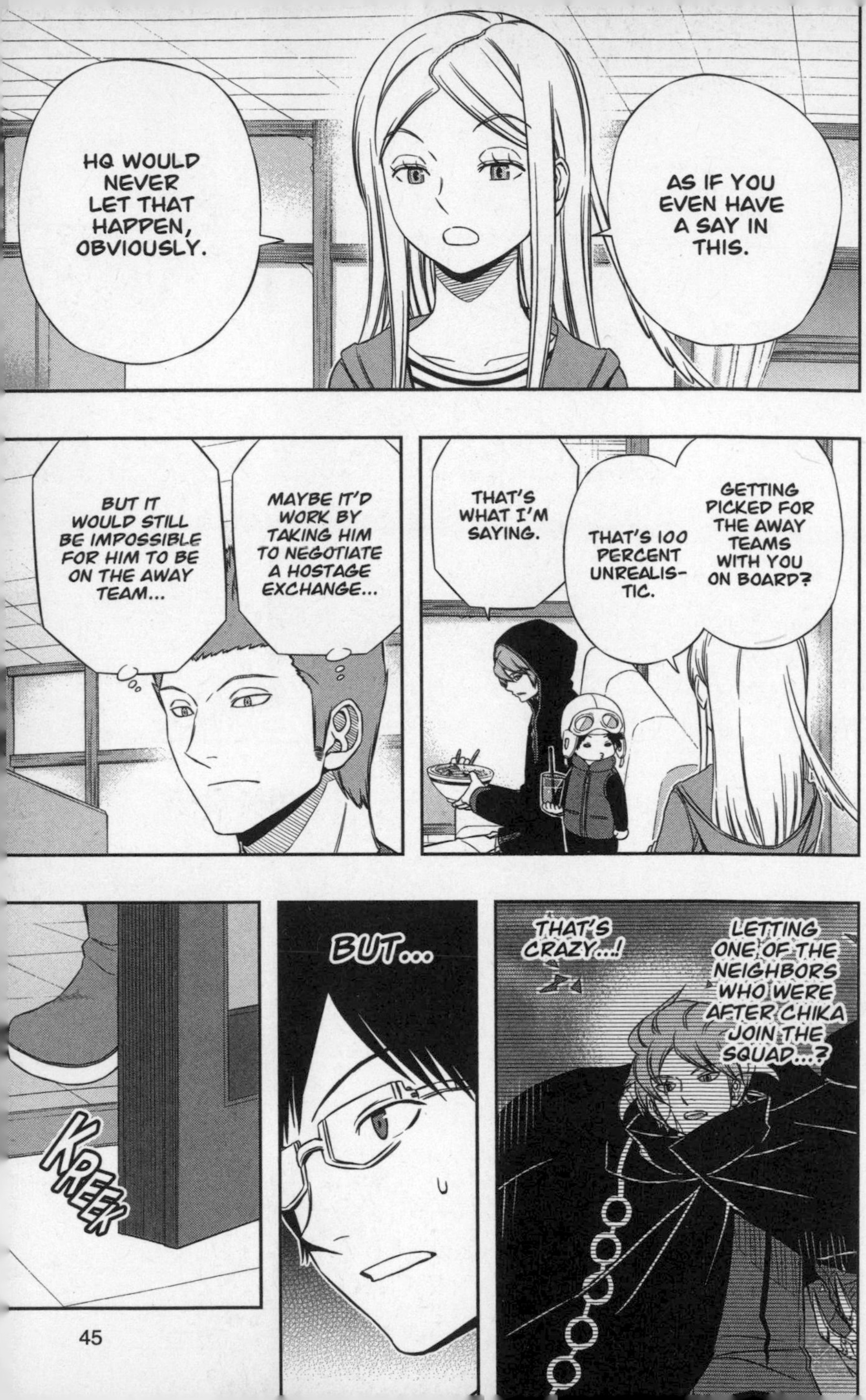
AS IF YOU EVEN HAVE A SAY IN THIS.
HQ WOULD NEVER LET THAT HAPPEN, OBVIOUSLY.
GETTING PICKED FOR THE AWAY TEAMS WITH YOU ON BOARD?
THAT'S 100 PERCENT UNREALIS-TIC.
THAT'S WHAT I'M SAYING.
MAYBE IT'D WORK BY TAKING HIM TO NEGOTIATE A HOSTAGE EXCHANGE...
BUT IT WOULD STILL BE IMPOSSIBLE FOR HIM TO BE ON THE AWAY TEAM...
LETTING ONE OF THE NEIGHBORS WHO WERE AFTER CHIKA JOIN THE SQUAD...?
THAT'S CRAZY...!
BUT...
KREEK

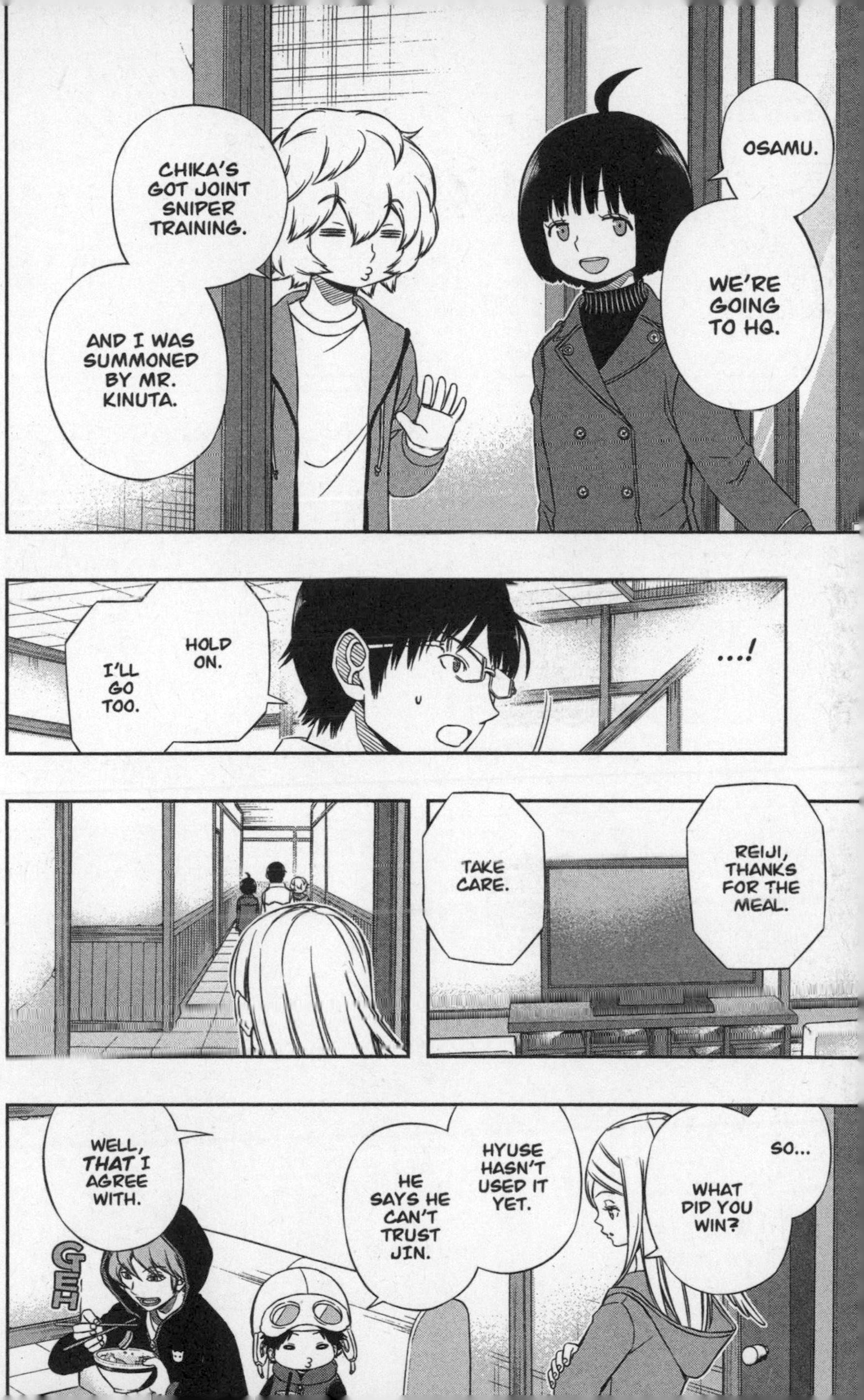
OSAMU.
WE'RE GOING TO HQ.
CHIKA'S GOT JOINT SNIPER TRAINING.
AND I WAS SUMMONED BY MR. KINUTA.
...!
HOLD ON.
I'LL GO TOO.
REIJI, THANKS FOR THE MEAL.
TAKE CARE.
SO...
WHAT DID YOU WIN?
HYUSE HASN'T USED IT YET.
HE SAYS HE CAN'T TRUST JIN.
WELL, THAT I AGREE WITH.
GEH

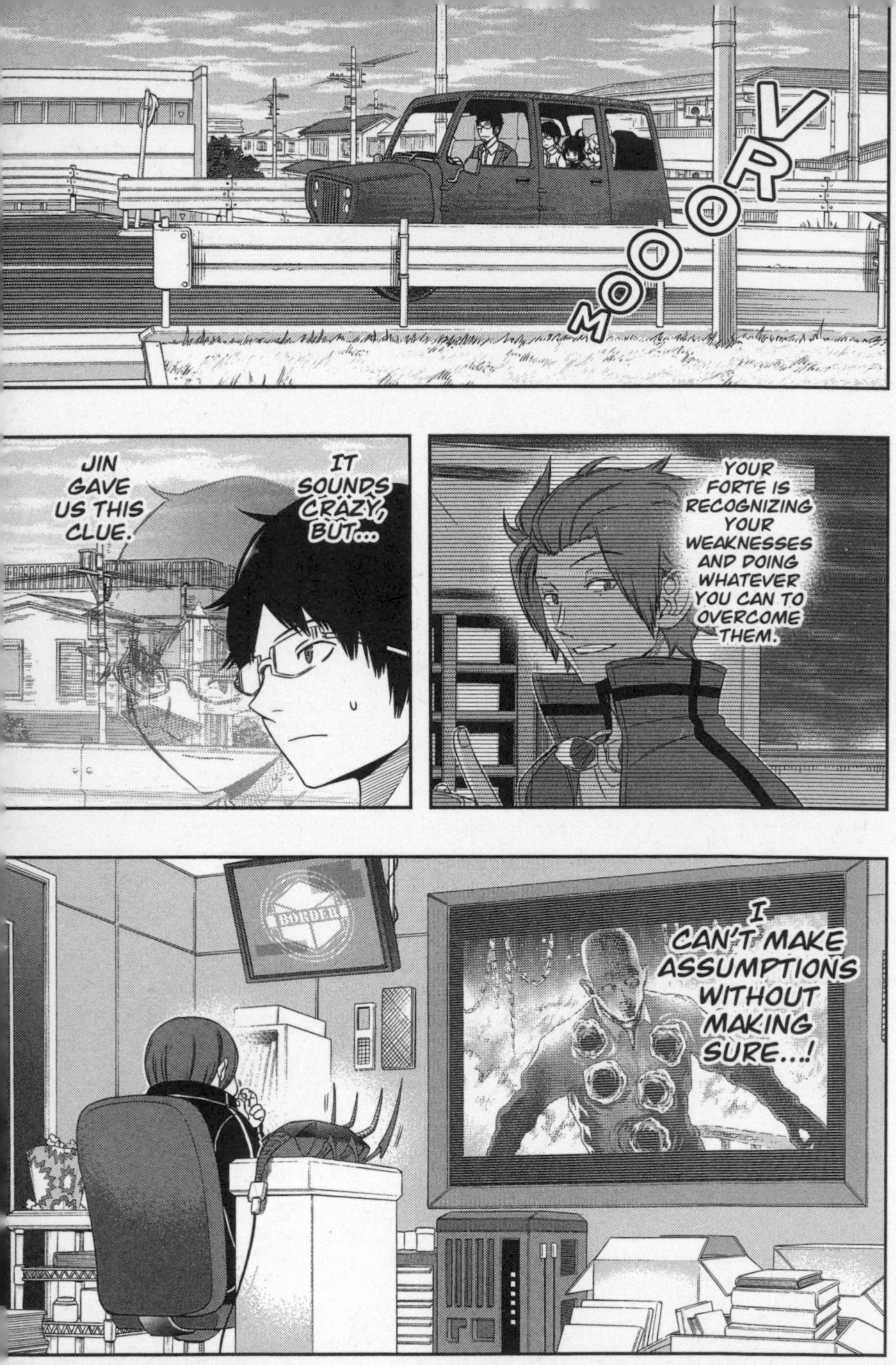
VROOOM
YOUR FORTE IS RECOGNIZING YOUR WEAKNESSES AND DOING WHATEVER YOU CAN TO OVERCOME THEM.
IT SOUNDS CRAZY, BUT...
JIN GAVE US THIS CLUE.
BORDER
I CAN'T MAKE ASSUMPTIONS WITHOUT MAKING SURE...!

Ninomiya Squad Strategy Room

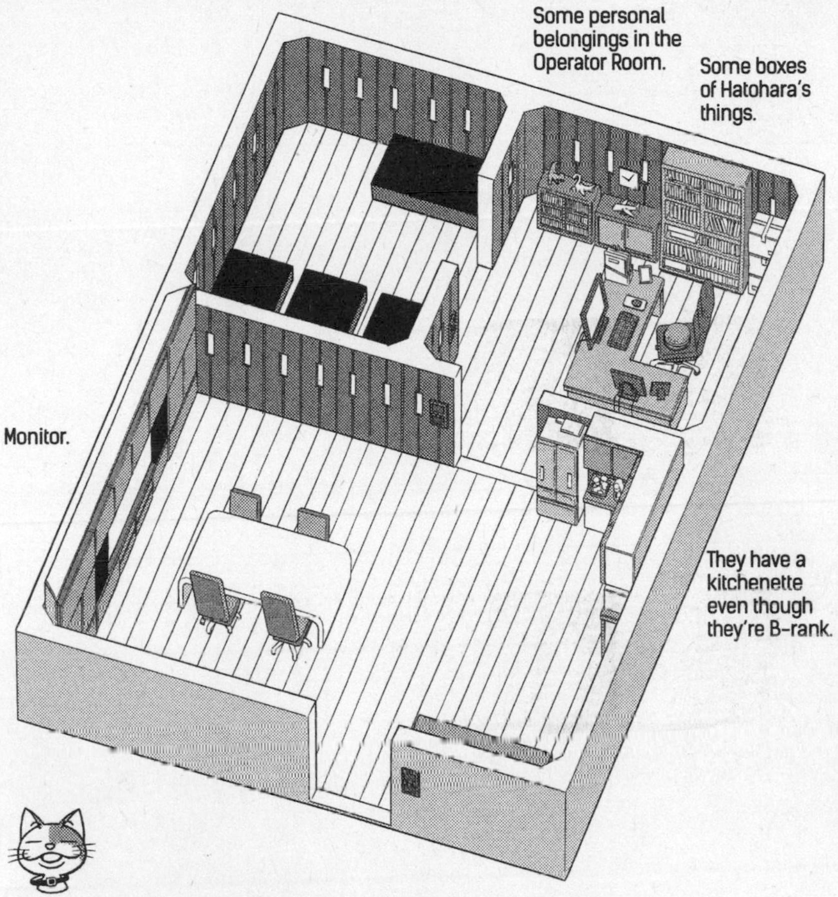
Some personal belongings in the Operator Room.
Some boxes of Hatohara's things.
Monitor.
They have a kitchenette even though they're B-rank.

The Ninomiya Squad Strategy Room has nothing in it and has a modern, stylish look. Ninomiya drinks ginger ale in this space. Hatohara used to clean regularly, but now that she's gone, everyone pitches in to clean. It's awkward to come in and see Ninomiya cleaning...

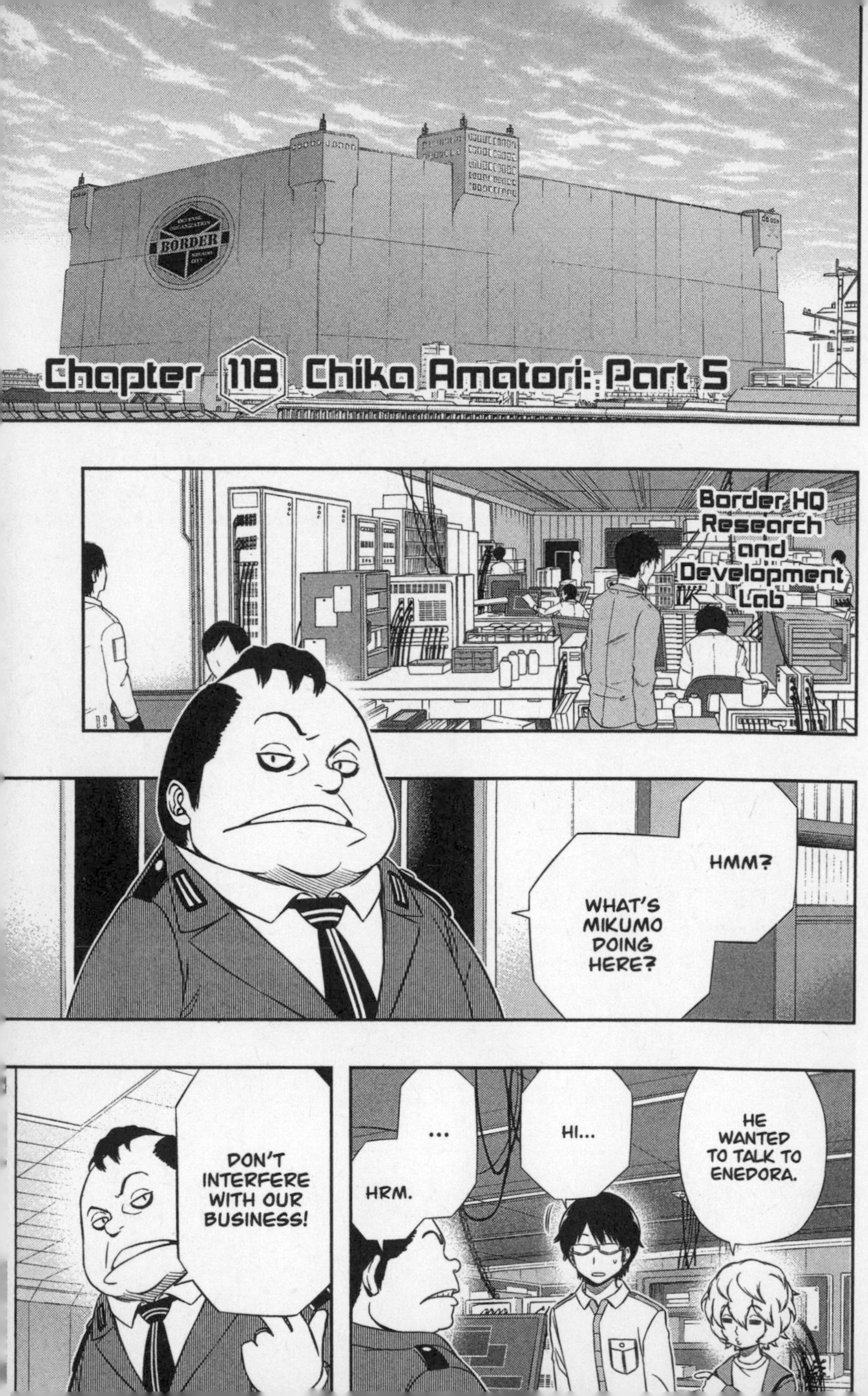
Chapter 118 Chika Amatori: Part 5
Border HQ Research and Development Lab
HMM?
WHAT'S MIKUMO DOING HERE?
HE WANTED TO TALK TO ENEDORA.
HI...
...
HRM.
DON'T INTERFERE WITH OUR BUSINESS!

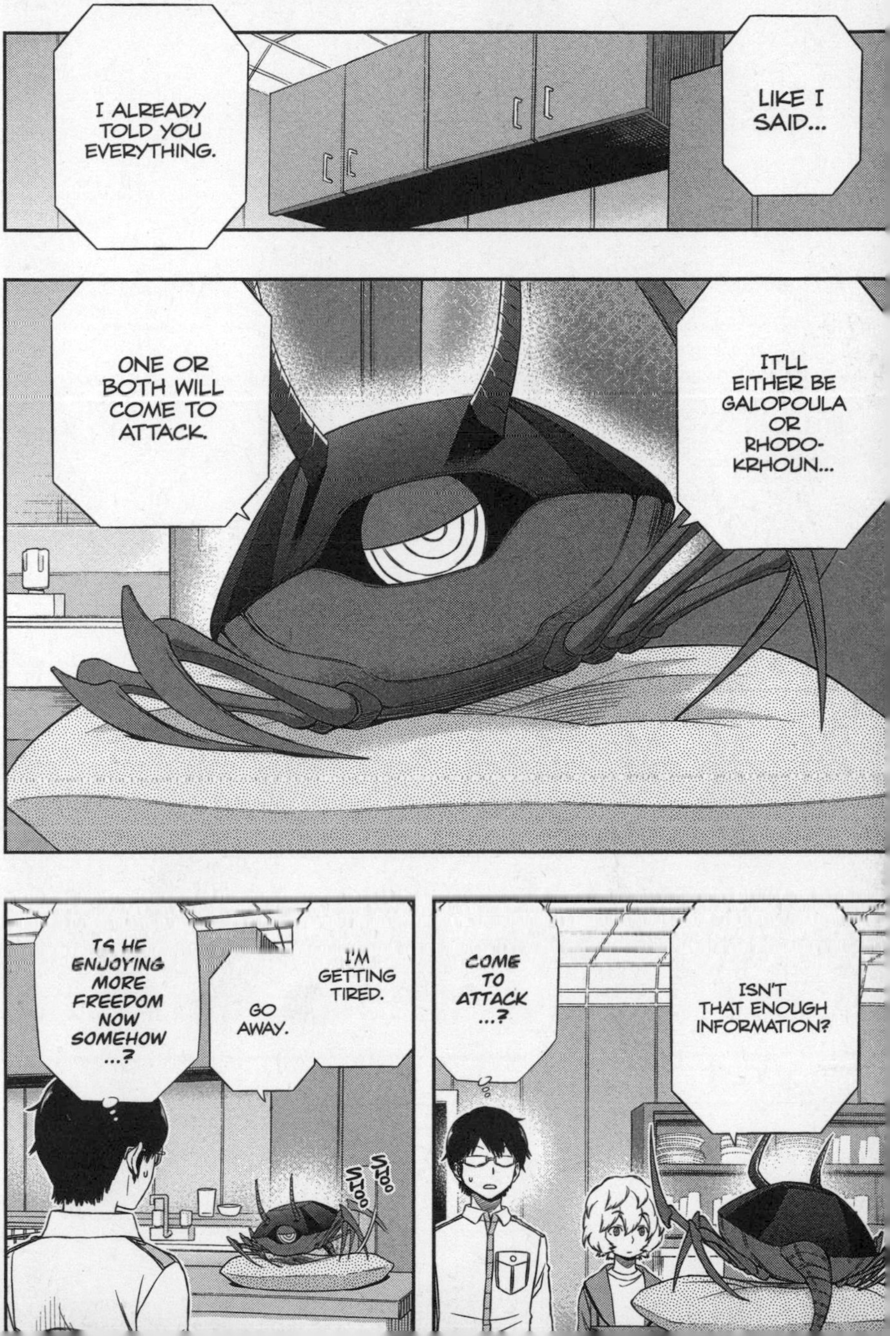
LIKE I SAID...
I ALREADY TOLD YOU EVERYTHING.
IT'LL EITHER BE GALOPOULA OR RHODO-KRHOUN...
ONE OR BOTH WILL COME TO ATTACK.
ISN'T THAT ENOUGH INFORMATION?
COME TO ATTACK ...?
I'M GETTING TIRED.
GO AWAY.
SHOO SHOO
IS HE ENJOYING MORE FREEDOM NOW SOMEHOW ...?

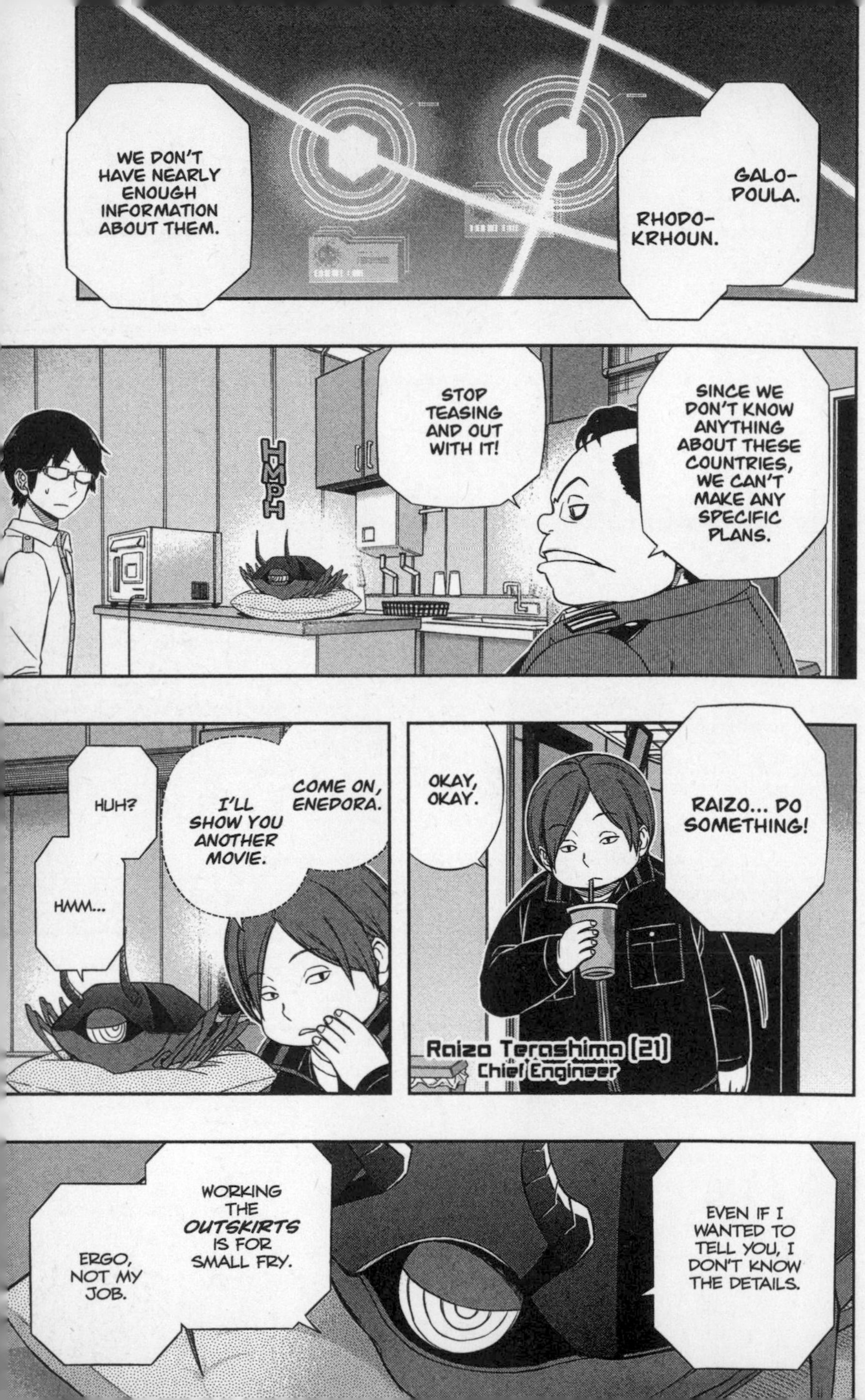
GALO-POULA.
RHODO-KRHOUN.
WE DON'T HAVE NEARLY ENOUGH INFORMATION ABOUT THEM.
SINCE WE DON'T KNOW ANYTHING ABOUT THESE COUNTRIES, WE CAN'T MAKE ANY SPECIFIC PLANS.
STOP TEASING AND OUT WITH IT!
HMPH
RAIZO... DO SOMETHING!
OKAY, OKAY.
Raizo Terashima (21)
Chief Engineer
COME ON, ENEDORA.
I'LL SHOW YOU ANOTHER MOVIE.
HUH?
HMM...
EVEN IF I WANTED TO TELL YOU, I DON'T KNOW THE DETAILS.
WORKING THE *OUTSKIRTS* IS FOR SMALL FRY.
ERGO, NOT MY JOB.

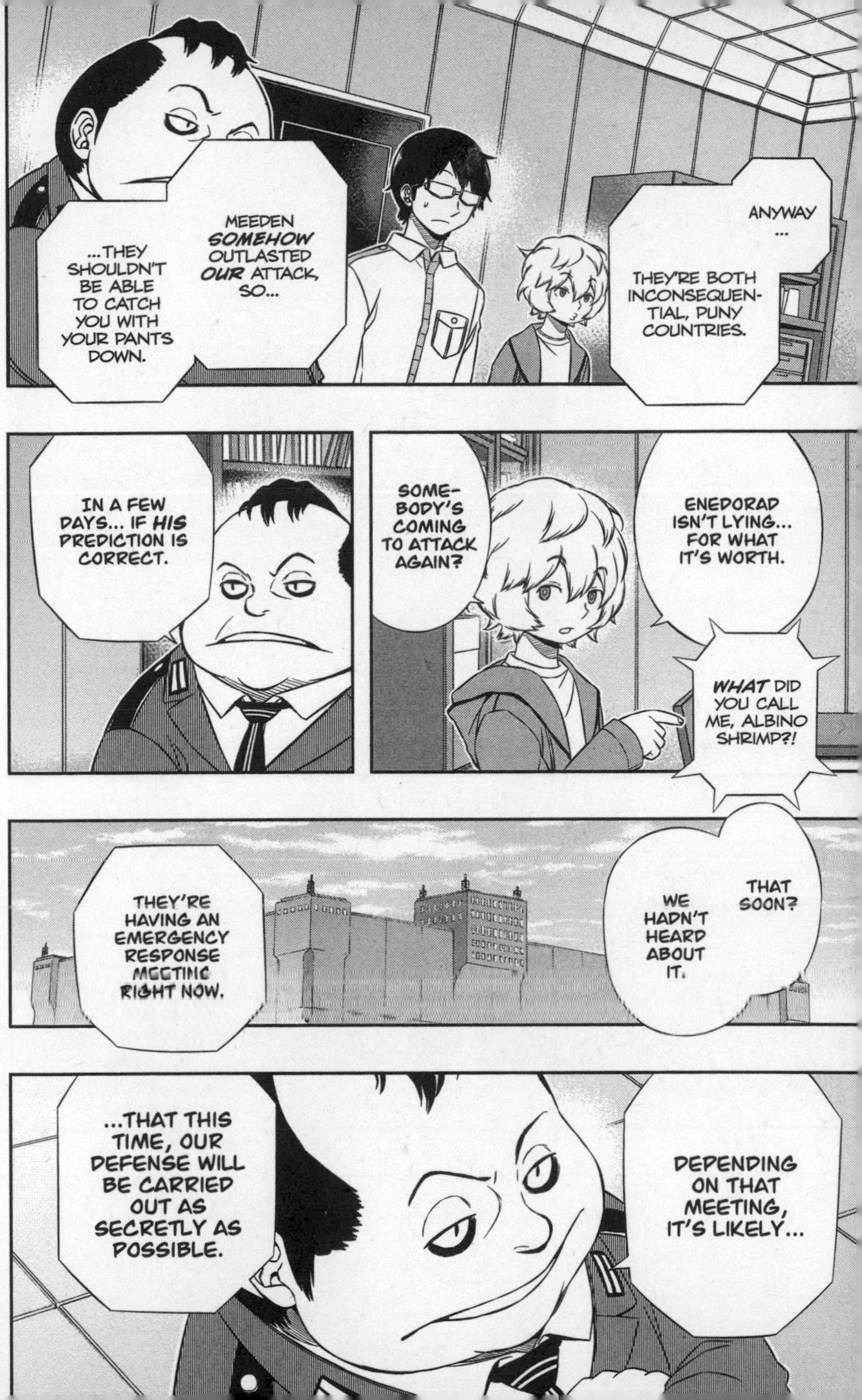
ANYWAY... THEY'RE BOTH INCONSEQUENTIAL, PUNY COUNTRIES.
MEEDEN SOMEHOW OUTLASTED OUR ATTACK, SO...
...THEY SHOULDN'T BE ABLE TO CATCH YOU WITH YOUR PANTS DOWN.
ENEDORAD ISN'T LYING... FOR WHAT IT'S WORTH.
WHAT DID YOU CALL ME, ALBINO SHRIMP?!
SOMEBODY'S COMING TO ATTACK AGAIN?
IN A FEW DAYS... IF HIS PREDICTION IS CORRECT.
THAT SOON? WE HADN'T HEARD ABOUT IT.
THEY'RE HAVING AN EMERGENCY RESPONSE MEETING RIGHT NOW.
DEPENDING ON THAT MEETING, IT'S LIKELY...
...THAT THIS TIME, OUR DEFENSE WILL BE CARRIED OUT AS SECRETLY AS POSSIBLE.

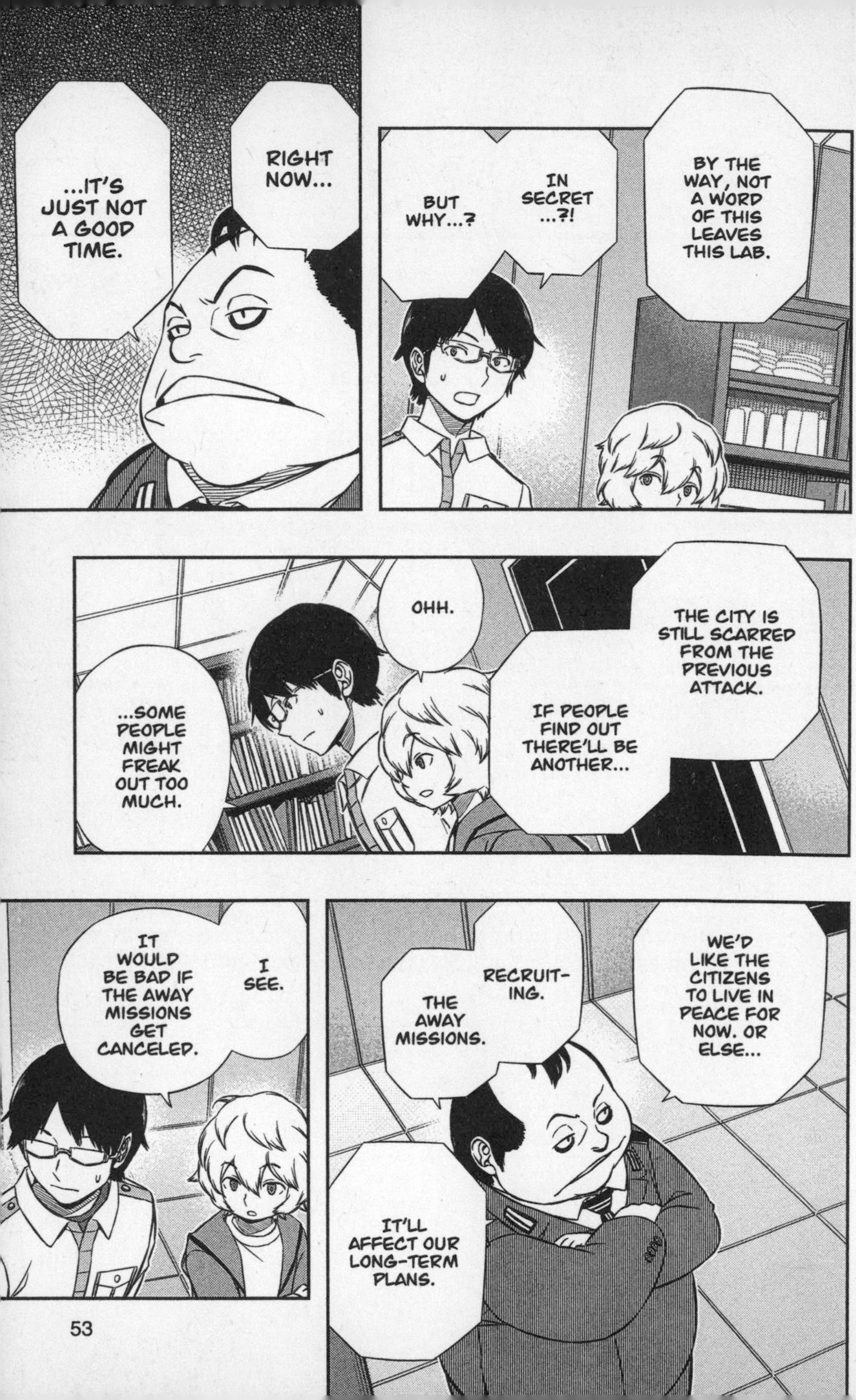
BY THE WAY, NOT A WORD OF THIS LEAVES THIS LAB.
IN SECRET ...?!
BUT WHY...?
RIGHT NOW...
...IT'S JUST NOT A GOOD TIME.
THE CITY IS STILL SCARRED FROM THE PREVIOUS ATTACK.
IF PEOPLE FIND OUT THERE'LL BE ANOTHER...
OHH.
...SOME PEOPLE MIGHT FREAK OUT TOO MUCH.
WE'D LIKE THE CITIZENS TO LIVE IN PEACE FOR NOW. OR ELSE...
RECRUIT-ING.
THE AWAY MISSIONS.
IT'LL AFFECT OUR LONG-TERM PLANS.
I SEE.
IT WOULD BE BAD IF THE AWAY MISSIONS GET CANCELED.

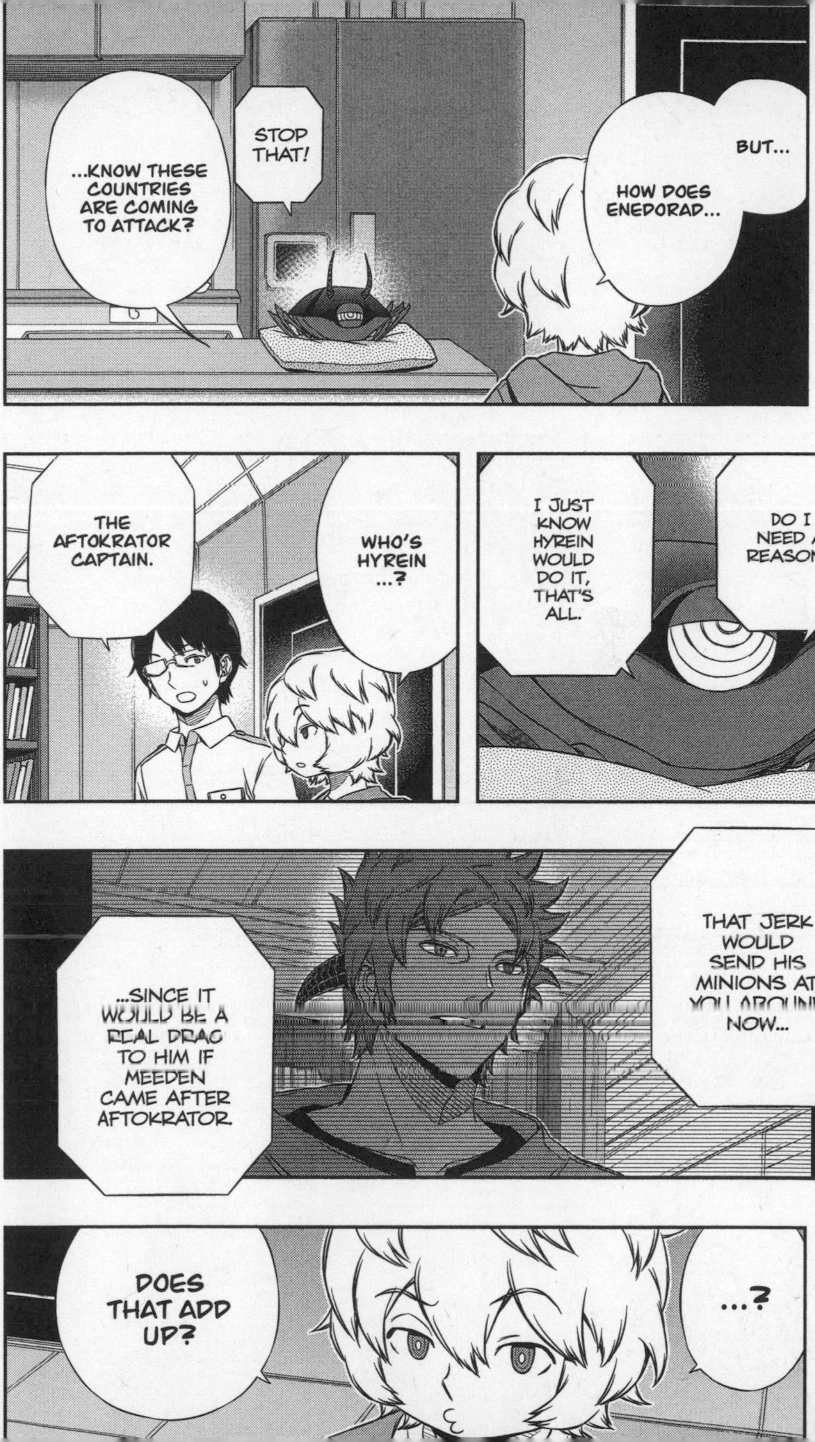
BUT...
HOW DOES ENEDORAD...
STOP THAT!
...KNOW THESE COUNTRIES ARE COMING TO ATTACK?
DO I NEED A REASON?
I JUST KNOW HYREIN WOULD DO IT, THAT'S ALL.
WHO'S HYREIN ...?
THE AFTOKRATOR CAPTAIN.
THAT JERK WOULD SEND HIS MINIONS AT YOU AROUND NOW...
...SINCE IT WOULD BE A REAL DRAG TO HIM IF MEEDEN CAME AFTER AFTOKRATOR.
...?
DOES THAT ADD UP?

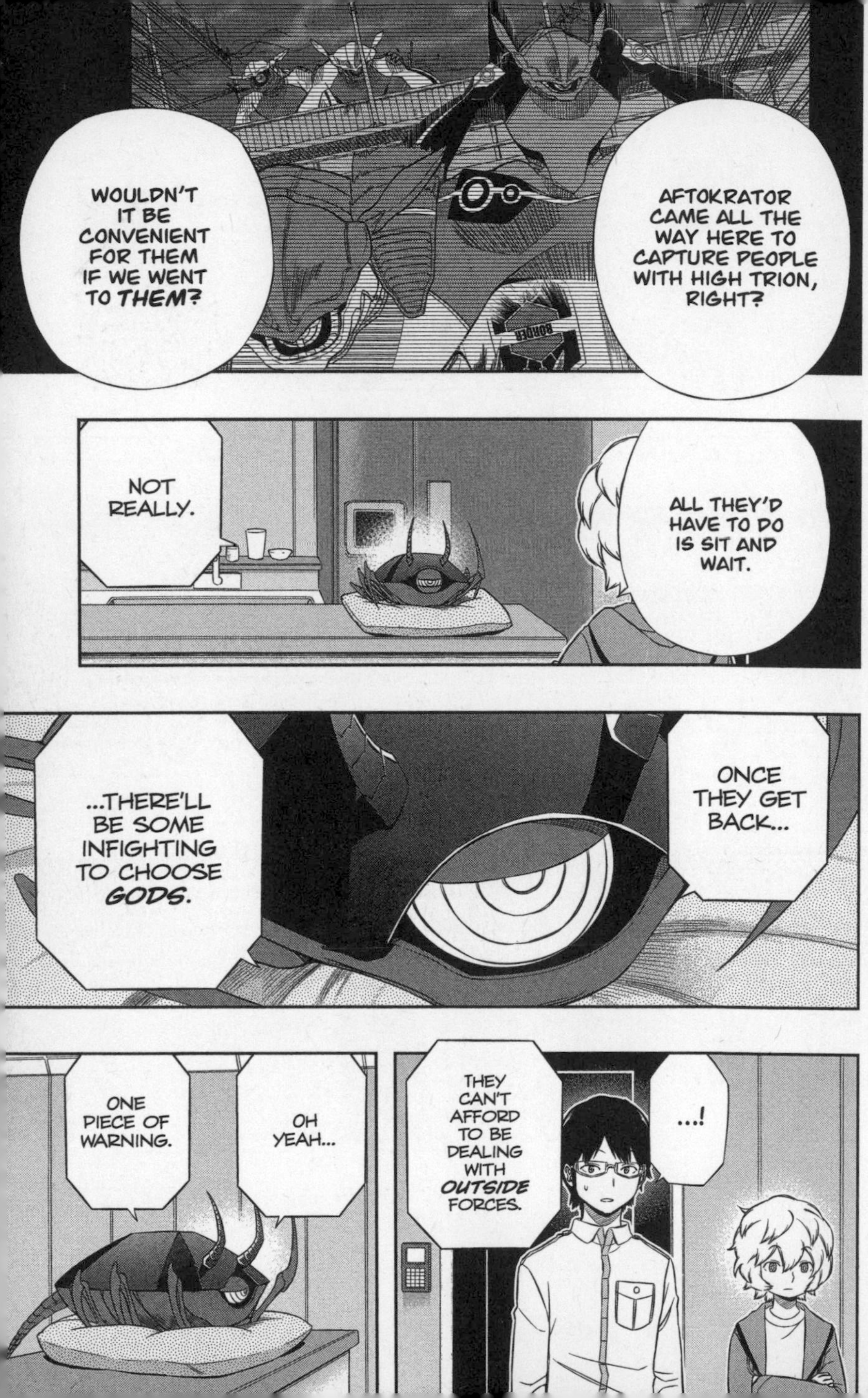
AFTOKRATOR CAME ALL THE WAY HERE TO CAPTURE PEOPLE WITH HIGH TRION, RIGHT?
WOULDN'T IT BE CONVENIENT FOR THEM IF WE WENT TO *THEM*?
BORDER
ALL THEY'D HAVE TO DO IS SIT AND WAIT.
NOT REALLY.
ONCE THEY GET BACK...
...THERE'LL BE SOME INFIGHTING TO CHOOSE *GODS*.
...!
THEY CAN'T AFFORD TO BE DEALING WITH *OUTSIDE* FORCES.
OH YEAH...
ONE PIECE OF WARNING.

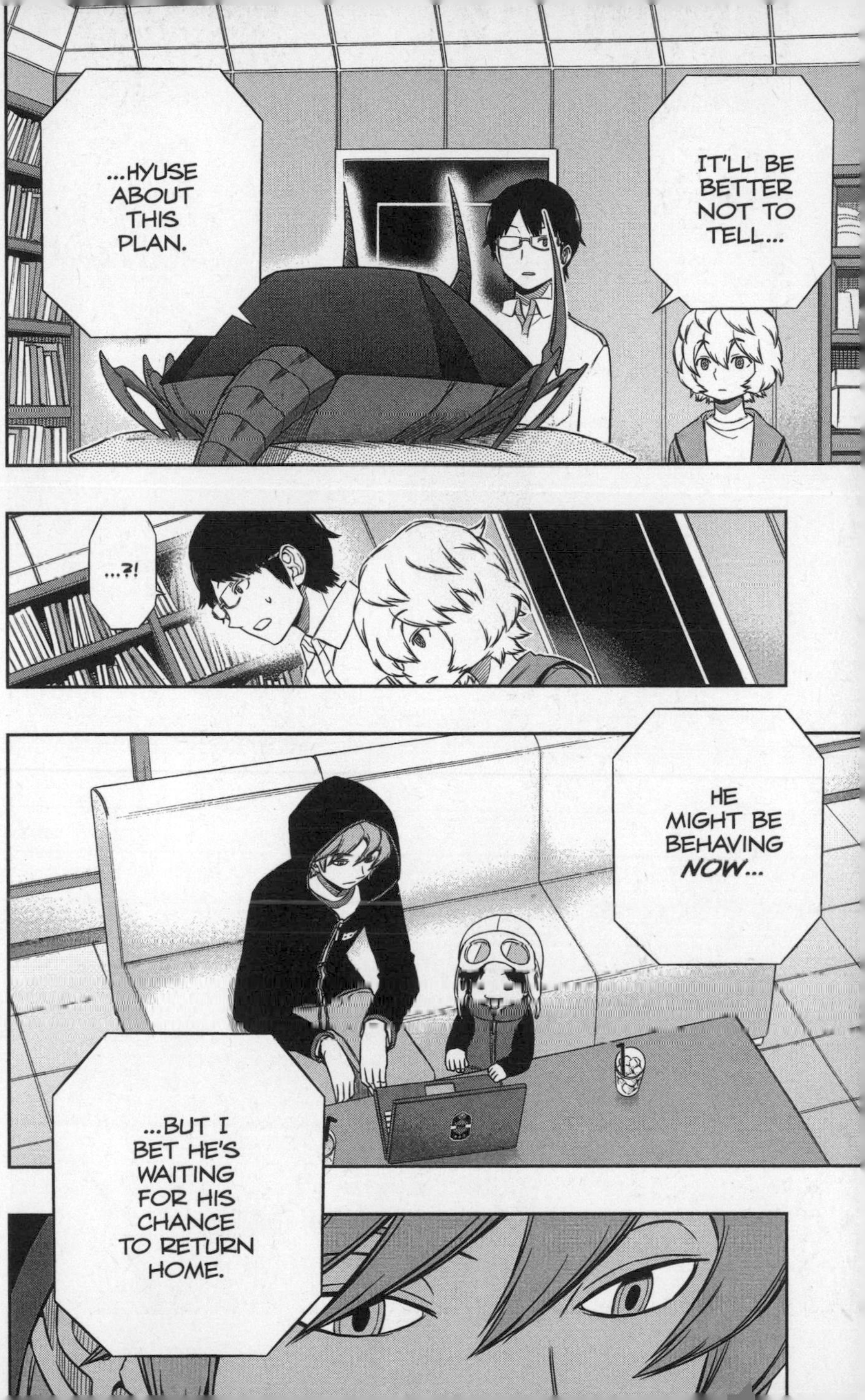
IT'LL BE BETTER NOT TO TELL...
...HYUSE ABOUT THIS PLAN.
...?!
HE MIGHT BE BEHAVING *NOW*...
...BUT I BET HE'S WAITING FOR HIS CHANCE TO RETURN HOME.

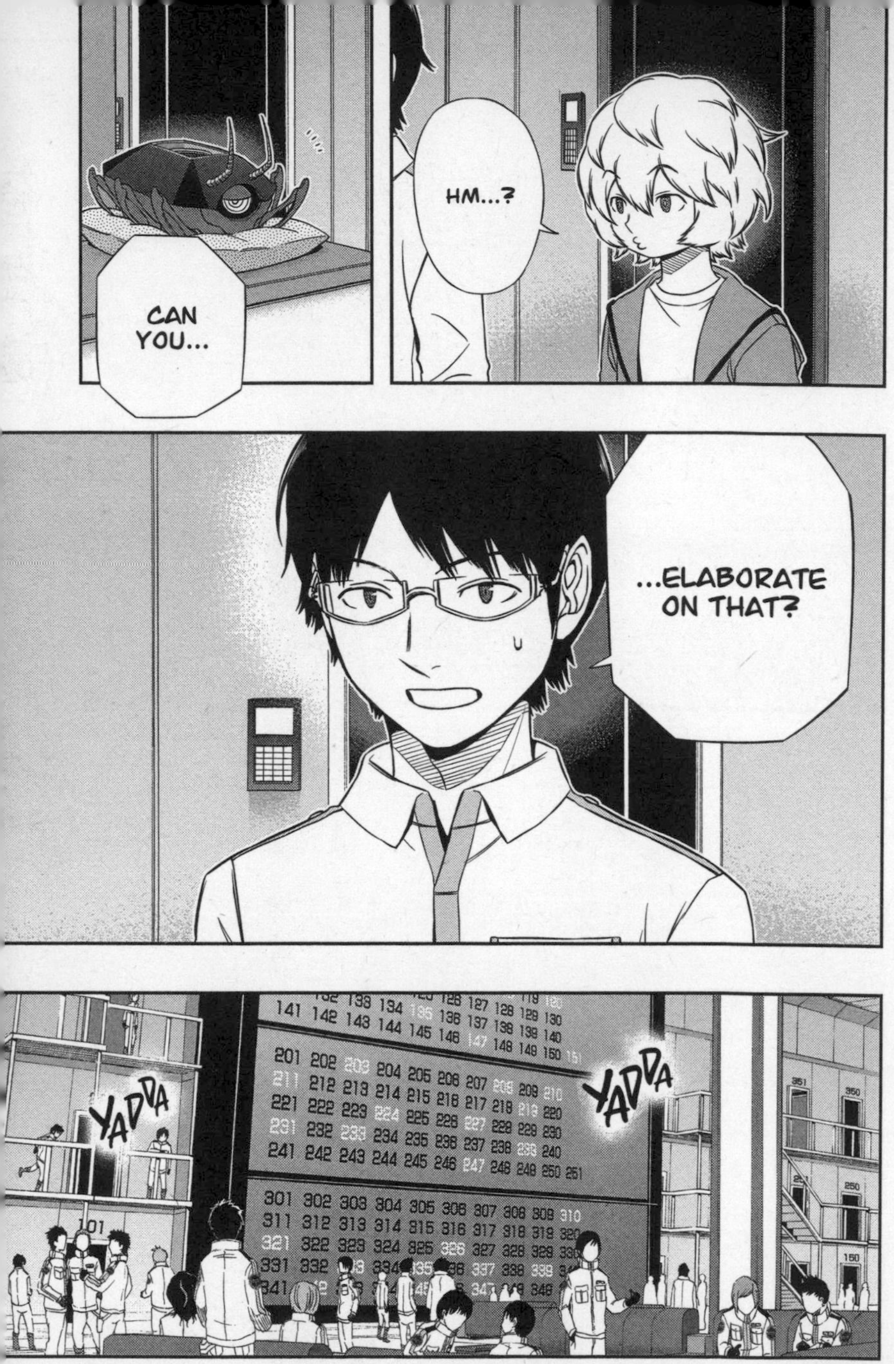
HM...?
CAN YOU...
...ELABORATE ON THAT?
YADDA
YADDA

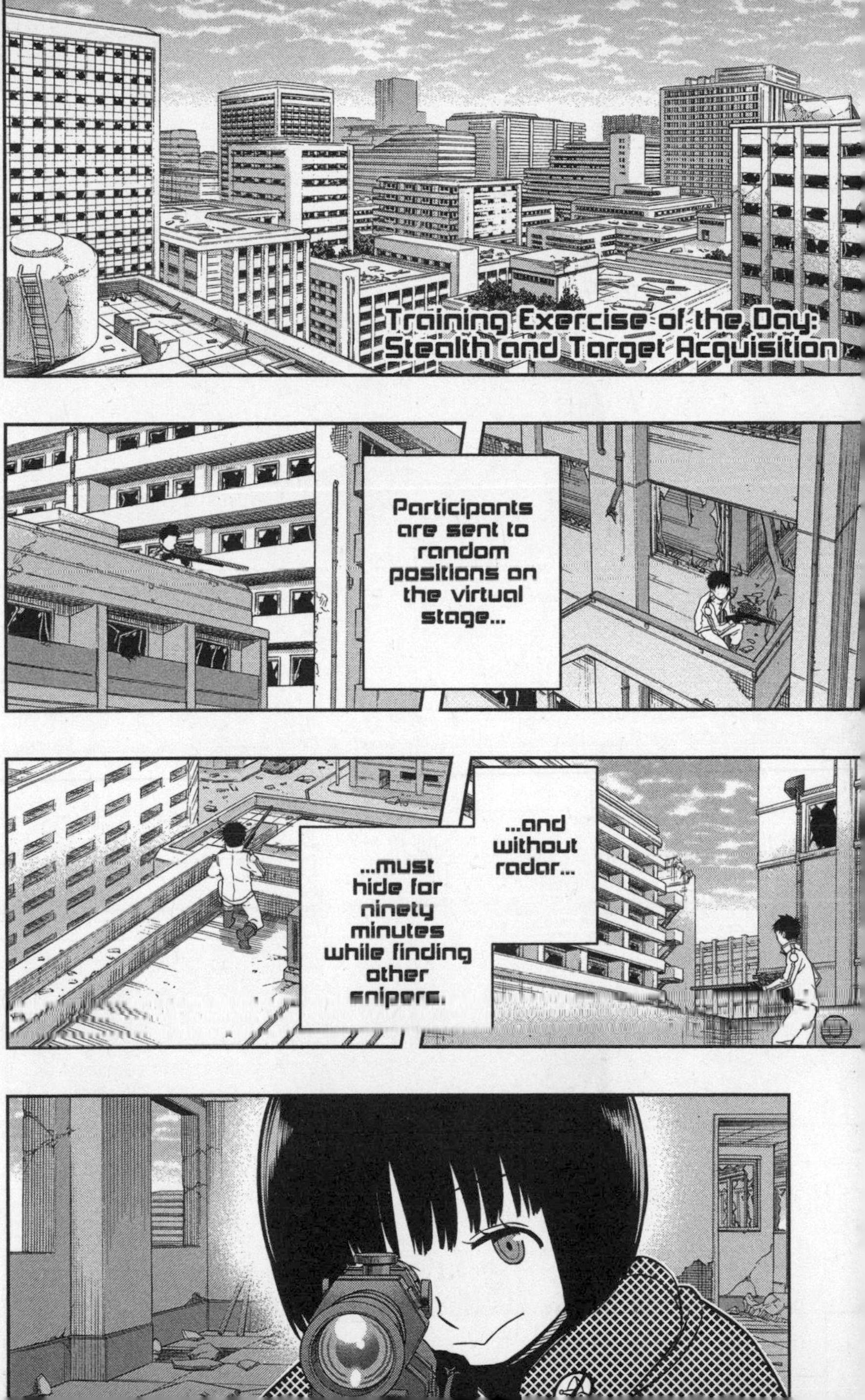
Training Exercise of the Day: Stealth and Target Acquisition
Participants are sent to random positions on the virtual stage...
...and without radar...
...must hide for ninety minutes while finding other snipers.

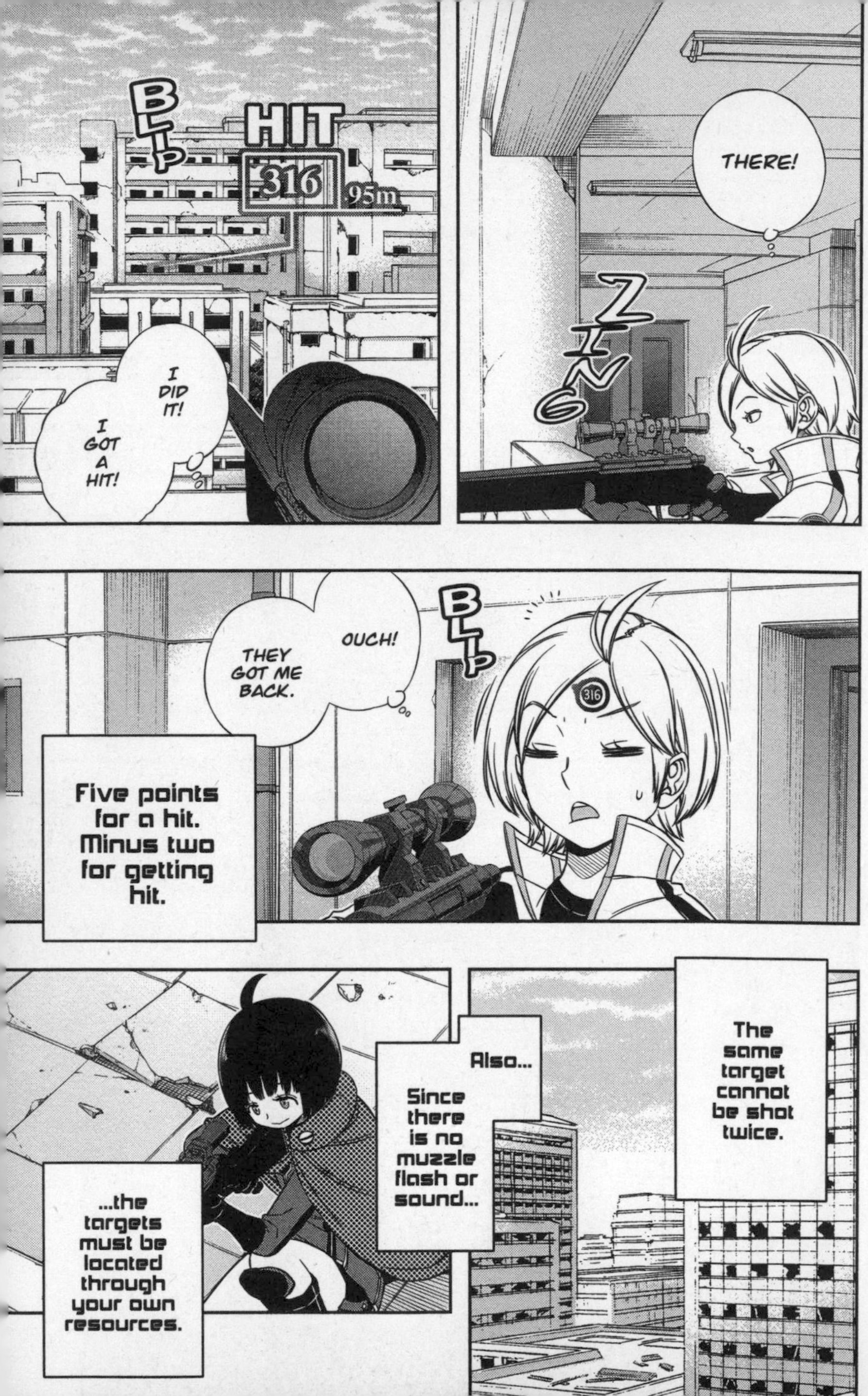
THERE!
ZING
BLIP
HIT
316
95m
I DID IT!
I GOT A HIT!
BLIP
OUCH!
THEY GOT ME BACK.
316
Five points for a hit. Minus two for getting hit.
The same target cannot be shot twice.
Also...
Since there is no muzzle flash or sound...
...the targets must be located through your own resources.

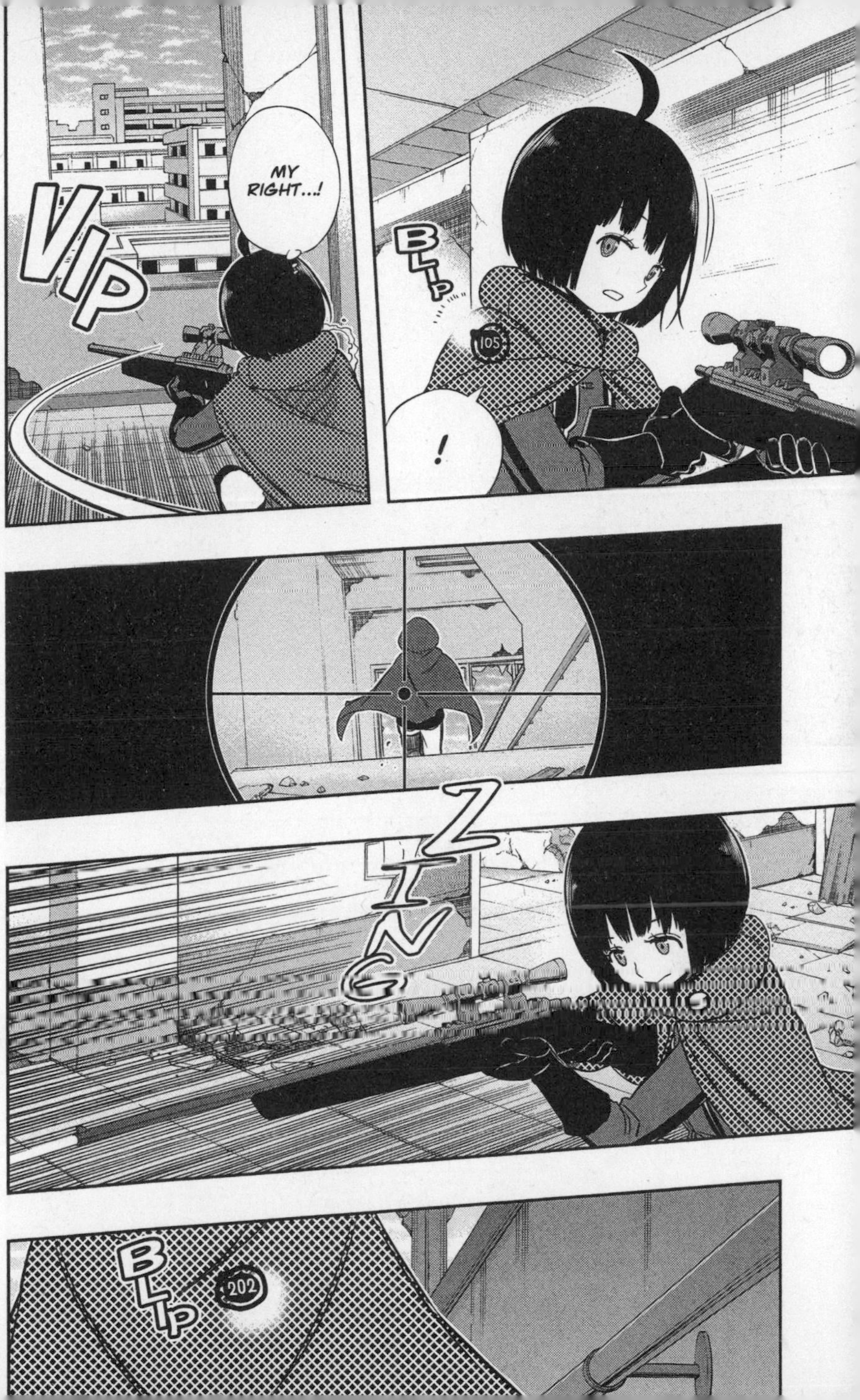

BLIP
105
!
MY RIGHT...!
VIP
ZING
BLIP
202

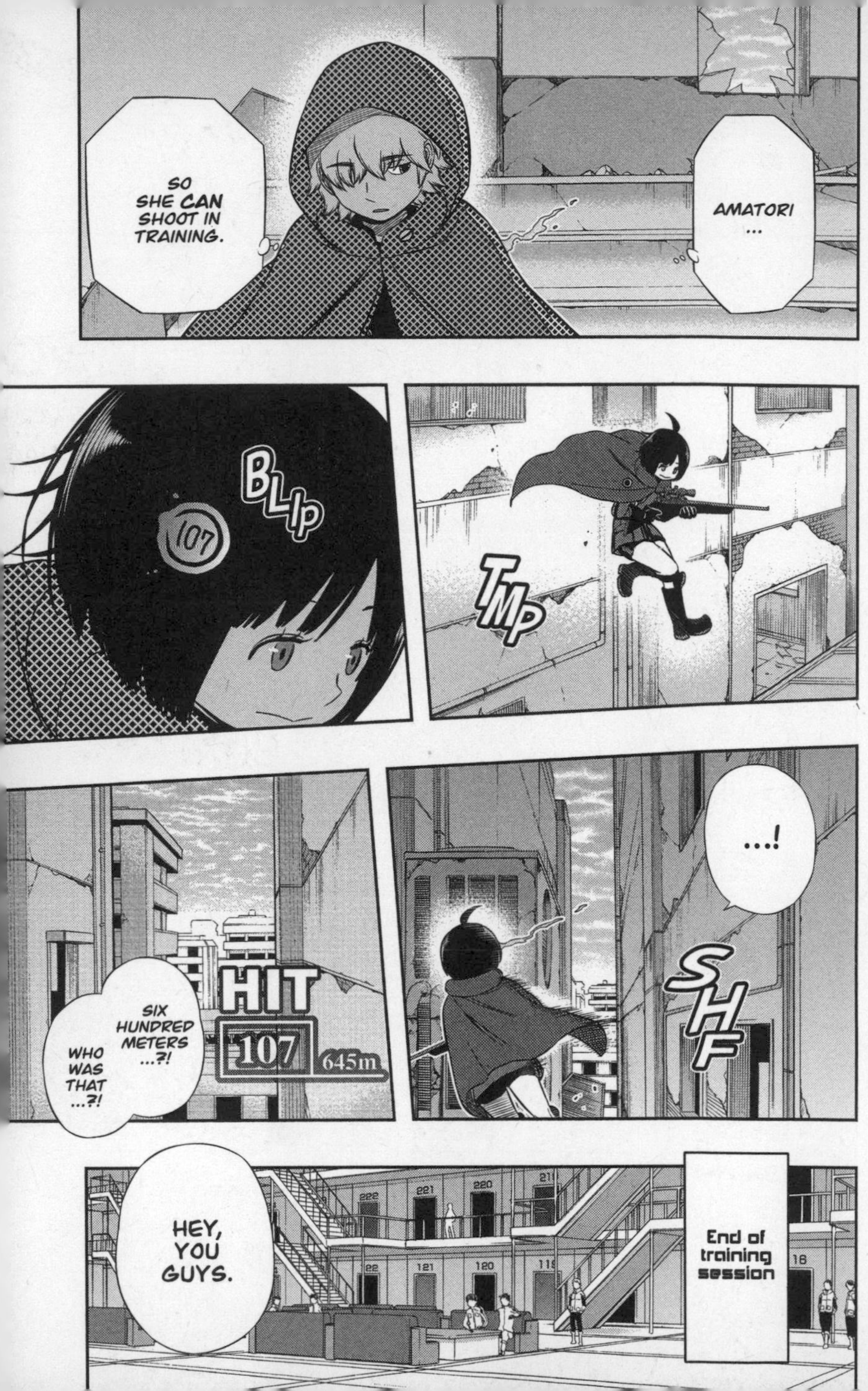

AMATORI ...
SO SHE CAN SHOOT IN TRAINING.
TMP
BLIP
107
...!
SHF
HIT
107
645m
SIX HUNDRED METERS ...?!
WHO WAS THAT ...?!
End of training session
HEY, YOU GUYS.

Booth No.

107 Isami Toma

60 points [51st out of 127]

Kills	Deaths
12	none
315	341
105	202
229	318
246	228
338	201
317	230

AREN'T YOU LEAVING YOURSELVES TOO OPEN?

HOW ARE WE SUPPOSED TO NOTICE ANYTHING 500 METERS AWAY?

I FIGURED IT WOULD BE TOMA.

201 Izuho Natsume

47 points [64th]

Kills	Deaths
15	14

202 Chika Amatori

104 points [19th]

Kills	Deaths
22	3

105 Yuzuru Ema

86 points [25th]

Kills	Deaths
18	2

IZUHO, YOU'RE FULL OF HOLES!

YOU'RE SO POPULAR.

WHEN WILL THIS *THING* DISAPPEAR?

229 Atsushi Hokari

147 points [5th]

Kills	Deaths
31	4

228 Tetsuji Arafune

141 points [7th]

Kills	Deaths
29	2

317 Shohei Kodera

136 points [9th]

230 Yoshito Hanzaki

148 points [4th]

316 Taichi Betsuyaku

125 points [13th]

315 Ken Satori

159 points [2nd]

CHIKAKO, YOU'RE AMAZING.

YOU'RE IN 19TH WITH OVER 100 POINTS.

341 Akane Hiura

129 points [11th]

246 Toru Narasaka

188 points [1st]

Kills	Deaths
38	1

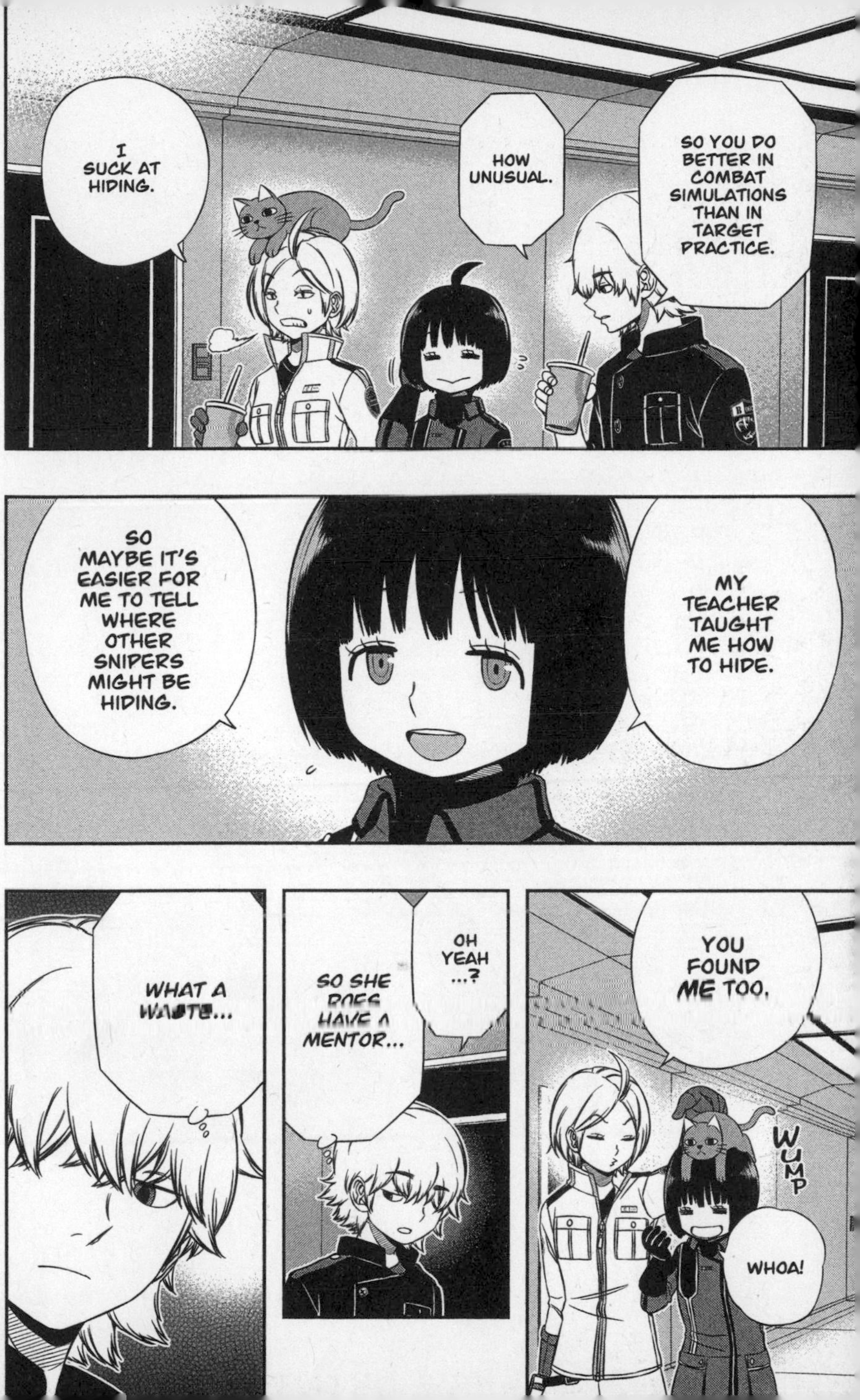
SO YOU DO BETTER IN COMBAT SIMULATIONS THAN IN TARGET PRACTICE.
HOW UNUSUAL.
I SUCK AT HIDING.
MY TEACHER TAUGHT ME HOW TO HIDE.
SO MAYBE IT'S EASIER FOR ME TO TELL WHERE OTHER SNIPERS MIGHT BE HIDING.
YOU FOUND ME TOO.
WUMP
WHOA!
OH YEAH ...?
SO SHE DOES HAVE A MENTOR...
WHAT A WASTE...

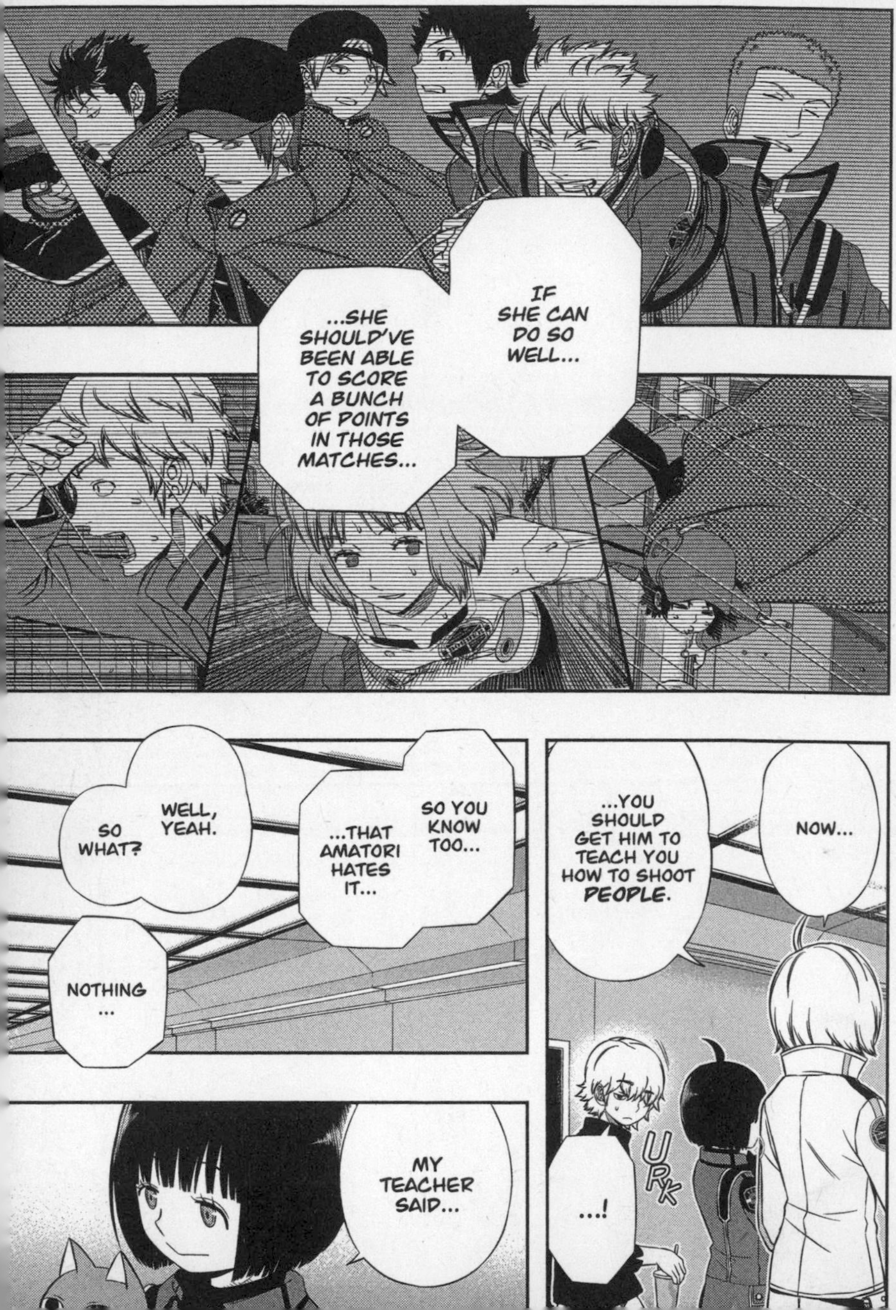
IF SHE CAN DO SO WELL...
...SHE SHOULD'VE BEEN ABLE TO SCORE A BUNCH OF POINTS IN THOSE MATCHES...
NOW...
...YOU SHOULD GET HIM TO TEACH YOU HOW TO SHOOT **PEOPLE**.
URK
...!
SO YOU KNOW TOO...
...THAT AMATORI HATES IT...
WELL, YEAH.
SO WHAT?
NOTHING ...
MY TEACHER SAID...

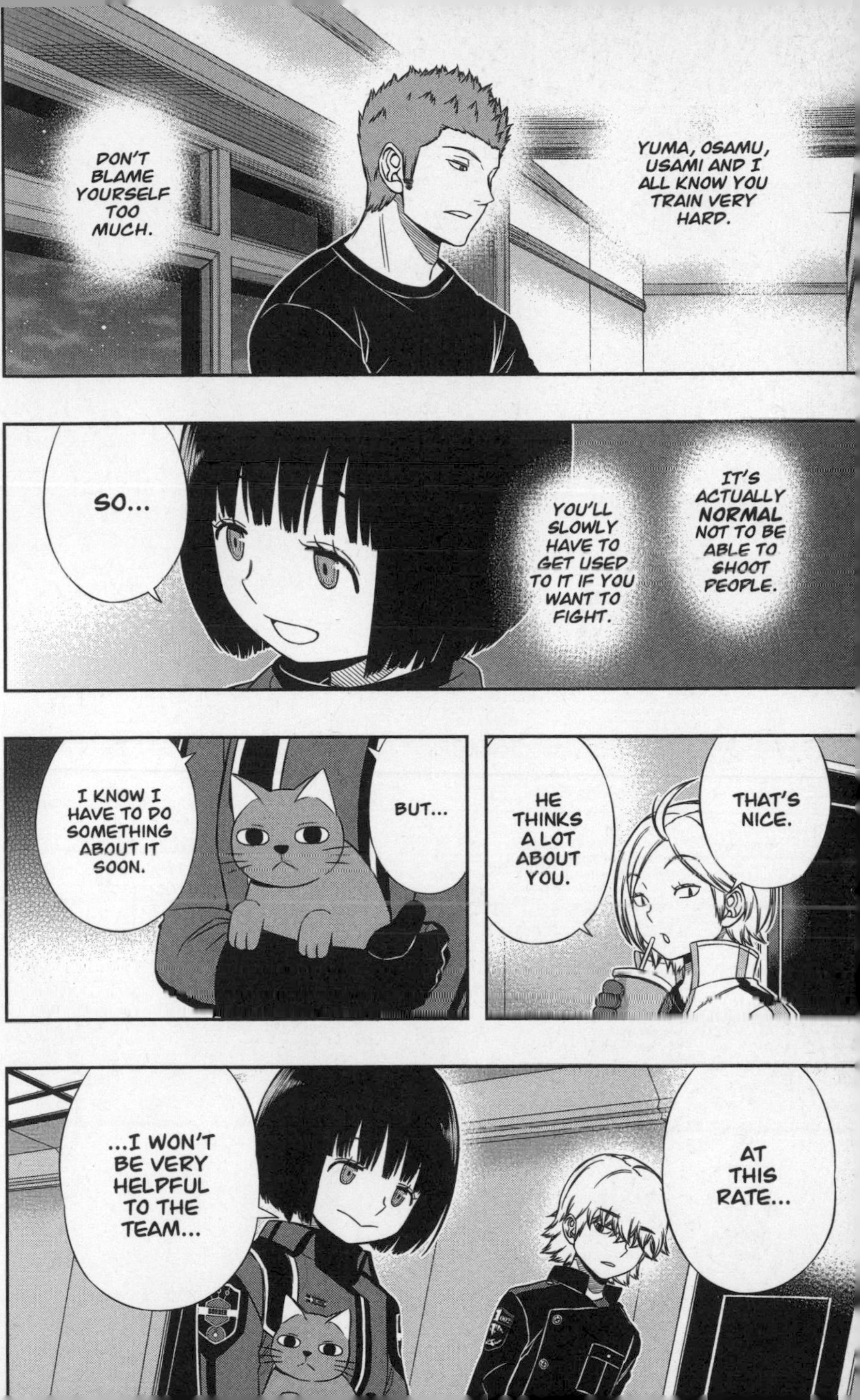
YUMA, OSAMU, USAMI AND I ALL KNOW YOU TRAIN VERY HARD.
DON'T BLAME YOURSELF TOO MUCH.
IT'S ACTUALLY NORMAL NOT TO BE ABLE TO SHOOT PEOPLE.
YOU'LL SLOWLY HAVE TO GET USED TO IT IF YOU WANT TO FIGHT.
SO...
THAT'S NICE.
HE THINKS A LOT ABOUT YOU.
BUT...
I KNOW I HAVE TO DO SOMETHING ABOUT IT SOON.
AT THIS RATE...
...I WON'T BE VERY HELPFUL TO THE TEAM...

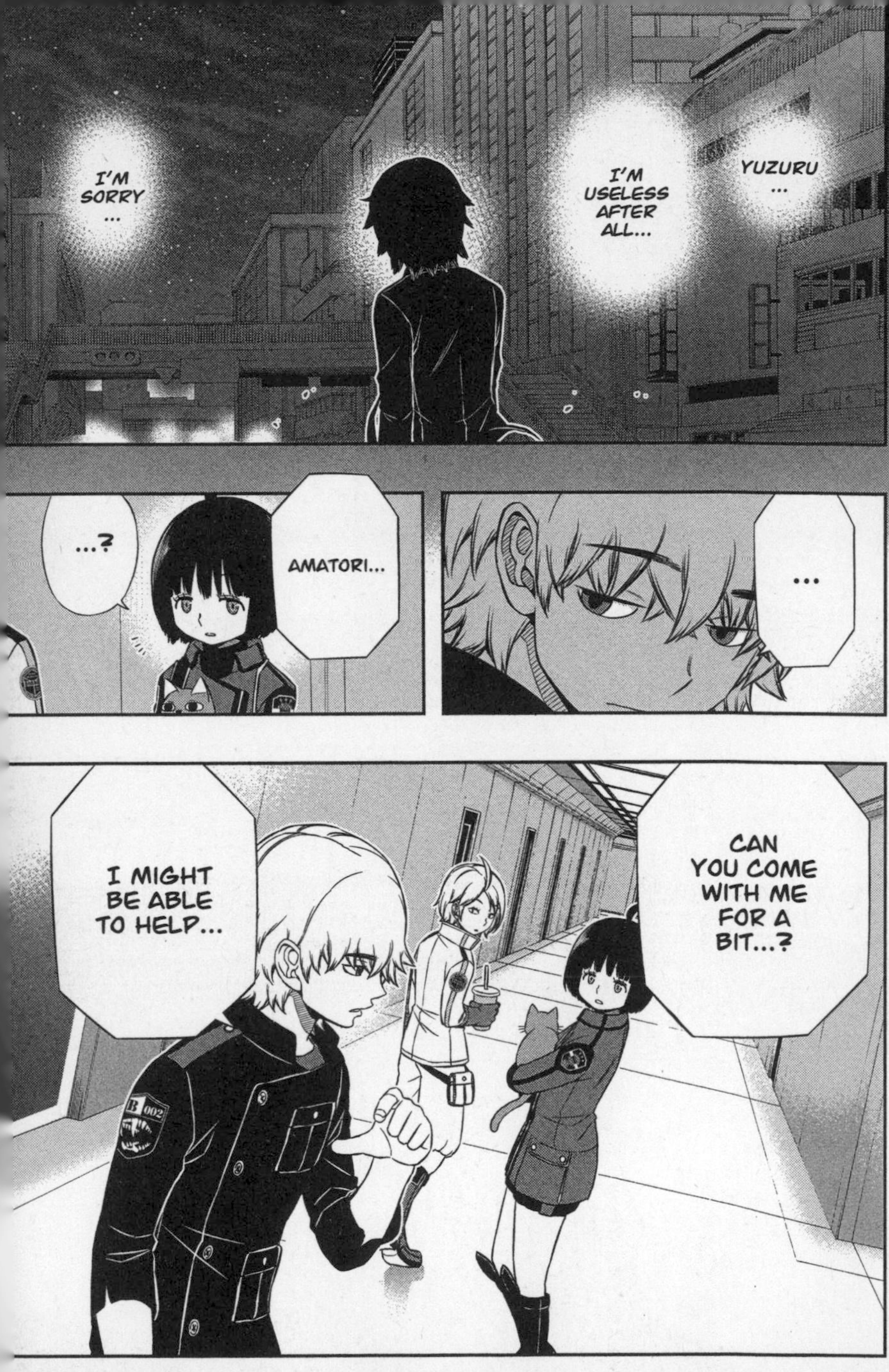
YUZURU...
I'M USELESS AFTER ALL...
I'M SORRY...
...
AMATORI...
...?
CAN YOU COME WITH ME FOR A BIT...?
I MIGHT BE ABLE TO HELP...

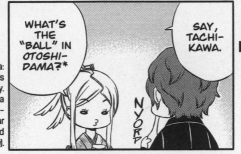

■ 2016 *Weekly Shonen Jump* 5-6 combined issue

New Year's Comic Strip

SAY, TACHIKAWA.
NYORP
WHAT'S THE "BALL" IN OTOSHIDAMA?*
WELL, SINCE COINS ARE ROUND AND SHINY...
NOM NOM
IT'S GOTTA BE FAMILY JEWELS!
NOM NOM
WHAT?!
REALLY?!
THEY'RE TESTICLES?!
FMP FMP
HM.
SOUNDS LOGICAL.
...?!

*Otoshidama: New Year's money. Literally a combination of year (*otoshi*) and ball (*dama*).

We were told to draw a comic strip about New Year's money. I first drew them in the usual style, but then switched them to the chibi version so they could say crazier things.

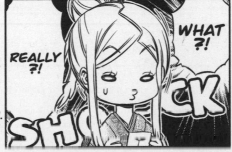

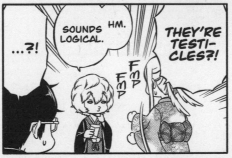

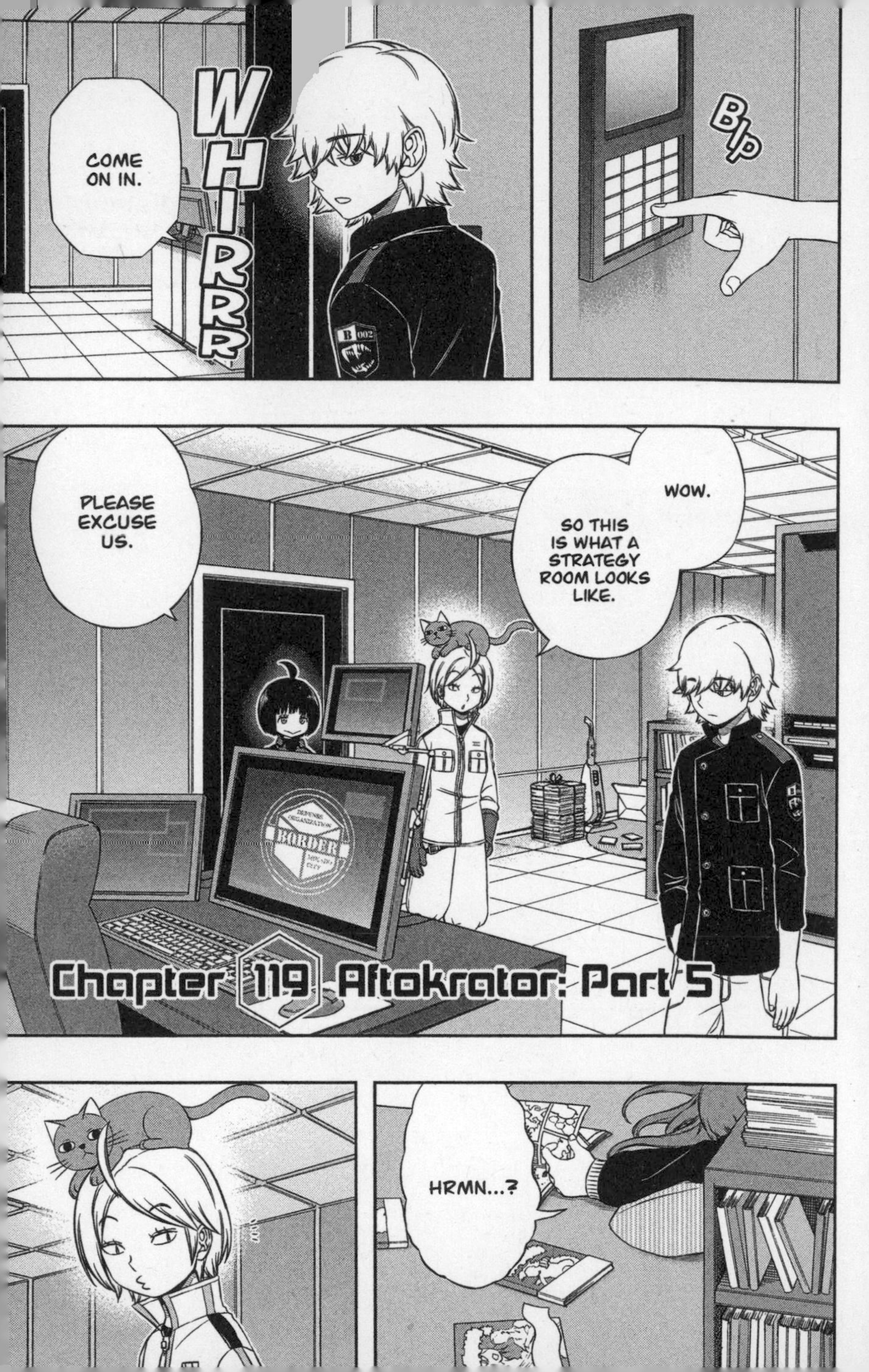
BIP
WHIRRR
COME ON IN.
WOW.
SO THIS IS WHAT A STRATEGY ROOM LOOKS LIKE.
PLEASE EXCUSE US.
Chapter 119 Aftokrator: Part 5
HRMN...?

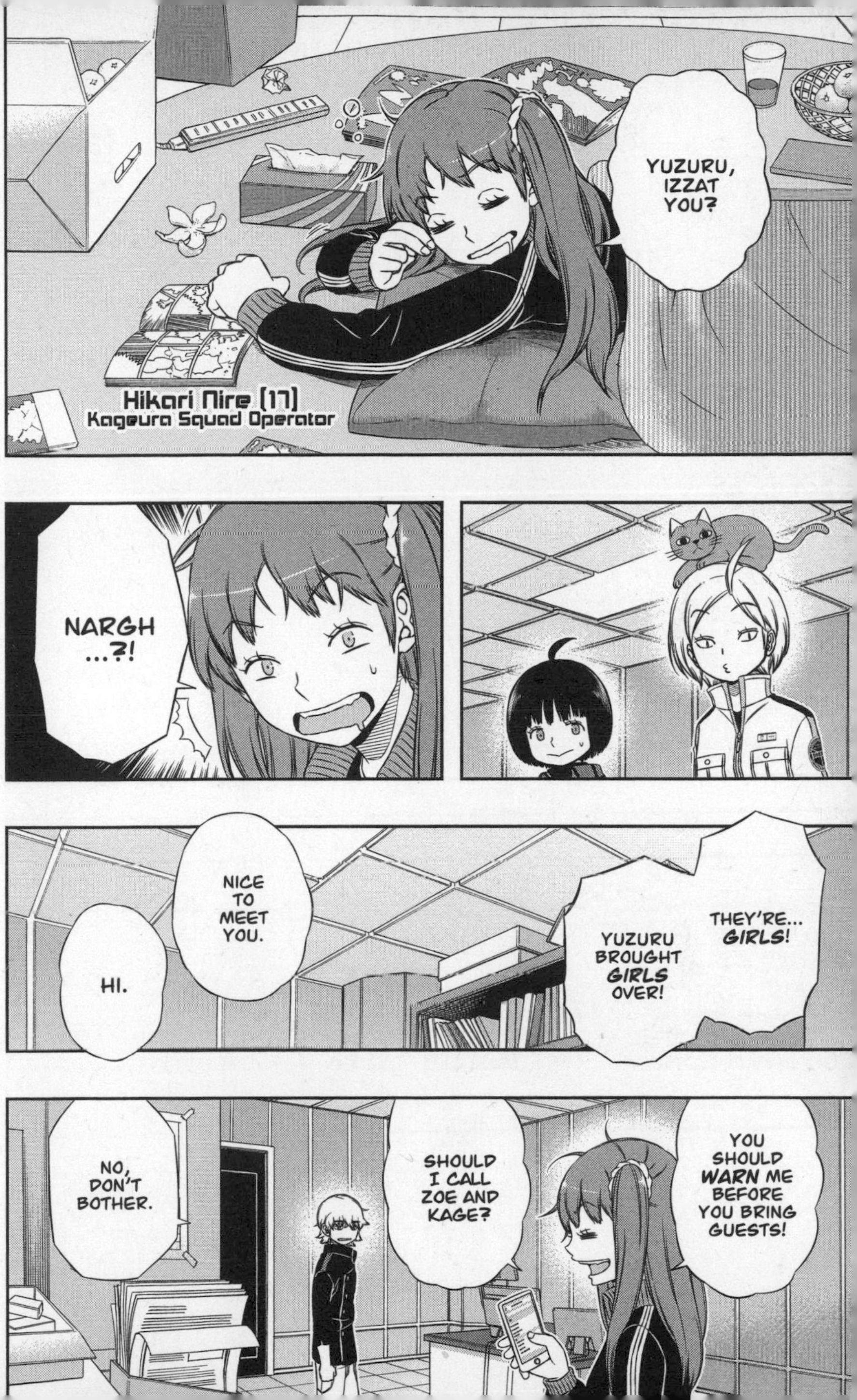
YUZURU, IZZAT YOU?
Hikari Nire (17)
Kageura Squad Operator
NARGH ...?!
THEY'RE... GIRLS!
YUZURU BROUGHT GIRLS OVER!
NICE TO MEET YOU.
HI.
YOU SHOULD WARN ME BEFORE YOU BRING GUESTS!
SHOULD I CALL ZOE AND KAGE?
NO, DON'T BOTHER.

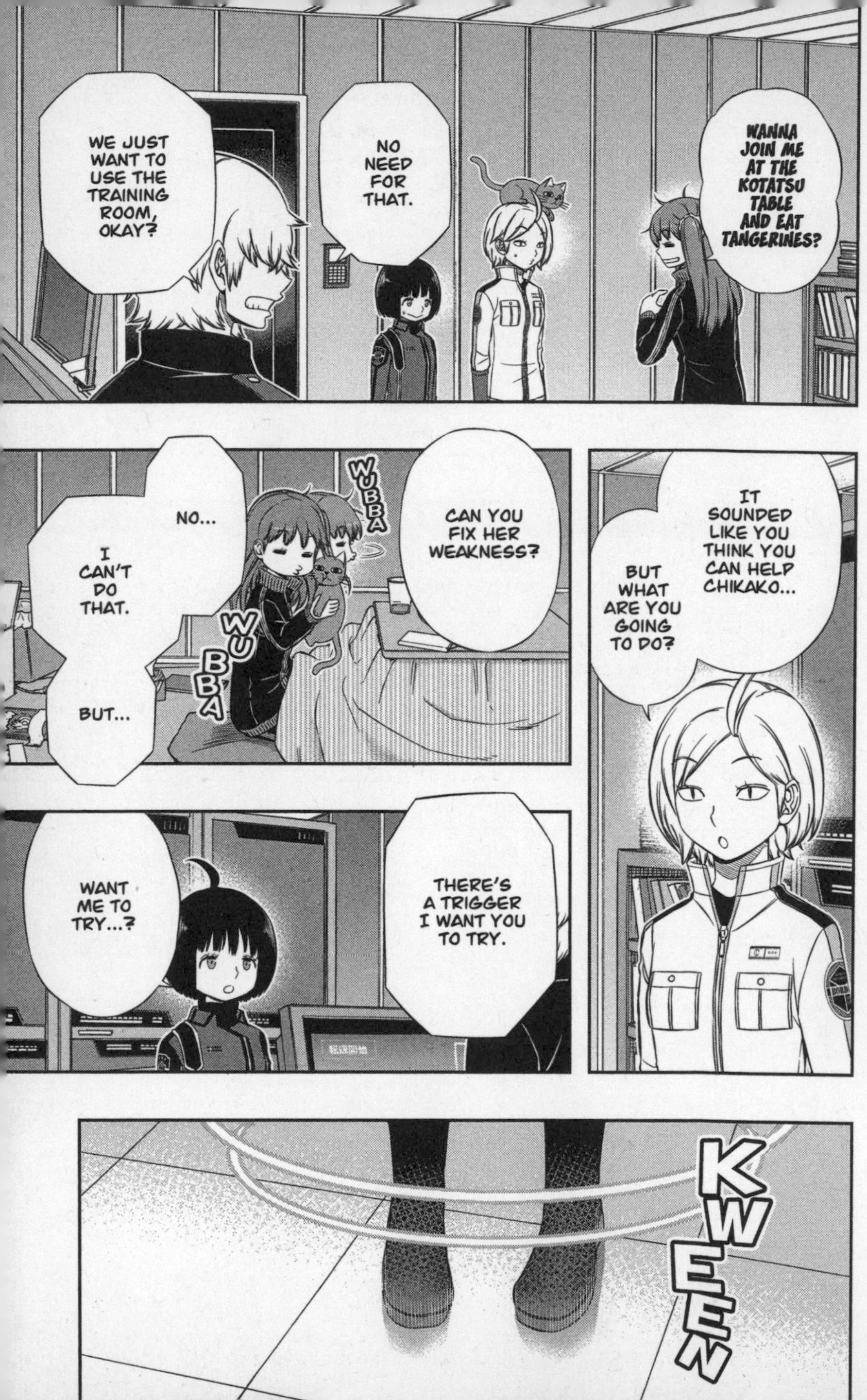
WANNA JOIN ME AT THE KOTATSU TABLE AND EAT TANGERINES?
NO NEED FOR THAT.
WE JUST WANT TO USE THE TRAINING ROOM, OKAY?
IT SOUNDED LIKE YOU THINK YOU CAN HELP CHIKAKO...
BUT WHAT ARE YOU GOING TO DO?
CAN YOU FIX HER WEAKNESS?
WUBBA
WUBBA
NO...
I CAN'T DO THAT.
BUT...
THERE'S A TRIGGER I WANT YOU TO TRY.
WANT ME TO TRY...?
KWEEN

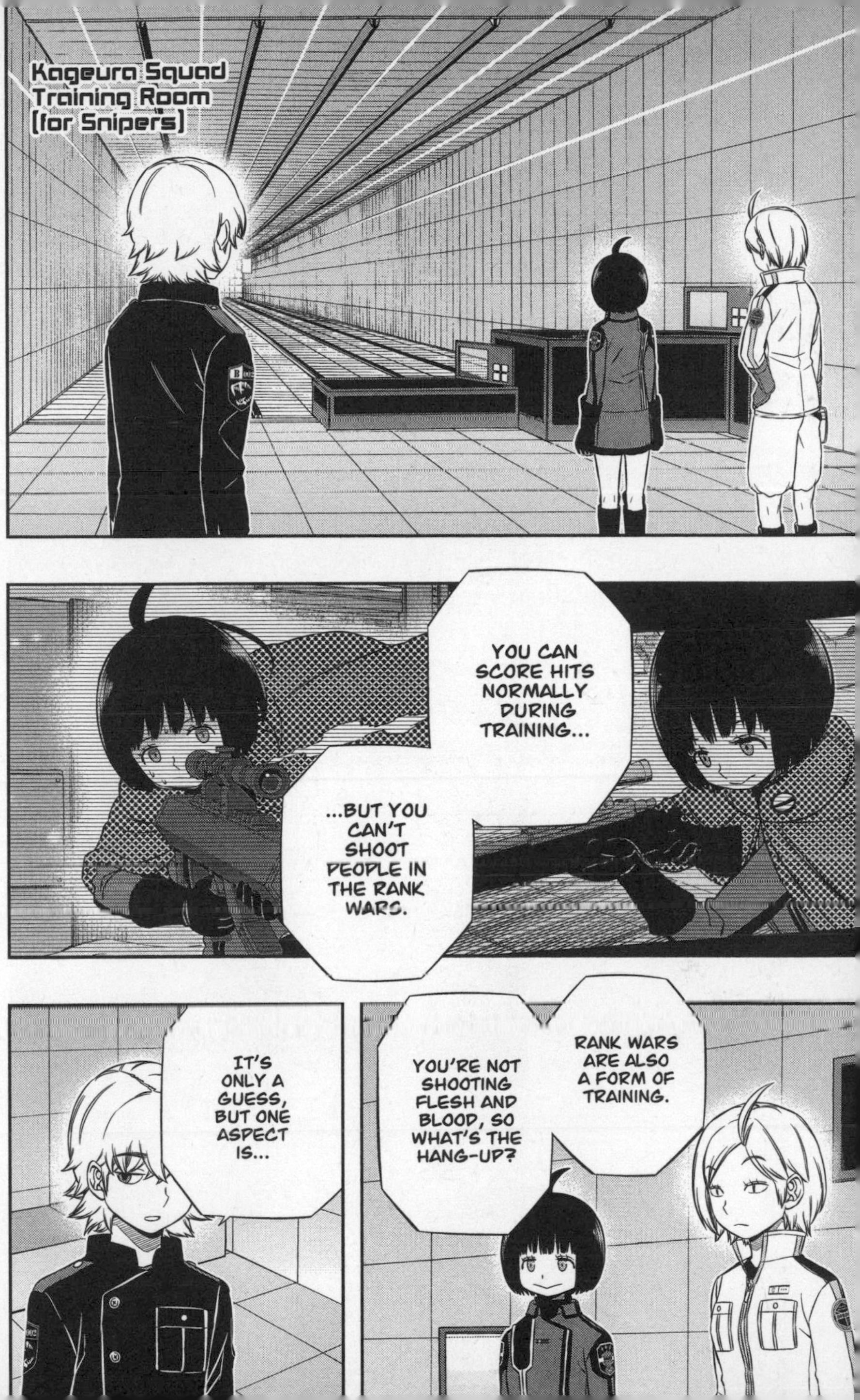
Kageura Squad Training Room (for Snipers)
YOU CAN SCORE HITS NORMALLY DURING TRAINING...
...BUT YOU CAN'T SHOOT PEOPLE IN THE RANK WARS.
RANK WARS ARE ALSO A FORM OF TRAINING.
YOU'RE NOT SHOOTING FLESH AND BLOOD, SO WHAT'S THE HANG-UP?
IT'S ONLY A GUESS, BUT ONE ASPECT IS...

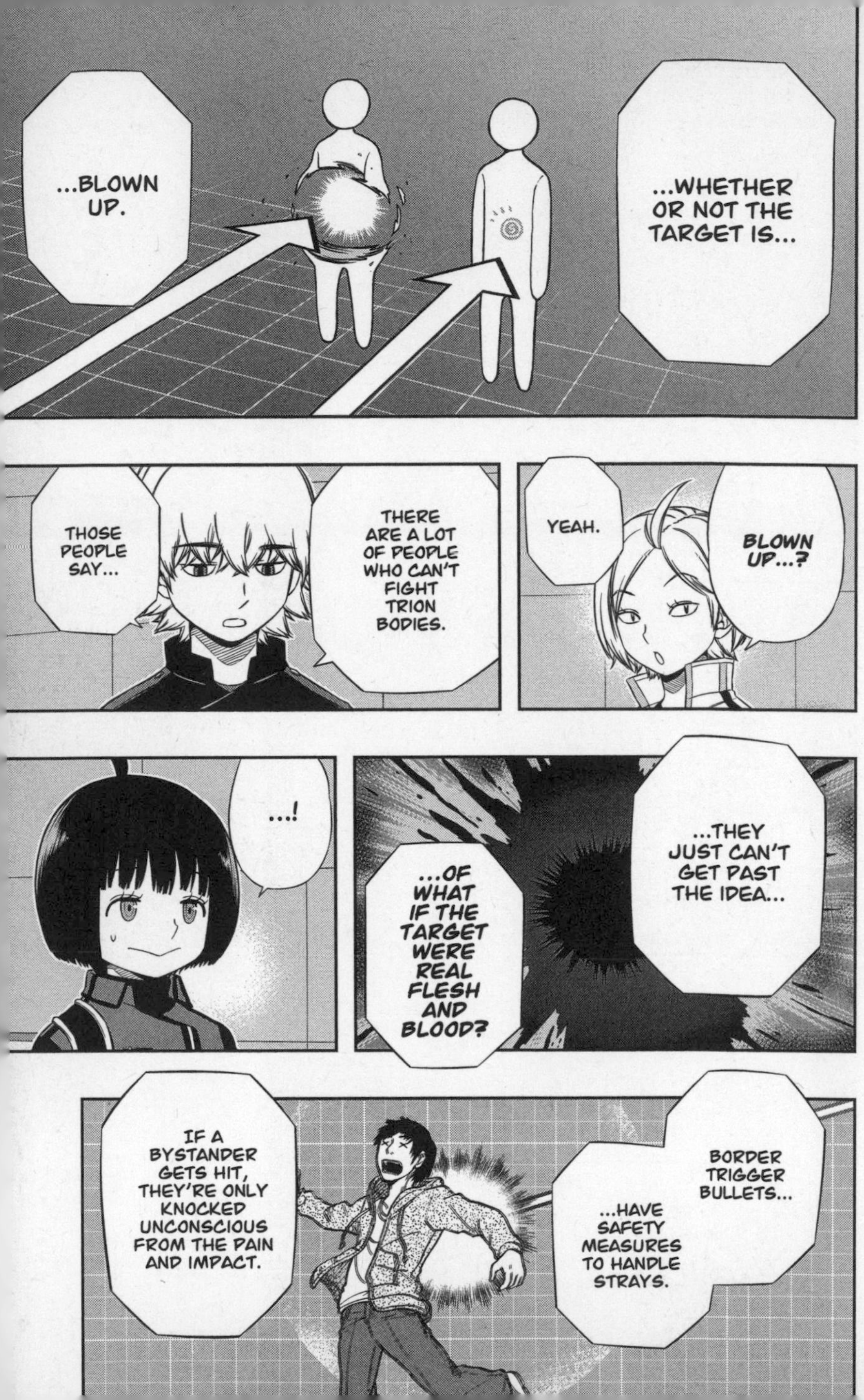
...WHETHER OR NOT THE TARGET IS...
...BLOWN UP.
BLOWN UP...?
YEAH.
THERE ARE A LOT OF PEOPLE WHO CAN'T FIGHT TRION BODIES.
THOSE PEOPLE SAY...
...THEY JUST CAN'T GET PAST THE IDEA...
...OF WHAT IF THE TARGET WERE REAL FLESH AND BLOOD?
...!
BORDER TRIGGER BULLETS...
...HAVE SAFETY MEASURES TO HANDLE STRAYS.
IF A BYSTANDER GETS HIT, THEY'RE ONLY KNOCKED UNCONSCIOUS FROM THE PAIN AND IMPACT.

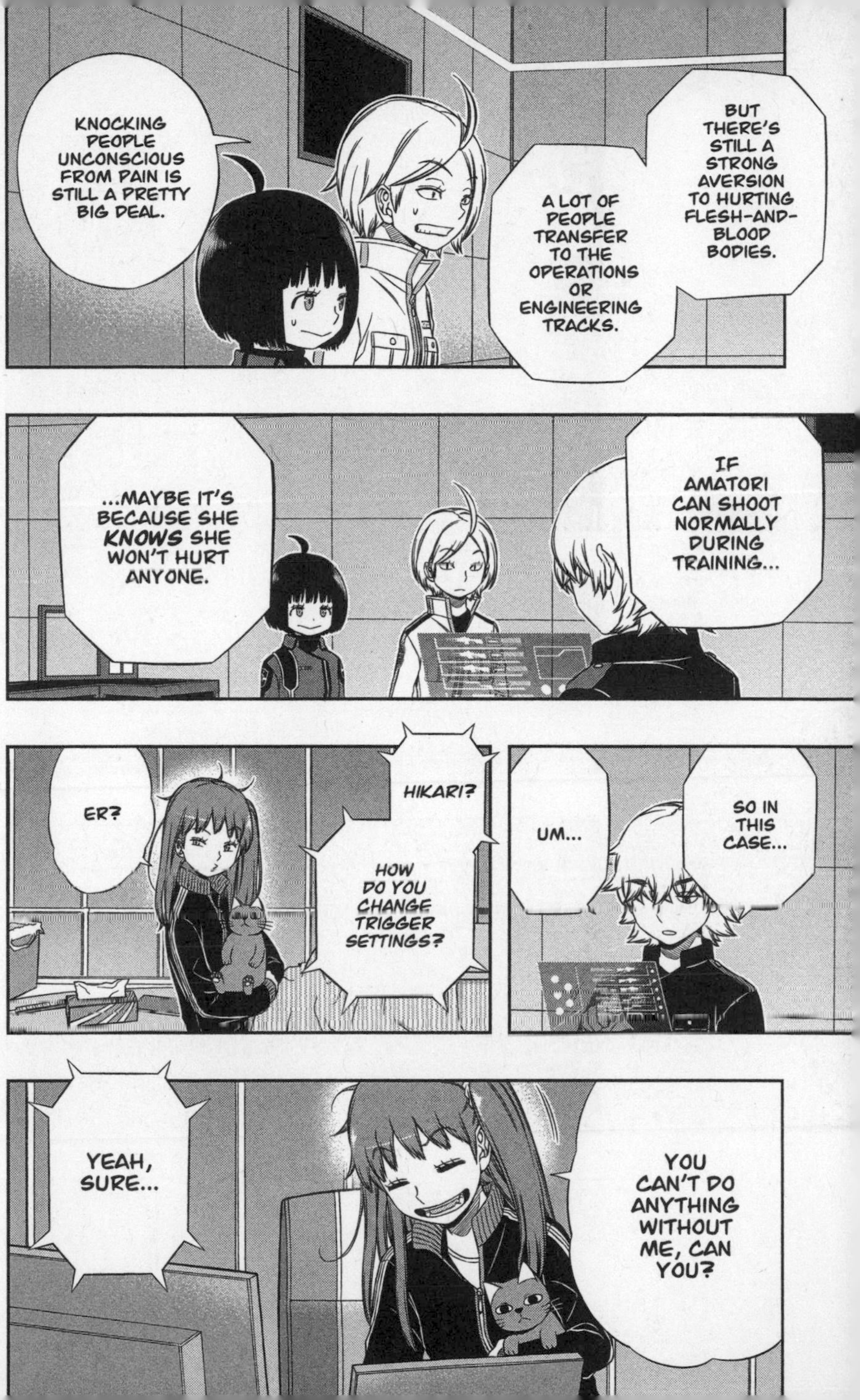
BUT THERE'S STILL A STRONG AVERSION TO HURTING FLESH-AND-BLOOD BODIES.
A LOT OF PEOPLE TRANSFER TO THE OPERATIONS OR ENGINEERING TRACKS.
KNOCKING PEOPLE UNCONSCIOUS FROM PAIN IS STILL A PRETTY BIG DEAL.
IF AMATORI CAN SHOOT NORMALLY DURING TRAINING...
...MAYBE IT'S BECAUSE SHE *KNOWS* SHE WON'T HURT ANYONE.
SO IN THIS CASE...
UM...
HIKARI?
HOW DO YOU CHANGE TRIGGER SETTINGS?
ER?
YOU CAN'T DO ANYTHING WITHOUT ME, CAN YOU?
YEAH, SURE...

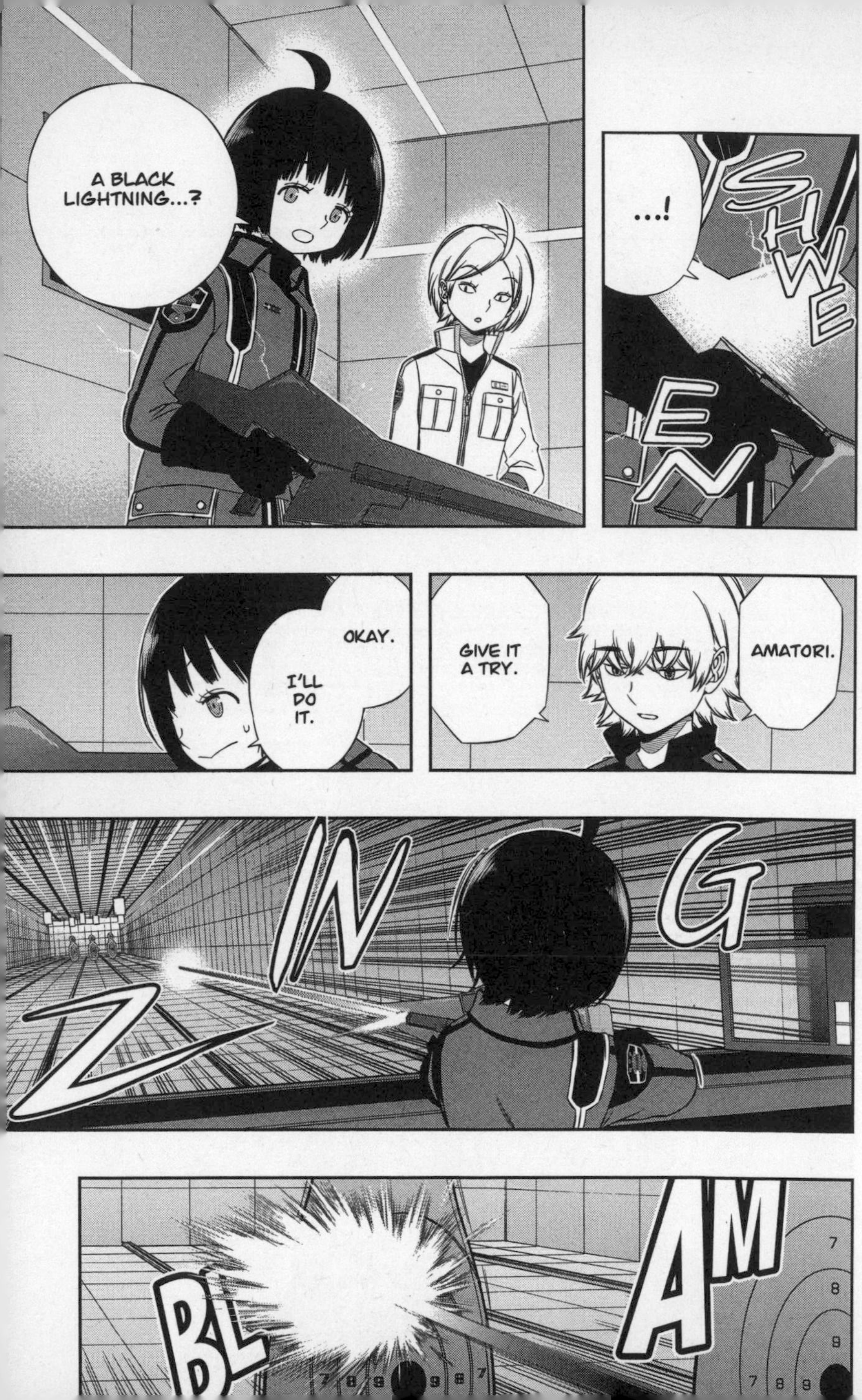

...!
SHWEEM
A BLACK LIGHTNING...?
AMATORI.
GIVE IT A TRY.
OKAY.
I'LL DO IT.
ZING
BLAM

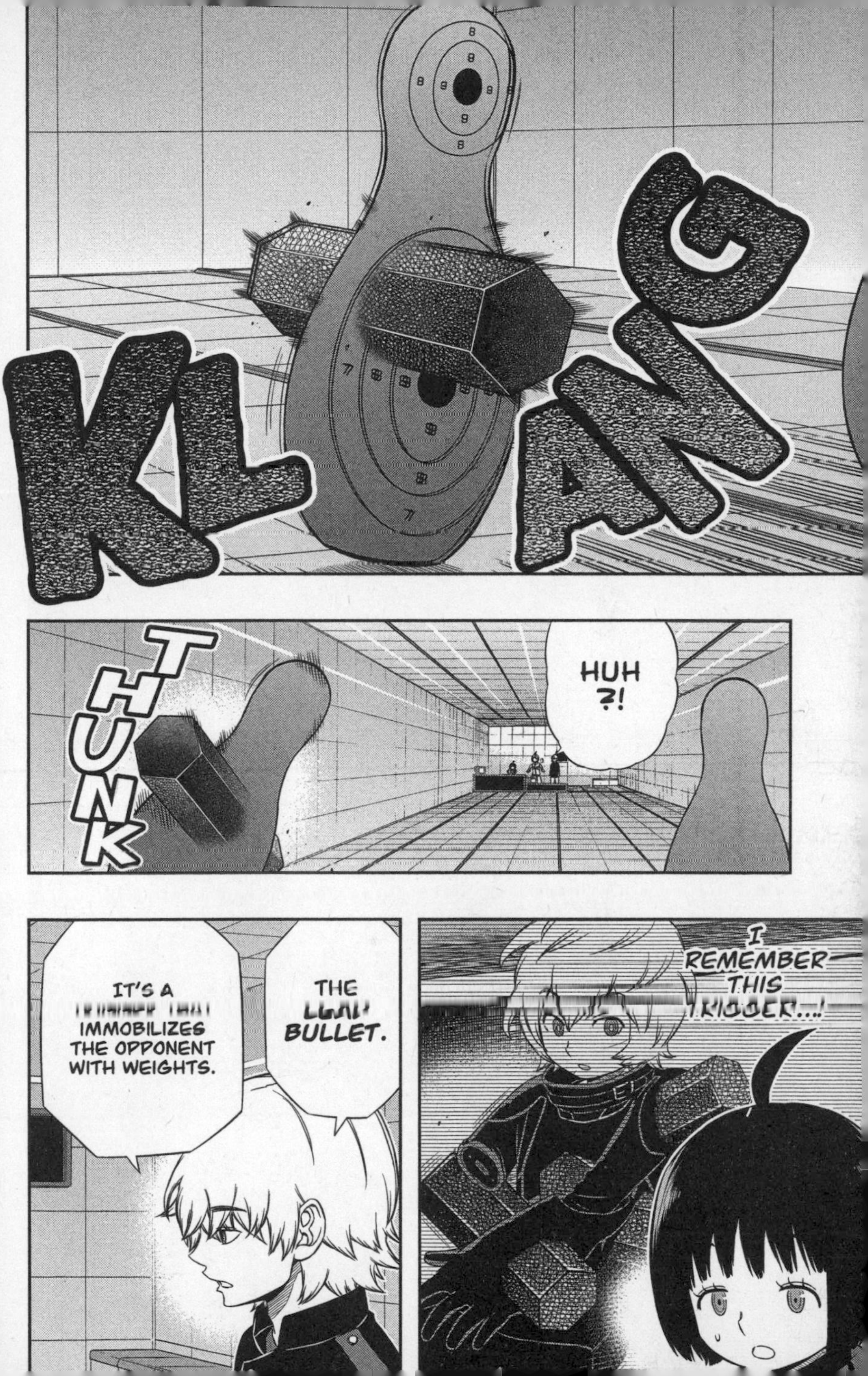
KLANG
HUH ?!
THUNK
I REMEMBER THIS
THE
BULLET.
IT'S A
IMMOBILIZES THE OPPONENT WITH WEIGHTS.

REALLY?! SUCH A THING EXISTS?!

SO I THINK EVEN AMATORI WOULD BE ABLE TO SHOOT IT.

THIS WON'T HURT ANYONE, EVEN IF THEY'RE FLESH AND BLOOD.

IT'S NOT THAT CONVENIENT.

WHAT?! THAT'S SUPER POWERFUL! WHY DOESN'T EVERYONE USE IT?!

IT ALSO CAN'T BE BLOCKED WITH A SHIELD, SO IT'S EASIER TO GET A HIT.

IT'S BETTER THAN SHOOTING BULLETS THAT WON'T HIT.

BUT WHEN YOU MISS, YOU'LL BE FOUND ANYWAY.

LET'S GO GET HER.

SHE'S DEFENSELESS NOW.

YOU'LL BE FOUND ON RADAR IF YOU'RE SNIPING WITH LEAD BULLETS.

...IS YOU CAN'T USE IT WITH A BAGWORM.

ONE OF ITS FLAWS...

Main	Sub
Egret	Lead Bullets
Shield	Shield
Ibis	Bagworm

THE OTHER PROBLEM IS...
...MUZZLE VELOCITY.
LEAD BULLETS USE A TON OF TRION BECAUSE OF THE WEIGHT EFFECT...
SO RANGE AND SPEED ARE DECREASED.
Normal + Lead Bullet
Weight Effect
Speed
Range
SNIPER TRIGGERS...
...GUARANTEE RANGE THROUGH THE GUN STRUCTURE ITSELF.
BUT IF THE BULLET IS TOO SLOW, IT WON'T HIT.
SPEED
POWER
WEIGHT
BUT AMATORI HAS...
...EXTRAOR-DINARY LEVELS OF TRION.
THE THREE SNIPING RIFLES...
...IMPROVE IN PERFORMANCE DIFFERENTLY ACCORDING TO THE USER'S TRION LEVELS...
Ibis
More Trion, more power
Egret
More Trion, more range
Lightning
More Trion, more velocity

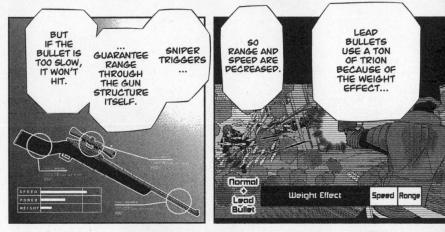

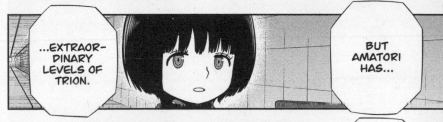

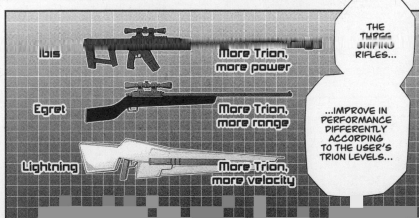

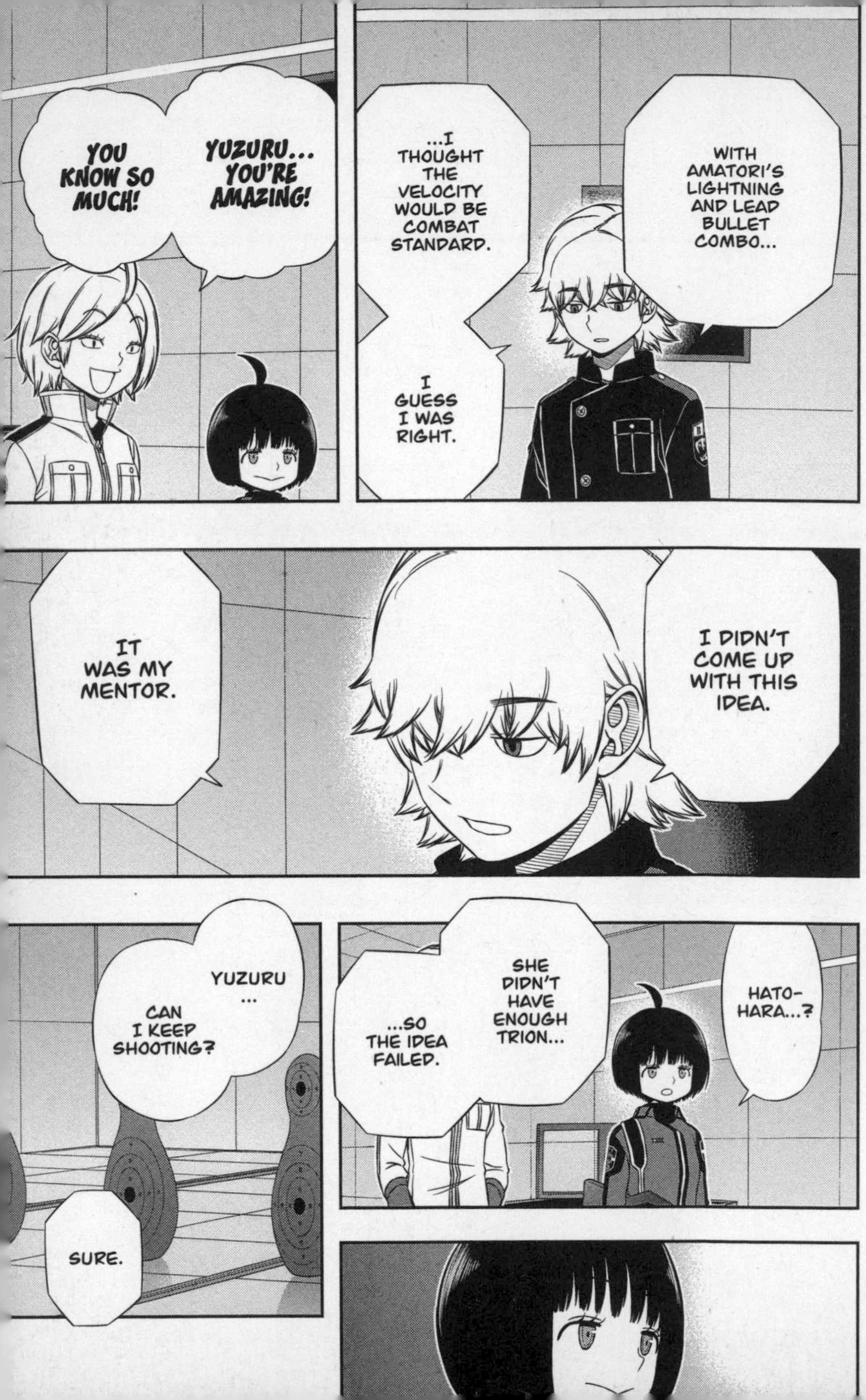
WITH AMATORI'S LIGHTNING AND LEAD BULLET COMBO...
...I THOUGHT THE VELOCITY WOULD BE COMBAT STANDARD.
I GUESS I WAS RIGHT.
YUZURU... YOU'RE AMAZING!
YOU KNOW SO MUCH!
I DIDN'T COME UP WITH THIS IDEA.
IT WAS MY MENTOR.
HATO-HARA...?
SHE DIDN'T HAVE ENOUGH TRION...
...SO THE IDEA FAILED.
YUZURU ...
CAN I KEEP SHOOTING?
SURE.

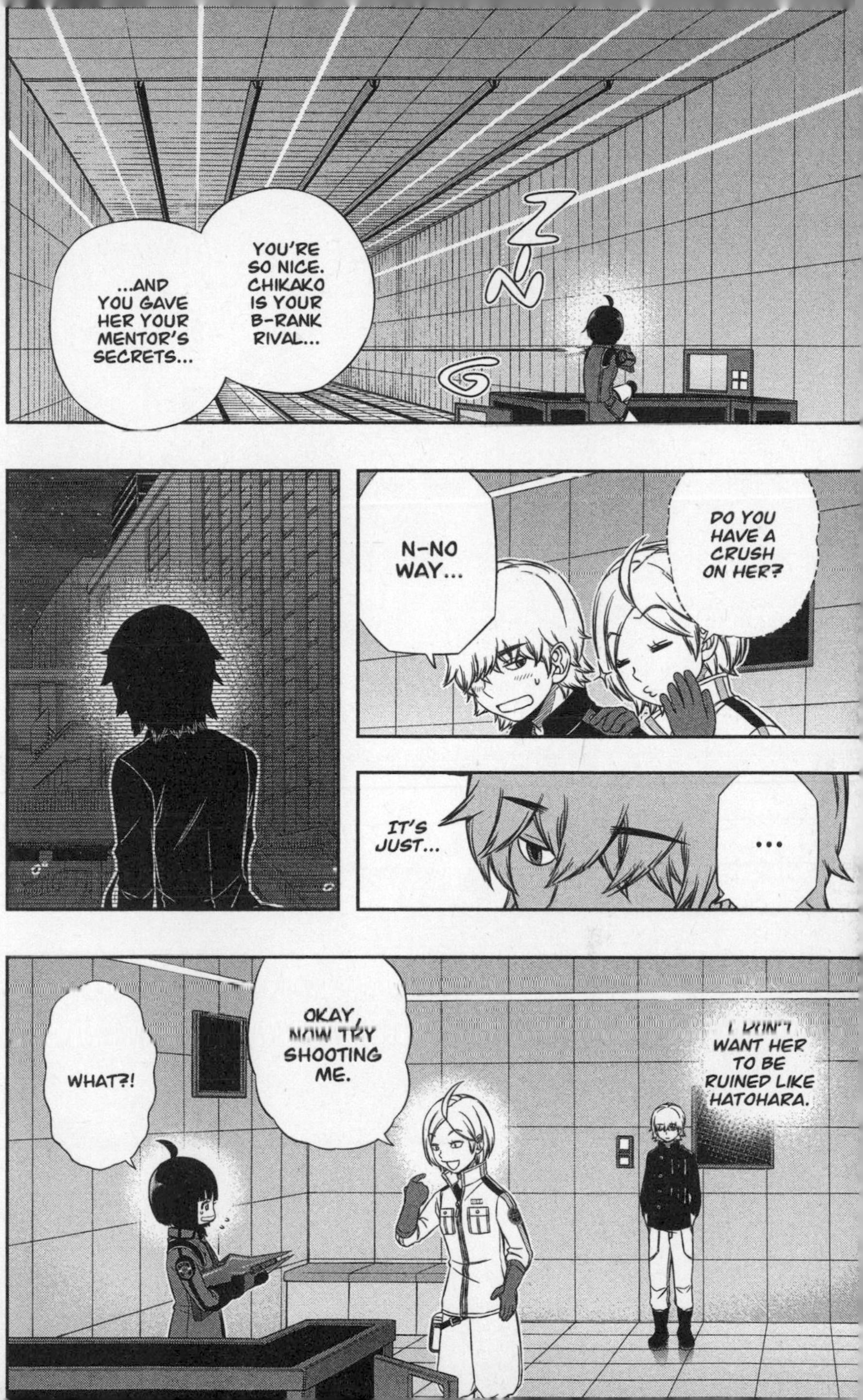
YOU'RE SO NICE. CHIKAKO IS YOUR B-RANK RIVAL...
...AND YOU GAVE HER YOUR MENTOR'S SECRETS...
DO YOU HAVE A CRUSH ON HER?
N-NO WAY...
...
IT'S JUST...
I DON'T WANT HER TO BE RUINED LIKE HATOHARA.
OKAY, NOW TRY SHOOTING ME.
WHAT?!

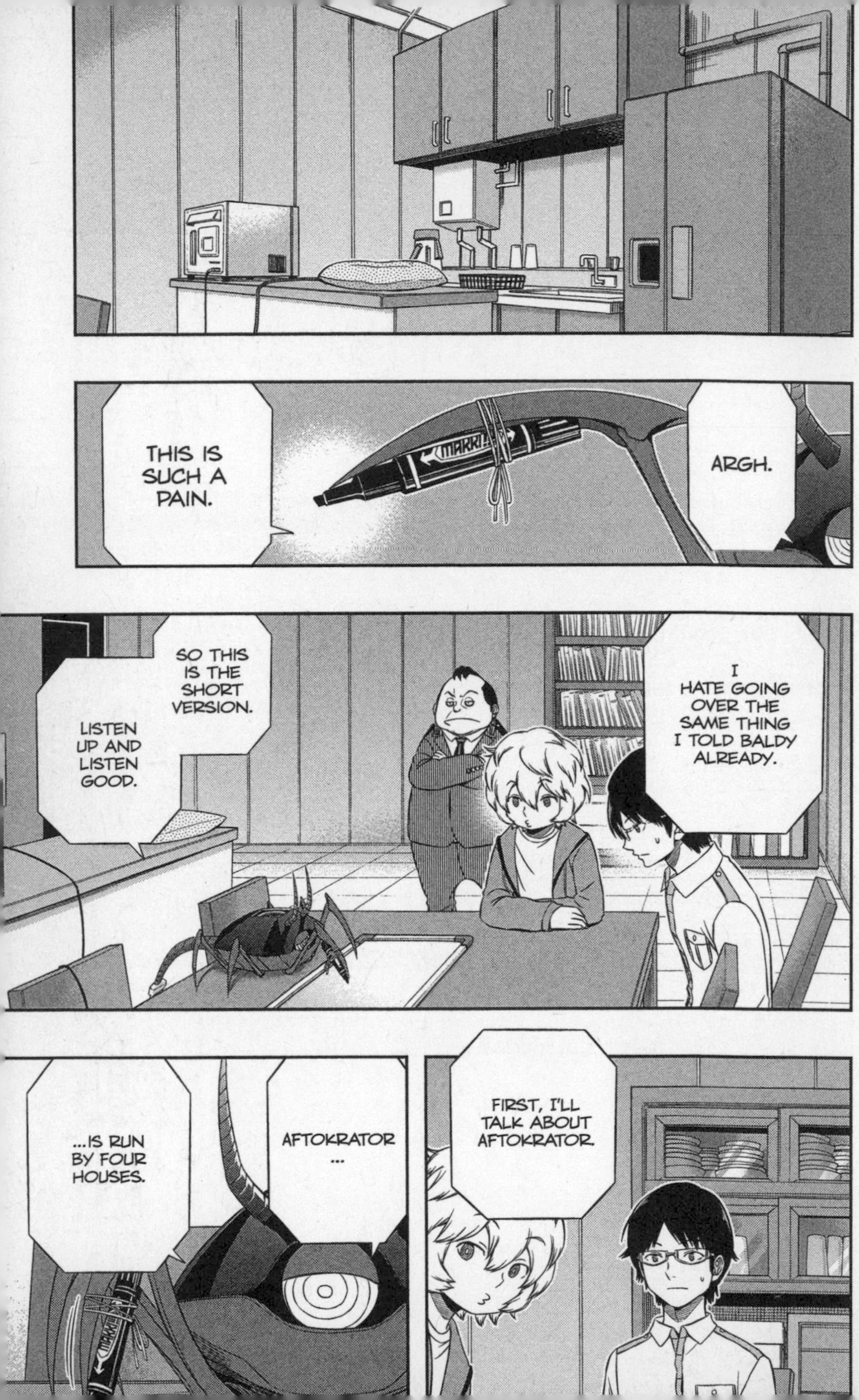
ARGH.
THIS IS SUCH A PAIN.
I HATE GOING OVER THE SAME THING I TOLD BALDY ALREADY.
SO THIS IS THE SHORT VERSION.
LISTEN UP AND LISTEN GOOD.
FIRST, I'LL TALK ABOUT AFTOKRATOR.
AFTOKRATOR...
...IS RUN BY FOUR HOUSES.

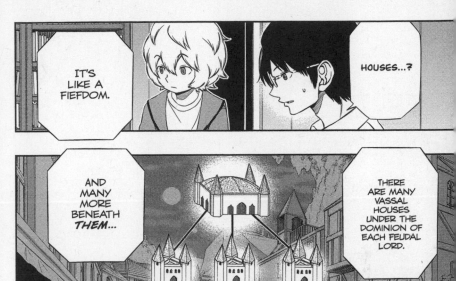

HOUSES...?
IT'S LIKE A FIEFDOM.
THERE ARE MANY VASSAL HOUSES UNDER THE DOMINION OF EACH FEUDAL LORD.
AND MANY MORE BENEATH *THEM*...
THERE ARE FOUR BIG GROUPS OF SMALLER HOUSES.
AND ALL OF THEM CLAIM THEIR OWN TERRITORIES.

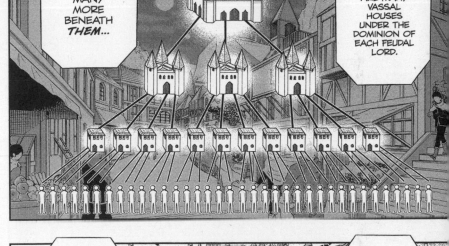

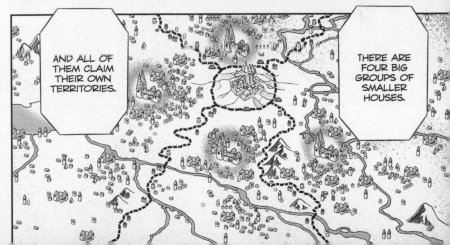

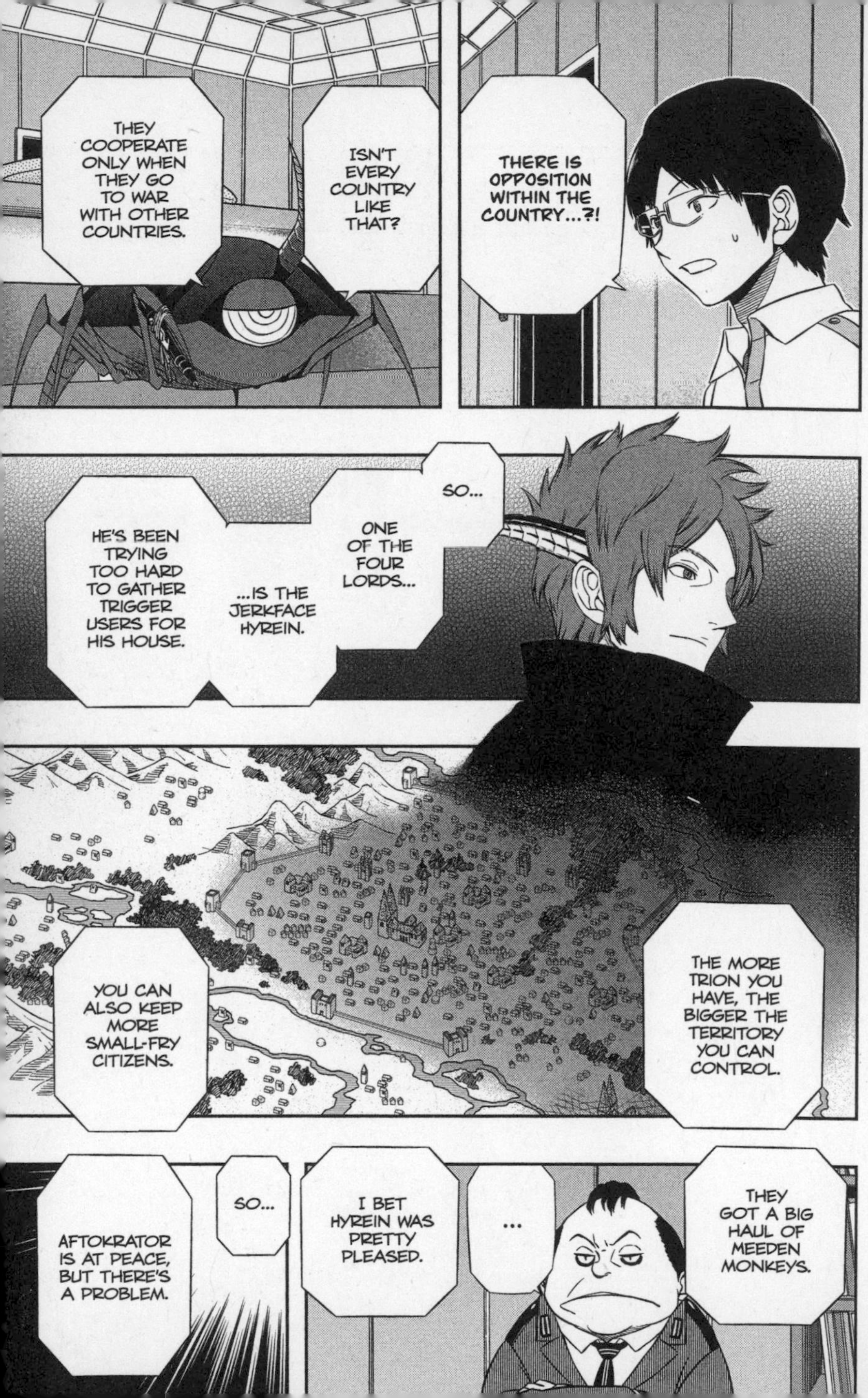
THERE IS OPPOSITION WITHIN THE COUNTRY...?!
ISN'T EVERY COUNTRY LIKE THAT?
THEY COOPERATE ONLY WHEN THEY GO TO WAR WITH OTHER COUNTRIES.
SO...
ONE OF THE FOUR LORDS...
...IS THE JERKFACE HYREIN.
HE'S BEEN TRYING TOO HARD TO GATHER TRIGGER USERS FOR HIS HOUSE.
THE MORE TRION YOU HAVE, THE BIGGER THE TERRITORY YOU CAN CONTROL.
YOU CAN ALSO KEEP MORE SMALL-FRY CITIZENS.
THEY GOT A BIG HAUL OF MEEDEN MONKEYS.
...
I BET HYREIN WAS PRETTY PLEASED.
SO...
AFTOKRATOR IS AT PEACE, BUT THERE'S A PROBLEM.

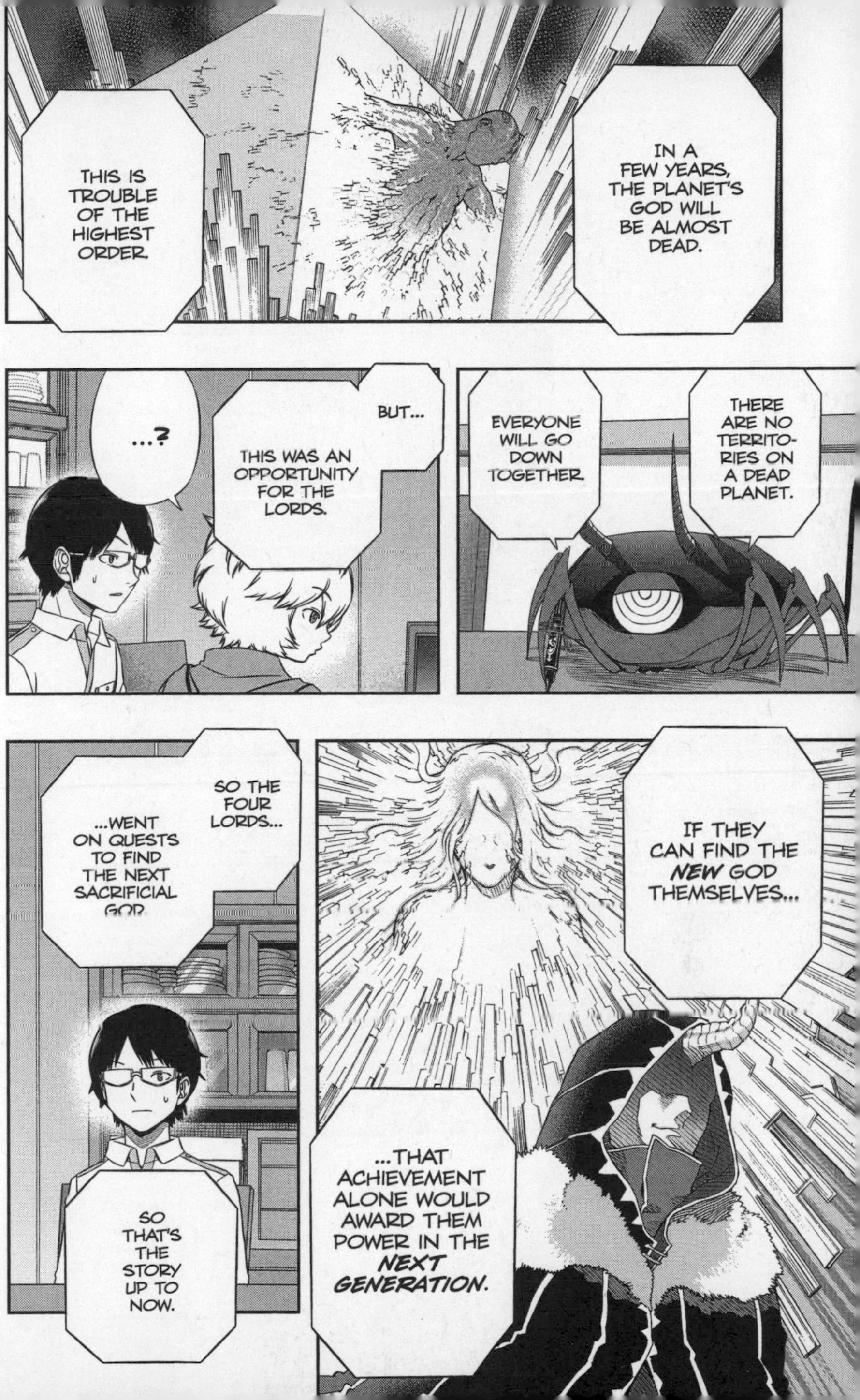
IN A FEW YEARS, THE PLANET'S GOD WILL BE ALMOST DEAD.
THIS IS TROUBLE OF THE HIGHEST ORDER.
THERE ARE NO TERRITORIES ON A DEAD PLANET.
EVERYONE WILL GO DOWN TOGETHER.
BUT...
THIS WAS AN OPPORTUNITY FOR THE LORDS.
...?
IF THEY CAN FIND THE *NEW* GOD THEMSELVES...
...THAT ACHIEVEMENT ALONE WOULD AWARD THEM POWER IN THE ***NEXT GENERATION***.
SO THE FOUR LORDS...
...WENT ON QUESTS TO FIND THE NEXT SACRIFICIAL GOD.
SO THAT'S THE STORY UP TO NOW.

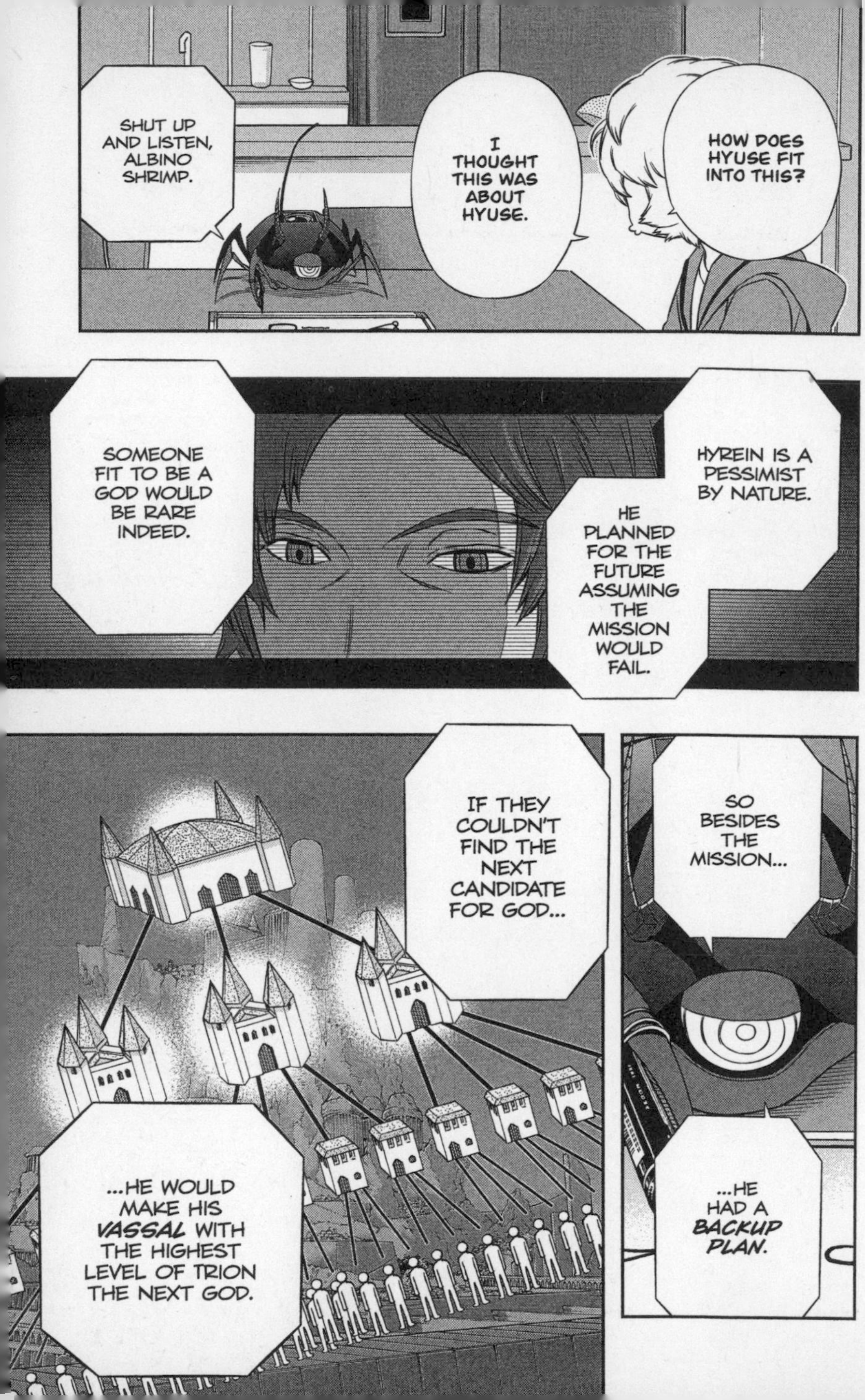
HOW DOES HYUSE FIT INTO THIS?
I THOUGHT THIS WAS ABOUT HYUSE.
SHUT UP AND LISTEN, ALBINO SHRIMP.
HYREIN IS A PESSIMIST BY NATURE.
HE PLANNED FOR THE FUTURE ASSUMING THE MISSION WOULD FAIL.
SOMEONE FIT TO BE A GOD WOULD BE RARE INDEED.
SO BESIDES THE MISSION...
...HE HAD A *BACKUP PLAN.*
IF THEY COULDN'T FIND THE NEXT CANDIDATE FOR GOD...
...HE WOULD MAKE HIS *VASSAL* WITH THE HIGHEST LEVEL OF TRION THE NEXT GOD.

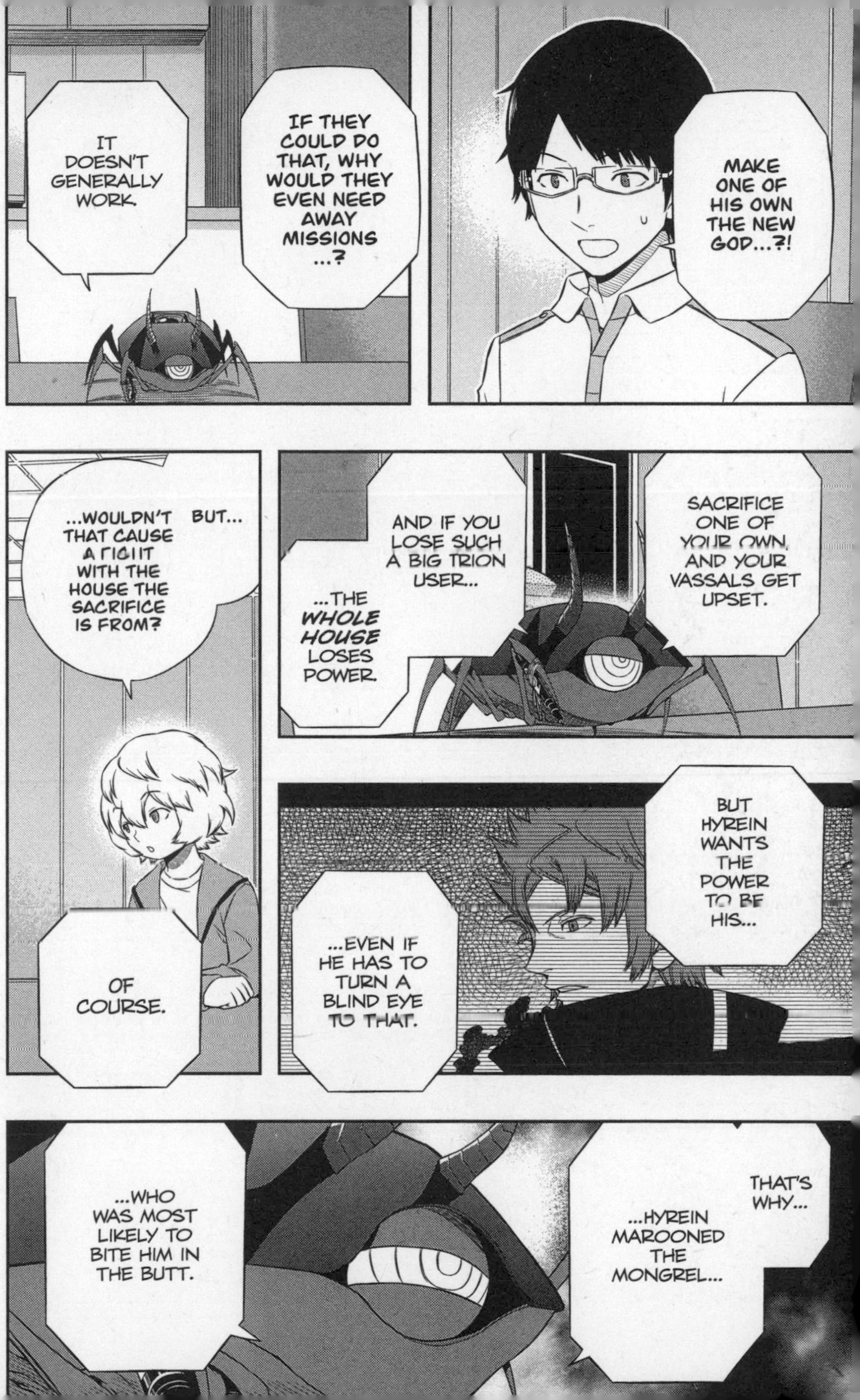
MAKE ONE OF HIS OWN THE NEW GOD...?!
IF THEY COULD DO THAT, WHY WOULD THEY EVEN NEED AWAY MISSIONS...?
IT DOESN'T GENERALLY WORK.
SACRIFICE ONE OF YOUR OWN, AND YOUR VASSALS GET UPSET.
AND IF YOU LOSE SUCH A BIG TRION USER...
...THE *WHOLE HOUSE* LOSES POWER.
BUT HYREIN WANTS THE POWER TO BE HIS...
...EVEN IF HE HAS TO TURN A BLIND EYE TO THAT.
BUT...
...WOULDN'T THAT CAUSE A FIGHT WITH THE HOUSE THE SACRIFICE IS FROM?
OF COURSE.
THAT'S WHY...
...HYREIN MAROONED THE MONGREL...
...WHO WAS MOST LIKELY TO BITE HIM IN THE BUTT.

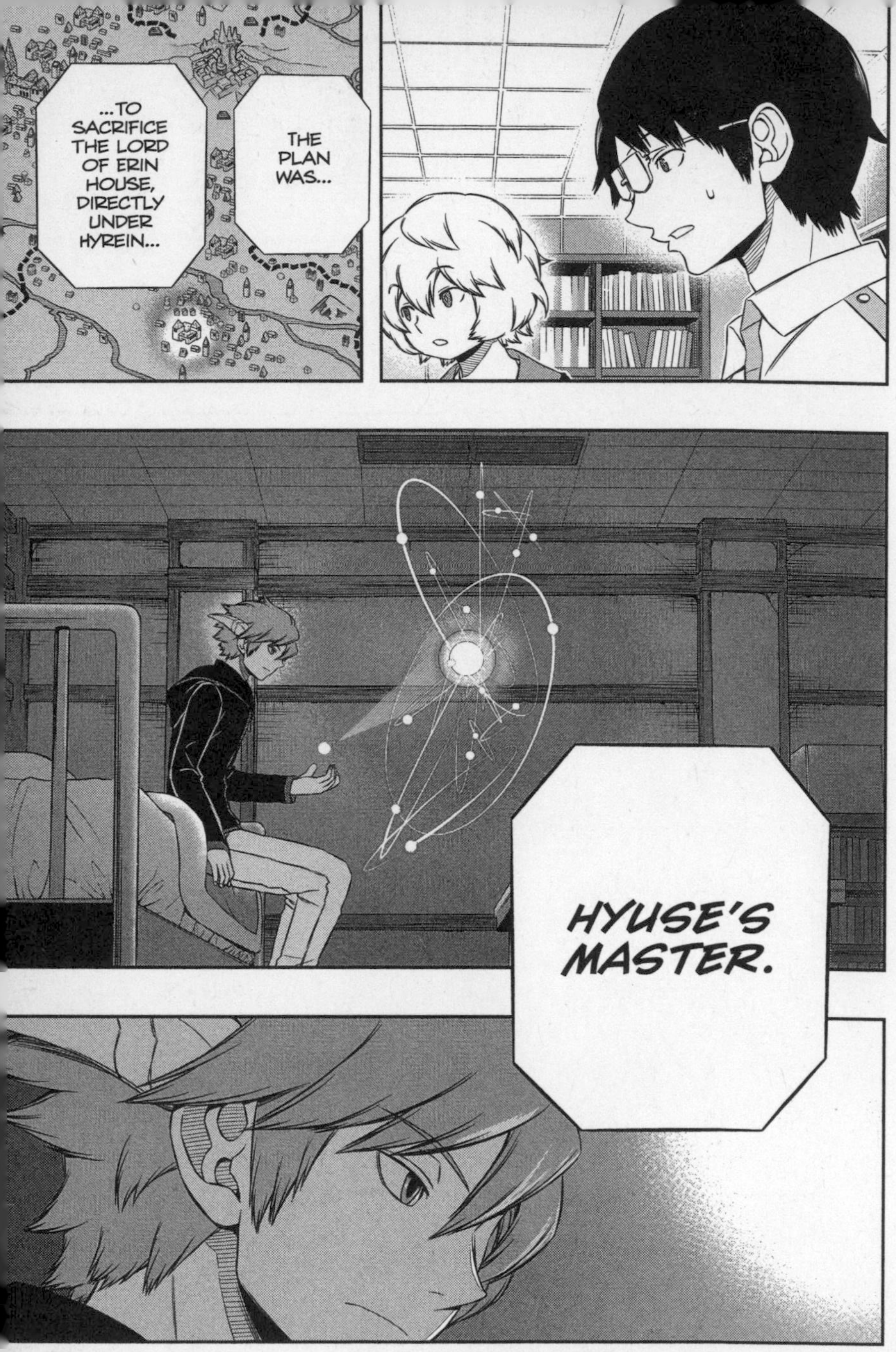
THE PLAN WAS...
...TO SACRIFICE THE LORD OF ERIN HOUSE, DIRECTLY UNDER HYREIN...
HYUSE'S MASTER.

Miwa Squad Strategy Room

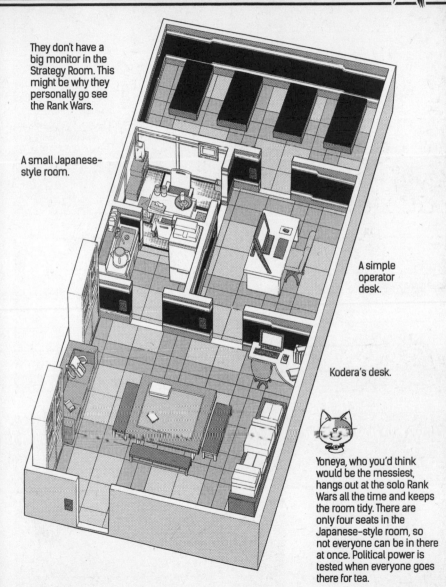

They don't have a big monitor in the Strategy Room. This might be why they personally go see the Rank Wars.

A small Japanese-style room.

A simple operator desk.

Kodera's desk.

Yoneya, who you'd think would be the messiest, hangs out at the solo Rank Wars all the time and keeps the room tidy. There are only four seats in the Japanese-style room, so not everyone can be in there at once. Political power is tested when everyone goes there for tea.

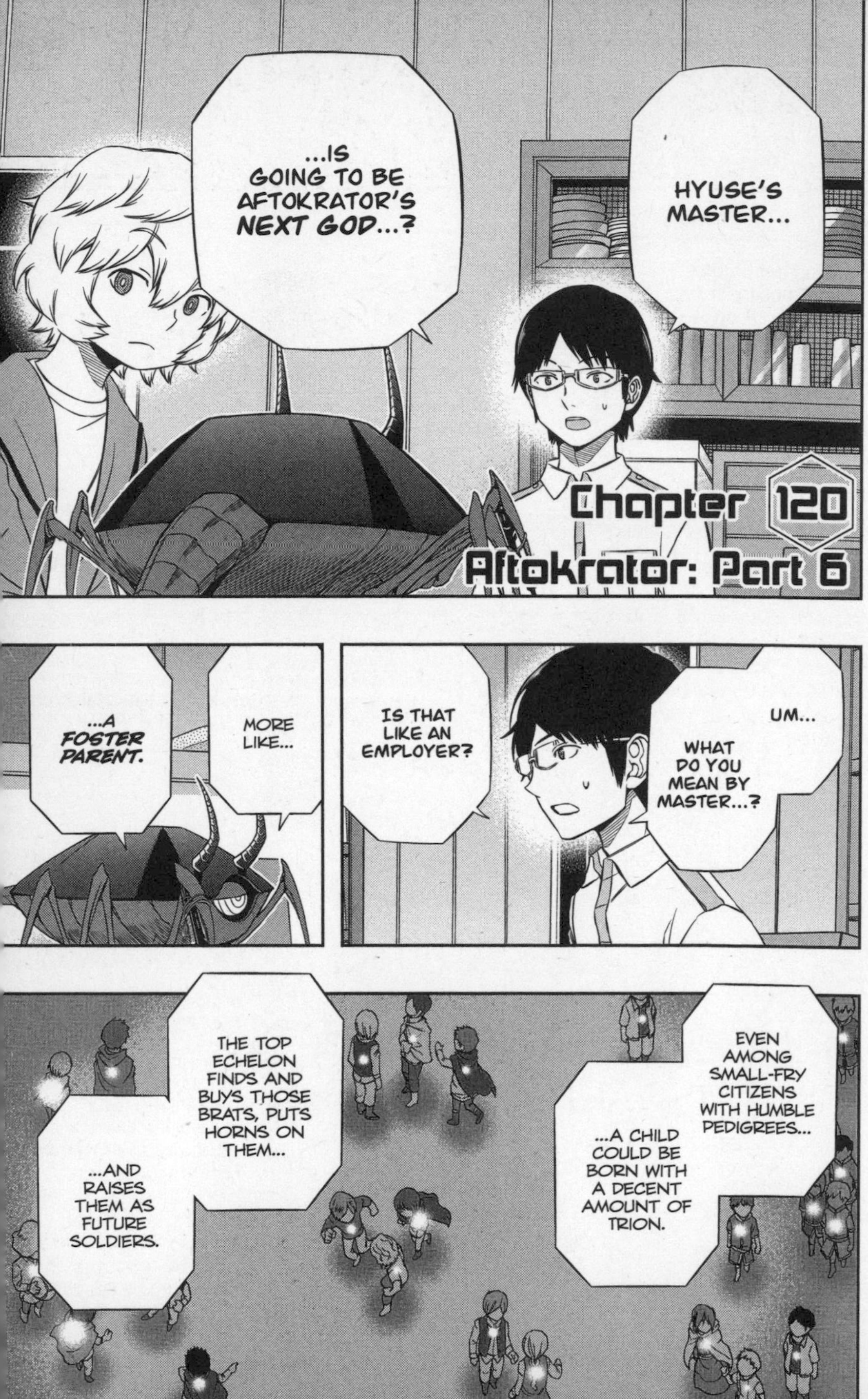
HYUSE'S MASTER...
...IS GOING TO BE AFTOKRATOR'S NEXT GOD...?
Chapter 120
Aftokrator: Part 6
UM...
WHAT DO YOU MEAN BY MASTER...?
IS THAT LIKE AN EMPLOYER?
MORE LIKE...
...A FOSTER PARENT.
EVEN AMONG SMALL-FRY CITIZENS WITH HUMBLE PEDIGREES...
...A CHILD COULD BE BORN WITH A DECENT AMOUNT OF TRION.
THE TOP ECHELON FINDS AND BUYS THOSE BRATS, PUTS HORNS ON THEM...
...AND RAISES THEM AS FUTURE SOLDIERS.

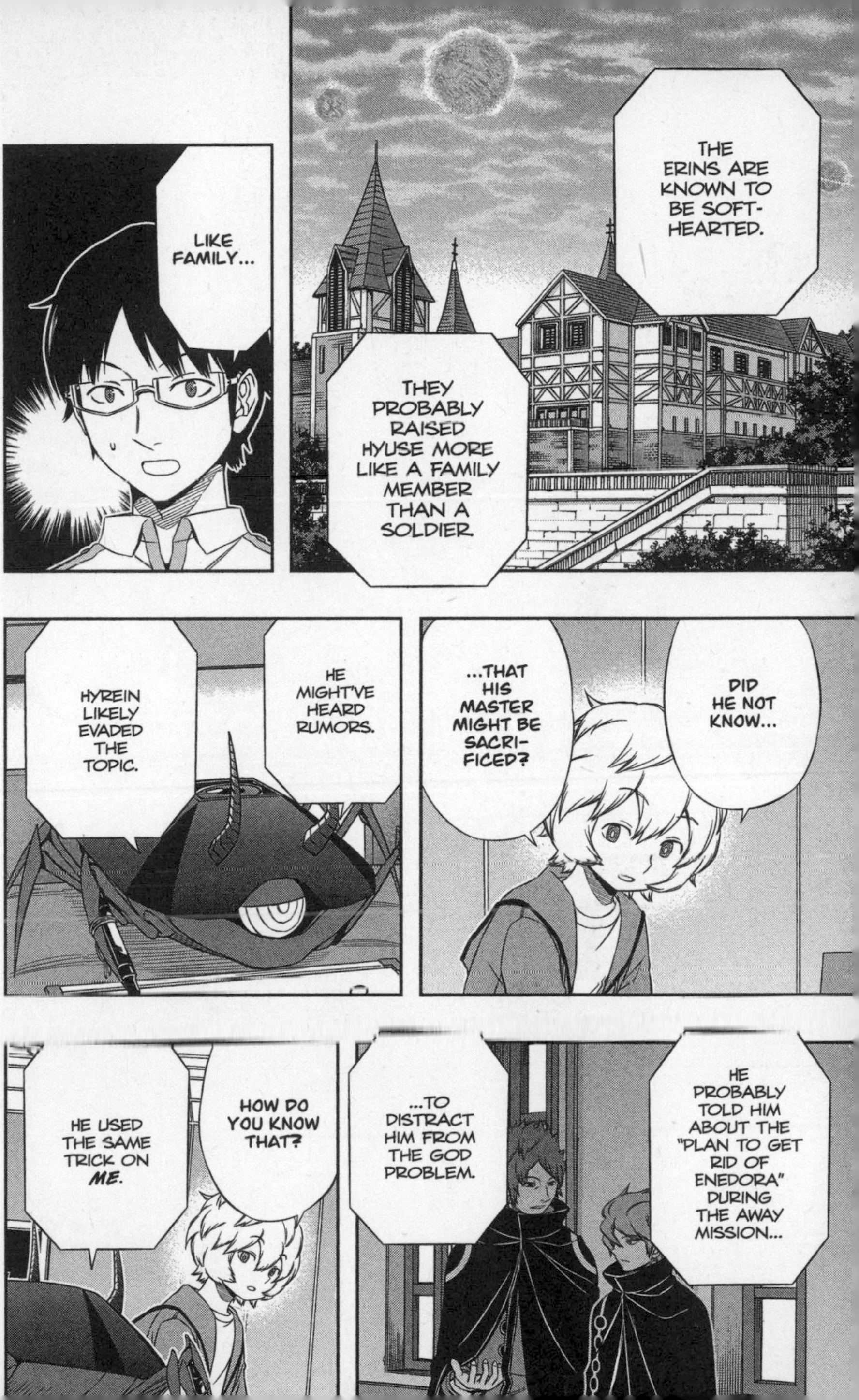
THE ERINS ARE KNOWN TO BE SOFT-HEARTED.
THEY PROBABLY RAISED HYUSE MORE LIKE A FAMILY MEMBER THAN A SOLDIER.
LIKE FAMILY...
DID HE NOT KNOW...
...THAT HIS MASTER MIGHT BE SACRI-FICED?
HE MIGHT'VE HEARD RUMORS.
HYREIN LIKELY EVADED THE TOPIC.
HE PROBABLY TOLD HIM ABOUT THE "PLAN TO GET RID OF ENEDORA" DURING THE AWAY MISSION...
...TO DISTRACT HIM FROM THE GOD PROBLEM.
HOW DO YOU KNOW THAT?
HE USED THE SAME TRICK ON *ME*.

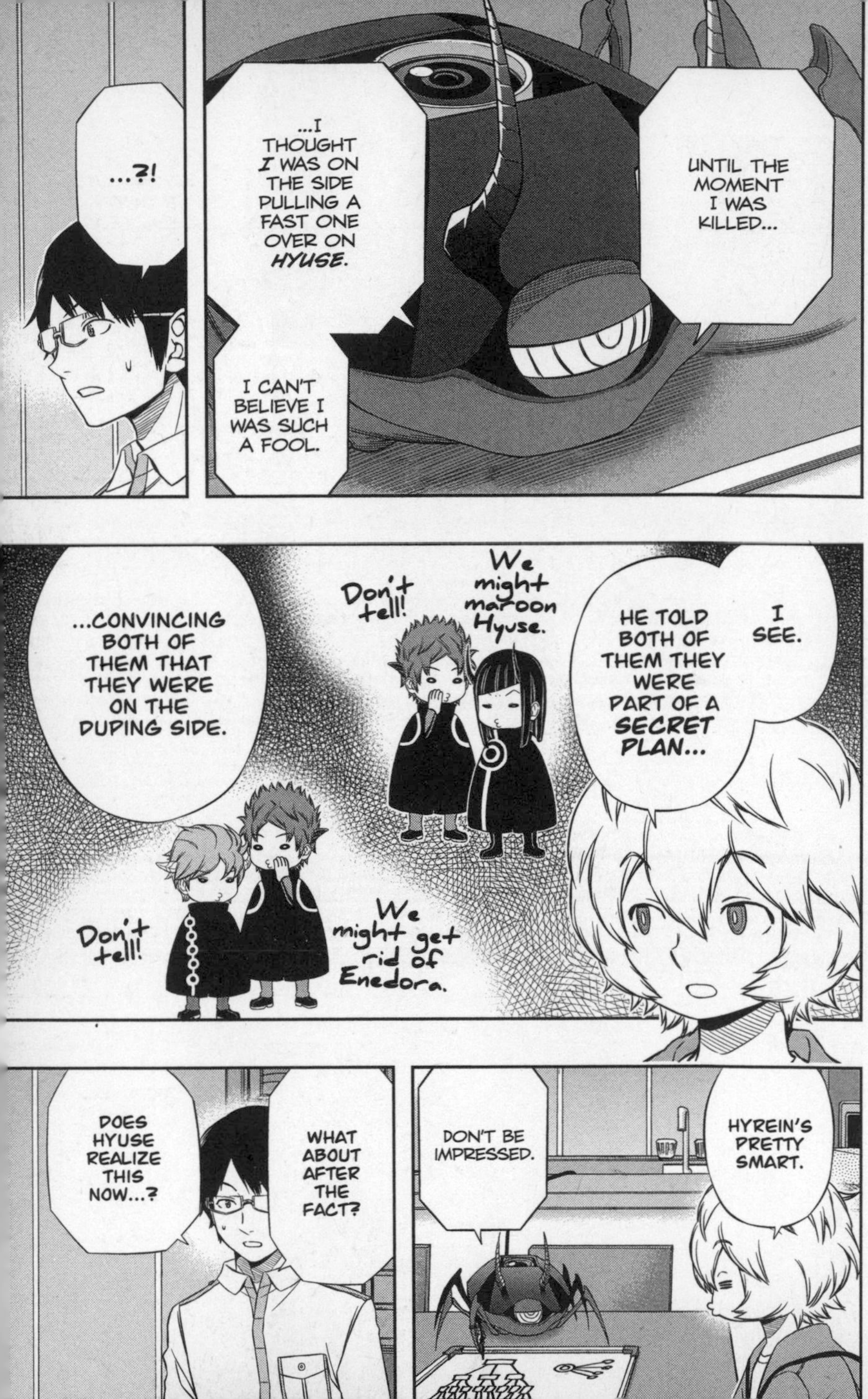
UNTIL THE MOMENT I WAS KILLED...
...I THOUGHT *I* WAS ON THE SIDE PULLING A FAST ONE OVER ON ***HYUSE***.
I CAN'T BELIEVE I WAS SUCH A FOOL.
...?!
I SEE.
HE TOLD BOTH OF THEM THEY WERE PART OF A **SECRET PLAN**...
We might maroon Hyuse.
Don't tell!
...CONVINCING BOTH OF THEM THAT THEY WERE ON THE DUPING SIDE.
We might get rid of Enedora.
Don't tell!
HYREIN'S PRETTY SMART.
DON'T BE IMPRESSED.
WHAT ABOUT AFTER THE FACT?
DOES HYUSE REALIZE THIS NOW...?

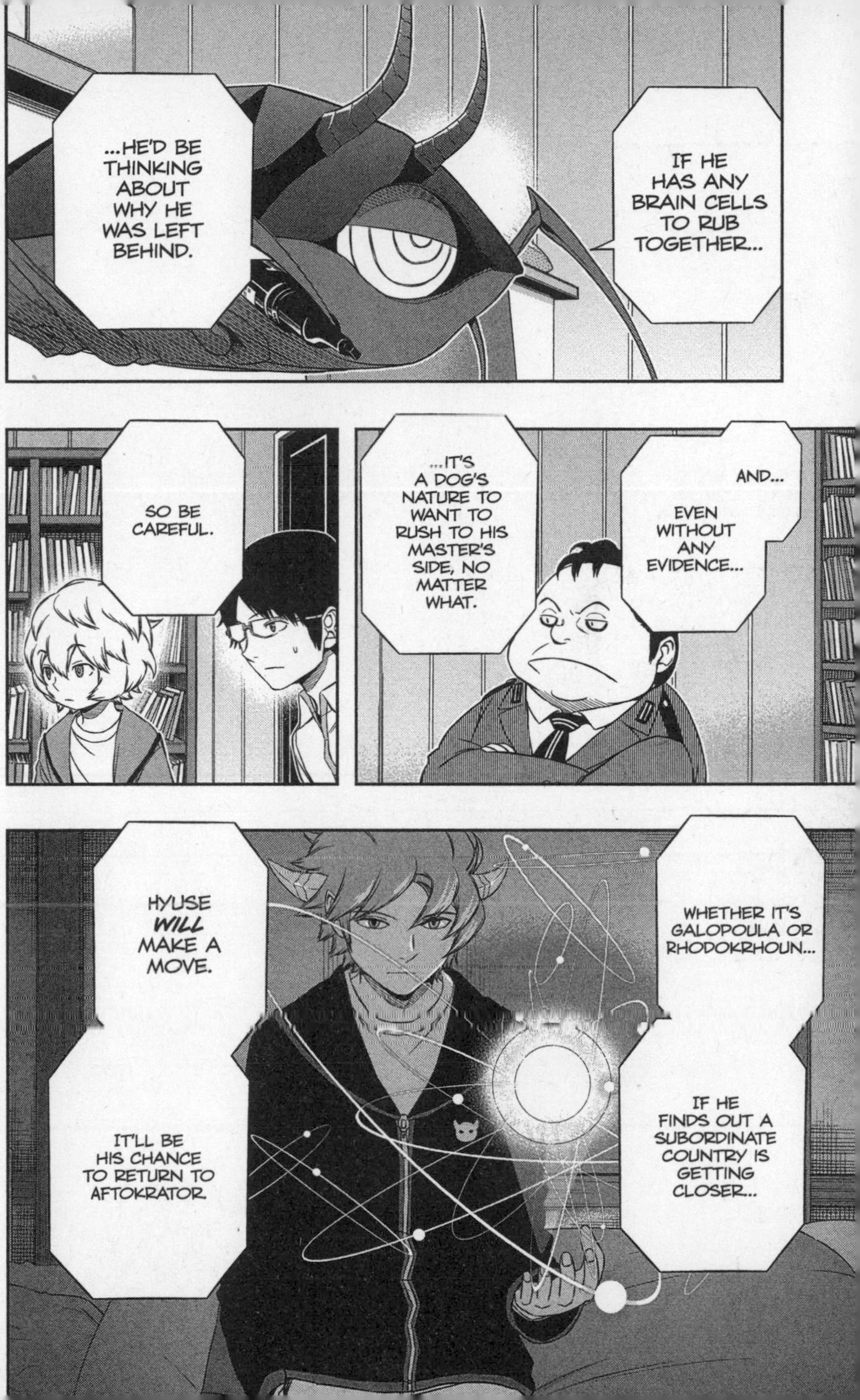
IF HE HAS ANY BRAIN CELLS TO RUB TOGETHER...
...HE'D BE THINKING ABOUT WHY HE WAS LEFT BEHIND.
AND...
EVEN WITHOUT ANY EVIDENCE...
...IT'S A DOG'S NATURE TO WANT TO RUSH TO HIS MASTER'S SIDE, NO MATTER WHAT.
SO BE CAREFUL.
WHETHER IT'S GALOPOULA OR RHODOKRHOUN...
IF HE FINDS OUT A SUBORDINATE COUNTRY IS GETTING CLOSER...
HYUSE *WILL* MAKE A MOVE.
IT'LL BE HIS CHANCE TO RETURN TO AFTOKRATOR.

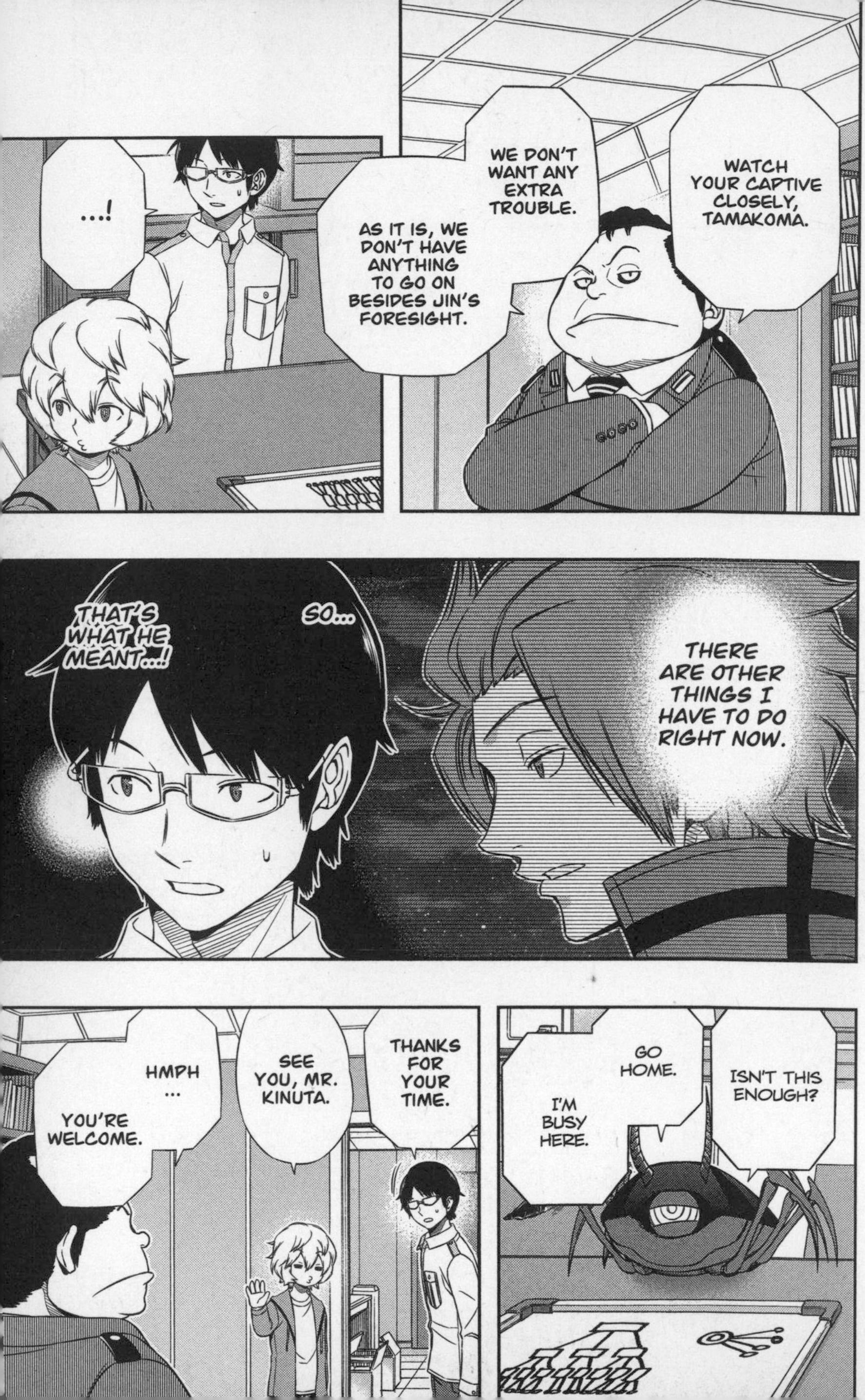
WATCH YOUR CAPTIVE CLOSELY, TAMAKOMA.
WE DON'T WANT ANY EXTRA TROUBLE.
AS IT IS, WE DON'T HAVE ANYTHING TO GO ON BESIDES JIN'S FORESIGHT.
...!
THERE ARE OTHER THINGS I HAVE TO DO RIGHT NOW.
SO...
THAT'S WHAT HE MEANT...!
ISN'T THIS ENOUGH?
GO HOME.
I'M BUSY HERE.
THANKS FOR YOUR TIME.
SEE YOU, MR. KINUTA.
HMPH ...
YOU'RE WELCOME.

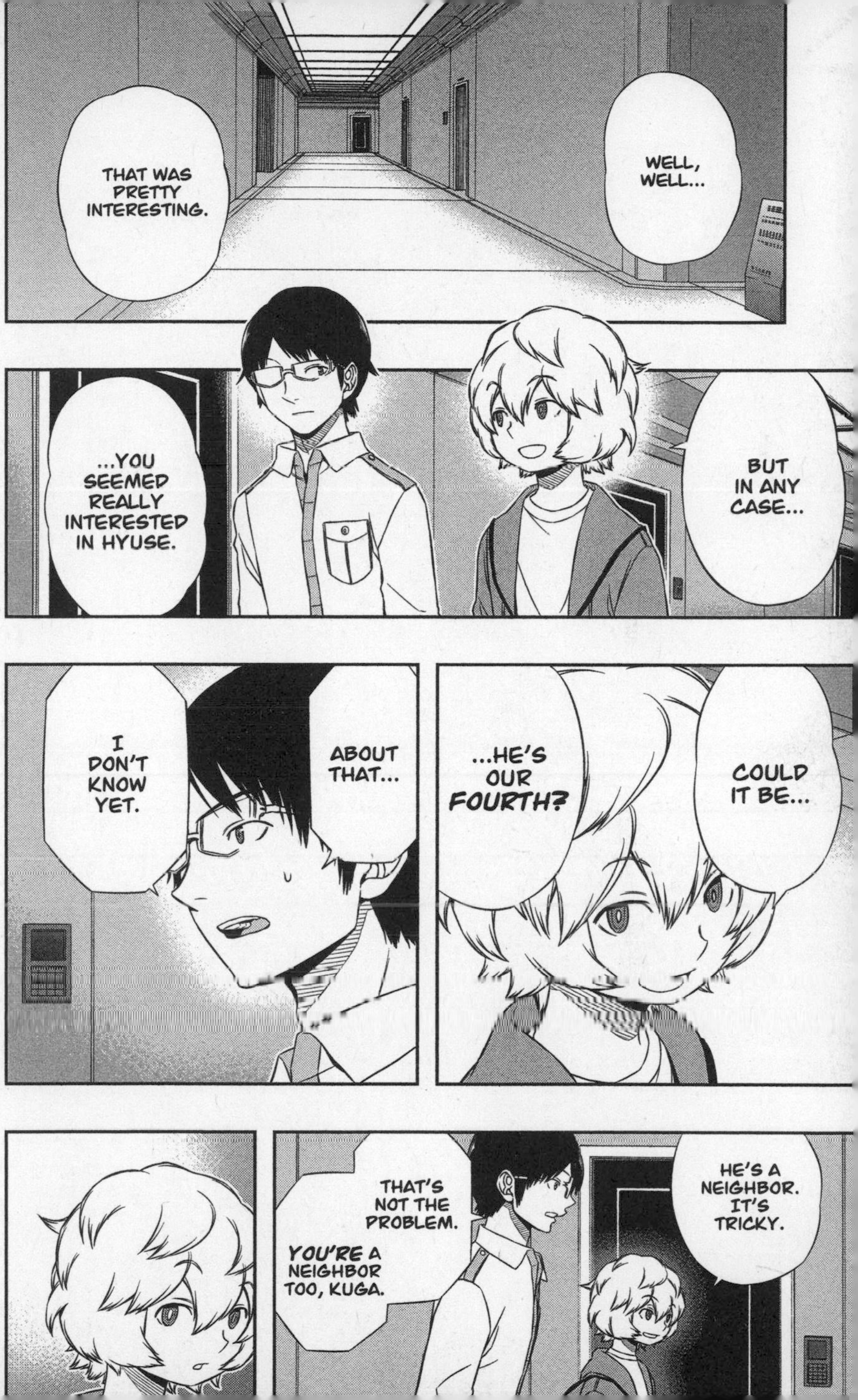
WELL, WELL...
THAT WAS PRETTY INTERESTING.
BUT IN ANY CASE...
...YOU SEEMED REALLY INTERESTED IN HYUSE.
COULD IT BE...
...HE'S OUR **FOURTH?**
ABOUT THAT...
I DON'T KNOW YET.
HE'S A NEIGHBOR. IT'S TRICKY.
THAT'S NOT THE PROBLEM.
YOU'RE A NEIGHBOR TOO, KUGA.

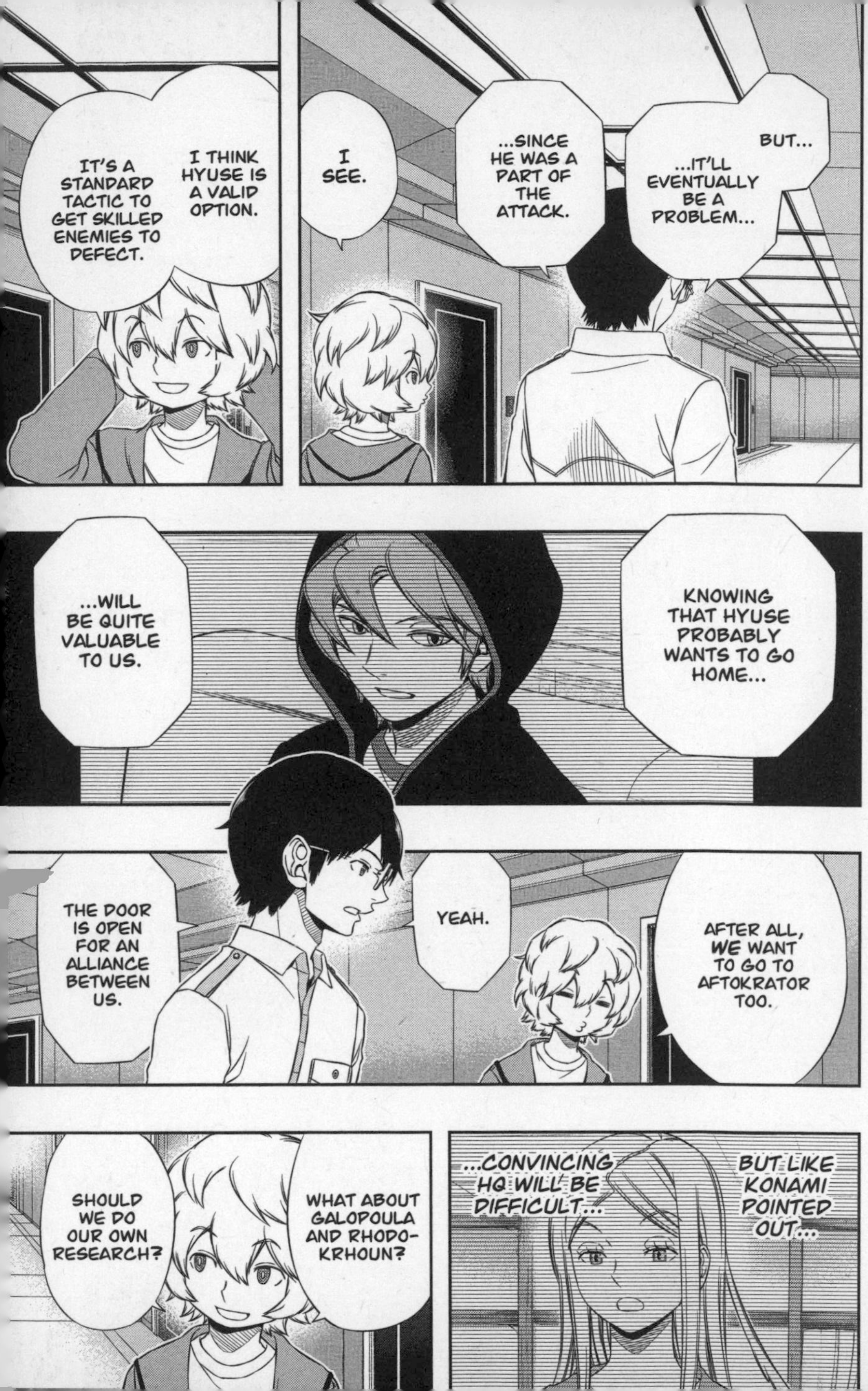
BUT... ...IT'LL EVENTUALLY BE A PROBLEM...
...SINCE HE WAS A PART OF THE ATTACK.
I SEE.
I THINK HYUSE IS A VALID OPTION.
IT'S A STANDARD TACTIC TO GET SKILLED ENEMIES TO DEFECT.
KNOWING THAT HYUSE PROBABLY WANTS TO GO HOME...
...WILL BE QUITE VALUABLE TO US.
AFTER ALL, WE WANT TO GO TO AFTOKRATOR TOO.
YEAH.
THE DOOR IS OPEN FOR AN ALLIANCE BETWEEN US.
BUT LIKE KONAMI POINTED OUT...
...CONVINCING HQ WILL BE DIFFICULT...
WHAT ABOUT GALOPOULA AND RHODO-KRHOUN?
SHOULD WE DO OUR OWN RESEARCH?

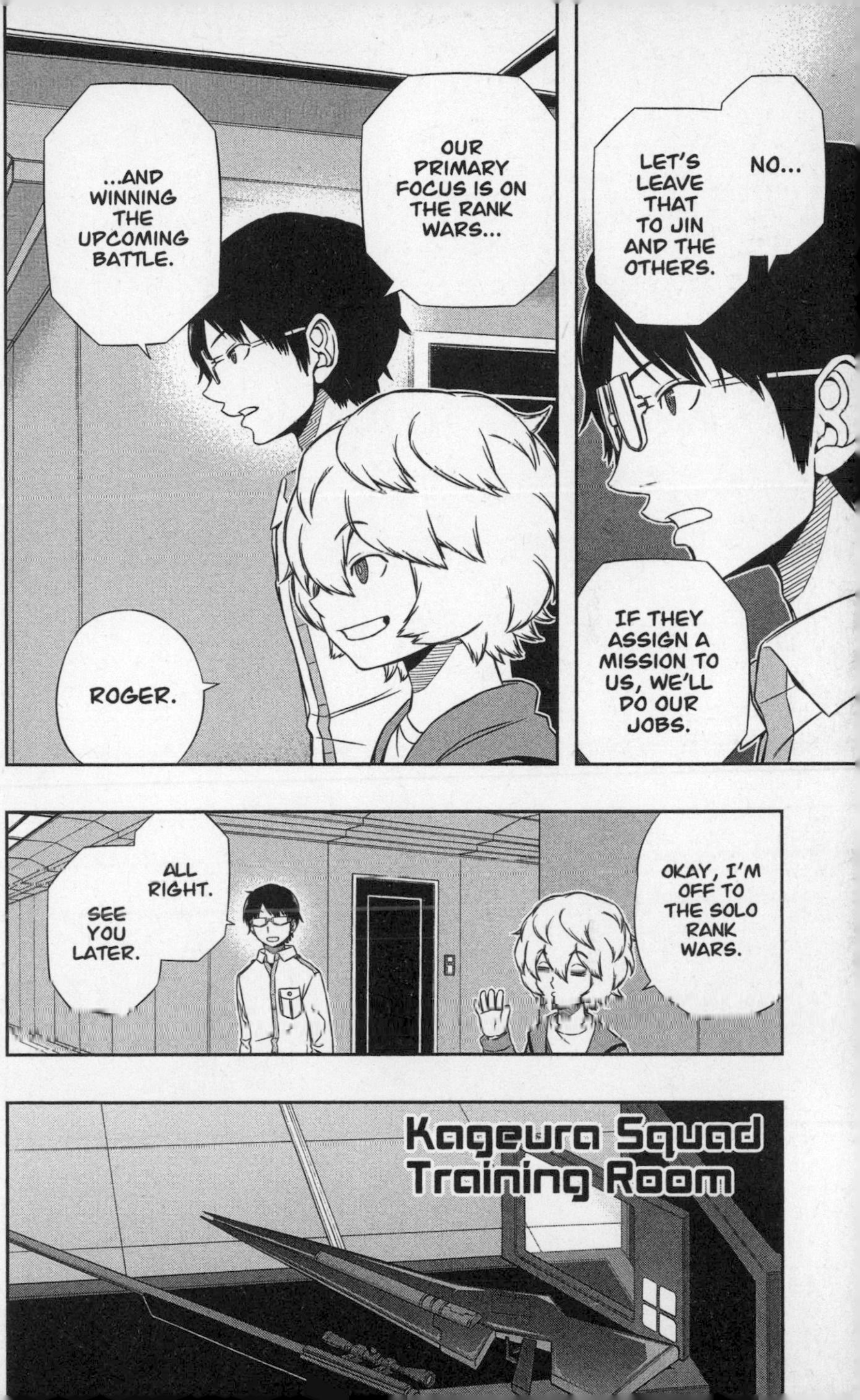
NO...
LET'S LEAVE THAT TO JIN AND THE OTHERS.
IF THEY ASSIGN A MISSION TO US, WE'LL DO OUR JOBS.
OUR PRIMARY FOCUS IS ON THE RANK WARS...
...AND WINNING THE UPCOMING BATTLE.
ROGER.
OKAY, I'M OFF TO THE SOLO RANK WARS.
ALL RIGHT. SEE YOU LATER.
Kageura Squad Training Room

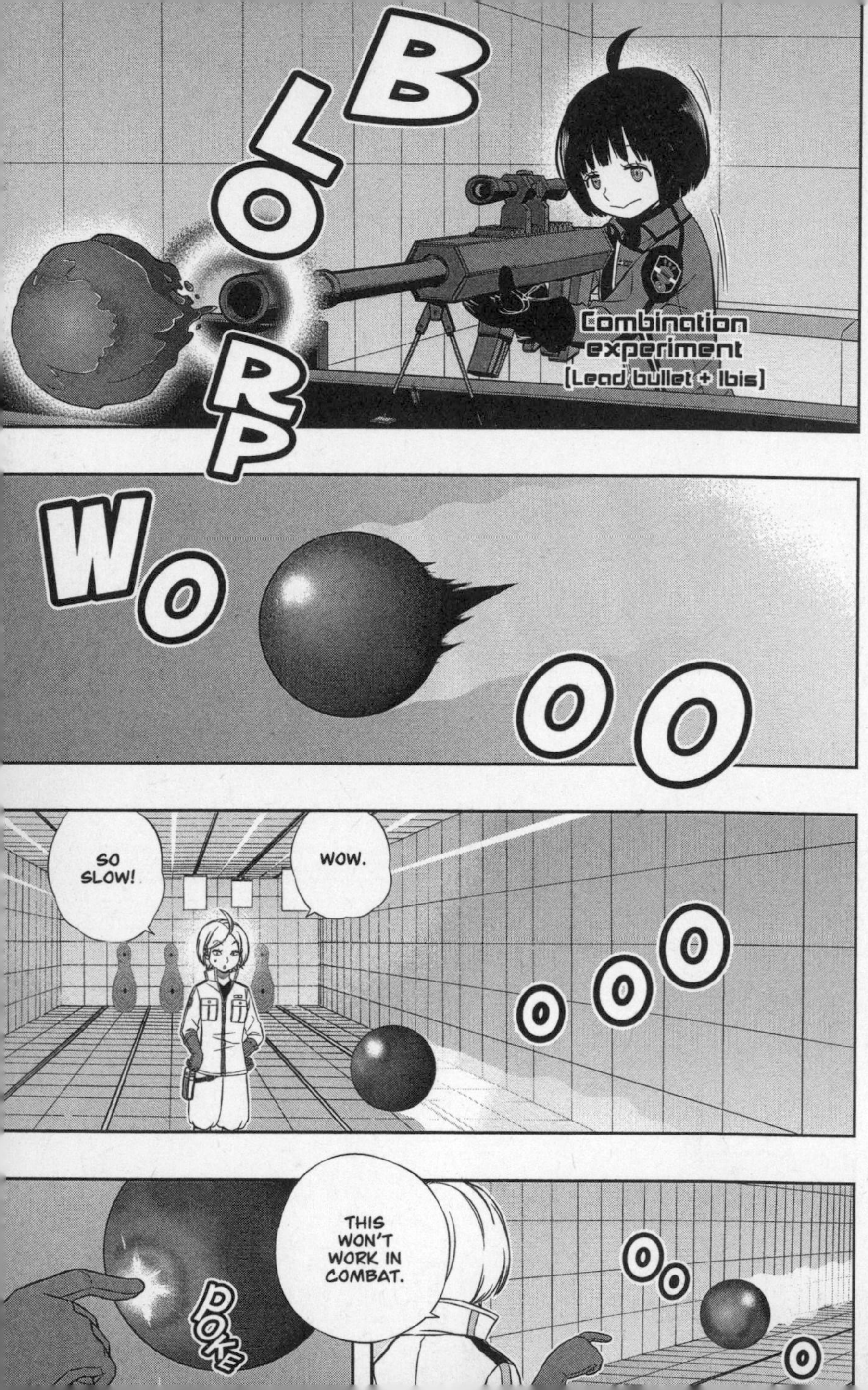
BLORP
Combination experiment
[Lead bullet + Ibis]
WOOO
WOW.
SO SLOW!
OOO
THIS WON'T WORK IN COMBAT.
POKE
OOO

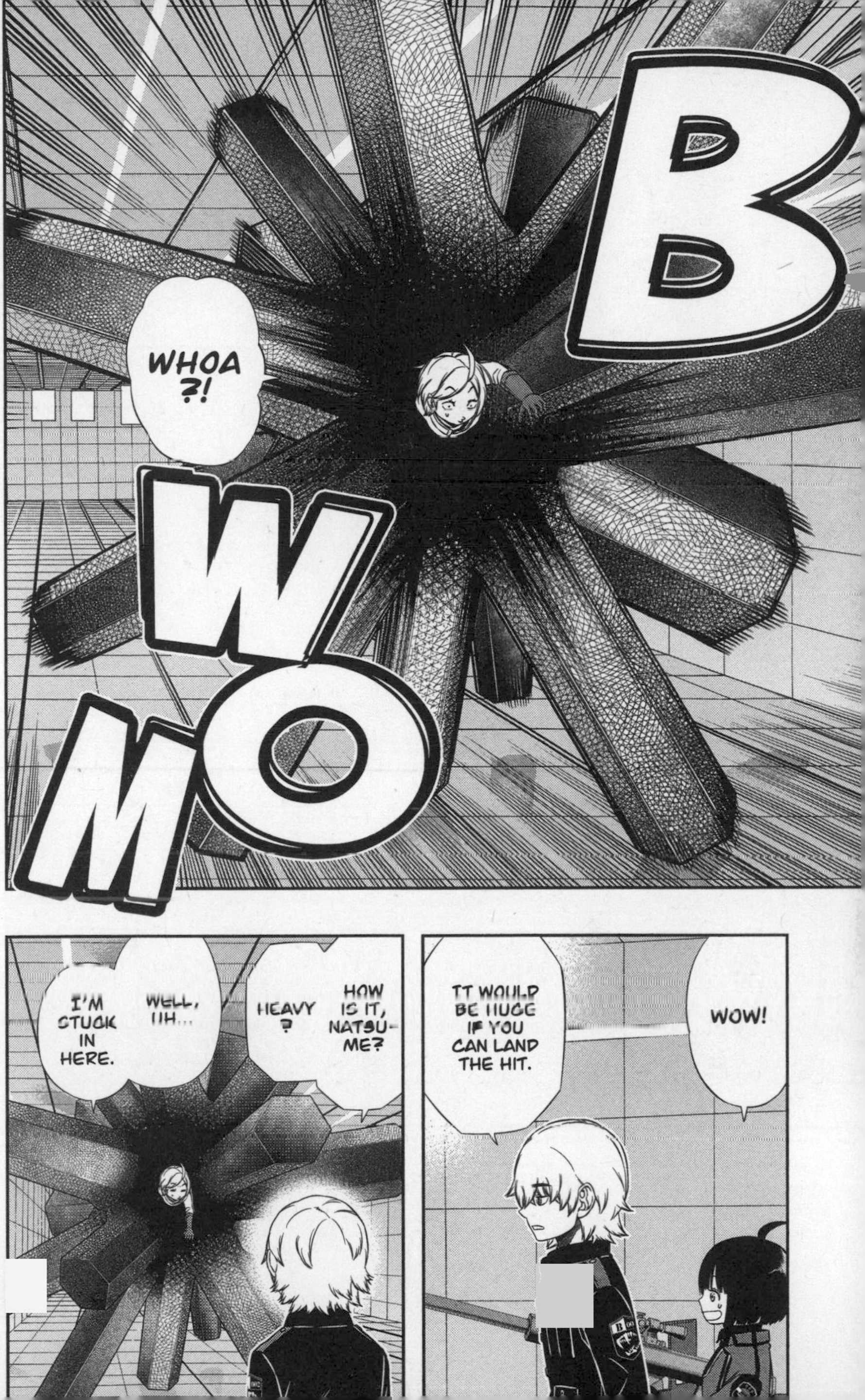
WHOA ?!
BWOM
WOW!
IT WOULD BE HUGE IF YOU CAN LAND THE HIT.
HOW IS IT, NATSUME?
HEAVY?
WELL, UH...
I'M STUCK IN HERE.

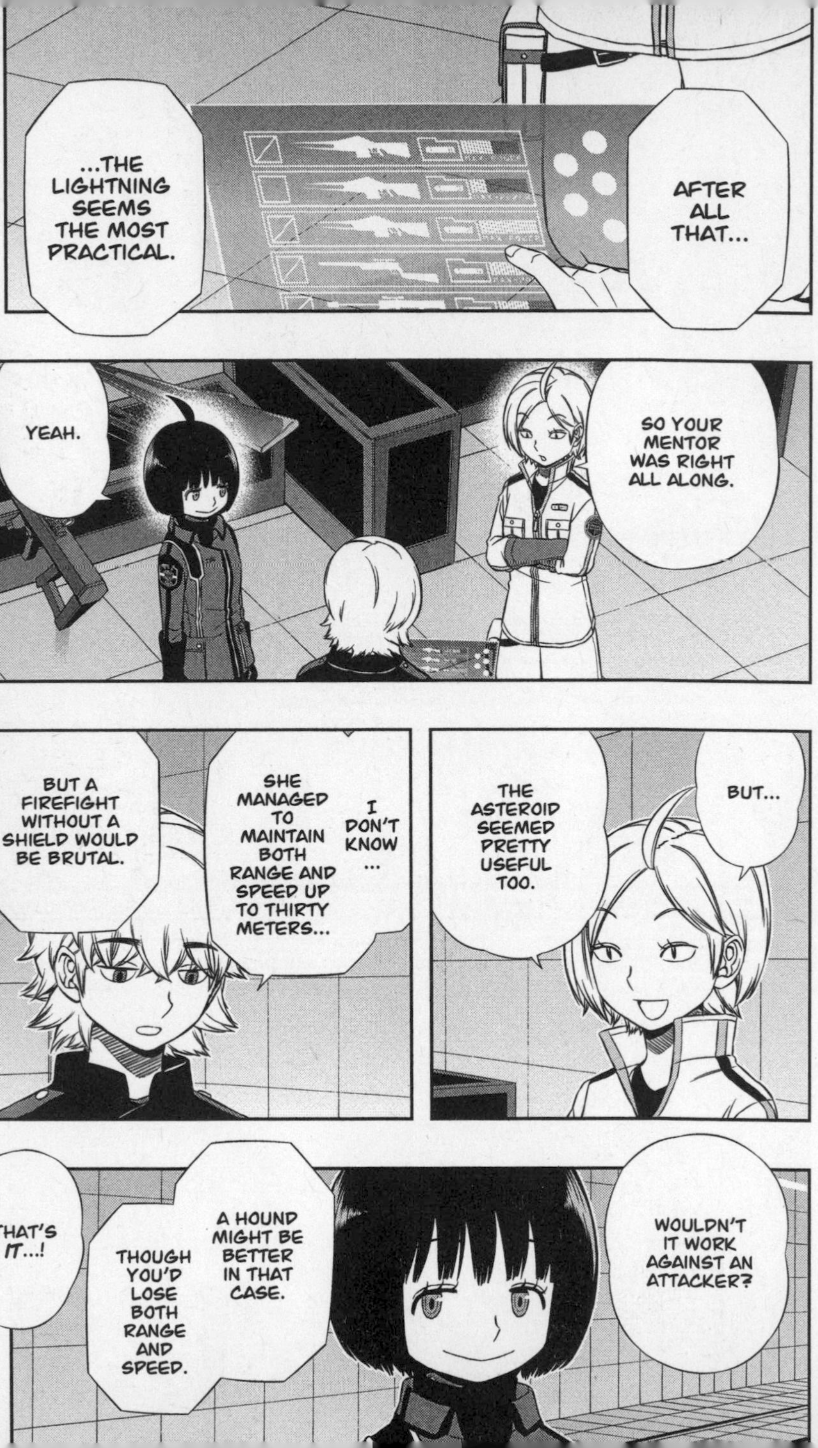
AFTER ALL THAT...
...THE LIGHTNING SEEMS THE MOST PRACTICAL.
SO YOUR MENTOR WAS RIGHT ALL ALONG.
YEAH.
BUT...
THE ASTEROID SEEMED PRETTY USEFUL TOO.
I DON'T KNOW...
SHE MANAGED TO MAINTAIN BOTH RANGE AND SPEED UP TO THIRTY METERS...
BUT A FIREFIGHT WITHOUT A SHIELD WOULD BE BRUTAL.
WOULDN'T IT WORK AGAINST AN ATTACKER?
A HOUND MIGHT BE BETTER IN THAT CASE.
THOUGH YOU'D LOSE BOTH RANGE AND SPEED.
THAT'S IT...!

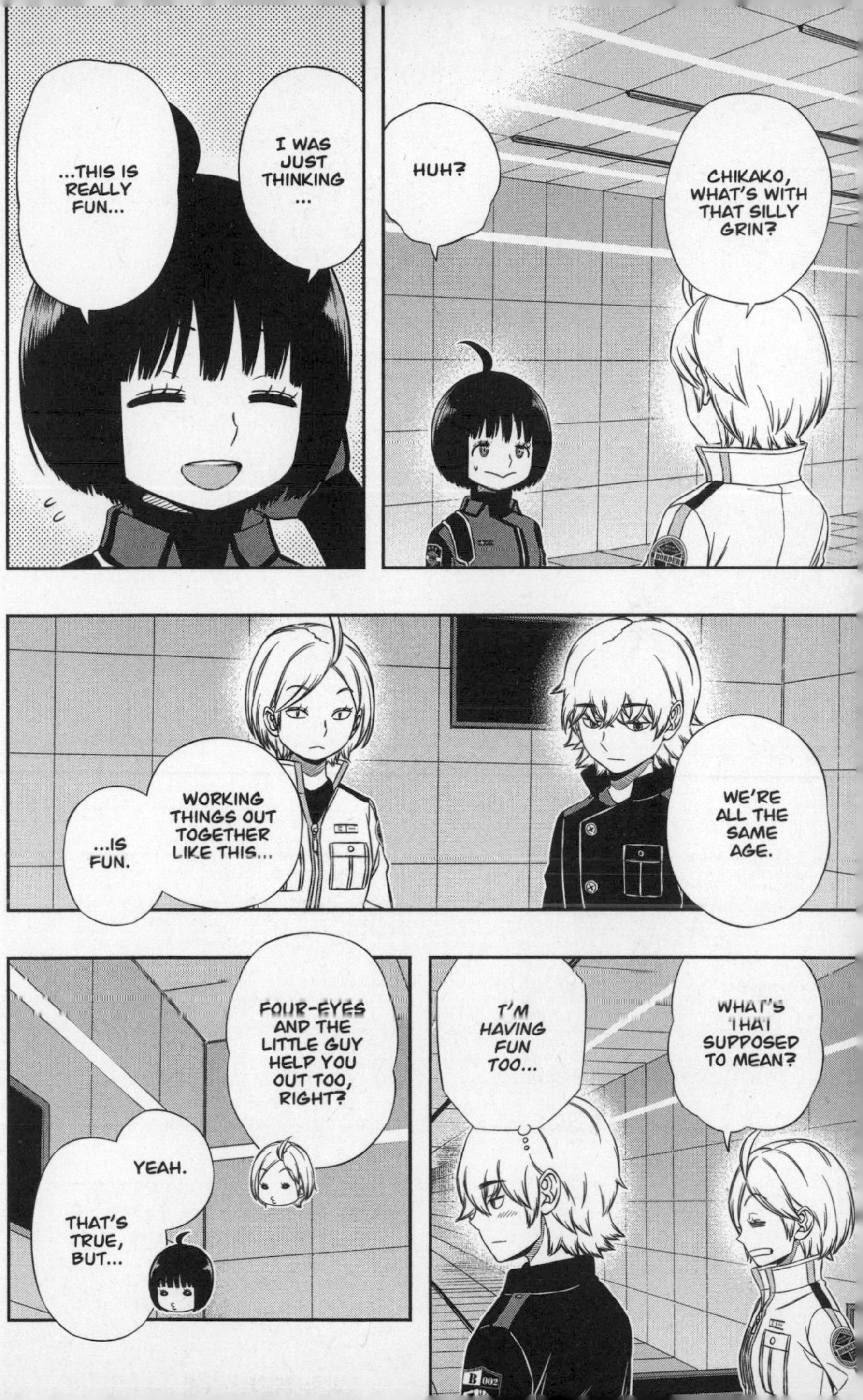
CHIKAKO, WHAT'S WITH THAT SILLY GRIN?
HUH?
I WAS JUST THINKING ...
...THIS IS REALLY FUN...
WE'RE ALL THE SAME AGE.
WORKING THINGS OUT TOGETHER LIKE THIS...
...IS FUN.
WHAT'S THAT SUPPOSED TO MEAN?
I'M HAVING FUN TOO...
FOUR-EYES AND THE LITTLE GUY HELP YOU OUT TOO, RIGHT?
YEAH.
THAT'S TRUE, BUT...

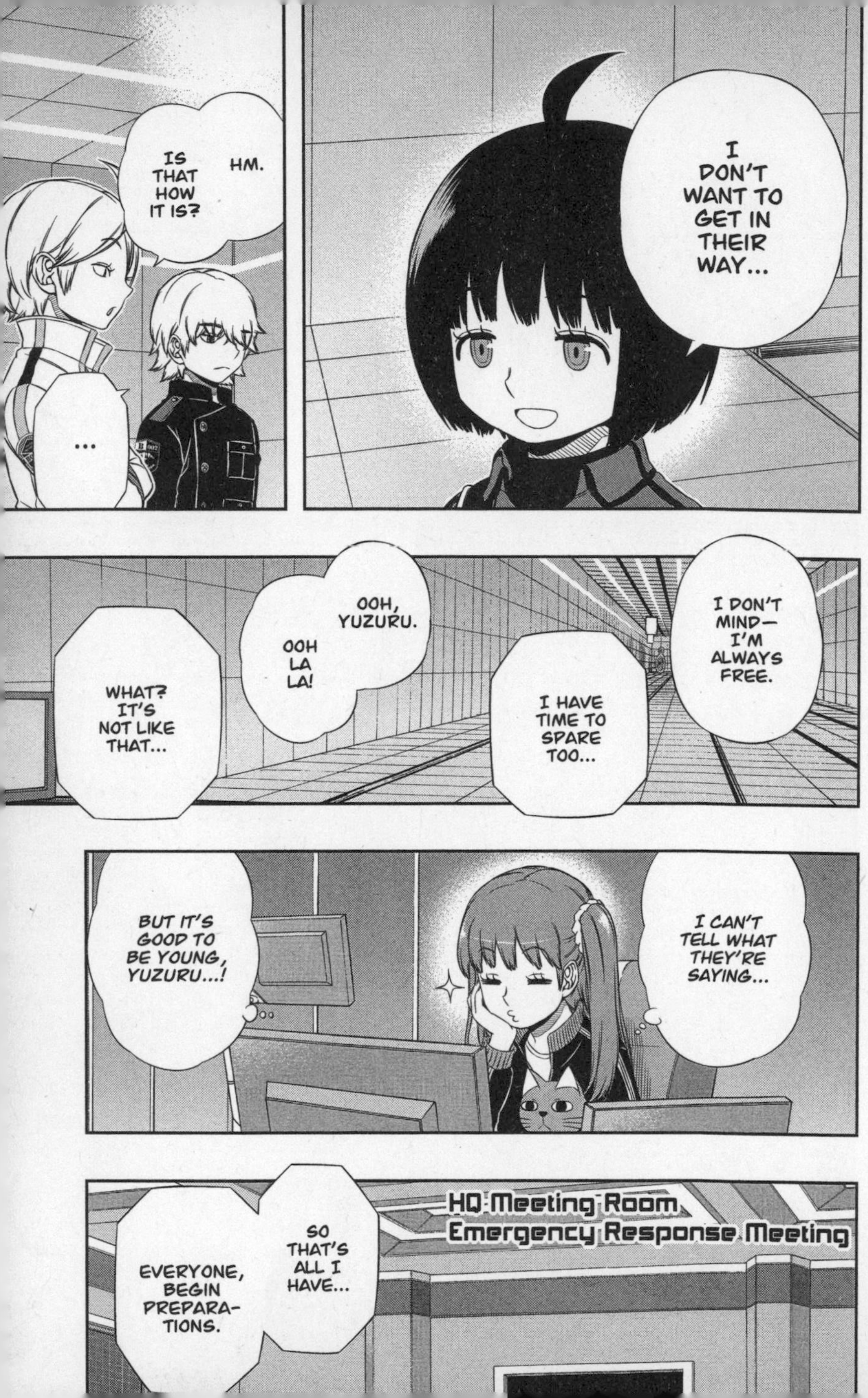
I DON'T WANT TO GET IN THEIR WAY...
HM.
IS THAT HOW IT IS?
...
I DON'T MIND—I'M ALWAYS FREE.
I HAVE TIME TO SPARE TOO...
OOH, YUZURU.
OOH LA LA!
WHAT? IT'S NOT LIKE THAT...
I CAN'T TELL WHAT THEY'RE SAYING...
BUT IT'S GOOD TO BE YOUNG, YUZURU...!
HQ Meeting Room
Emergency Response Meeting
SO THAT'S ALL I HAVE...
EVERYONE, BEGIN PREPARATIONS.

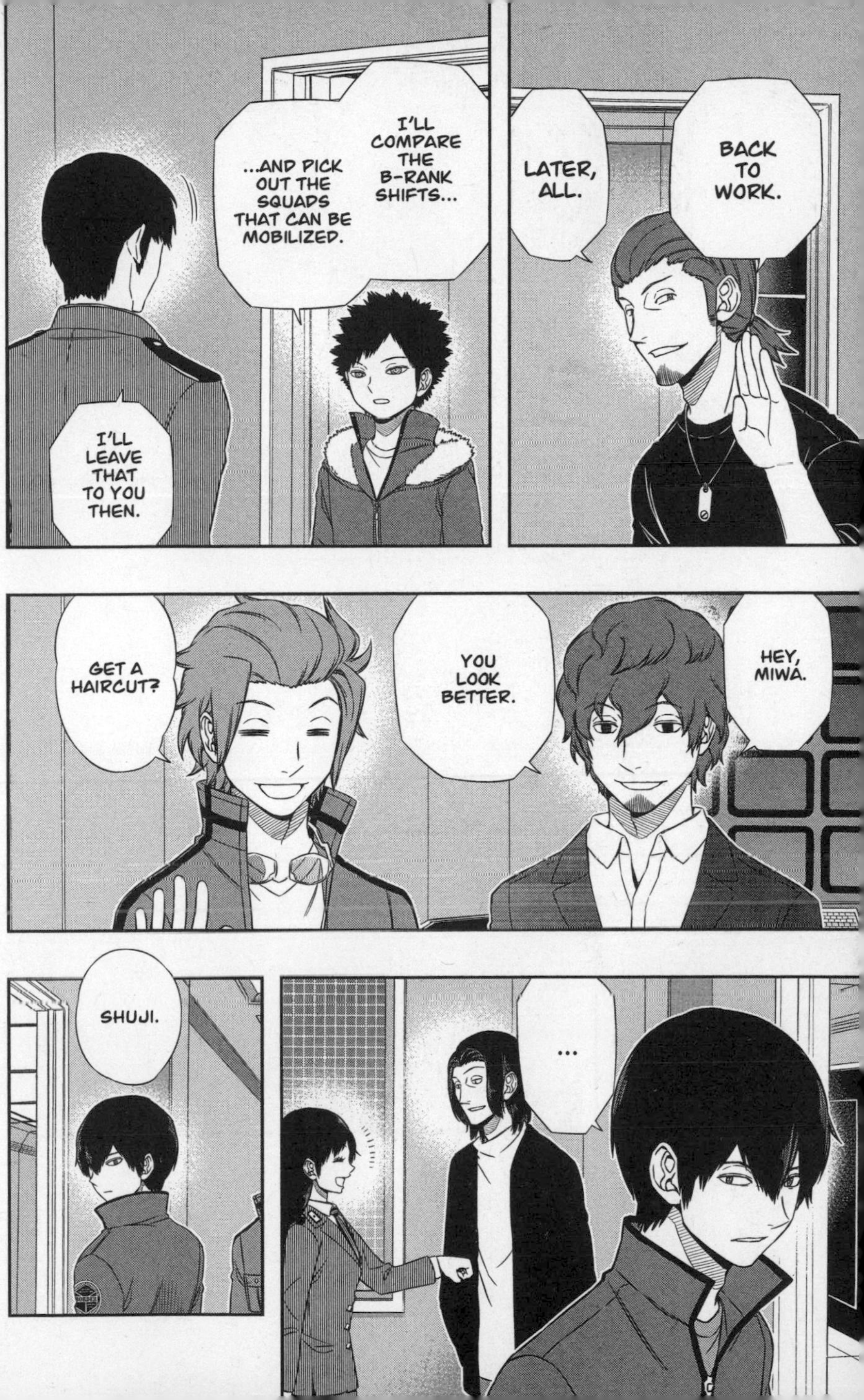
BACK TO WORK.
LATER, ALL.
I'LL COMPARE THE B-RANK SHIFTS...
...AND PICK OUT THE SQUADS THAT CAN BE MOBILIZED.
I'LL LEAVE THAT TO YOU THEN.
HEY, MIWA.
YOU LOOK BETTER.
GET A HAIRCUT?
...
SHUJI.

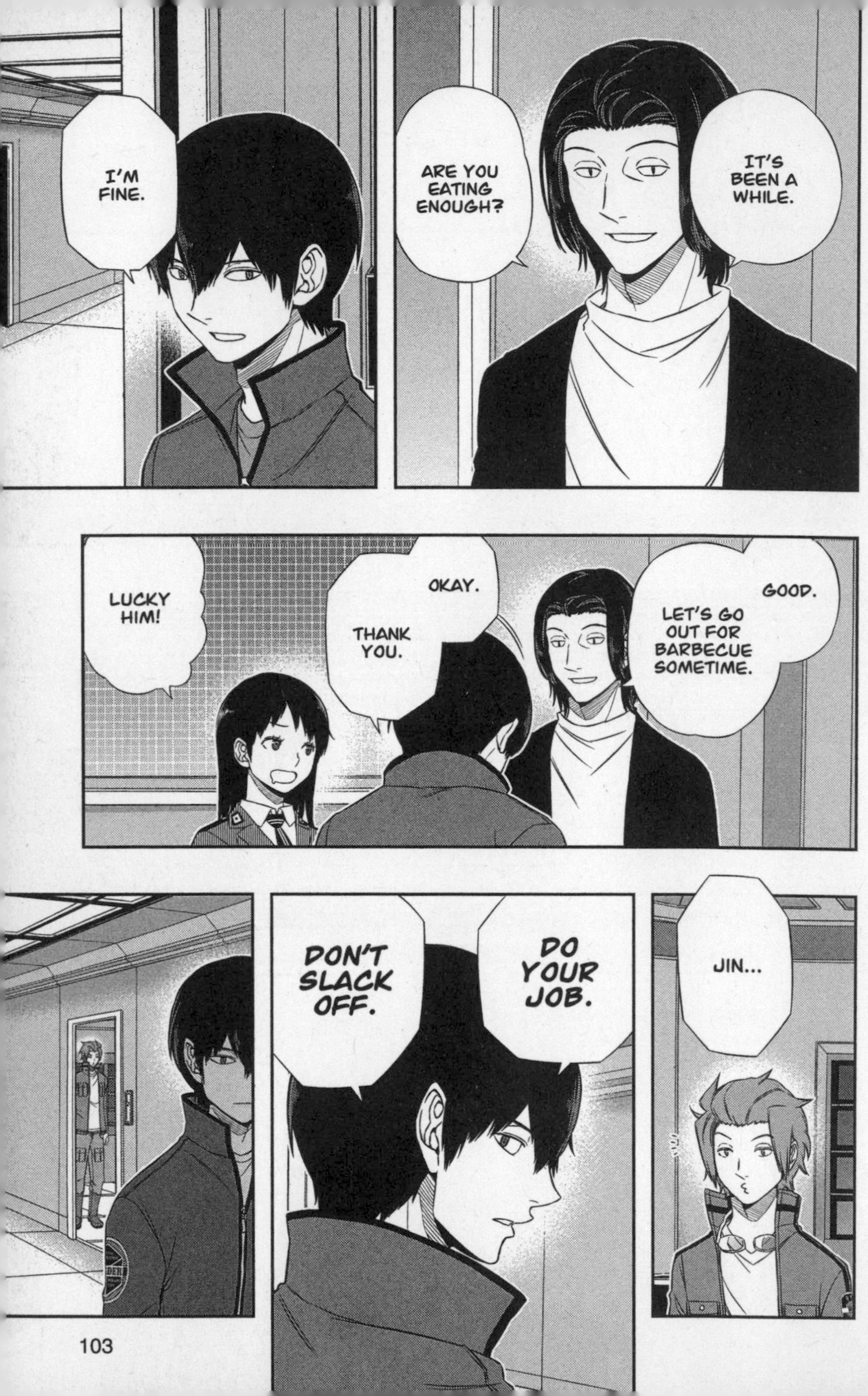
IT'S BEEN A WHILE.
ARE YOU EATING ENOUGH?
I'M FINE.
GOOD.
LET'S GO OUT FOR BARBECUE SOMETIME.
OKAY.
THANK YOU.
LUCKY HIM!
JIN...
DO YOUR JOB.
DON'T SLACK OFF.

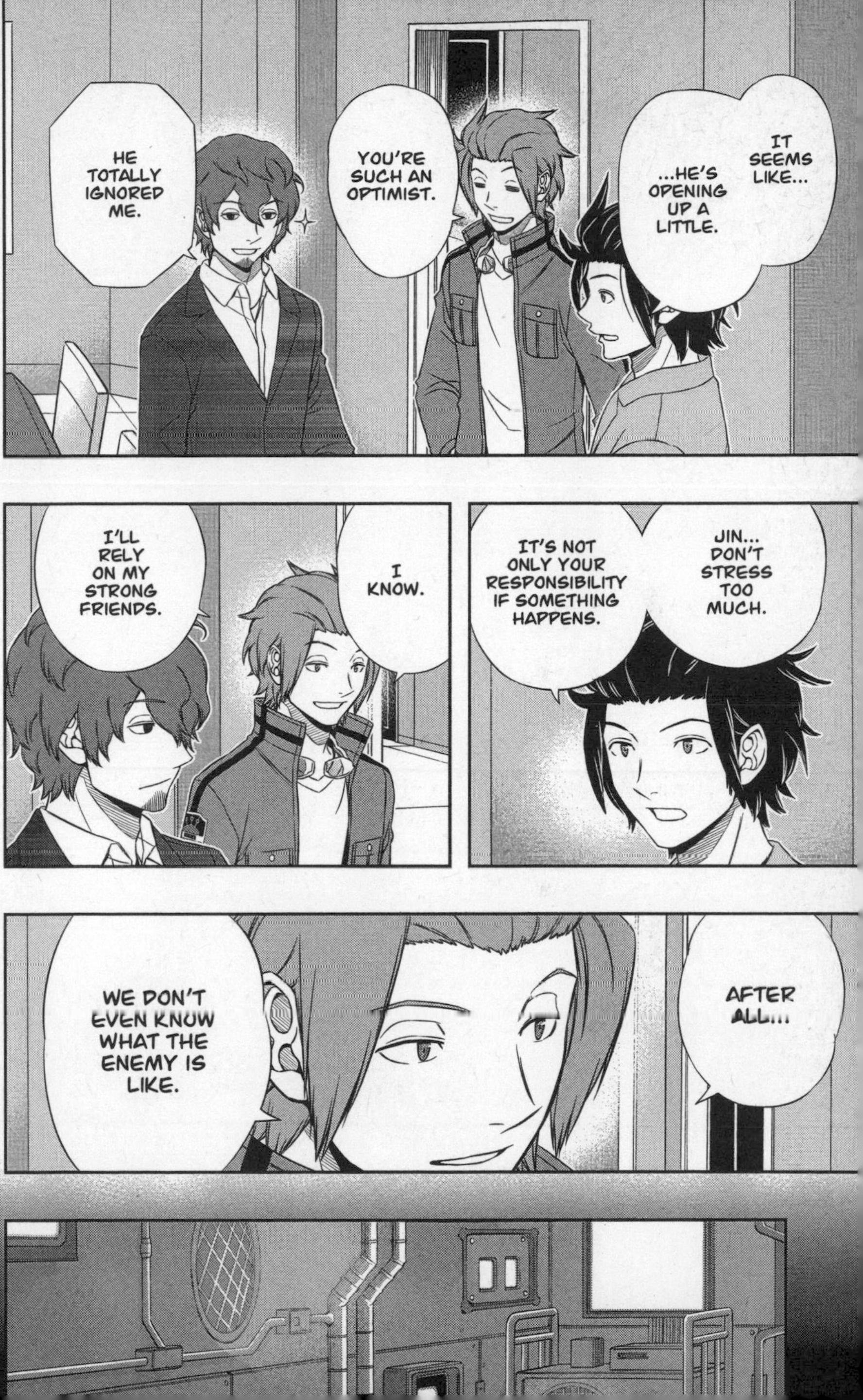
IT SEEMS LIKE...
...HE'S OPENING UP A LITTLE.
YOU'RE SUCH AN OPTIMIST.
HE TOTALLY IGNORED ME.
JIN... DON'T STRESS TOO MUCH.
IT'S NOT ONLY YOUR RESPONSIBILITY IF SOMETHING HAPPENS.
I KNOW.
I'LL RELY ON MY STRONG FRIENDS.
AFTER ALL...
WE DON'T EVEN KNOW WHAT THE ENEMY IS LIKE.

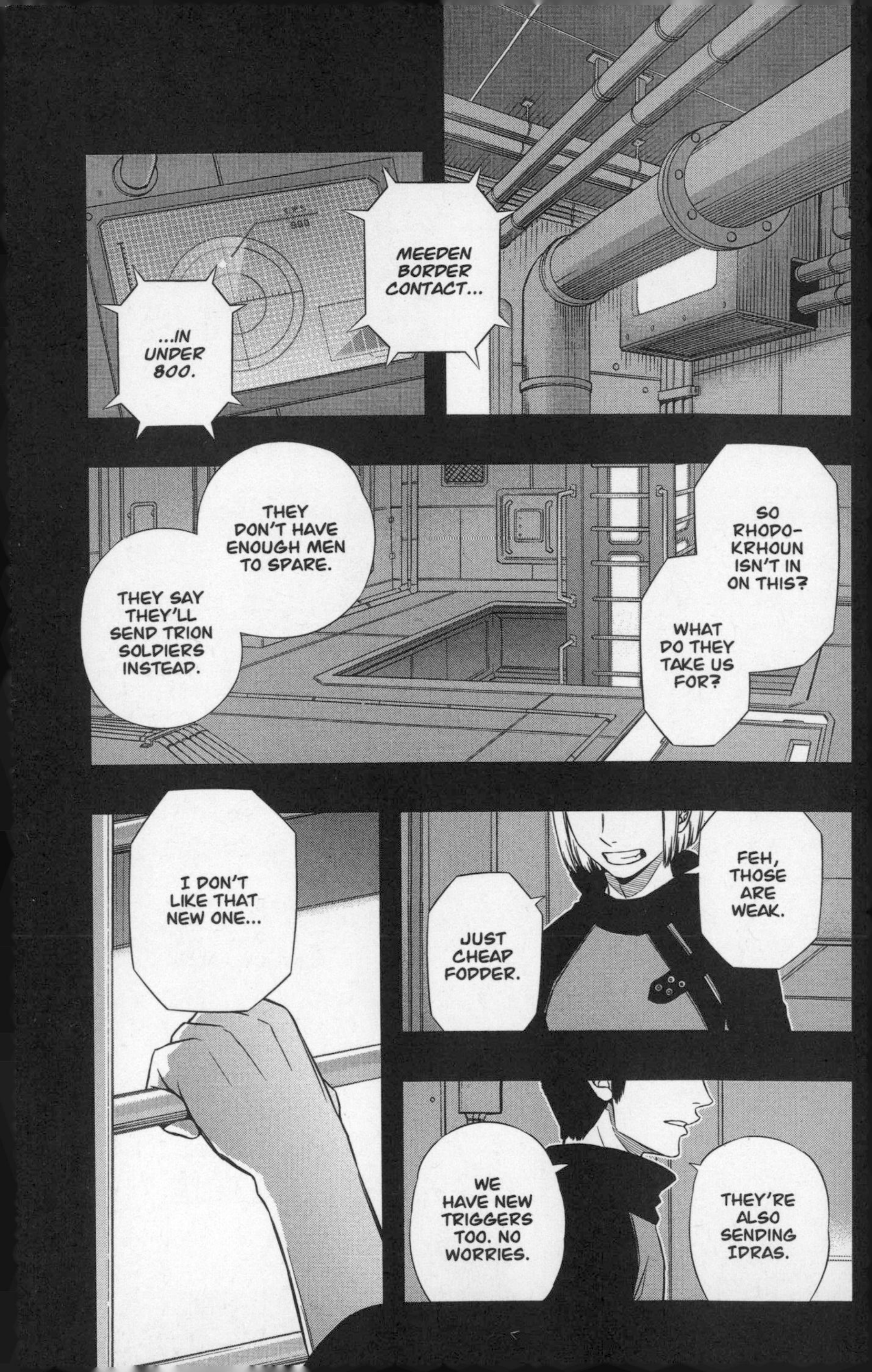
MEEDEN BORDER CONTACT...
...IN UNDER 800.
SO RHODO-KRHOUN ISN'T IN ON THIS?
WHAT DO THEY TAKE US FOR?
THEY DON'T HAVE ENOUGH MEN TO SPARE.
THEY SAY THEY'LL SEND TRION SOLDIERS INSTEAD.
FEH, THOSE ARE WEAK.
JUST CHEAP FODDER.
THEY'RE ALSO SENDING IDRAS.
WE HAVE NEW TRIGGERS TOO. NO WORRIES.
I DON'T LIKE THAT NEW ONE...

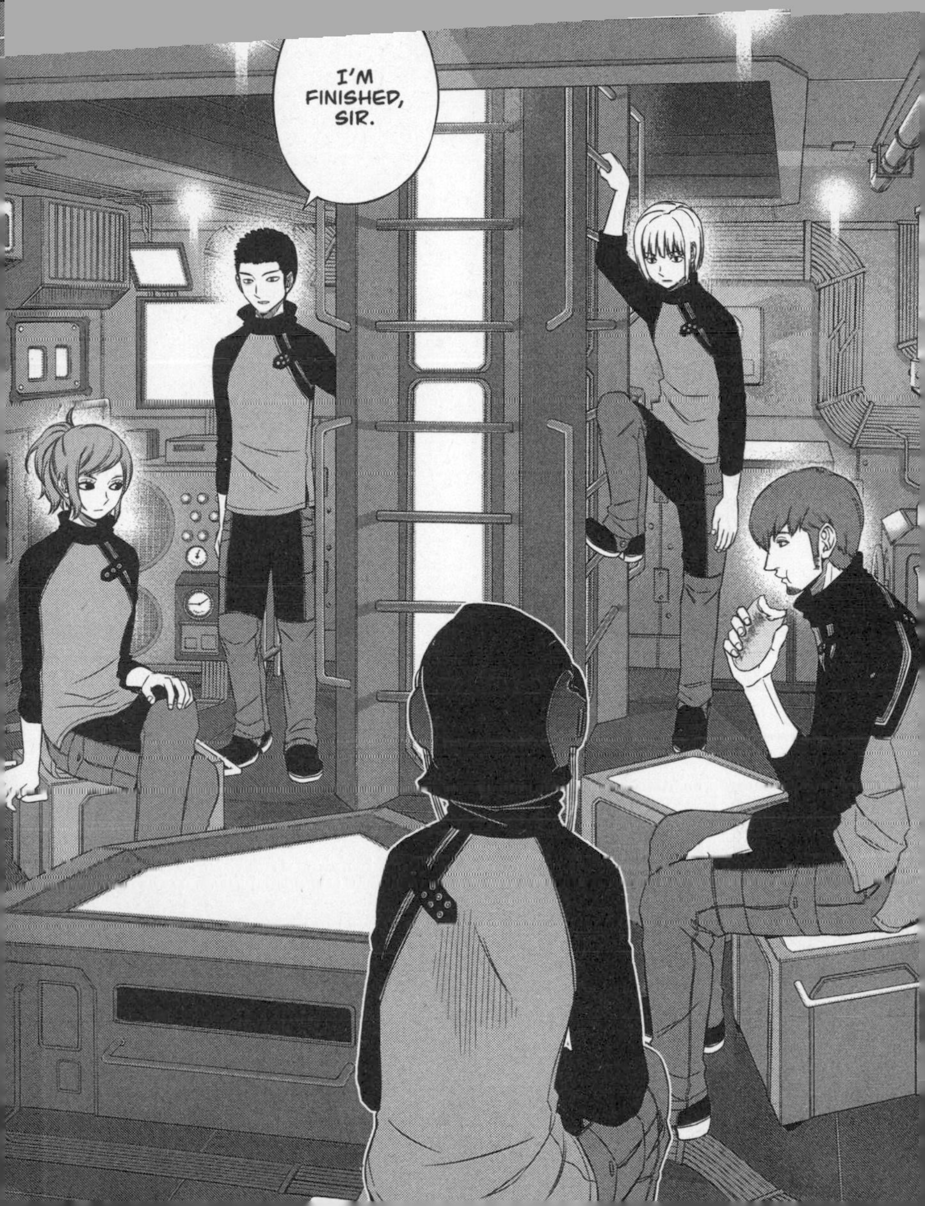
I'M FINISHED, SIR.

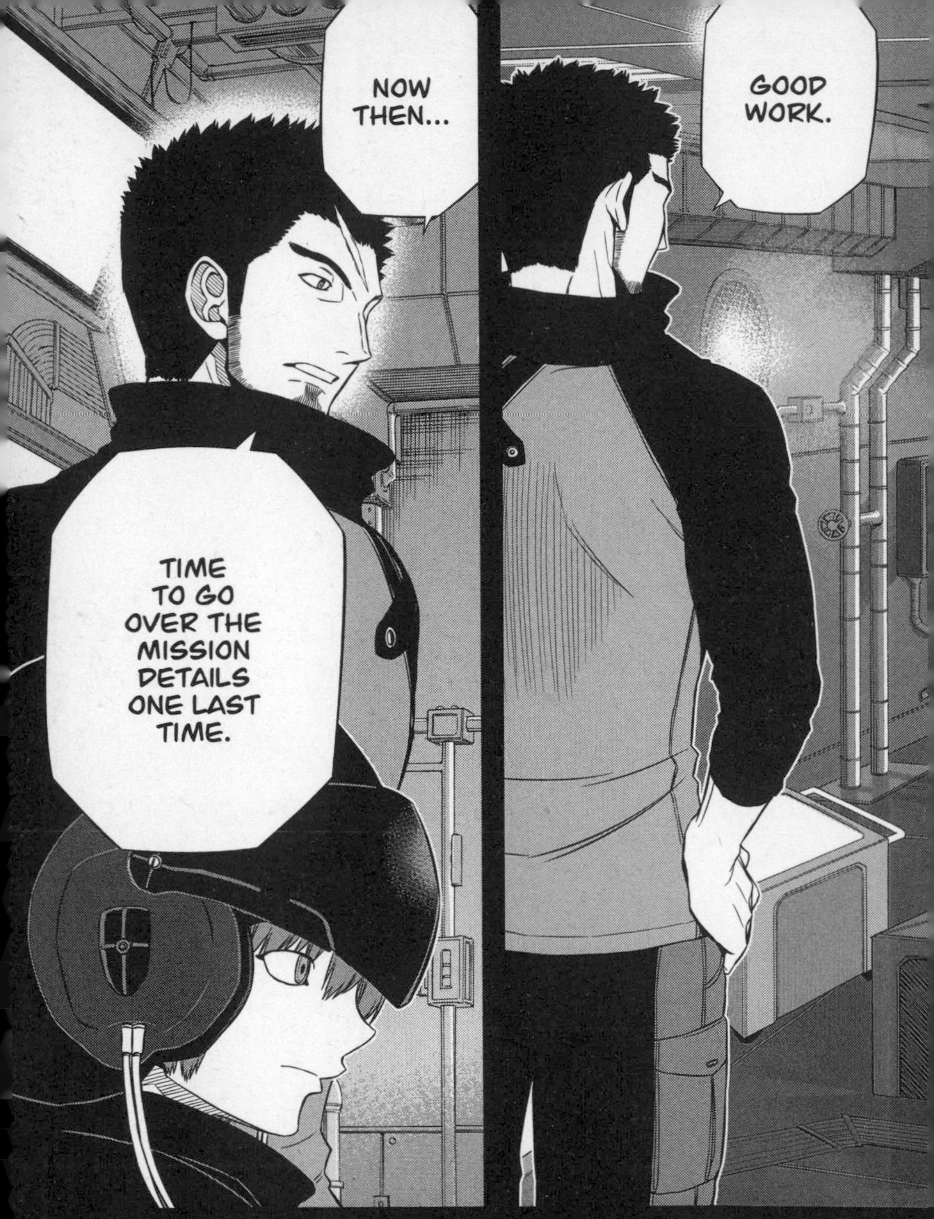
GOOD WORK.
NOW THEN...
TIME TO GO OVER THE MISSION DETAILS ONE LAST TIME.

Kazama Squad Strategy Room

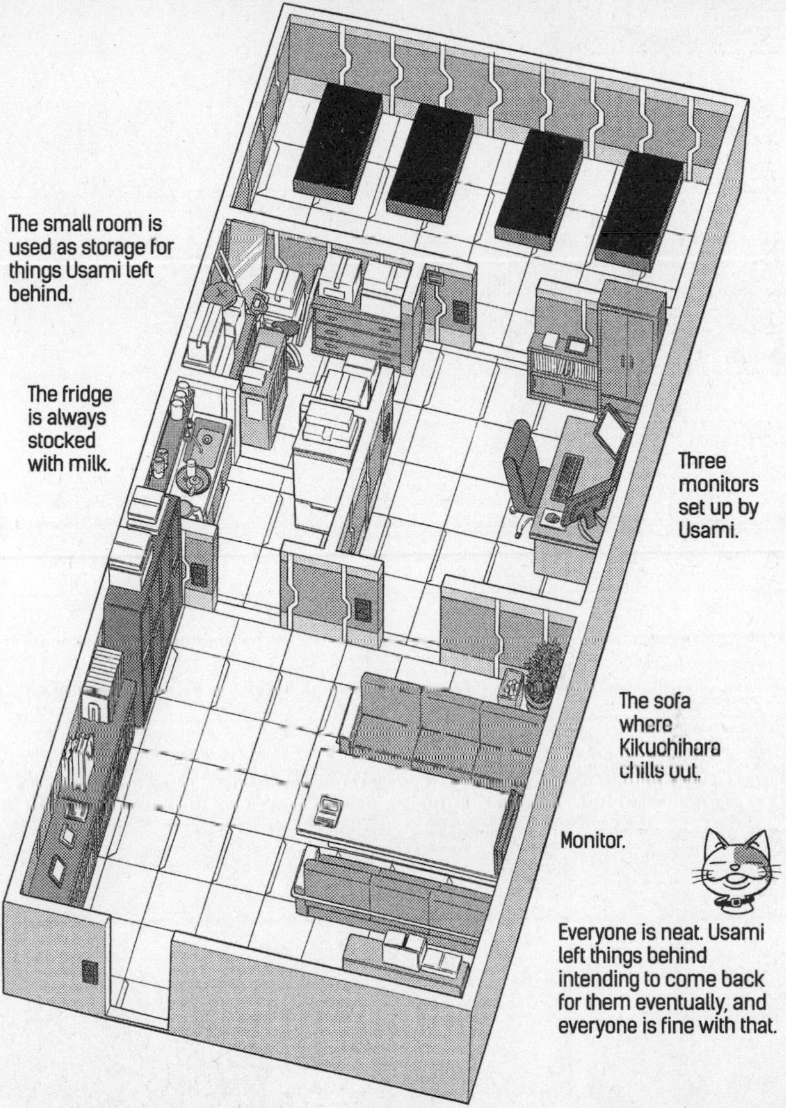

The small room is used as storage for things Usami left behind.
The fridge is always stocked with milk.
Three monitors set up by Usami.
The sofa where Kikuchihara chills out.
Monitor.
Everyone is neat. Usami left things behind intending to come back for them eventually, and everyone is fine with that.

Chapter 121 Galopoula

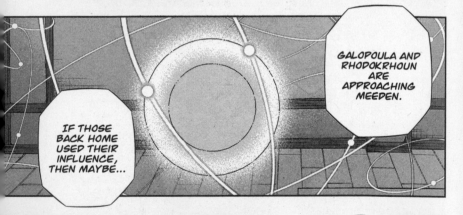

GALOPOULA AND RHODOKRHOUN ARE APPROACHING MEEDEN.

IF THOSE BACK HOME USED THEIR INFLUENCE, THEN MAYBE...

SQUK

FFT

....!

HYUSE, I'M COMING IN!

NOK NOK

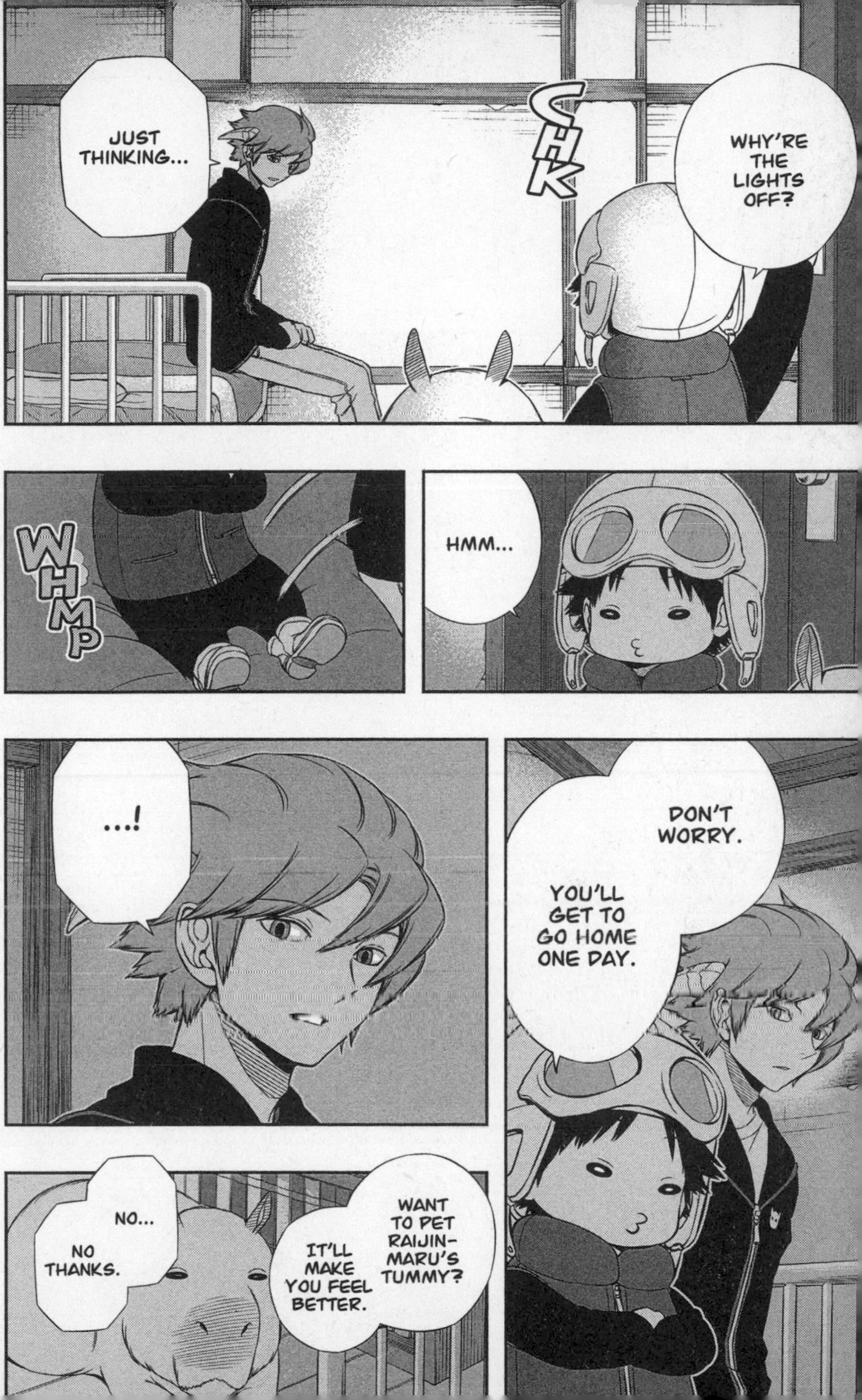
WHY'RE THE LIGHTS OFF?
CHK
JUST THINKING...
HMM...
WHMP
DON'T WORRY.
YOU'LL GET TO GO HOME ONE DAY.
...!
WANT TO PET RAIJIN-MARU'S TUMMY?
IT'LL MAKE YOU FEEL BETTER.
NO...
NO THANKS.

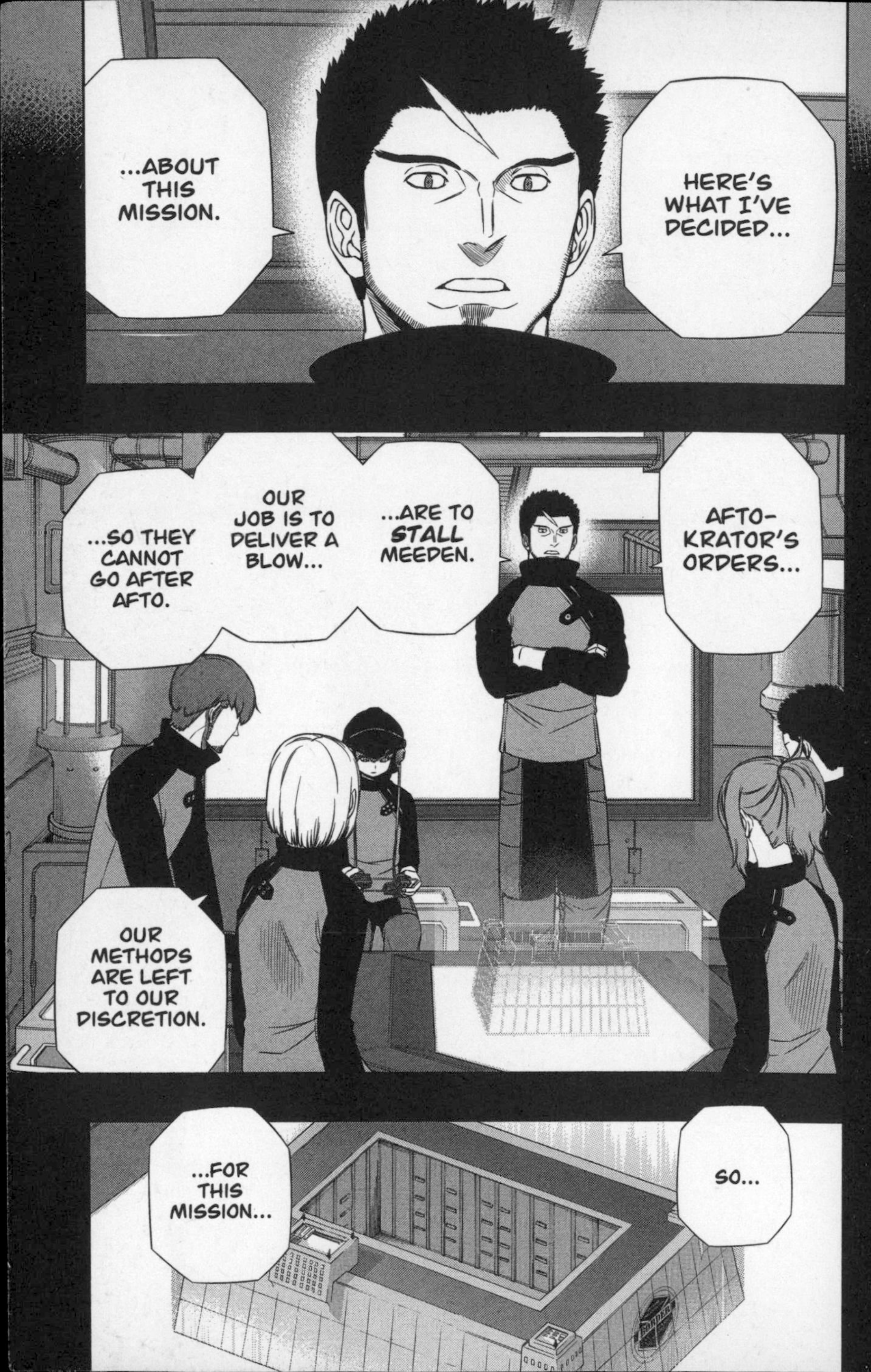
HERE'S WHAT I'VE DECIDED...
...ABOUT THIS MISSION.
AFTO-KRATOR'S ORDERS...
...ARE TO STALL MEEDEN.
OUR JOB IS TO DELIVER A BLOW...
...SO THEY CANNOT GO AFTER AFTO.
OUR METHODS ARE LEFT TO OUR DISCRETION.
SO...
...FOR THIS MISSION...

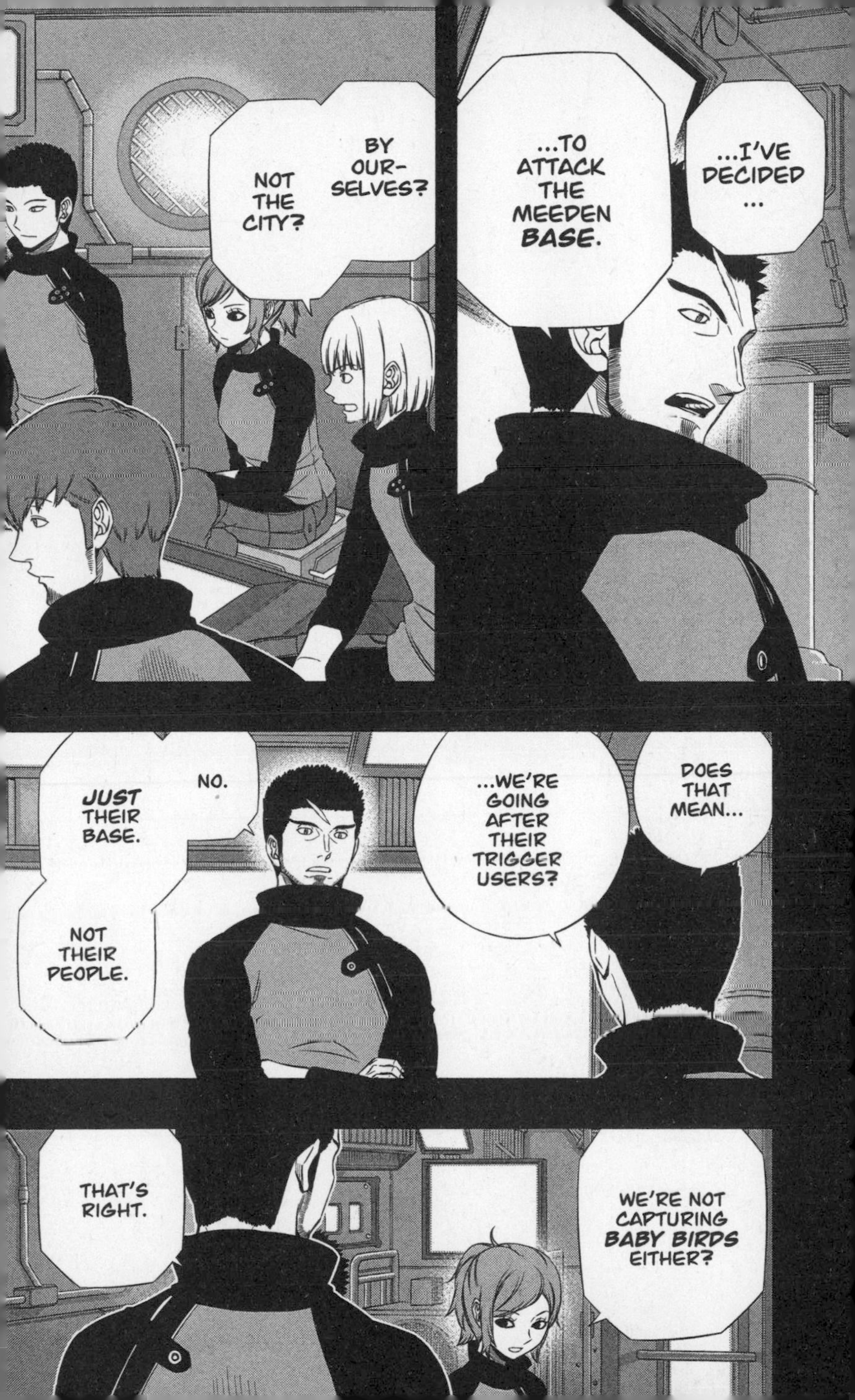
...I'VE DECIDED...
...TO ATTACK THE MEEDEN BASE.
BY OUR-SELVES?
NOT THE CITY?
DOES THAT MEAN...
...WE'RE GOING AFTER THEIR TRIGGER USERS?
NO.
JUST THEIR BASE.
NOT THEIR PEOPLE.
WE'RE NOT CAPTURING BABY BIRDS EITHER?
THAT'S RIGHT.

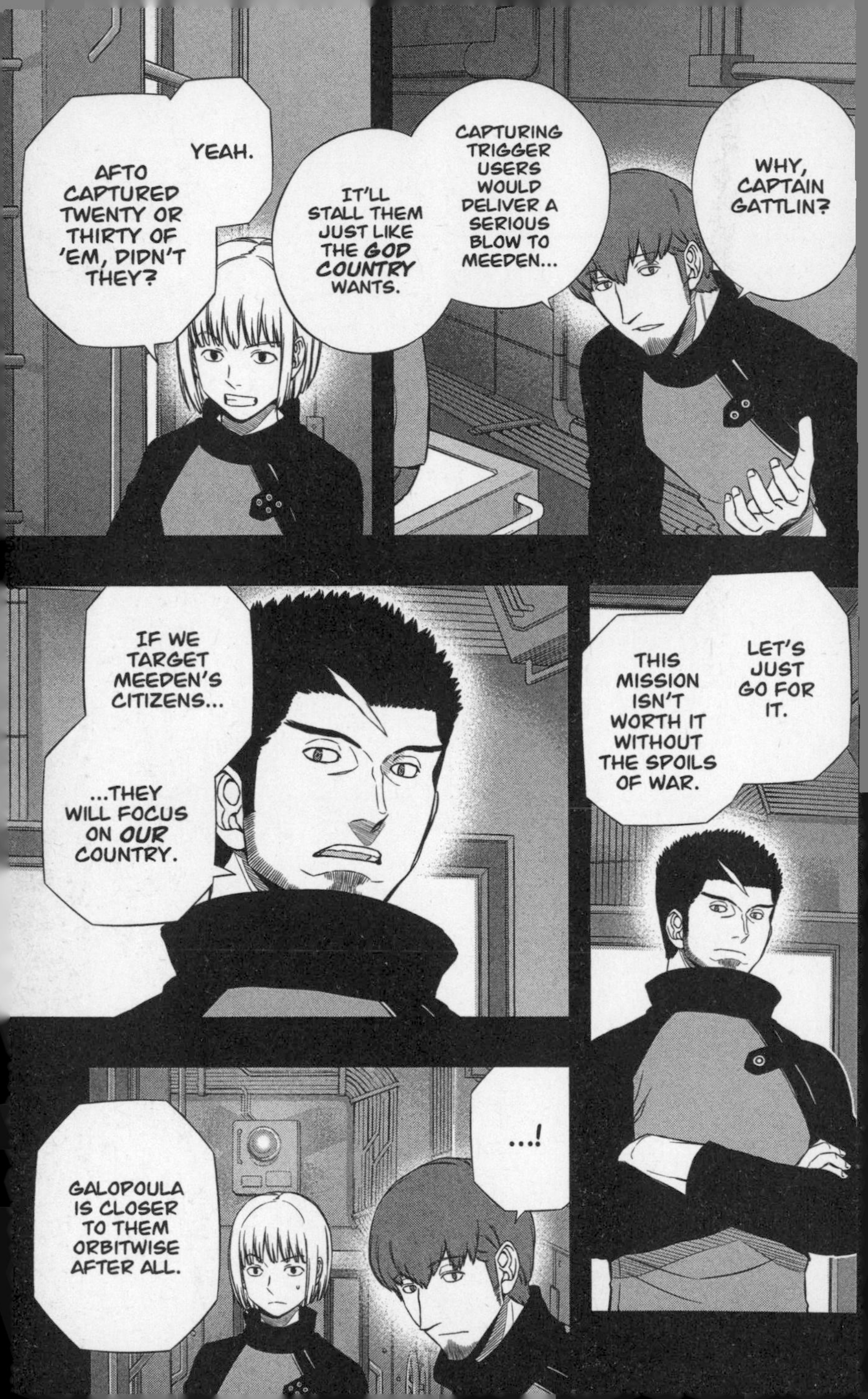
WHY, CAPTAIN GATTLIN?
CAPTURING TRIGGER USERS WOULD DELIVER A SERIOUS BLOW TO MEEDEN...
IT'LL STALL THEM JUST LIKE THE GOD COUNTRY WANTS.
YEAH.
AFTO CAPTURED TWENTY OR THIRTY OF 'EM, DIDN'T THEY?
LET'S JUST GO FOR IT.
THIS MISSION ISN'T WORTH IT WITHOUT THE SPOILS OF WAR.
IF WE TARGET MEEDEN'S CITIZENS...
...THEY WILL FOCUS ON OUR COUNTRY.
...!
GALOPOULA IS CLOSER TO THEM ORBITWISE AFTER ALL.

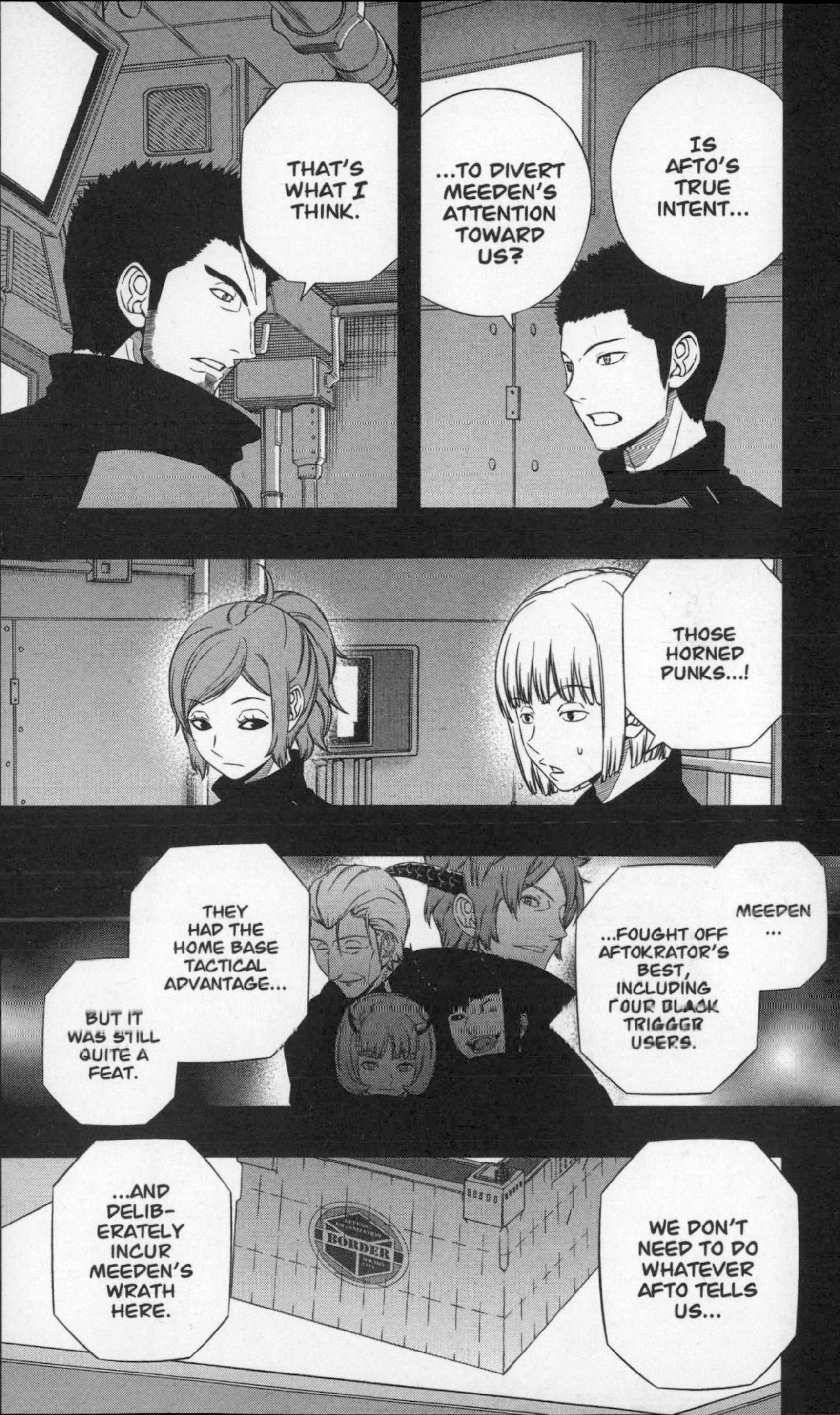
IS AFTO'S TRUE INTENT...
...TO DIVERT MEEDEN'S ATTENTION TOWARD US?
THAT'S WHAT I THINK.
THOSE HORNED PUNKS...!
MEEDEN...
...FOUGHT OFF AFTOKRATOR'S BEST, INCLUDING FOUR BLACK TRIGGER USERS.
THEY HAD THE HOME BASE TACTICAL ADVANTAGE...
BUT IT WAS STILL QUITE A FEAT.
WE DON'T NEED TO DO WHATEVER AFTO TELLS US...
BORDER
...AND DELIB-ERATELY INCUR MEEDEN'S WRATH HERE.

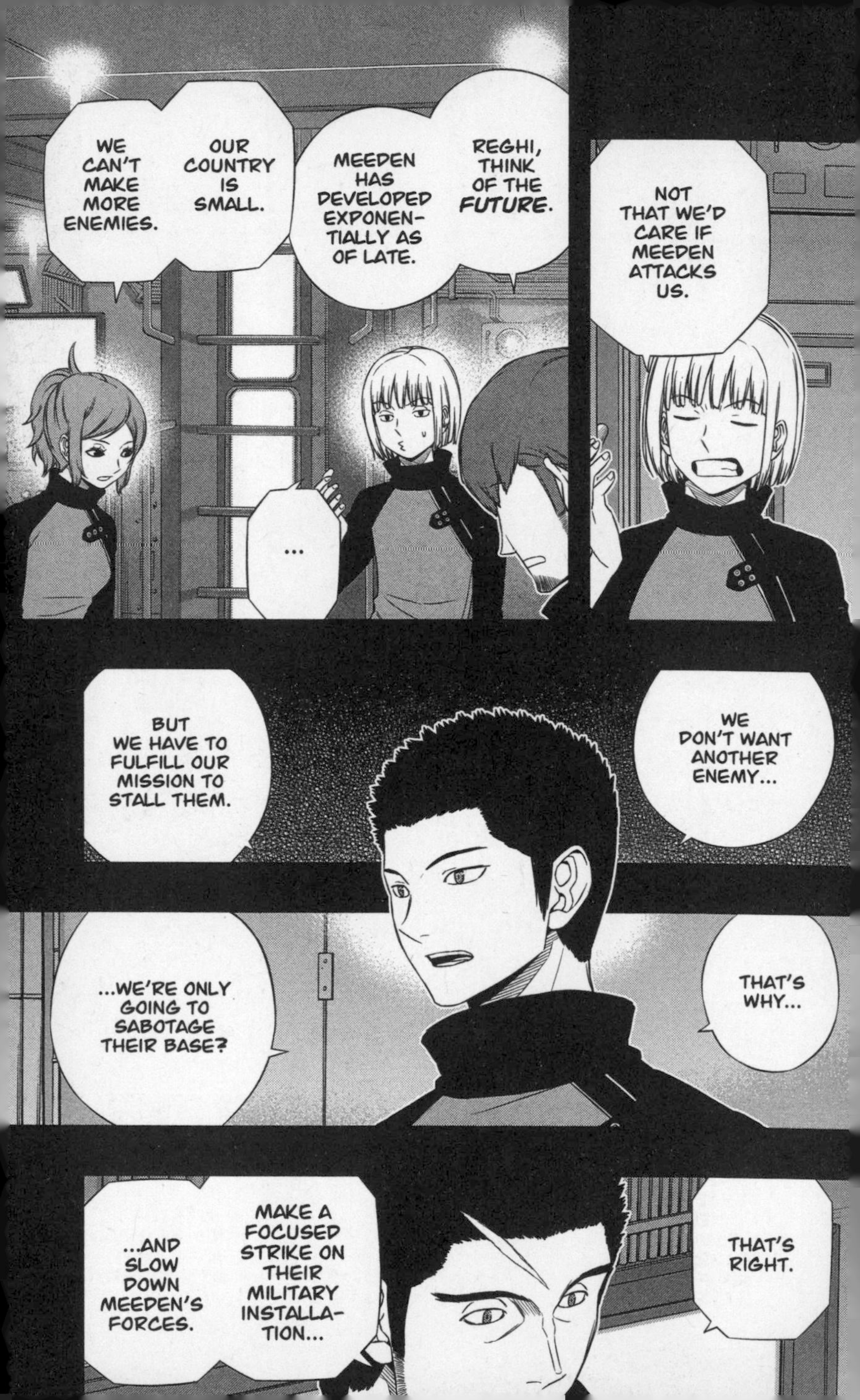
NOT THAT WE'D CARE IF MEEDEN ATTACKS US.
REGHI, THINK OF THE *FUTURE*.
MEEDEN HAS DEVELOPED EXPONEN- TIALLY AS OF LATE.
OUR COUNTRY IS SMALL.
WE CAN'T MAKE MORE ENEMIES.
...
WE DON'T WANT ANOTHER ENEMY...
BUT WE HAVE TO FULFILL OUR MISSION TO STALL THEM.
THAT'S WHY...
...WE'RE ONLY GOING TO SABOTAGE THEIR BASE?
THAT'S RIGHT.
MAKE A FOCUSED STRIKE ON THEIR MILITARY INSTALLA- TION...
...AND SLOW DOWN MEEDEN'S FORCES.

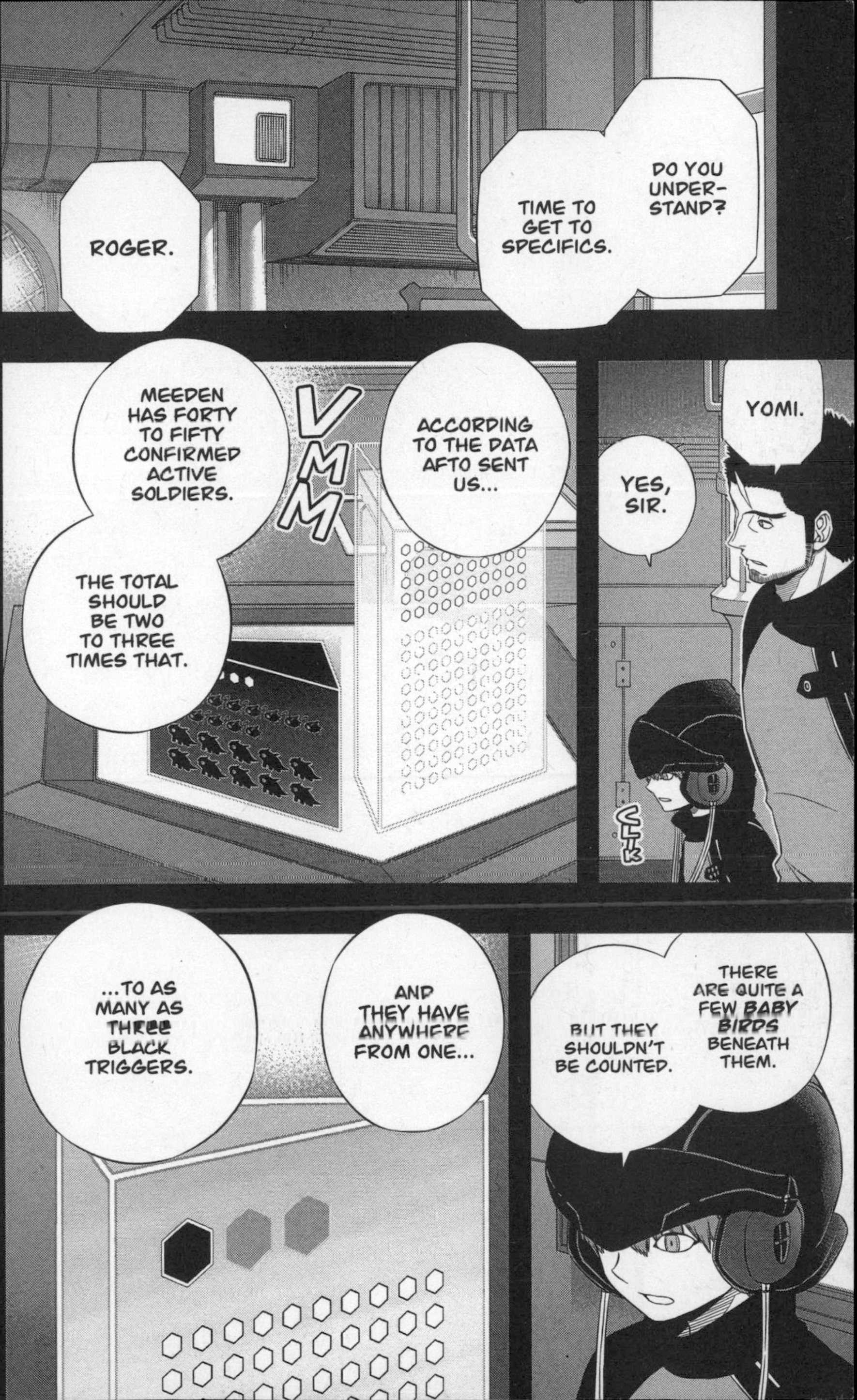
DO YOU UNDER-STAND?
TIME TO GET TO SPECIFICS.
ROGER.
YOMI.
YES, SIR.
CLIK
ACCORDING TO THE DATA AFTO SENT US...
VMM
MEEDEN HAS FORTY TO FIFTY CONFIRMED ACTIVE SOLDIERS.
THE TOTAL SHOULD BE TWO TO THREE TIMES THAT.
THERE ARE QUITE A FEW BABY BIRDS BENEATH THEM.
BUT THEY SHOULDN'T BE COUNTED.
AND THEY HAVE ANYWHERE FROM ONE...
...TO AS MANY AS THREE BLACK TRIGGERS.

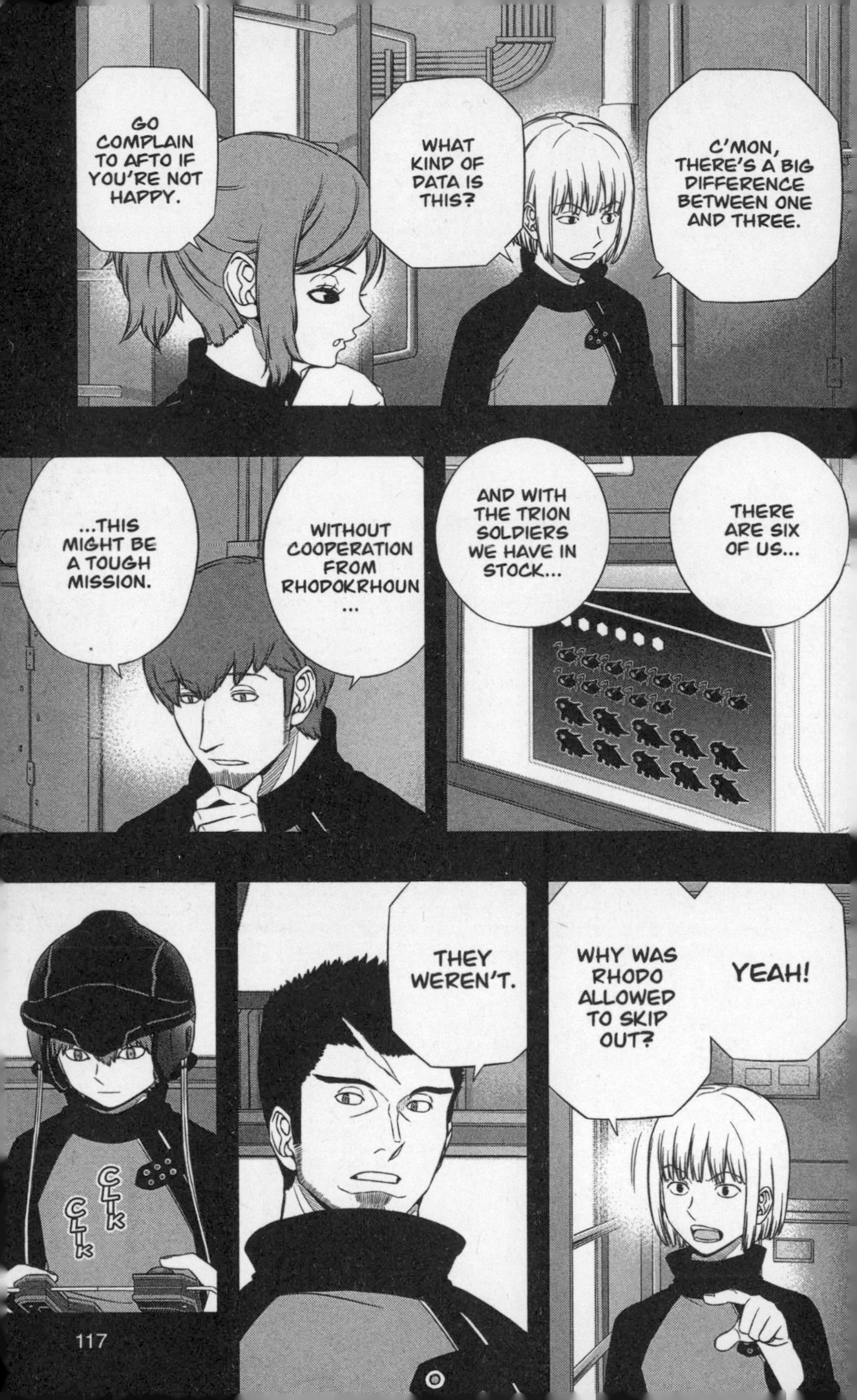
C'MON, THERE'S A BIG DIFFERENCE BETWEEN ONE AND THREE.
WHAT KIND OF DATA IS THIS?
GO COMPLAIN TO AFTO IF YOU'RE NOT HAPPY.
THERE ARE SIX OF US...
AND WITH THE TRION SOLDIERS WE HAVE IN STOCK...
WITHOUT COOPERATION FROM RHODOKRHOUN ...
...THIS MIGHT BE A TOUGH MISSION.
YEAH!
WHY WAS RHODO ALLOWED TO SKIP OUT?
THEY WEREN'T.
CLIK
CLIK

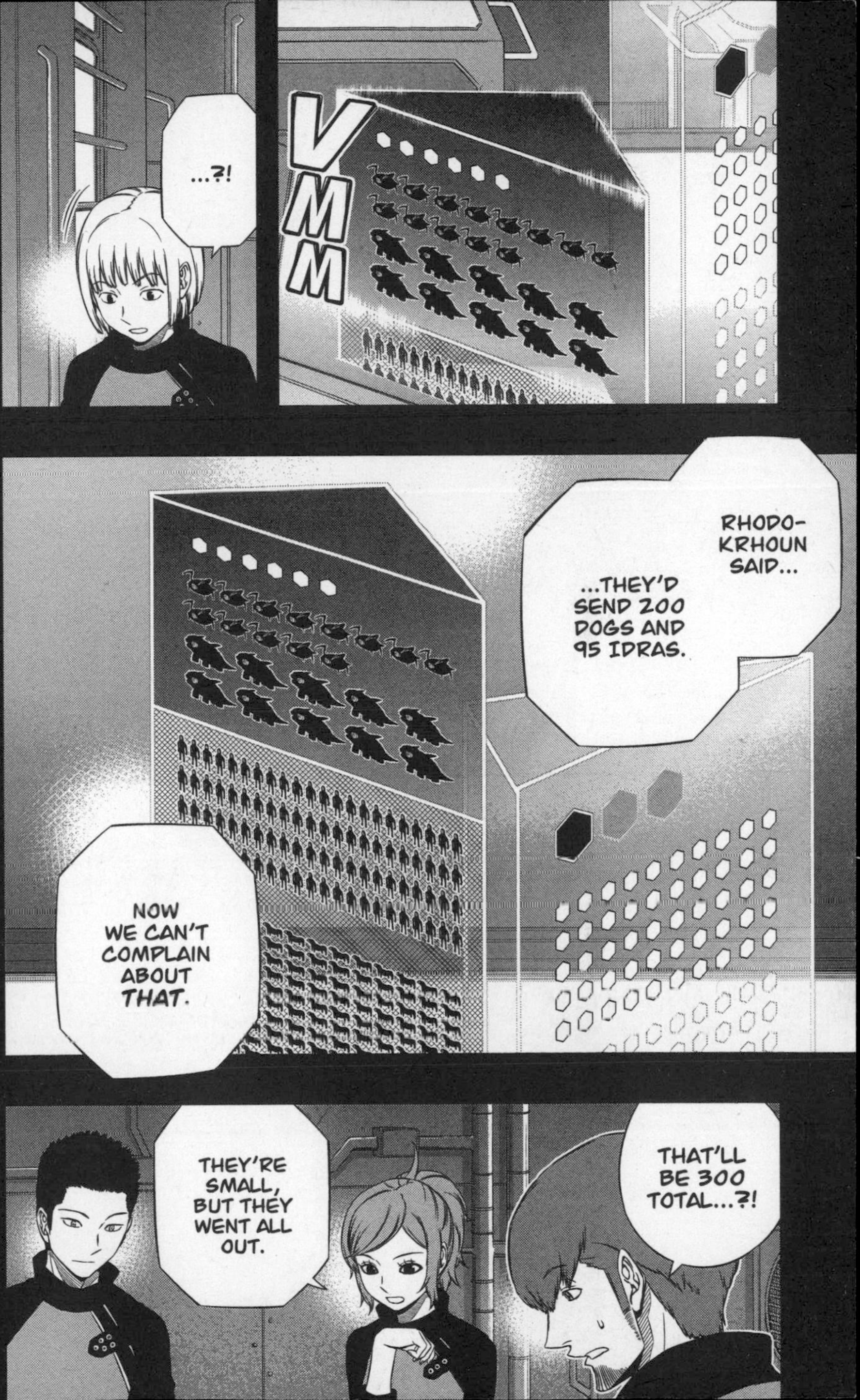
VMM
...?!
RHODO-KRHOUN SAID...
...THEY'D SEND 200 DOGS AND 95 IDRAS.
NOW WE CAN'T COMPLAIN ABOUT THAT.
THAT'LL BE 300 TOTAL...?!
THEY'RE SMALL, BUT THEY WENT ALL OUT.

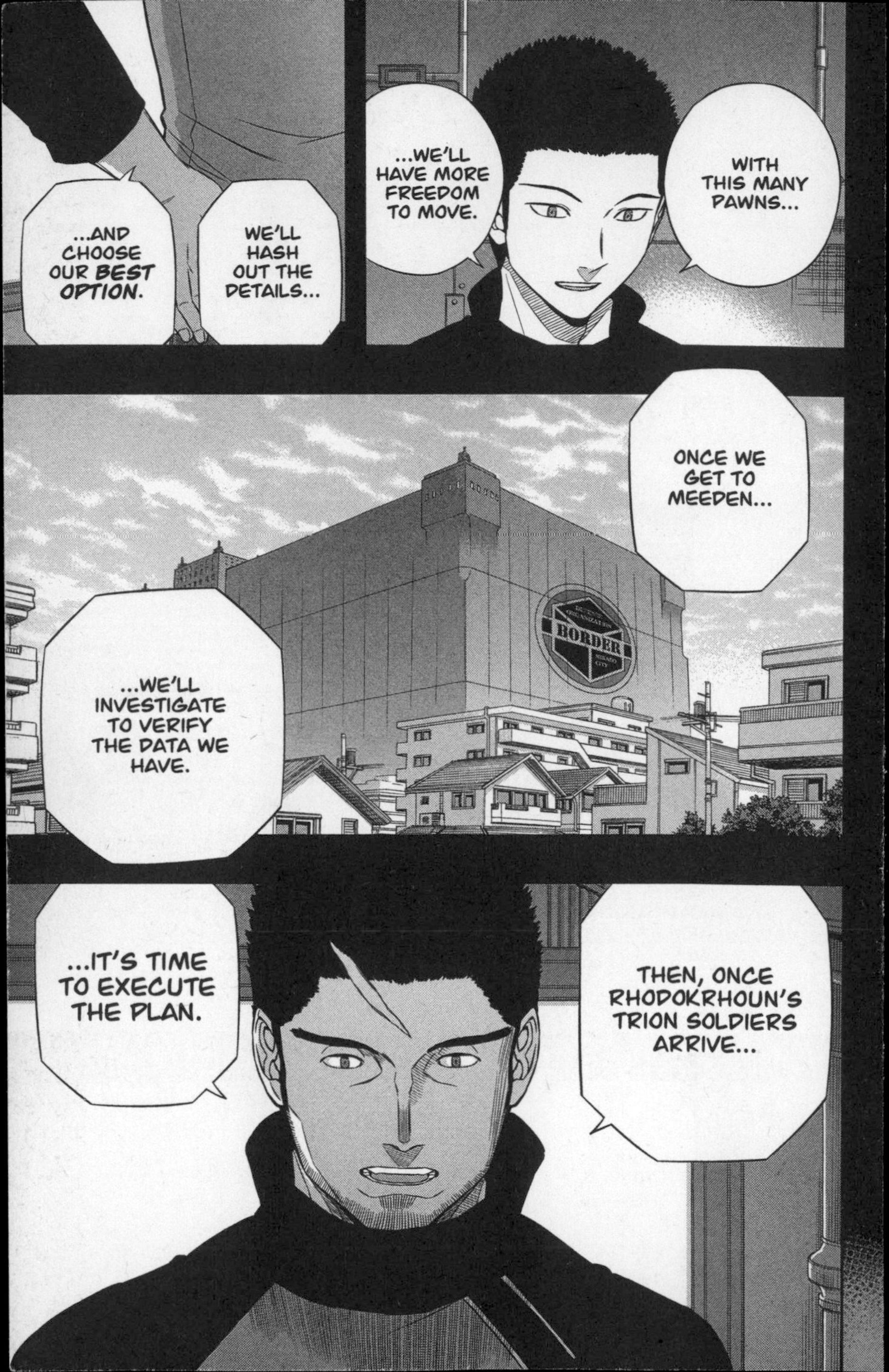
WITH THIS MANY PAWNS...
...WE'LL HAVE MORE FREEDOM TO MOVE.
WE'LL HASH OUT THE DETAILS...
...AND CHOOSE OUR BEST OPTION.
ONCE WE GET TO MEEDEN...
BORDER
...WE'LL INVESTIGATE TO VERIFY THE DATA WE HAVE.
THEN, ONCE RHODOKRHOUN'S TRION SOLDIERS ARRIVE...
...IT'S TIME TO EXECUTE THE PLAN.

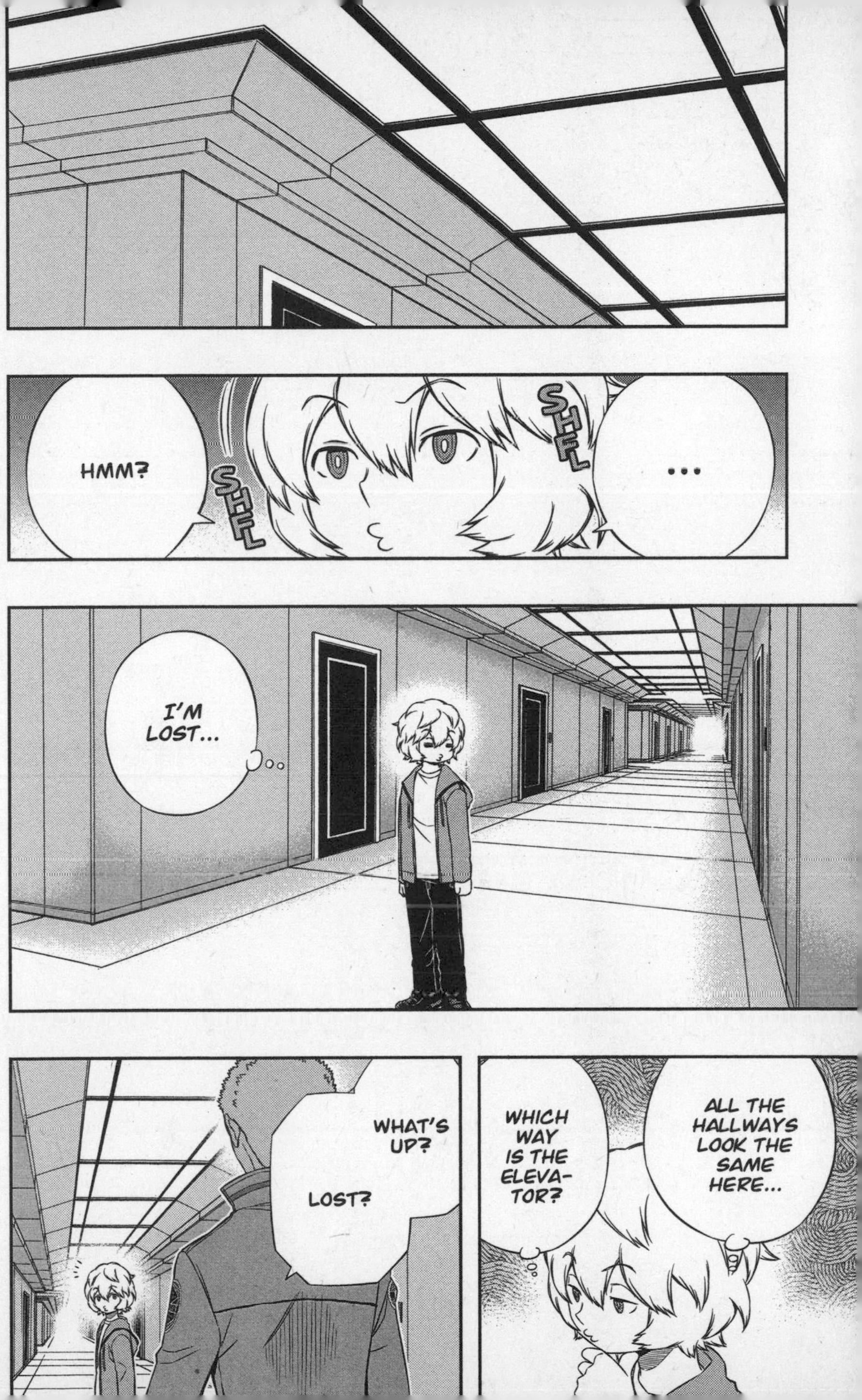
SHFL
...
HMM?
SHFL
I'M LOST...
ALL THE HALLWAYS LOOK THE SAME HERE...
WHICH WAY IS THE ELEVA-TOR?
WHAT'S UP?
LOST?

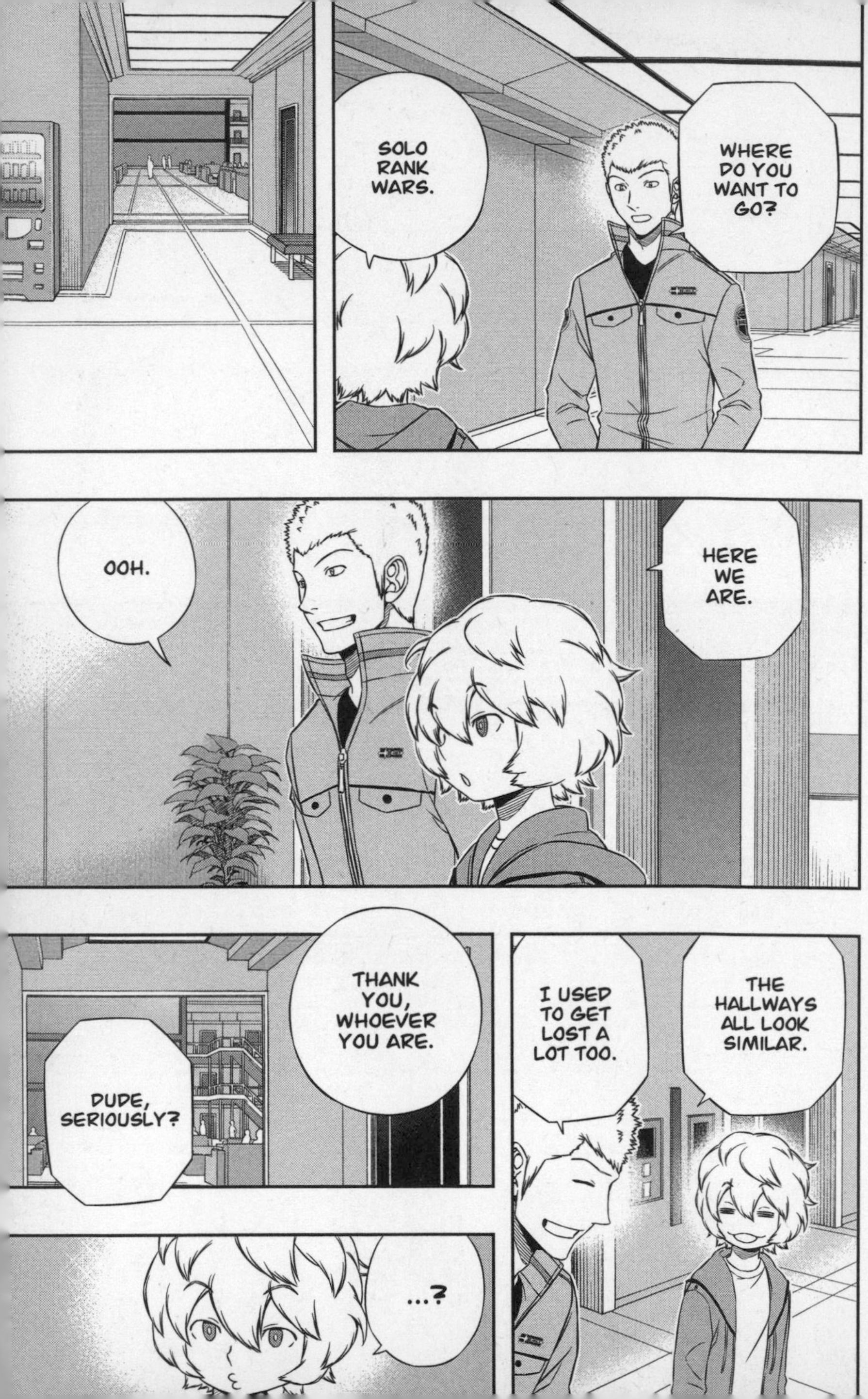
WHERE DO YOU WANT TO GO?
SOLO RANK WARS.
HERE WE ARE.
OOH.
THE HALLWAYS ALL LOOK SIMILAR.
I USED TO GET LOST A LOT TOO.
THANK YOU, WHOEVER YOU ARE.
DUDE, SERIOUSLY?
...?

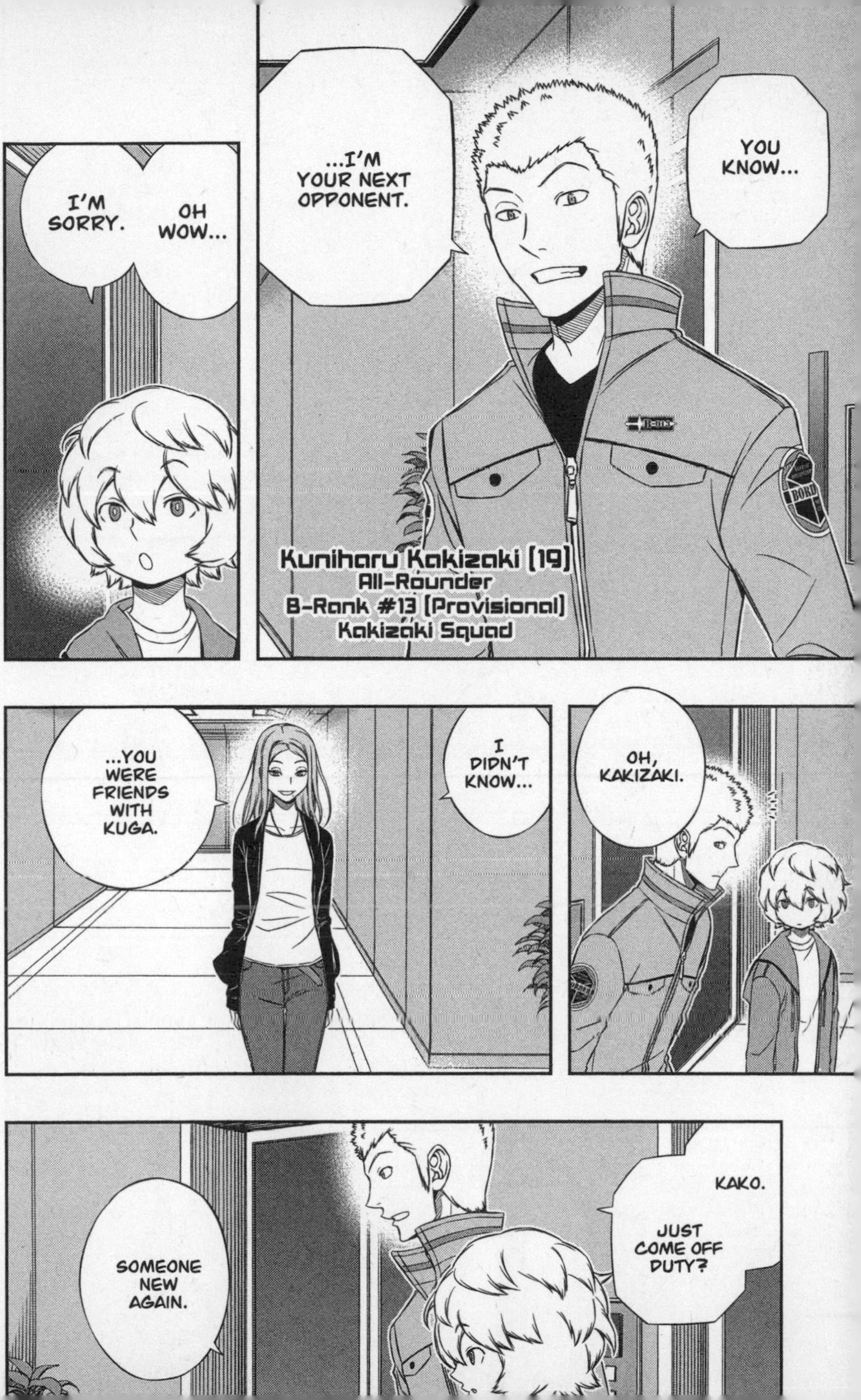
YOU KNOW...
...I'M YOUR NEXT OPPONENT.
Kuniharu Kakizaki (19)
All-Rounder
B-Rank #13 (Provisional)
Kakizaki Squad
OH WOW...
I'M SORRY.
OH, KAKIZAKI.
I DIDN'T KNOW...
...YOU WERE FRIENDS WITH KUGA.
KAKO.
JUST COME OFF DUTY?
SOMEONE NEW AGAIN.

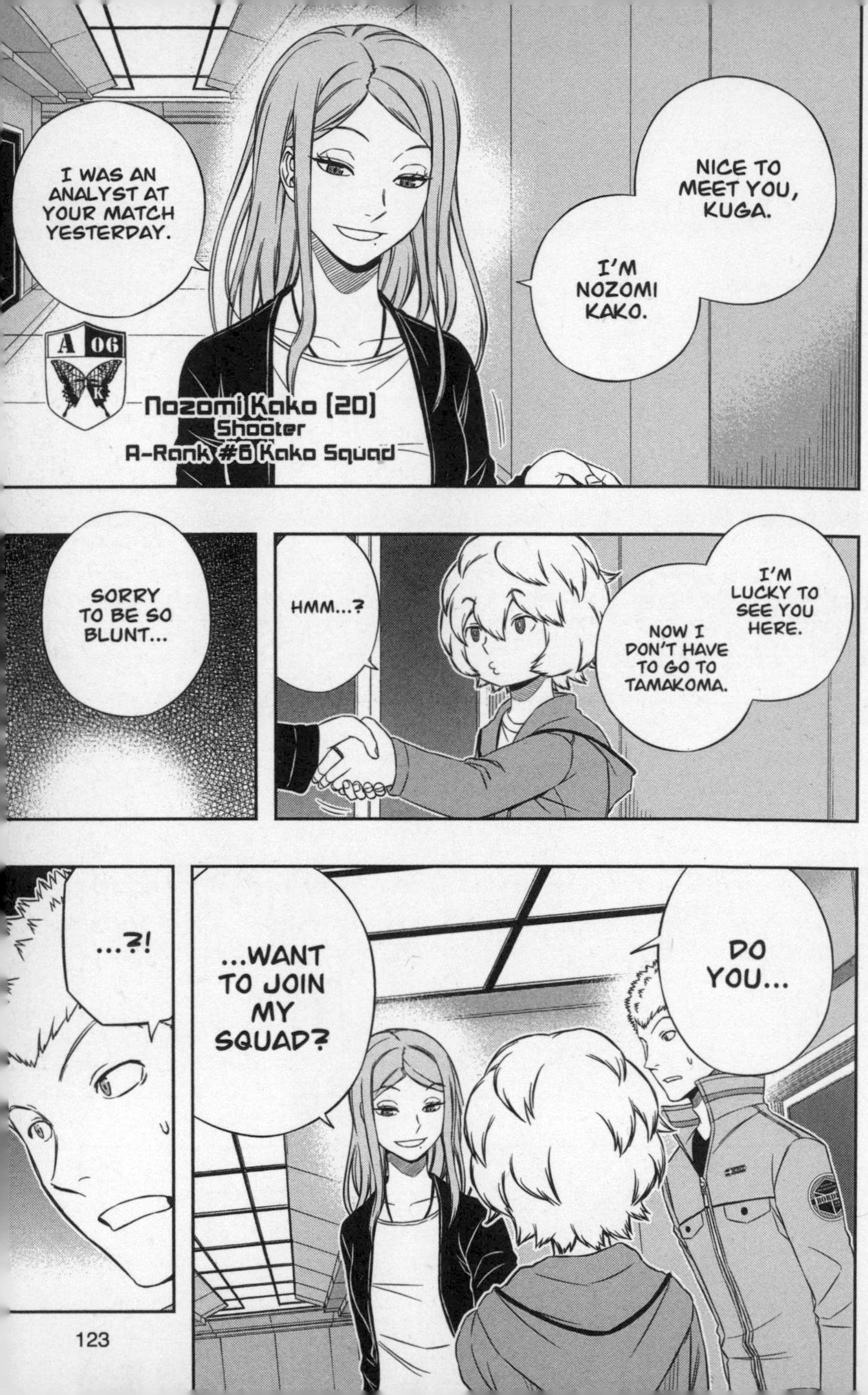
NICE TO MEET YOU, KUGA.
I'M NOZOMI KAKO.
I WAS AN ANALYST AT YOUR MATCH YESTERDAY.
Nozomi Kako (20)
Shooter
A-Rank #6 Kako Squad
I'M LUCKY TO SEE YOU HERE.
NOW I DON'T HAVE TO GO TO TAMAKOMA.
HMM...?
SORRY TO BE SO BLUNT...
DO YOU...
...WANT TO JOIN MY SQUAD?
...?!

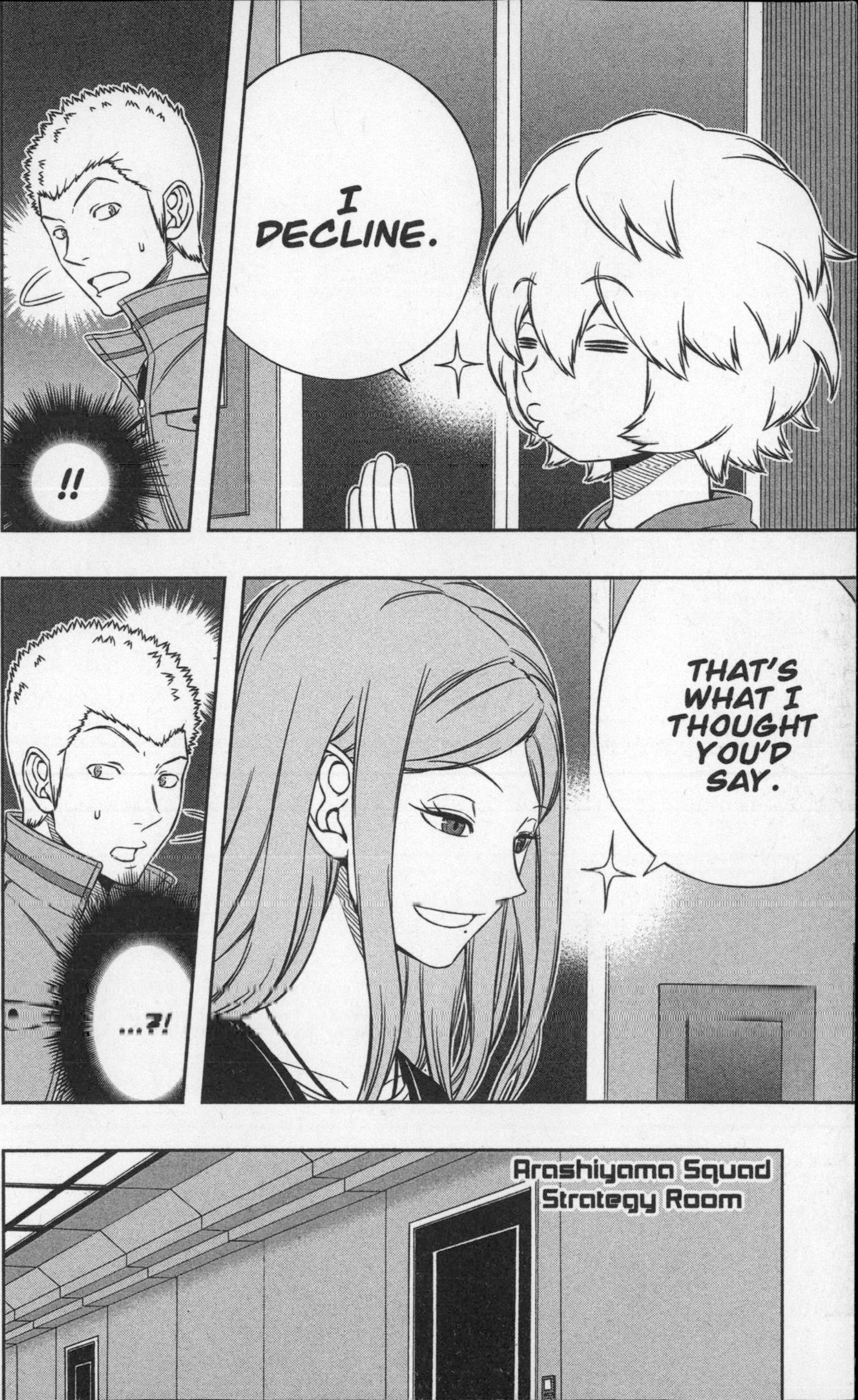
I DECLINE.
!!
THAT'S WHAT I THOUGHT YOU'D SAY.
...?!
Arashiyama Squad Strategy Room

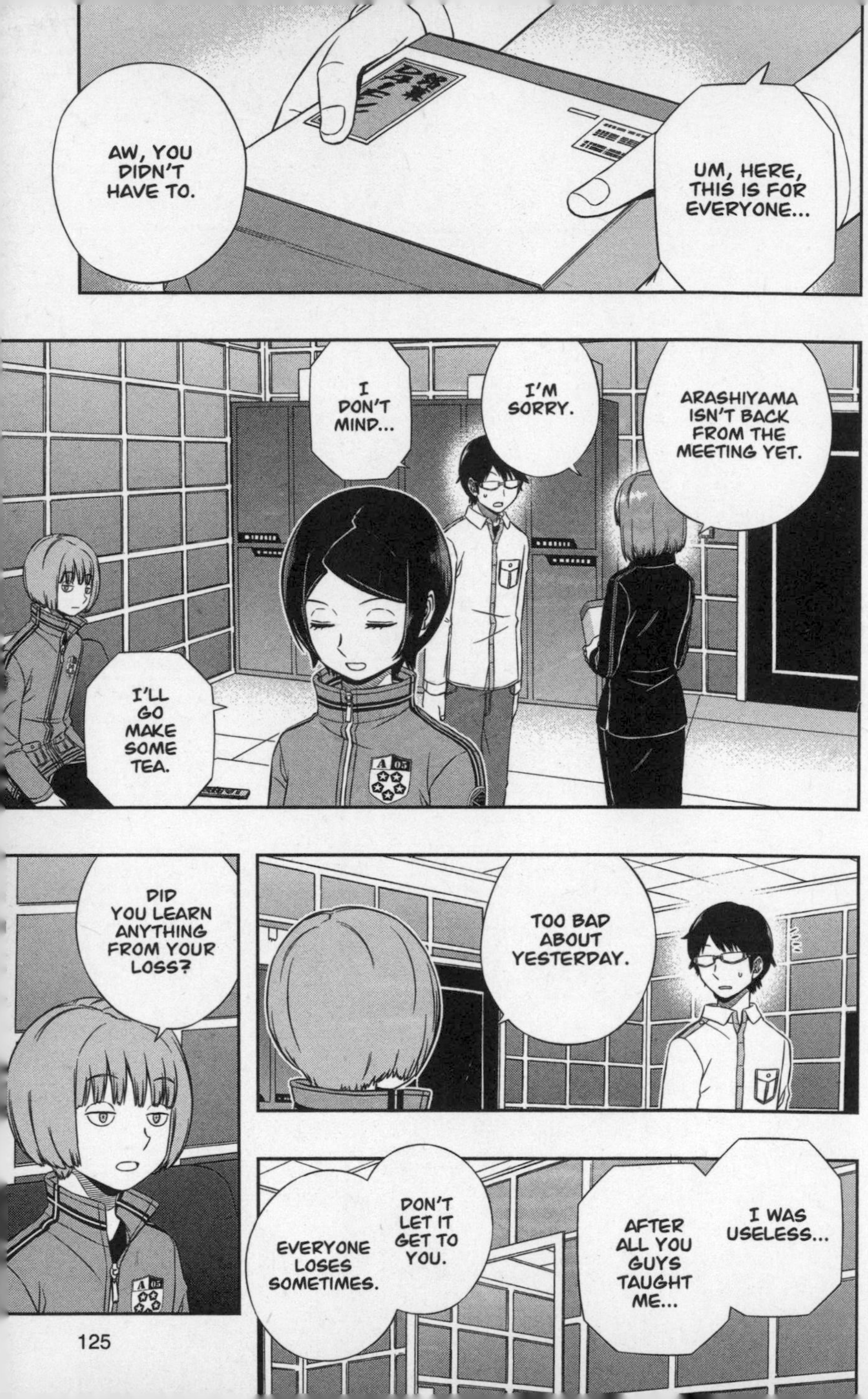
UM, HERE, THIS IS FOR EVERYONE...
AW, YOU DIDN'T HAVE TO.
ARASHIYAMA ISN'T BACK FROM THE MEETING YET.
I'M SORRY.
I DON'T MIND...
I'LL GO MAKE SOME TEA.
TOO BAD ABOUT YESTERDAY.
I WAS USELESS...
AFTER ALL YOU GUYS TAUGHT ME...
DON'T LET IT GET TO YOU.
EVERYONE LOSES SOMETIMES.
DID YOU LEARN ANYTHING FROM YOUR LOSS?

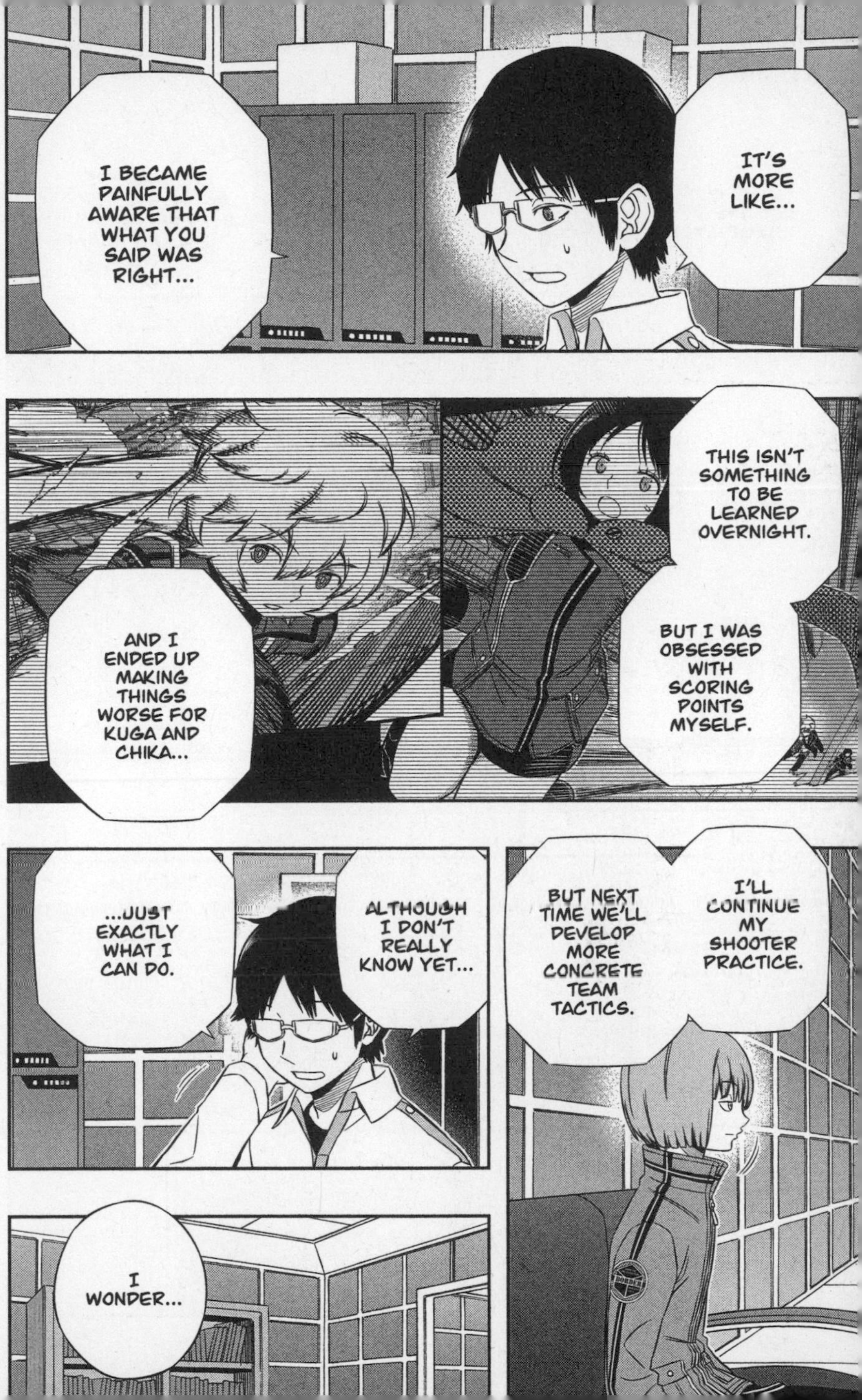
IT'S MORE LIKE...
I BECAME PAINFULLY AWARE THAT WHAT YOU SAID WAS RIGHT...
THIS ISN'T SOMETHING TO BE LEARNED OVERNIGHT.
BUT I WAS OBSESSED WITH SCORING POINTS MYSELF.
AND I ENDED UP MAKING THINGS WORSE FOR KUGA AND CHIKA...
I'LL CONTINUE MY SHOOTER PRACTICE.
BUT NEXT TIME WE'LL DEVELOP MORE CONCRETE TEAM TACTICS.
ALTHOUGH I DON'T REALLY KNOW YET...
...JUST EXACTLY WHAT I CAN DO.
I WONDER...

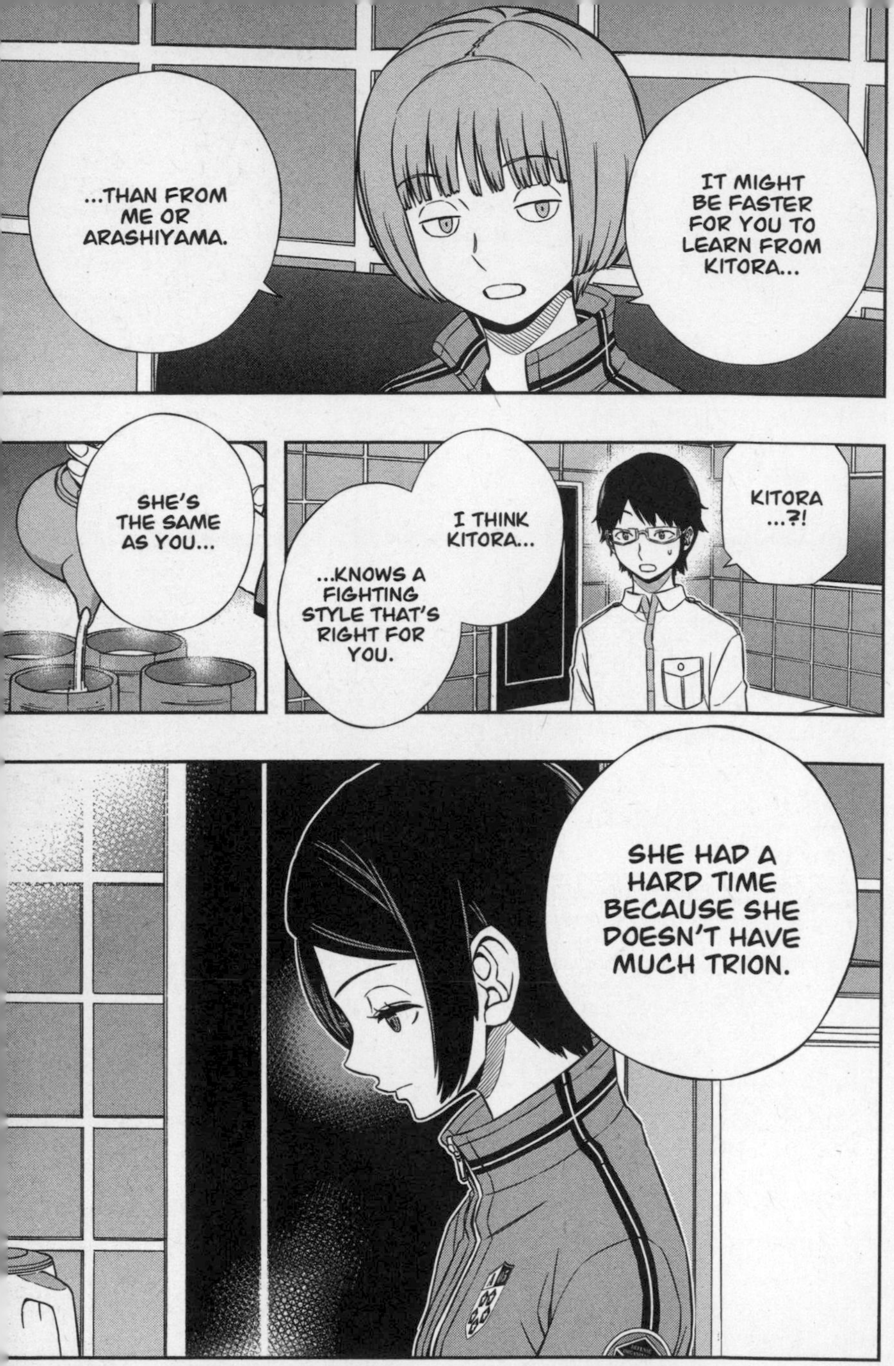
IT MIGHT BE FASTER FOR YOU TO LEARN FROM KITORA...
...THAN FROM ME OR ARASHIYAMA.
KITORA ...?!
I THINK KITORA...
...KNOWS A FIGHTING STYLE THAT'S RIGHT FOR YOU.
SHE'S THE SAME AS YOU...
SHE HAD A HARD TIME BECAUSE SHE DOESN'T HAVE MUCH TRION.

Mysterious Files 1

I don't even remember why I drew these. Probably for if figures of the characters were ever made. It looks like I was winging it. Maybe they were used for the anime?

■Jin's bag

A normal leather belt with a line of holes. Fujin fits perfectly into a pocket made especially for that trigger.

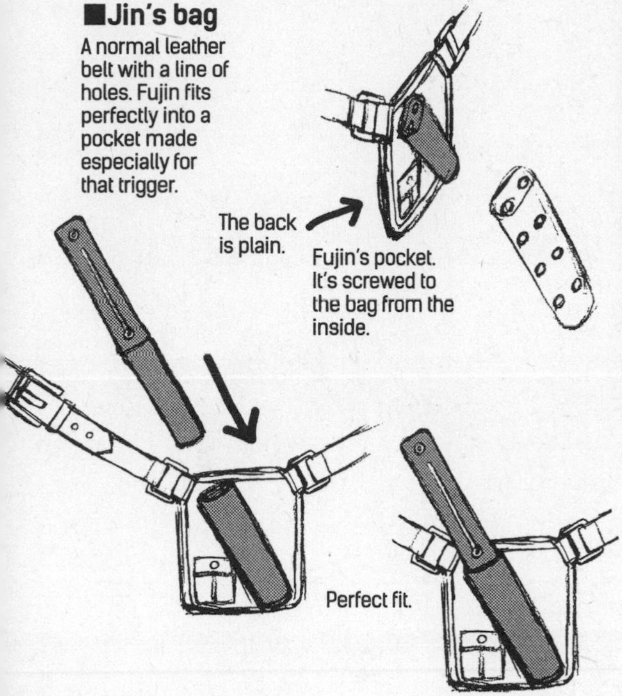
The back is plain.
Fujin's pocket. It's screwed to the bag from the inside.
Perfect fit.

■How the belt connects

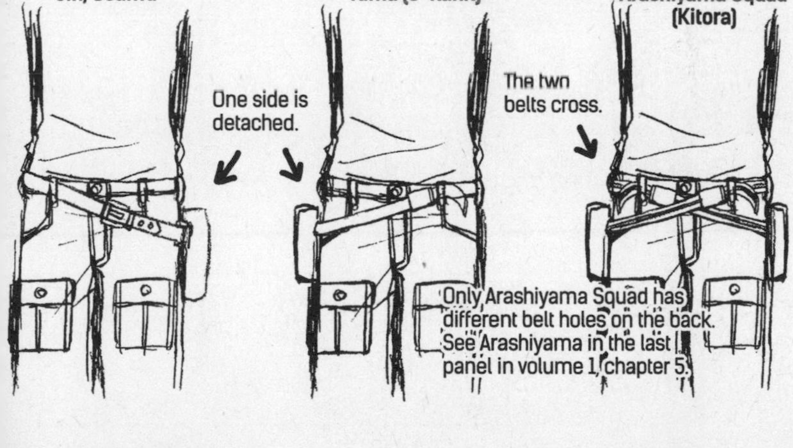
Jin, Osamu
Yuma (C-Rank)
Arashiyama Squad (Kitora)
One side is detached.
The two belts cross.
Only Arashiyama Squad has different belt holes on the back. See Arashiyama in the last panel in volume 1, chapter 5.

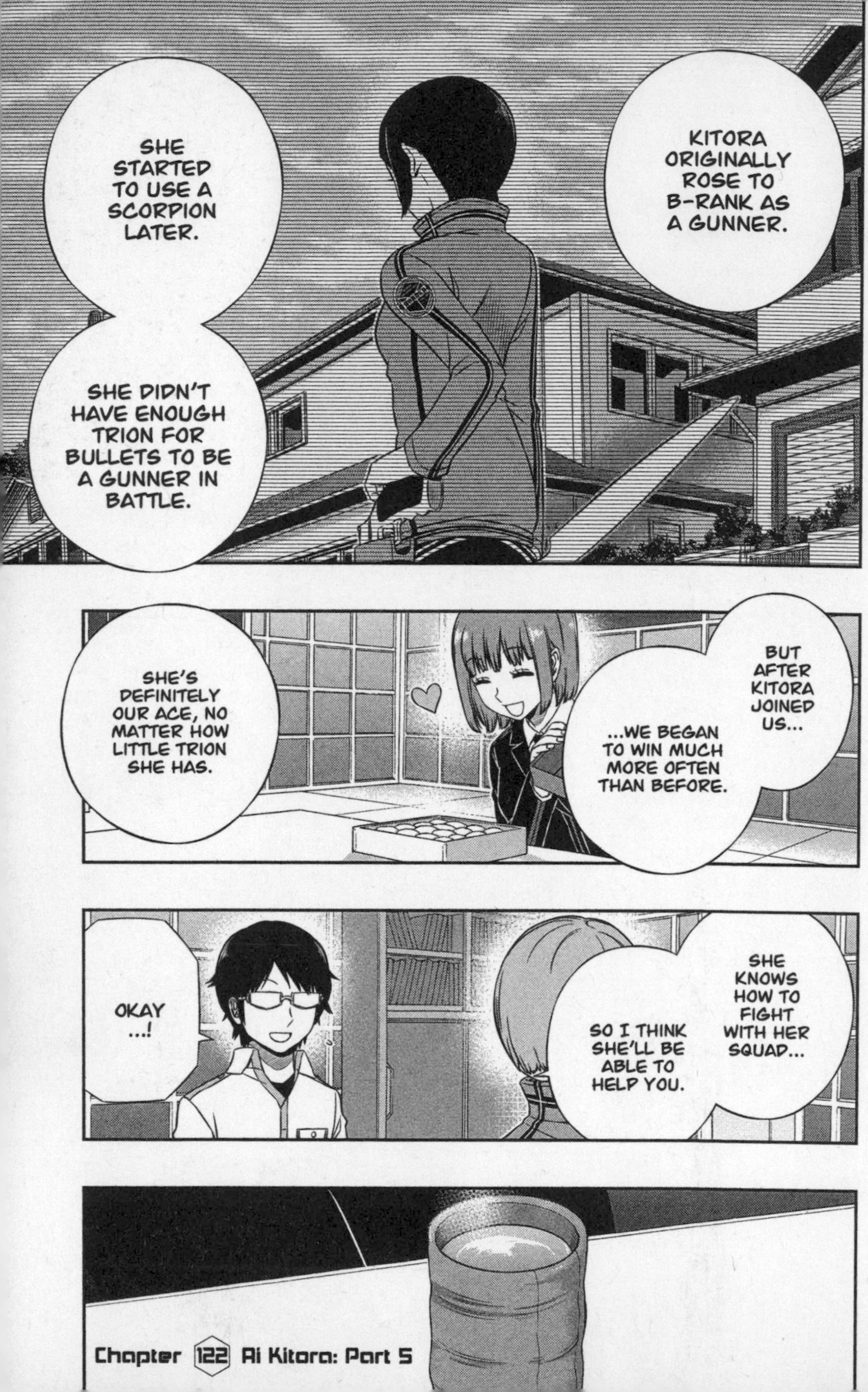
KITORA ORIGINALLY ROSE TO B-RANK AS A GUNNER.
SHE STARTED TO USE A SCORPION LATER.
SHE DIDN'T HAVE ENOUGH TRION FOR BULLETS TO BE A GUNNER IN BATTLE.
BUT AFTER KITORA JOINED US...
...WE BEGAN TO WIN MUCH MORE OFTEN THAN BEFORE.
SHE'S DEFINITELY OUR ACE, NO MATTER HOW LITTLE TRION SHE HAS.
SHE KNOWS HOW TO FIGHT WITH HER SQUAD...
SO I THINK SHE'LL BE ABLE TO HELP YOU.
OKAY ...!
Chapter 122 Ai Kitora: Part 5

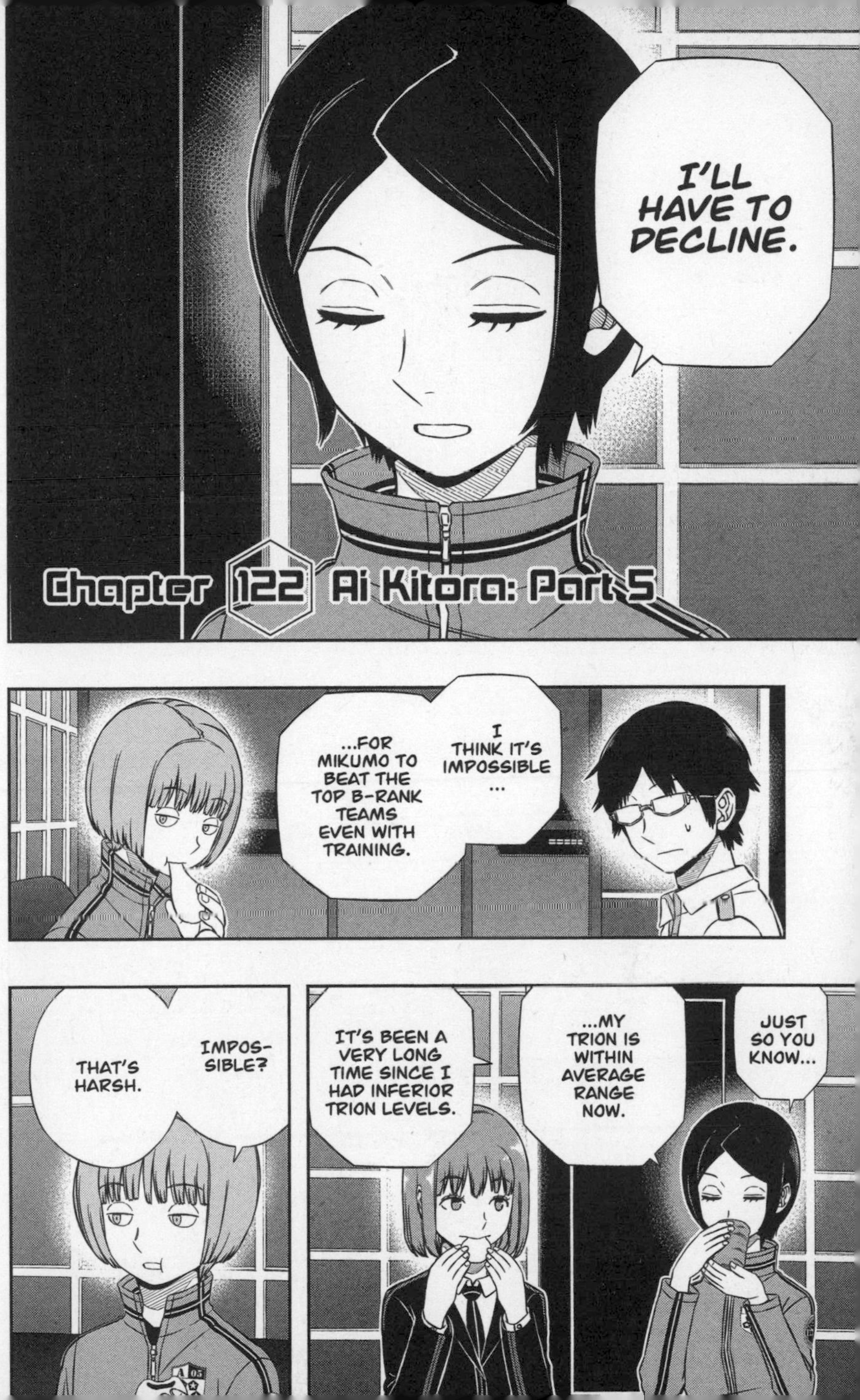
I'LL HAVE TO DECLINE.
Chapter 122 Ai Kitora: Part 5
I THINK IT'S IMPOSSIBLE ...
...FOR MIKUMO TO BEAT THE TOP B-RANK TEAMS EVEN WITH TRAINING.
JUST SO YOU KNOW...
...MY TRION IS WITHIN AVERAGE RANGE NOW.
IT'S BEEN A VERY LONG TIME SINCE I HAD INFERIOR TRION LEVELS.
IMPOS-SIBLE?
THAT'S HARSH.

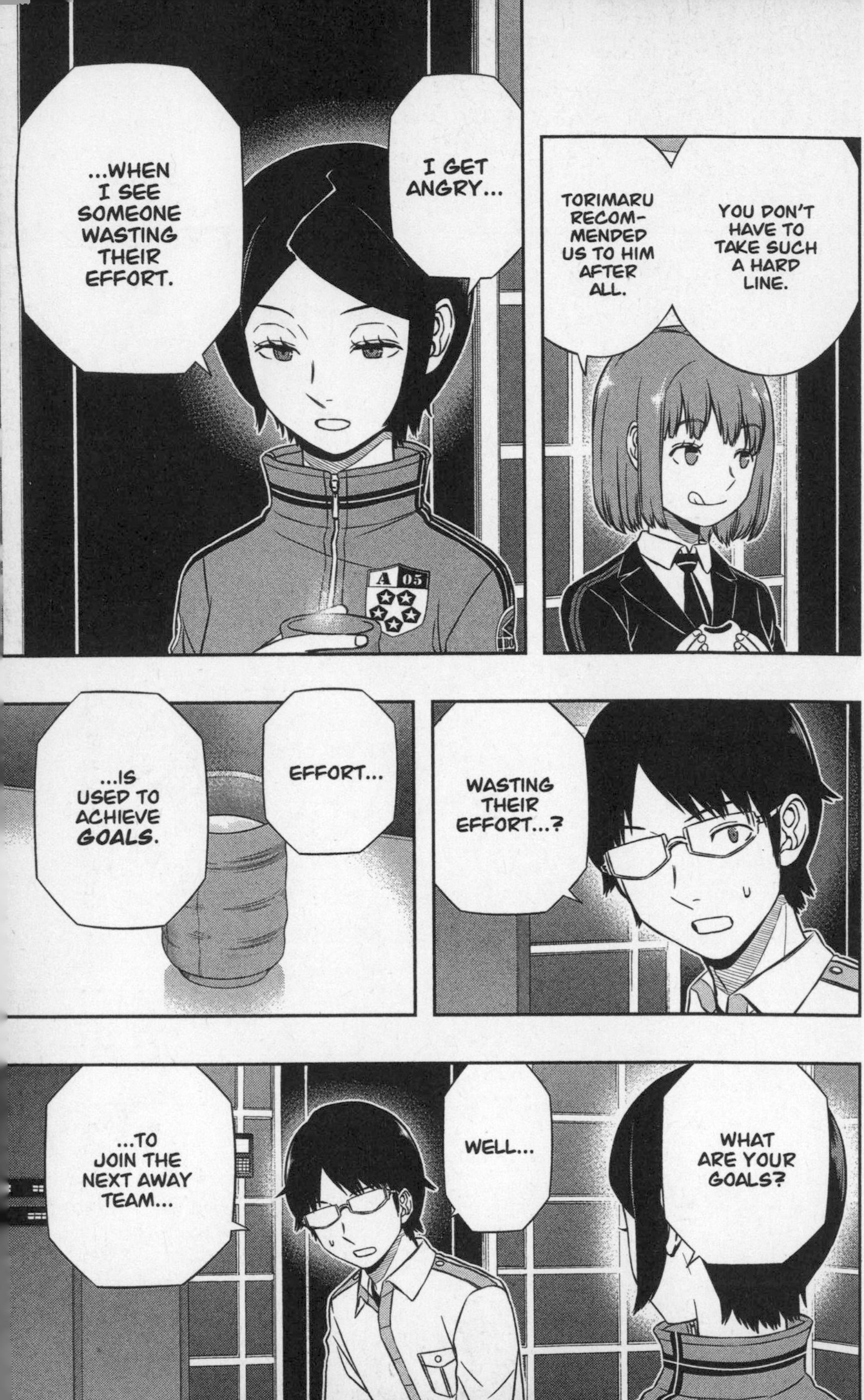
YOU DON'T HAVE TO TAKE SUCH A HARD LINE.
TORIMARU RECOMMENDED US TO HIM AFTER ALL.
I GET ANGRY...
...WHEN I SEE SOMEONE WASTING THEIR EFFORT.
WASTING THEIR EFFORT...?
EFFORT...
...IS USED TO ACHIEVE GOALS.
WHAT ARE YOUR GOALS?
WELL...
...TO JOIN THE NEXT AWAY TEAM...

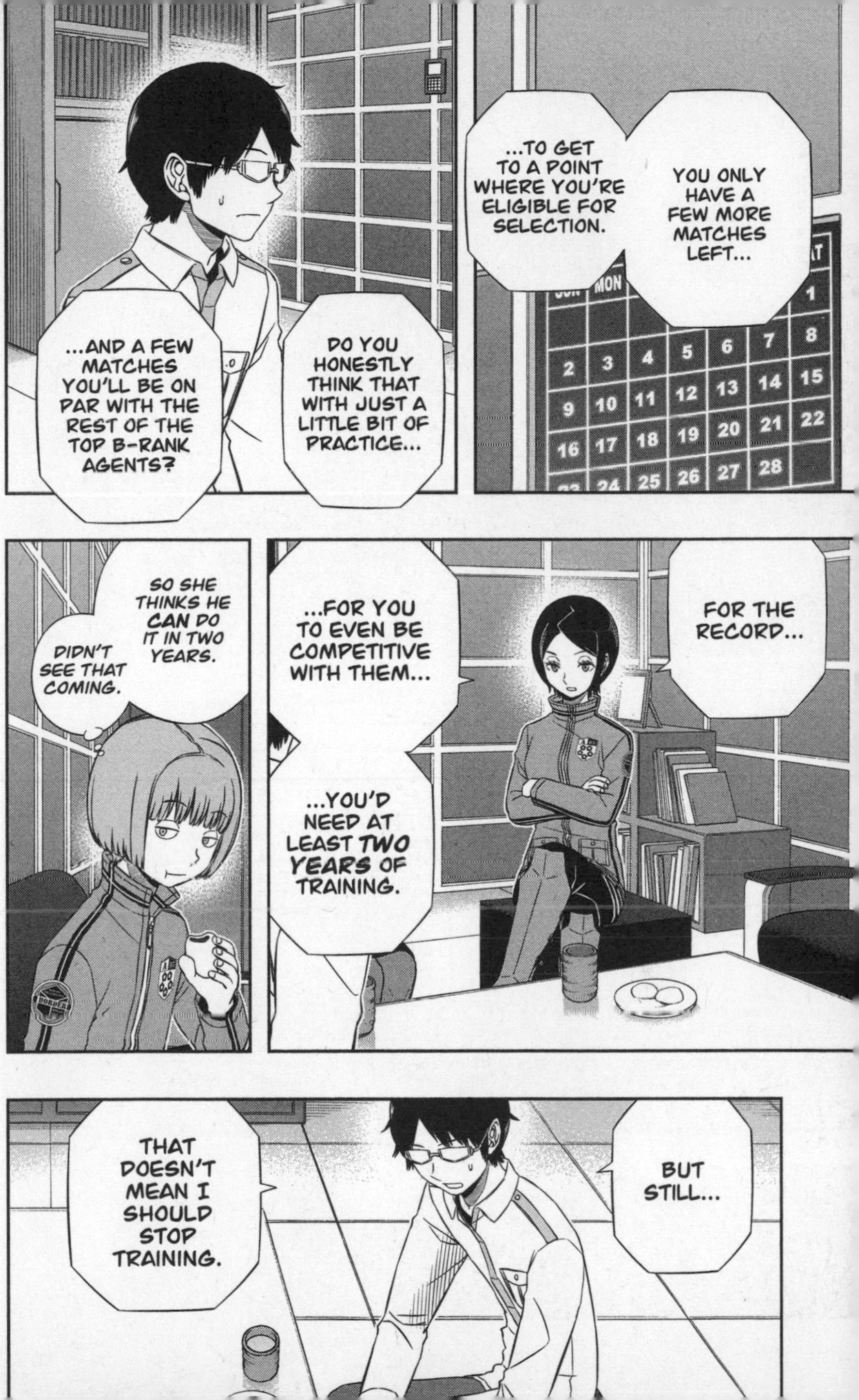
YOU ONLY HAVE A FEW MORE MATCHES LEFT...
...TO GET TO A POINT WHERE YOU'RE ELIGIBLE FOR SELECTION.
DO YOU HONESTLY THINK THAT WITH JUST A LITTLE BIT OF PRACTICE...
...AND A FEW MATCHES YOU'LL BE ON PAR WITH THE REST OF THE TOP B-RANK AGENTS?
FOR THE RECORD...
...FOR YOU TO EVEN BE COMPETITIVE WITH THEM...
...YOU'D NEED AT LEAST TWO YEARS OF TRAINING.
SO SHE THINKS HE CAN DO IT IN TWO YEARS.
DIDN'T SEE THAT COMING.
BUT STILL...
THAT DOESN'T MEAN I SHOULD STOP TRAINING.

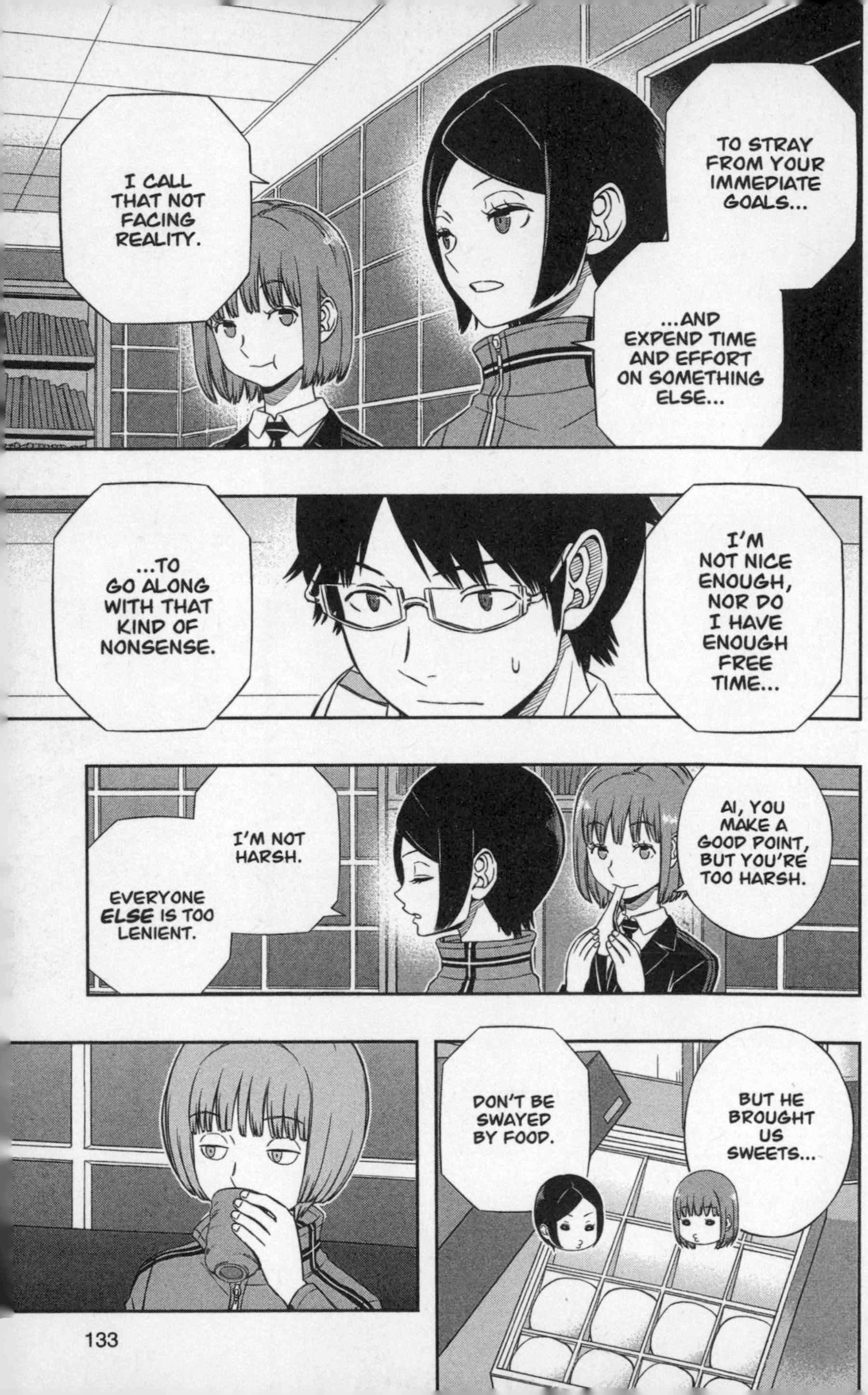
TO STRAY FROM YOUR IMMEDIATE GOALS...
...AND EXPEND TIME AND EFFORT ON SOMETHING ELSE...
I CALL THAT NOT FACING REALITY.
I'M NOT NICE ENOUGH, NOR DO I HAVE ENOUGH FREE TIME...
...TO GO ALONG WITH THAT KIND OF NONSENSE.
AI, YOU MAKE A GOOD POINT, BUT YOU'RE TOO HARSH.
I'M NOT HARSH.
EVERYONE ELSE IS TOO LENIENT.
BUT HE BROUGHT US SWEETS...
DON'T BE SWAYED BY FOOD.

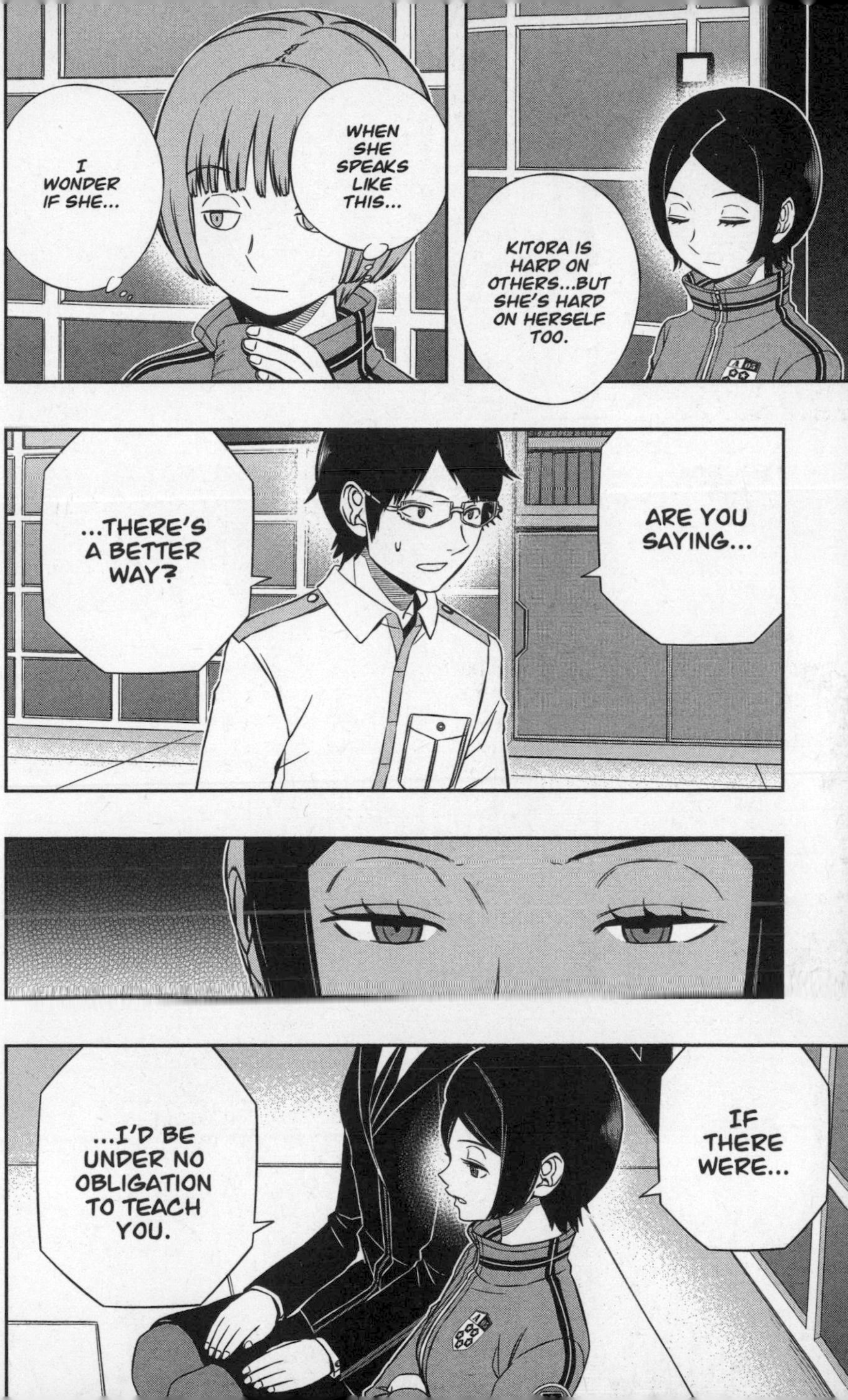
KITORA IS HARD ON OTHERS...BUT SHE'S HARD ON HERSELF TOO.
WHEN SHE SPEAKS LIKE THIS...
I WONDER IF SHE...
ARE YOU SAYING...
...THERE'S A BETTER WAY?
IF THERE WERE...
...I'D BE UNDER NO OBLIGATION TO TEACH YOU.

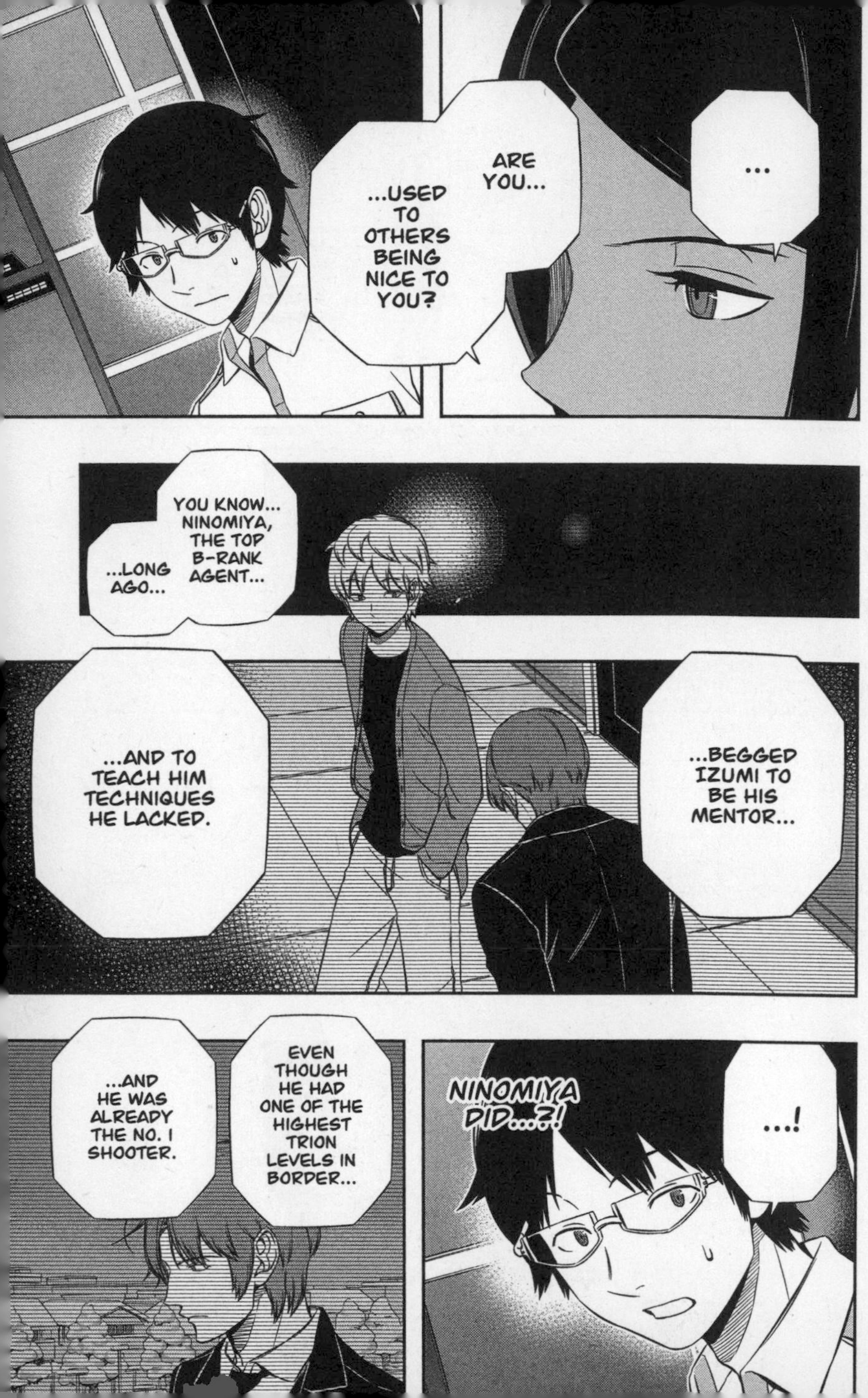
...
ARE YOU...
...USED TO OTHERS BEING NICE TO YOU?
YOU KNOW... NINOMIYA, THE TOP B-RANK AGENT...
...LONG AGO...
...BEGGED IZUMI TO BE HIS MENTOR...
...AND TO TEACH HIM TECHNIQUES HE LACKED.
...!
NINOMIYA DID...?!
EVEN THOUGH HE HAD ONE OF THE HIGHEST TRION LEVELS IN BORDER...
...AND HE WAS ALREADY THE NO. 1 SHOOTER.

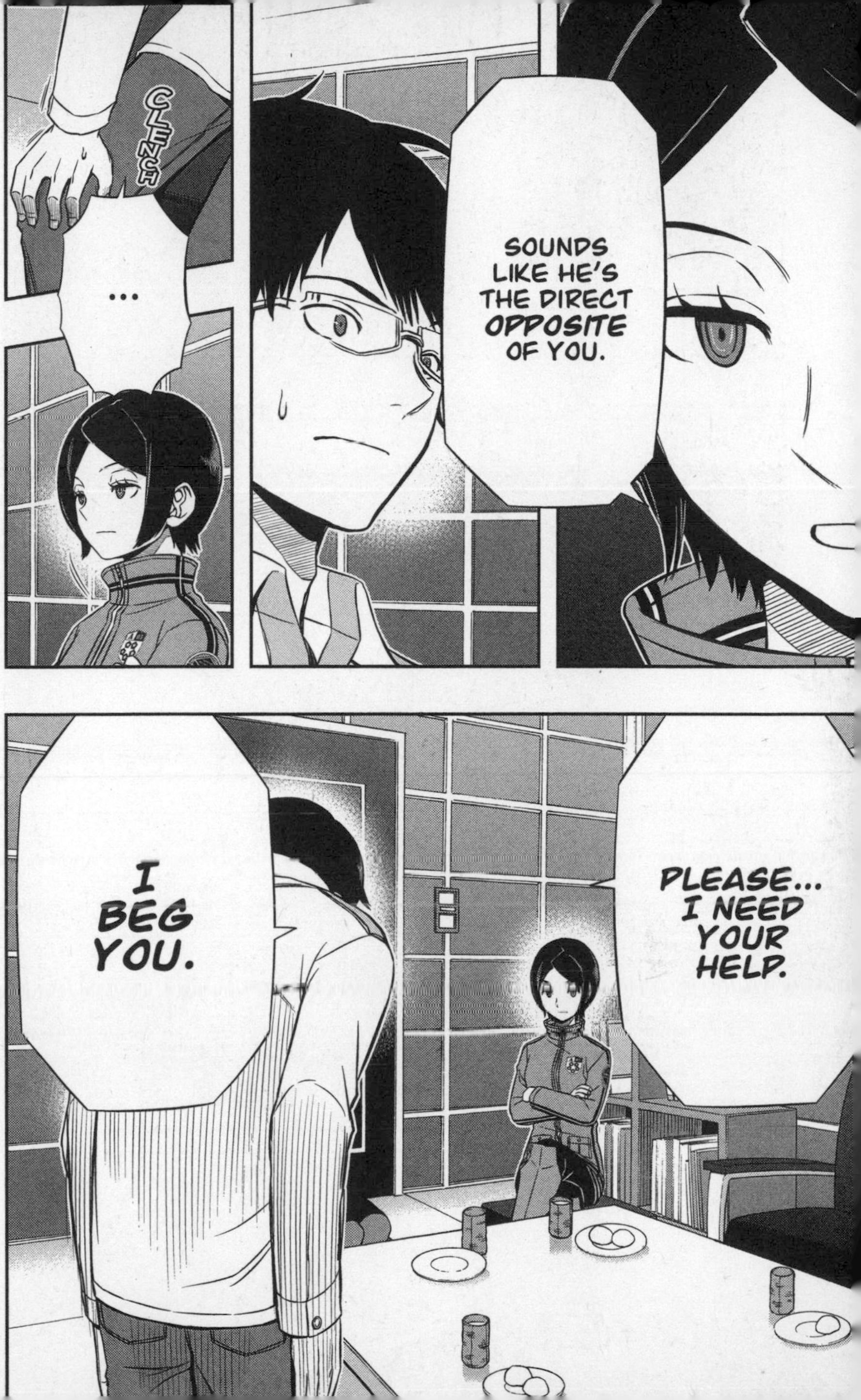
SOUNDS LIKE HE'S THE DIRECT OPPOSITE OF YOU.
CLENCH
...
PLEASE... I NEED YOUR HELP.
I BEG YOU.

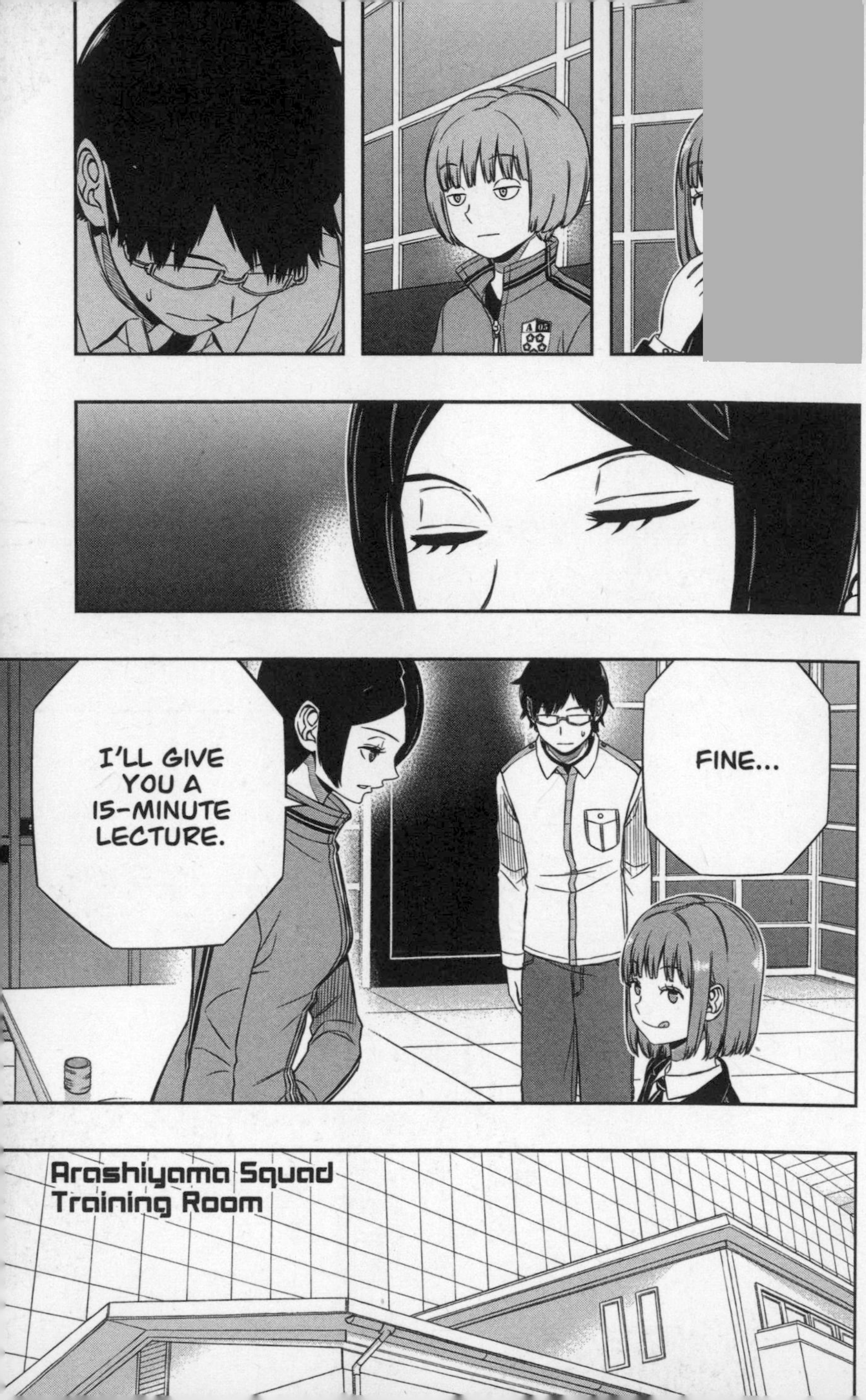
FINE...
I'LL GIVE YOU A 15-MINUTE LECTURE.
Arashiyama Squad Training Room

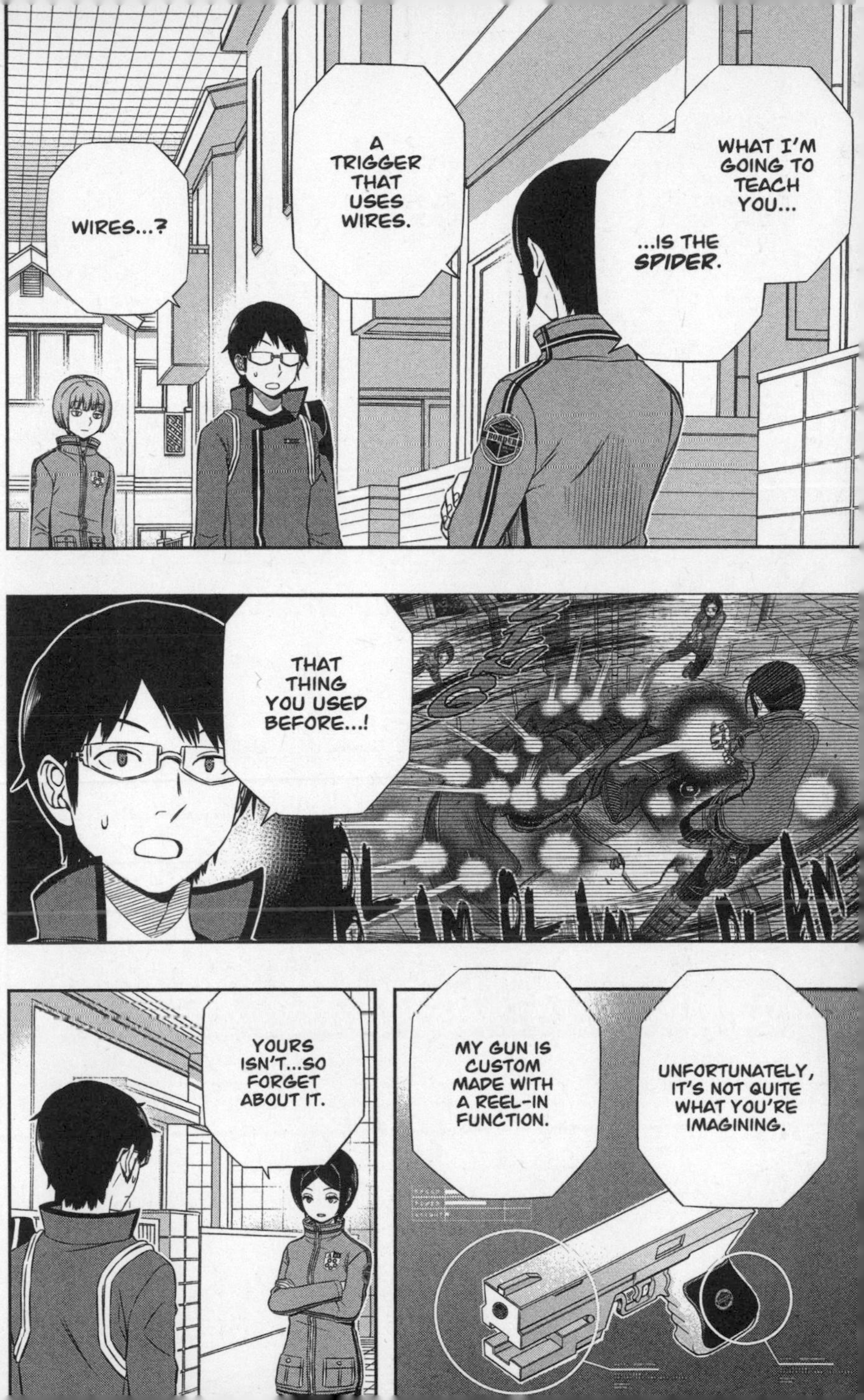
WHAT I'M GOING TO TEACH YOU...
...IS THE SPIDER.
A TRIGGER THAT USES WIRES.
WIRES...?
THAT THING YOU USED BEFORE...!
UNFORTUNATELY, IT'S NOT QUITE WHAT YOU'RE IMAGINING.
MY GUN IS CUSTOM MADE WITH A REEL-IN FUNCTION.
YOURS ISN'T...SO FORGET ABOUT IT.

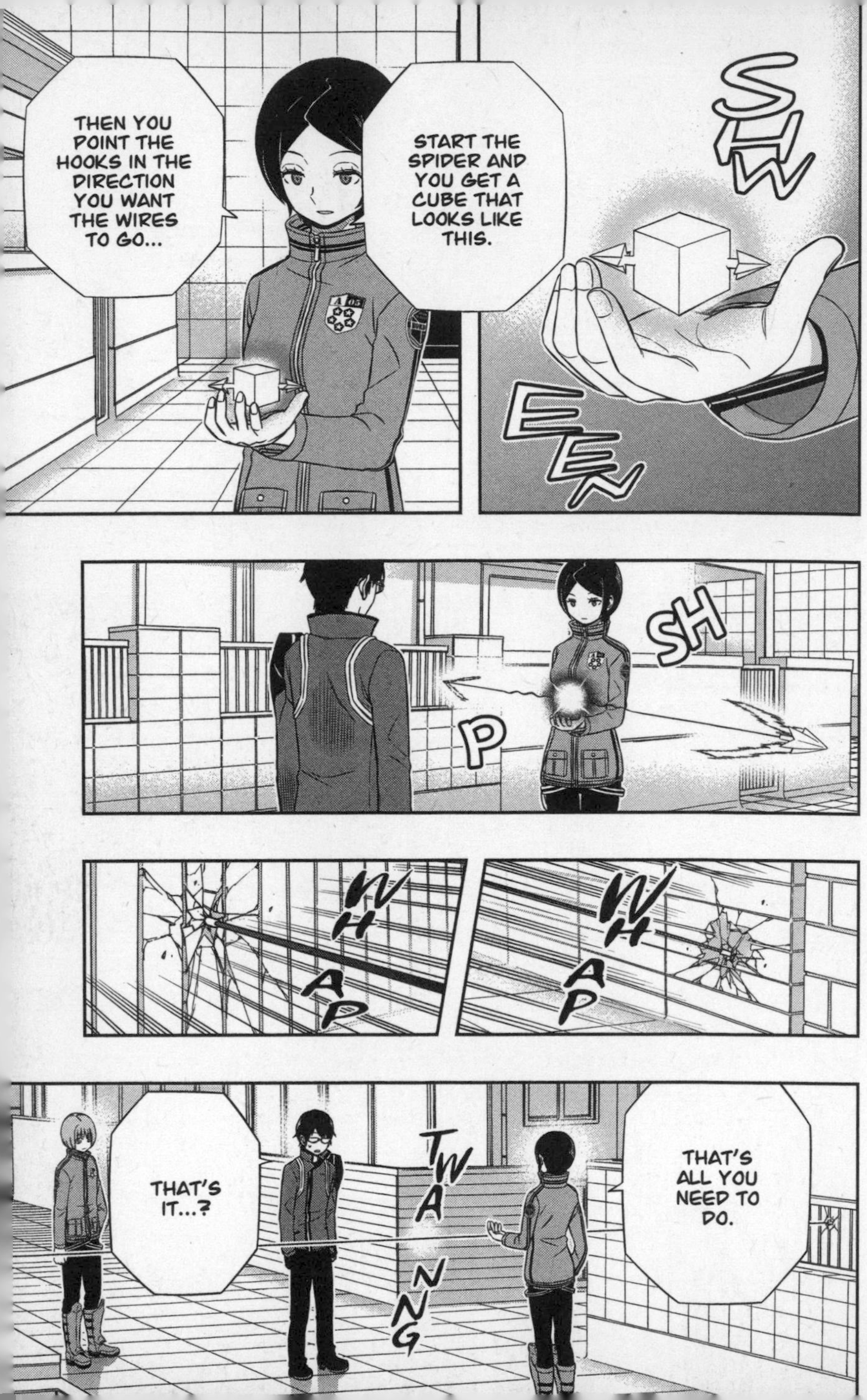
SHWEEEN
START THE SPIDER AND YOU GET A CUBE THAT LOOKS LIKE THIS.
THEN YOU POINT THE HOOKS IN THE DIRECTION YOU WANT THE WIRES TO GO...
SH
P
WHAP
WHAP
THAT'S ALL YOU NEED TO DO.
TWANNG
THAT'S IT...?

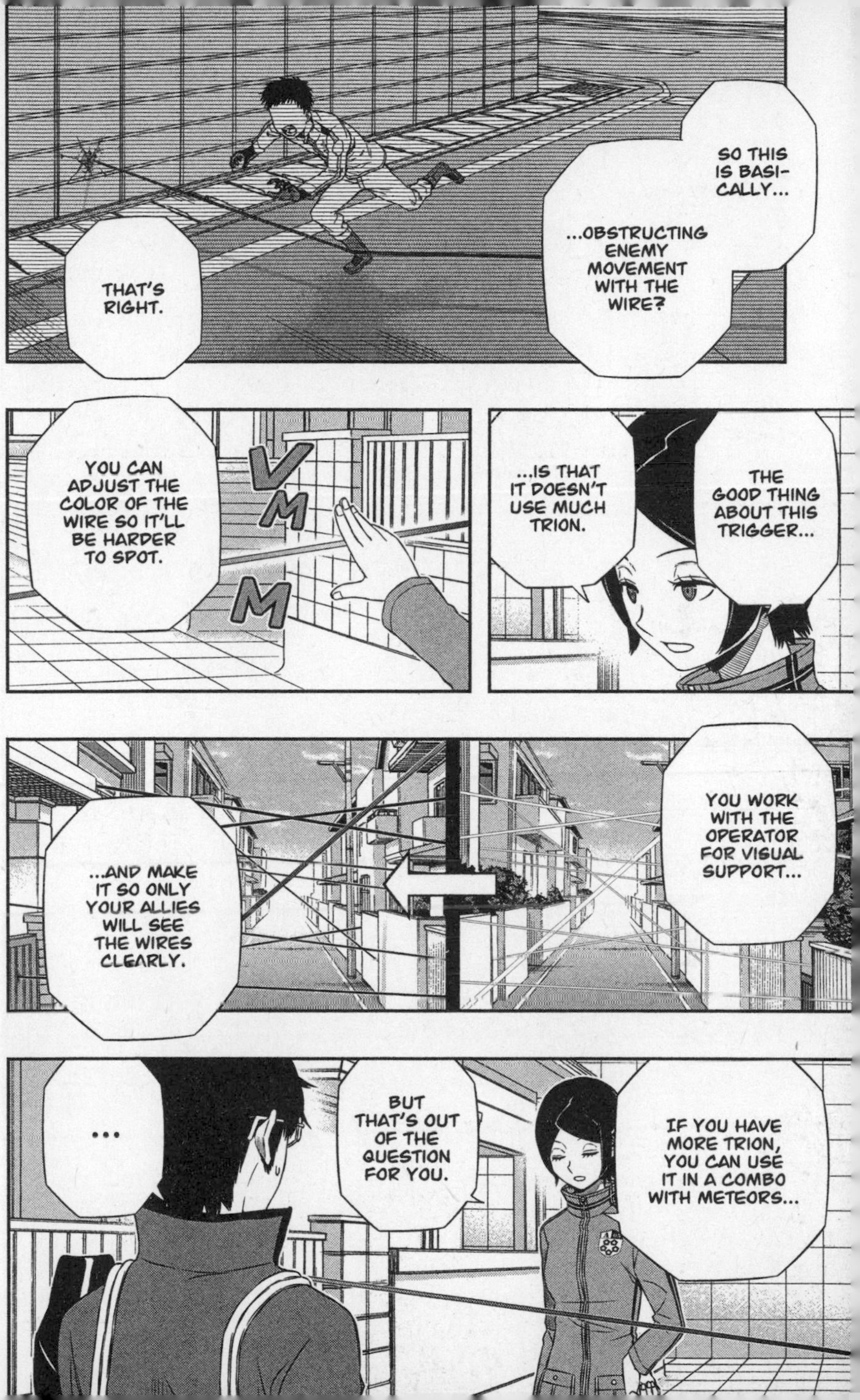
SO THIS IS BASICALLY...
...OBSTRUCTING ENEMY MOVEMENT WITH THE WIRE?
THAT'S RIGHT.
THE GOOD THING ABOUT THIS TRIGGER...
...IS THAT IT DOESN'T USE MUCH TRION.
VMM
YOU CAN ADJUST THE COLOR OF THE WIRE SO IT'LL BE HARDER TO SPOT.
YOU WORK WITH THE OPERATOR FOR VISUAL SUPPORT...
...AND MAKE IT SO ONLY YOUR ALLIES WILL SEE THE WIRES CLEARLY.
IF YOU HAVE MORE TRION, YOU CAN USE IT IN A COMBO WITH METEORS...
BUT THAT'S OUT OF THE QUESTION FOR YOU.
...

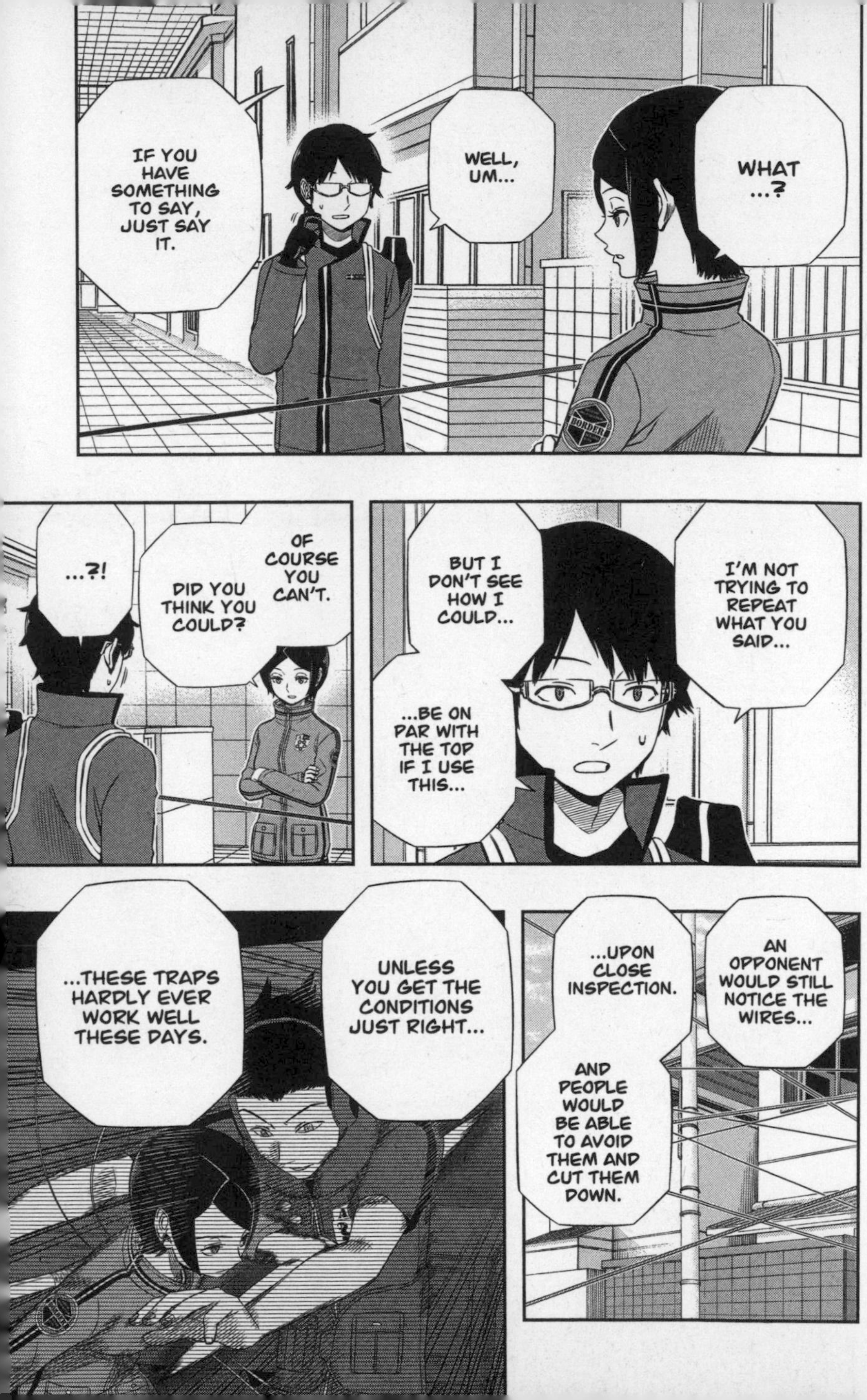
WHAT ...?
WELL, UM...
IF YOU HAVE SOMETHING TO SAY, JUST SAY IT.
I'M NOT TRYING TO REPEAT WHAT YOU SAID...
BUT I DON'T SEE HOW I COULD...
...BE ON PAR WITH THE TOP IF I USE THIS...
OF COURSE YOU CAN'T.
DID YOU THINK YOU COULD?
...?!
AN OPPONENT WOULD STILL NOTICE THE WIRES...
...UPON CLOSE INSPECTION.
AND PEOPLE WOULD BE ABLE TO AVOID THEM AND CUT THEM DOWN.
UNLESS YOU GET THE CONDITIONS JUST RIGHT...
...THESE TRAPS HARDLY EVER WORK WELL THESE DAYS.

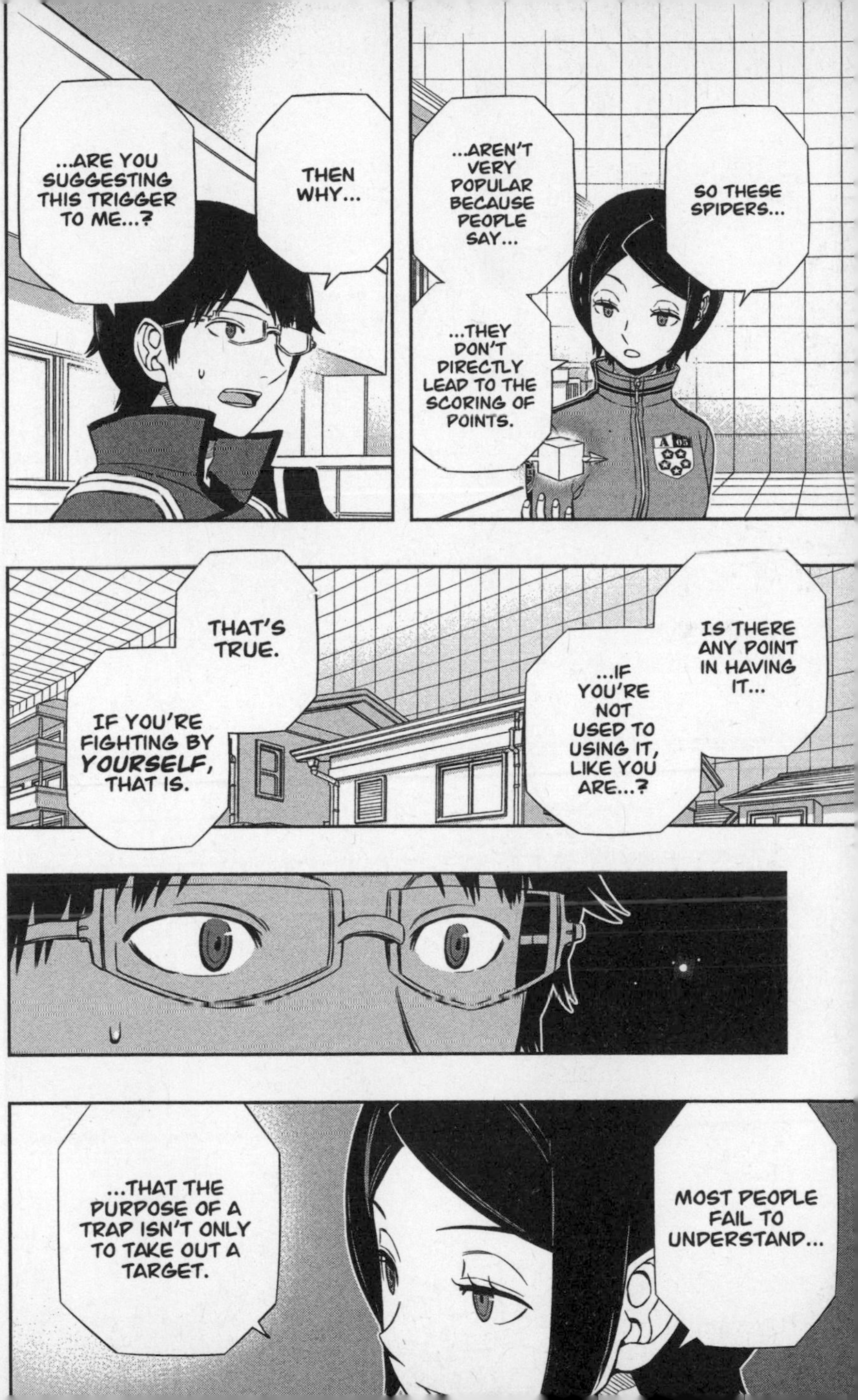
SO THESE SPIDERS...
...AREN'T VERY POPULAR BECAUSE PEOPLE SAY...
...THEY DON'T DIRECTLY LEAD TO THE SCORING OF POINTS.
THEN WHY...
...ARE YOU SUGGESTING THIS TRIGGER TO ME...?
IS THERE ANY POINT IN HAVING IT...
...IF YOU'RE NOT USED TO USING IT, LIKE YOU ARE...?
THAT'S TRUE.
IF YOU'RE FIGHTING BY *YOURSELF*, THAT IS.
MOST PEOPLE FAIL TO UNDERSTAND...
...THAT THE PURPOSE OF A TRAP ISN'T ONLY TO TAKE OUT A TARGET.

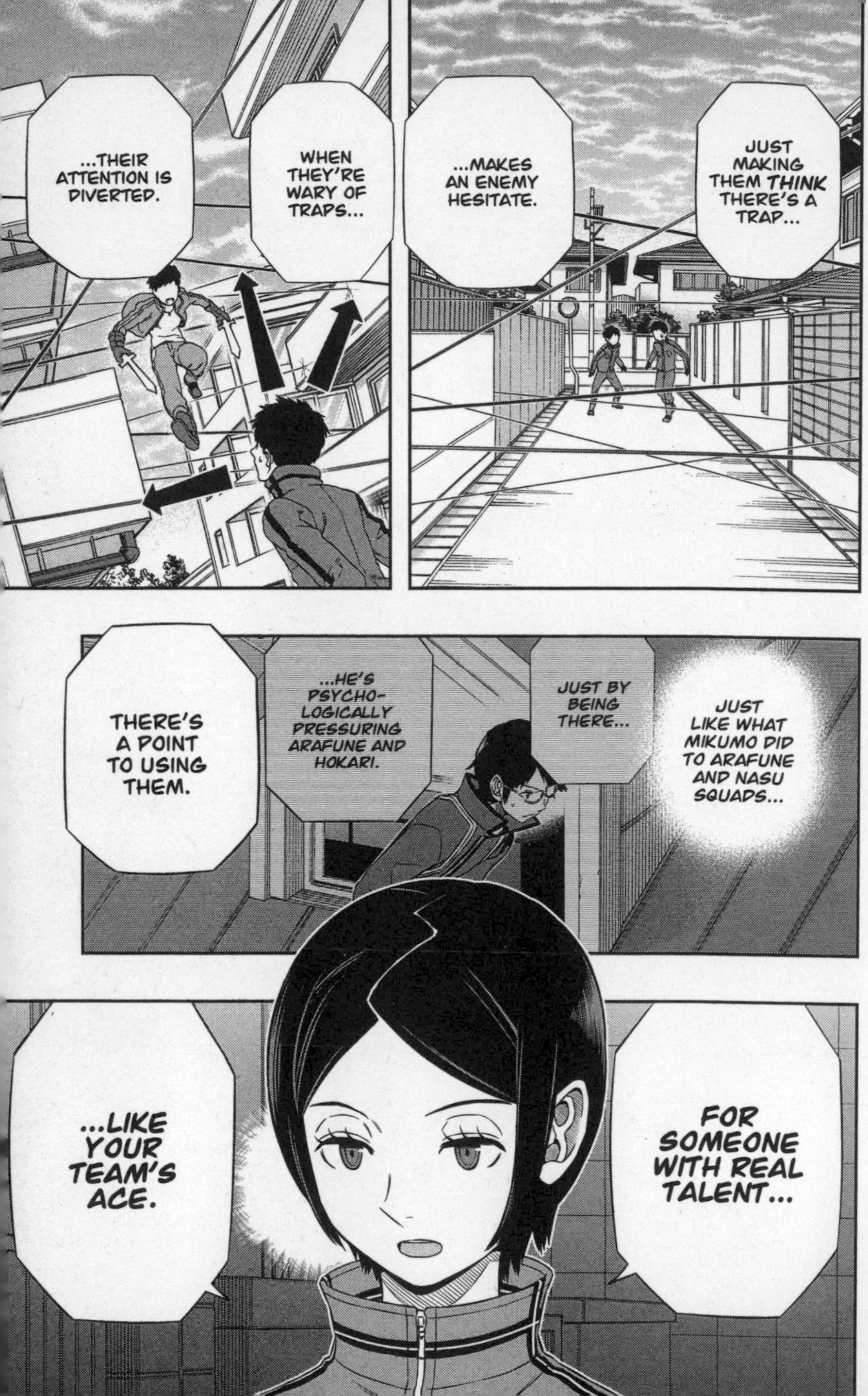
JUST MAKING THEM THINK THERE'S A TRAP...
...MAKES AN ENEMY HESITATE.
WHEN THEY'RE WARY OF TRAPS...
...THEIR ATTENTION IS DIVERTED.
JUST LIKE WHAT MIKUMO DID TO ARAFUNE AND NASU SQUADS...
JUST BY BEING THERE...
...HE'S PSYCHO-LOGICALLY PRESSURING ARAFUNE AND HOKARI.
THERE'S A POINT TO USING THEM.
FOR SOMEONE WITH REAL TALENT...
...LIKE YOUR TEAM'S ACE.

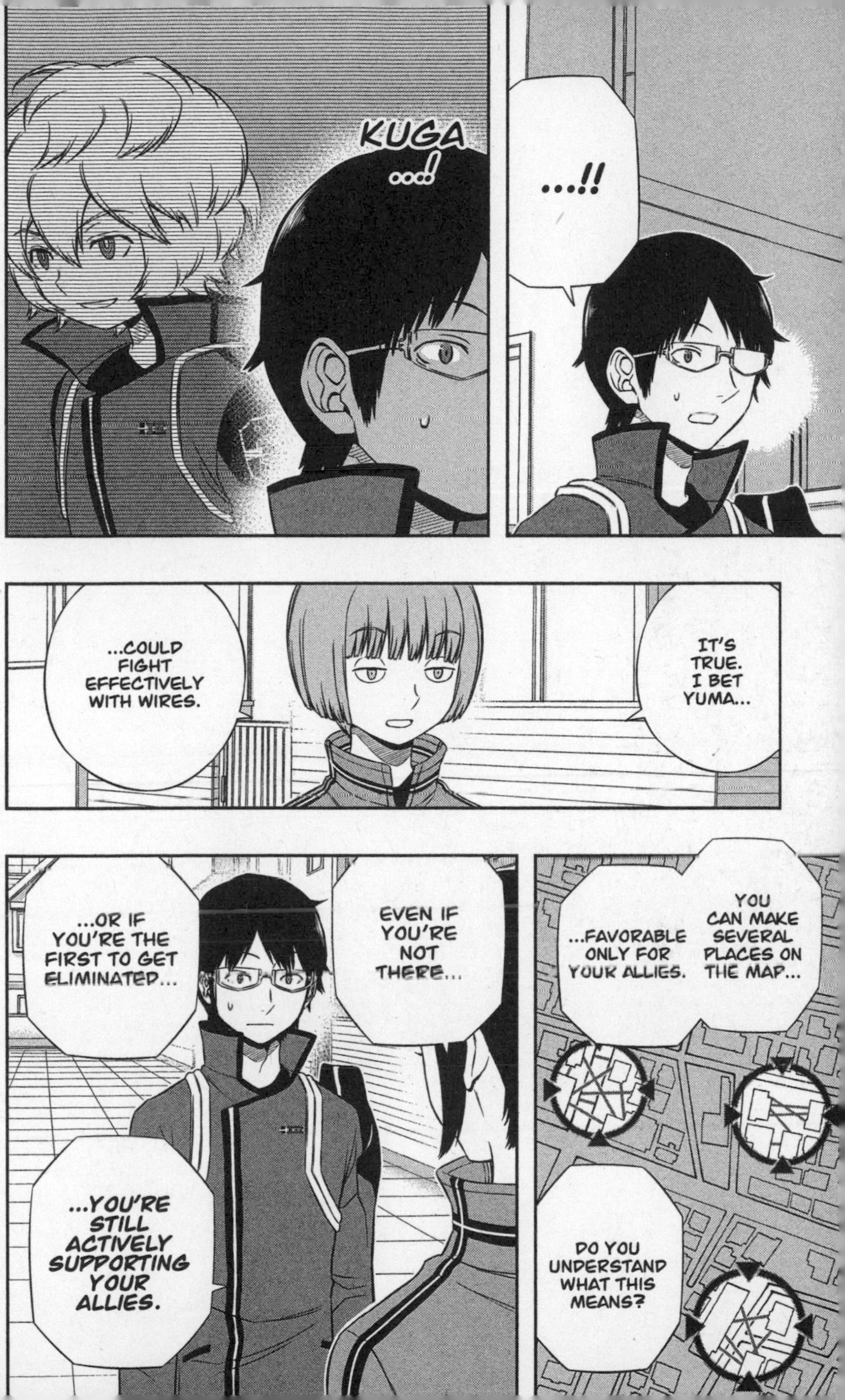
...!!
KUGA ...!
IT'S TRUE. I BET YUMA...
...COULD FIGHT EFFECTIVELY WITH WIRES.
YOU CAN MAKE SEVERAL PLACES ON THE MAP...
...FAVORABLE ONLY FOR YOUR ALLIES.
DO YOU UNDERSTAND WHAT THIS MEANS?
EVEN IF YOU'RE NOT THERE...
...OR IF YOU'RE THE FIRST TO GET ELIMINATED...
...YOU'RE STILL ACTIVELY SUPPORTING YOUR ALLIES.

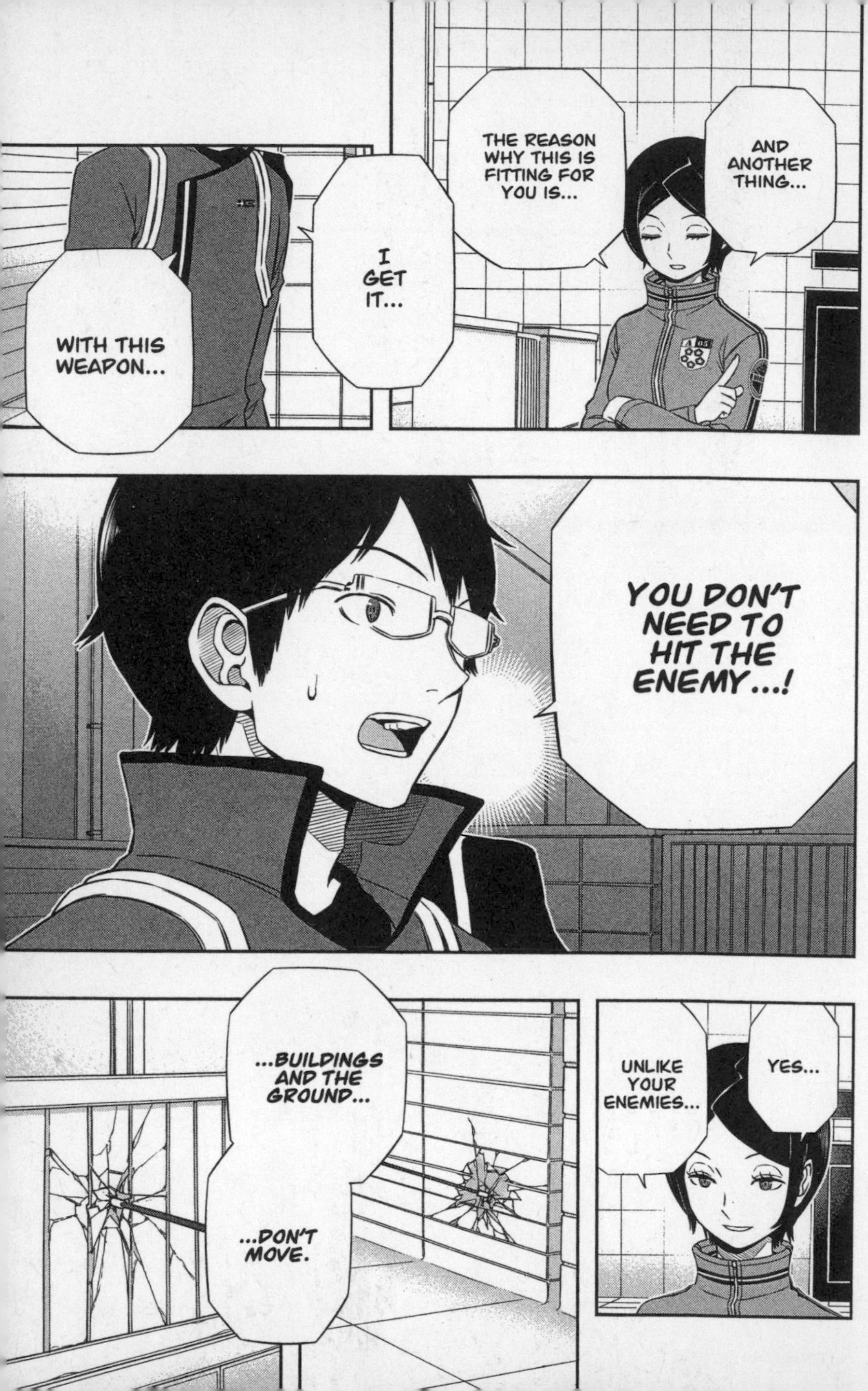
AND ANOTHER THING...
THE REASON WHY THIS IS FITTING FOR YOU IS...
I GET IT...
WITH THIS WEAPON...
YOU DON'T NEED TO HIT THE ENEMY...!
YES...
UNLIKE YOUR ENEMIES...
...BUILDINGS AND THE GROUND...
...DON'T MOVE.

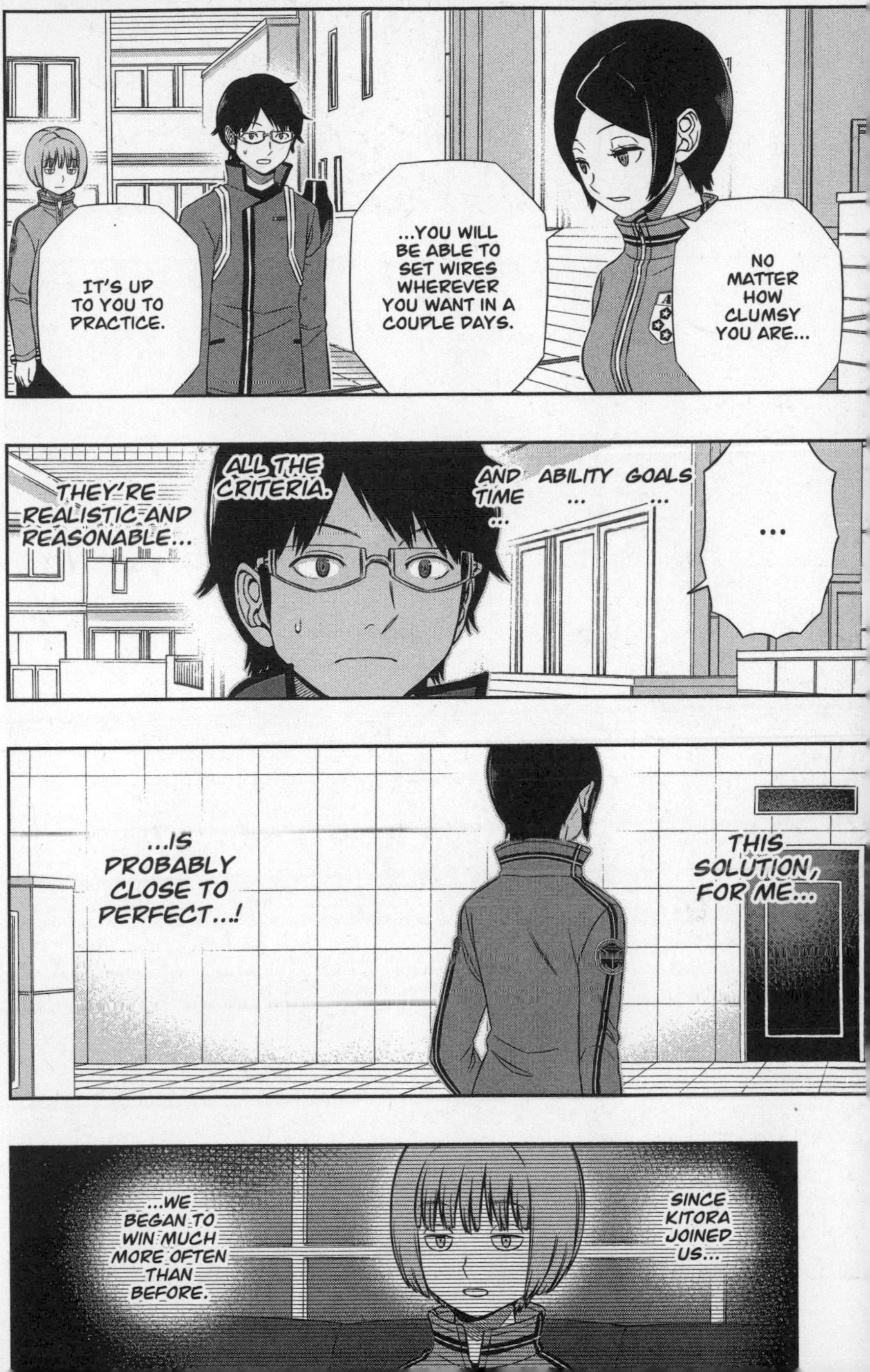
NO MATTER HOW CLUMSY YOU ARE...
...YOU WILL BE ABLE TO SET WIRES WHEREVER YOU WANT IN A COUPLE DAYS.
IT'S UP TO YOU TO PRACTICE.
...
GOALS ...
ABILITY ...
AND TIME ...
ALL THE CRITERIA.
THEY'RE REALISTIC AND REASONABLE...
THIS SOLUTION, FOR ME...
...IS PROBABLY CLOSE TO PERFECT...!
SINCE KITORA JOINED US...
...WE BEGAN TO WIN MUCH MORE OFTEN THAN BEFORE.

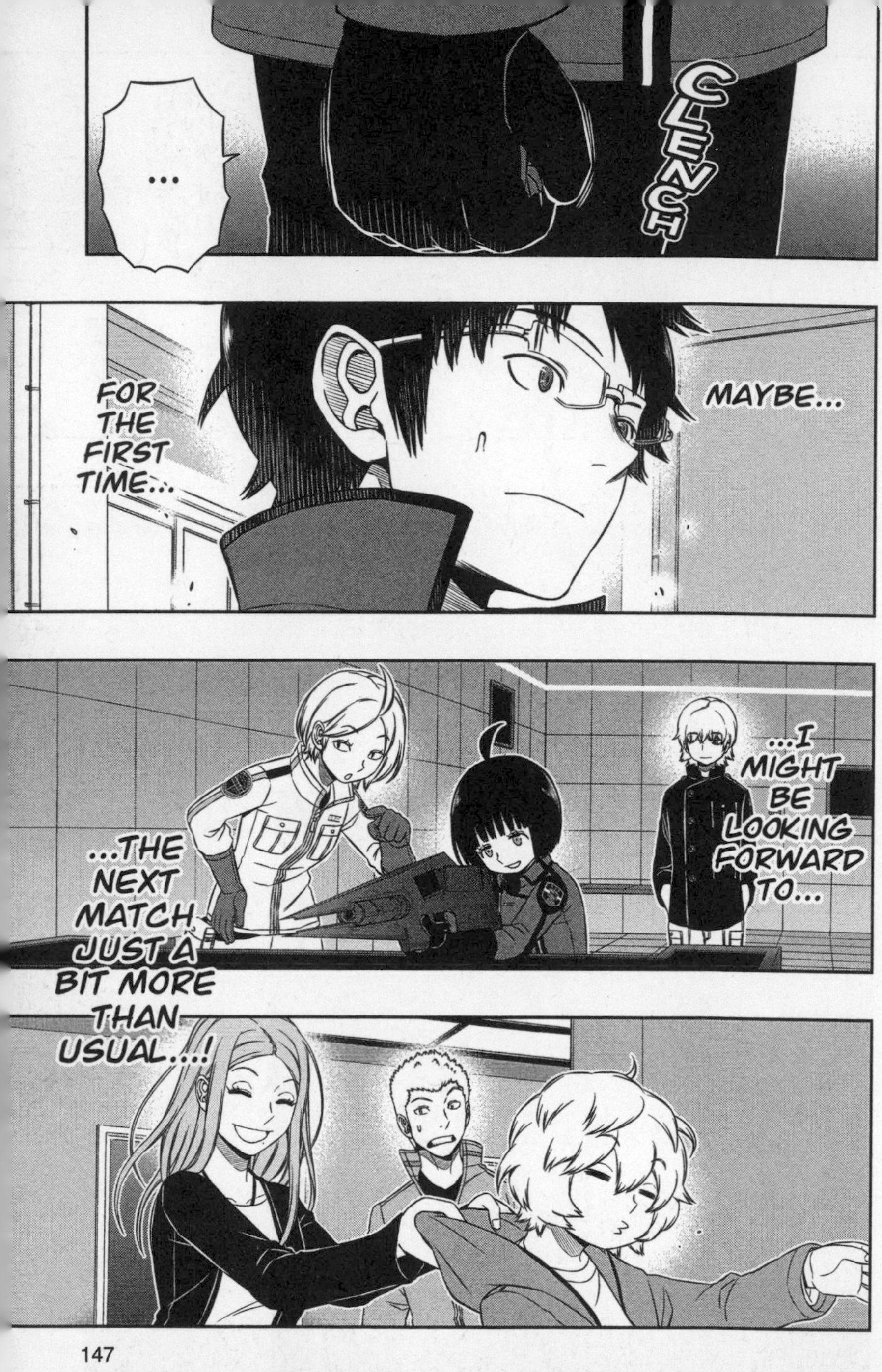
CLENCH
...
MAYBE...
FOR THE FIRST TIME...
...I MIGHT BE LOOKING FORWARD TO...
...THE NEXT MATCH JUST A BIT MORE THAN USUAL...!

■Osamu's holster.

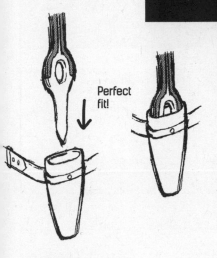

Perfect fit!

The belt is the same as Jin's. In volume 2, it was the same belt as Arashiyama Squad's, but it has changed since then.

There's a secure snap on the back.

■Kitora's gun

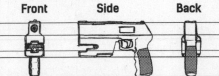

Front　　Side　　Back

The sides are open.

Beveled corners.

■Kitora's holster

Secured by snaps just like Osamu's.

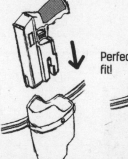

Perfect fit!

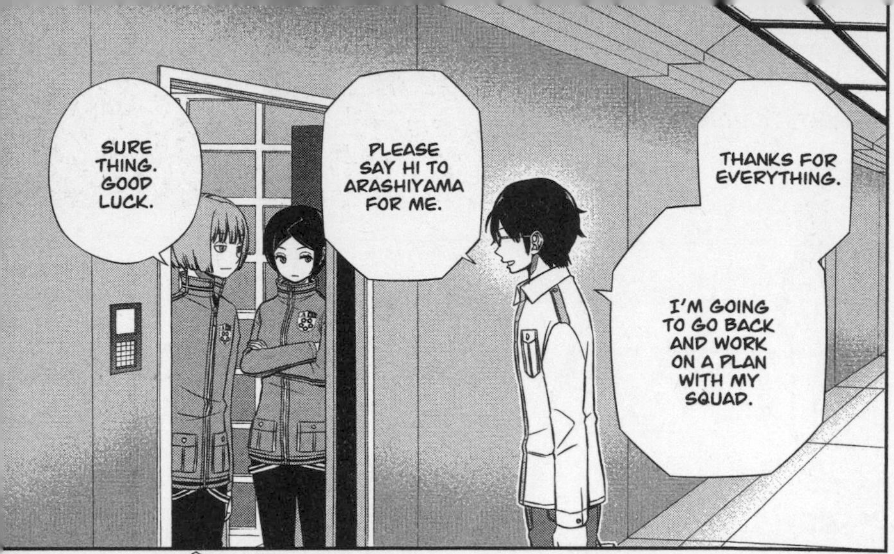
THANKS FOR EVERYTHING.
I'M GOING TO GO BACK AND WORK ON A PLAN WITH MY SQUAD.
PLEASE SAY HI TO ARASHIYAMA FOR ME.
SURE THING. GOOD LUCK.

Chapter 123 Galopoula: Part 2

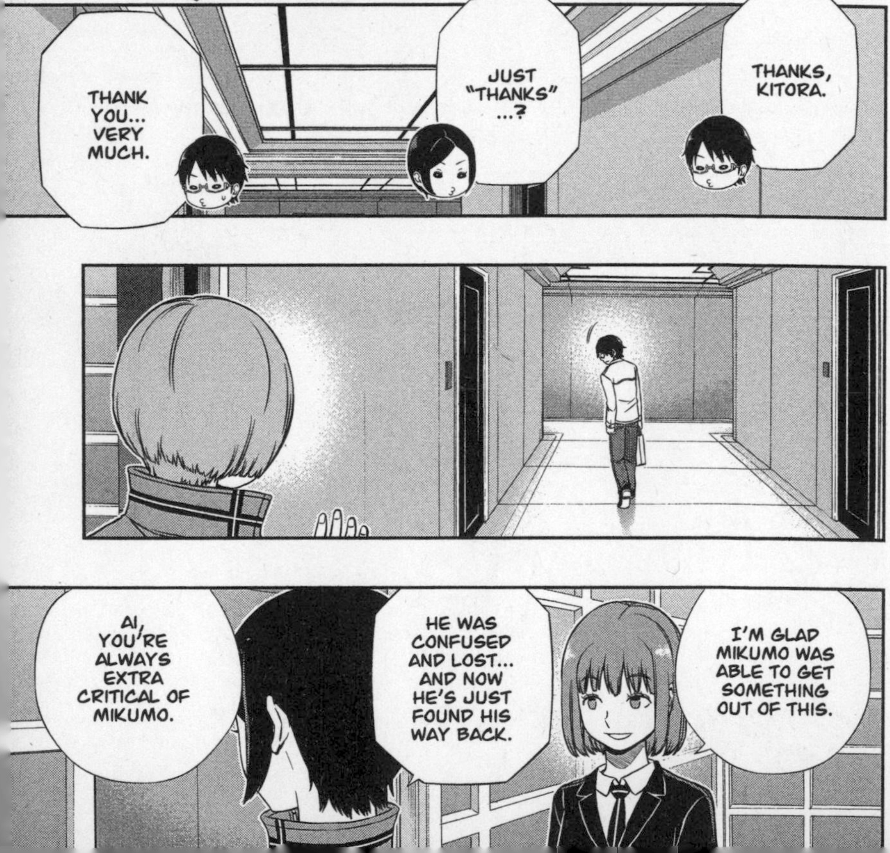
THANKS, KITORA.
JUST "THANKS" ...?
THANK YOU... VERY MUCH.
I'M GLAD MIKUMO WAS ABLE TO GET SOMETHING OUT OF THIS.
HE WAS CONFUSED AND LOST... AND NOW HE'S JUST FOUND HIS WAY BACK.
AI, YOU'RE ALWAYS EXTRA CRITICAL OF MIKUMO.

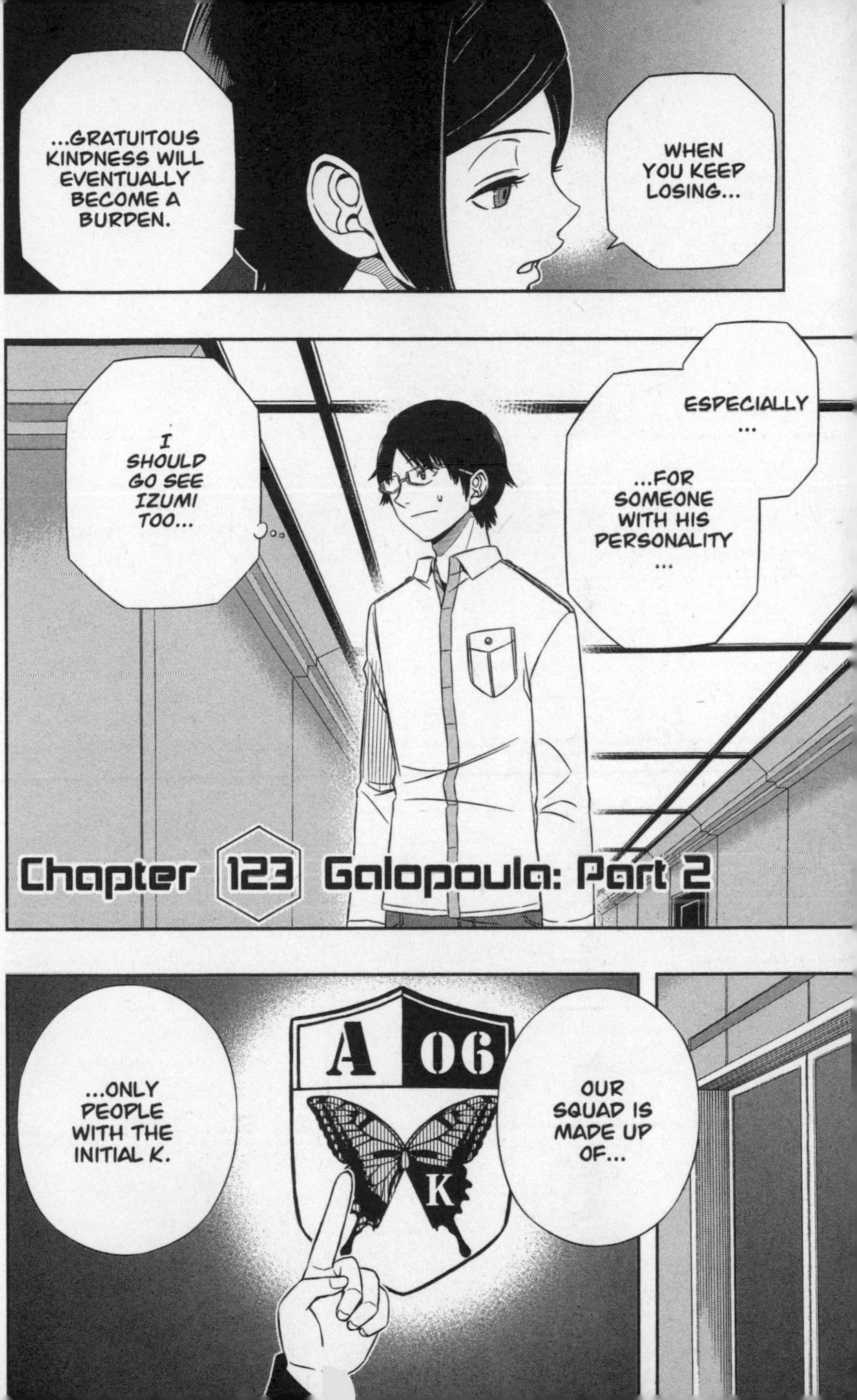
WHEN YOU KEEP LOSING...
...GRATUITOUS KINDNESS WILL EVENTUALLY BECOME A BURDEN.
ESPECIALLY ...
...FOR SOMEONE WITH HIS PERSONALITY ...
I SHOULD GO SEE IZUMI TOO...
Chapter 123 Galopoula: Part 2
A 06
K
OUR SQUAD IS MADE UP OF...
...ONLY PEOPLE WITH THE INITIAL K.

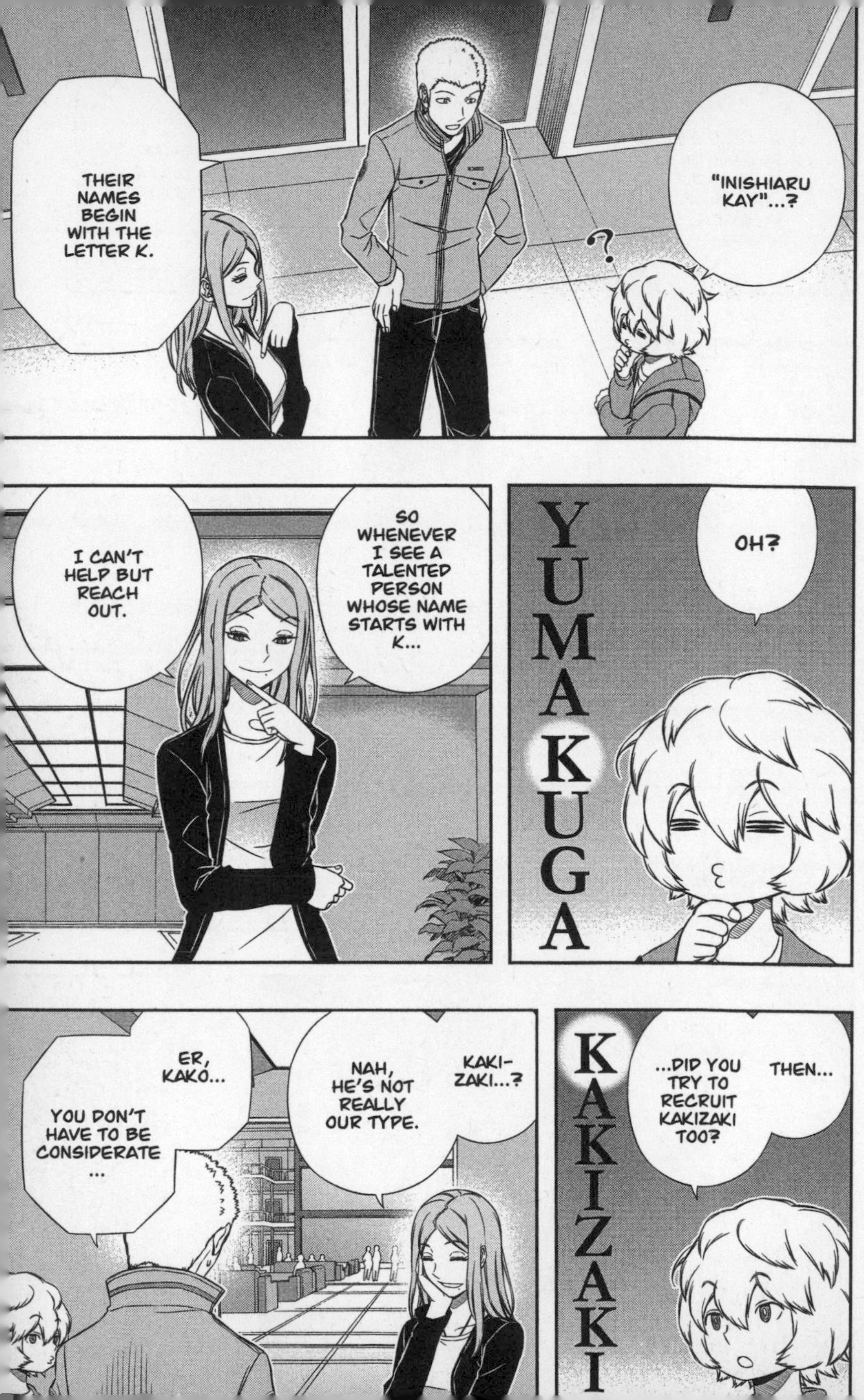
"INISHIARU KAY"...?
?
THEIR NAMES BEGIN WITH THE LETTER K.
OH?
YUMA KUGA
SO WHENEVER I SEE A TALENTED PERSON WHOSE NAME STARTS WITH K...
I CAN'T HELP BUT REACH OUT.
THEN...
...DID YOU TRY TO RECRUIT KAKIZAKI TOO?
KAKIZAKI
KAKI-ZAKI...?
NAH, HE'S NOT REALLY OUR TYPE.
ER, KAKO...
YOU DON'T HAVE TO BE CONSIDERATE...

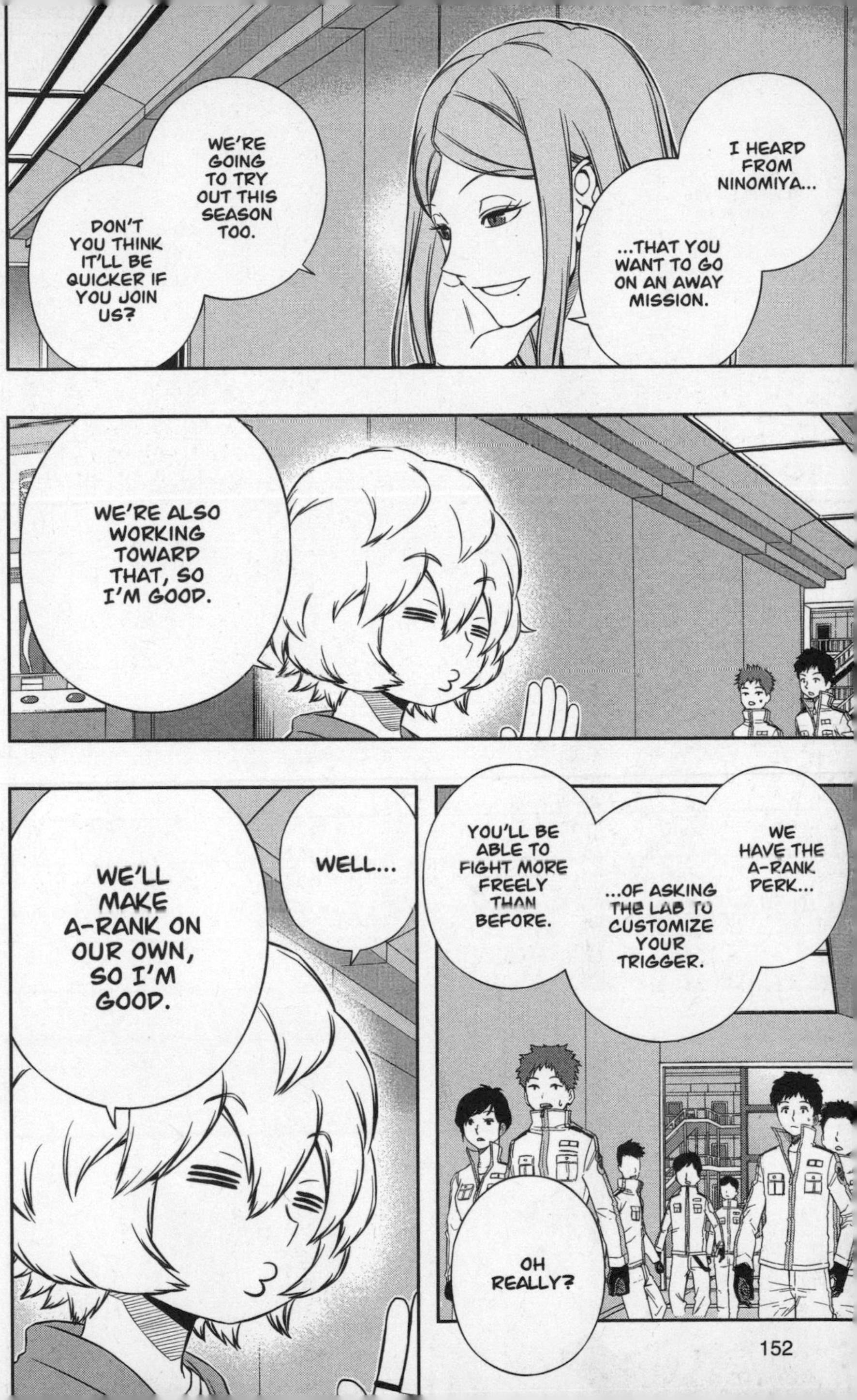
I HEARD FROM NINOMIYA...
...THAT YOU WANT TO GO ON AN AWAY MISSION.
WE'RE GOING TO TRY OUT THIS SEASON TOO.
DON'T YOU THINK IT'LL BE QUICKER IF YOU JOIN US?
WE'RE ALSO WORKING TOWARD THAT, SO I'M GOOD.
WE HAVE THE A-RANK PERK...
...OF ASKING THE LAB TO CUSTOMIZE YOUR TRIGGER.
YOU'LL BE ABLE TO FIGHT MORE FREELY THAN BEFORE.
OH REALLY?
WELL...
WE'LL MAKE A-RANK ON OUR OWN, SO I'M GOOD.

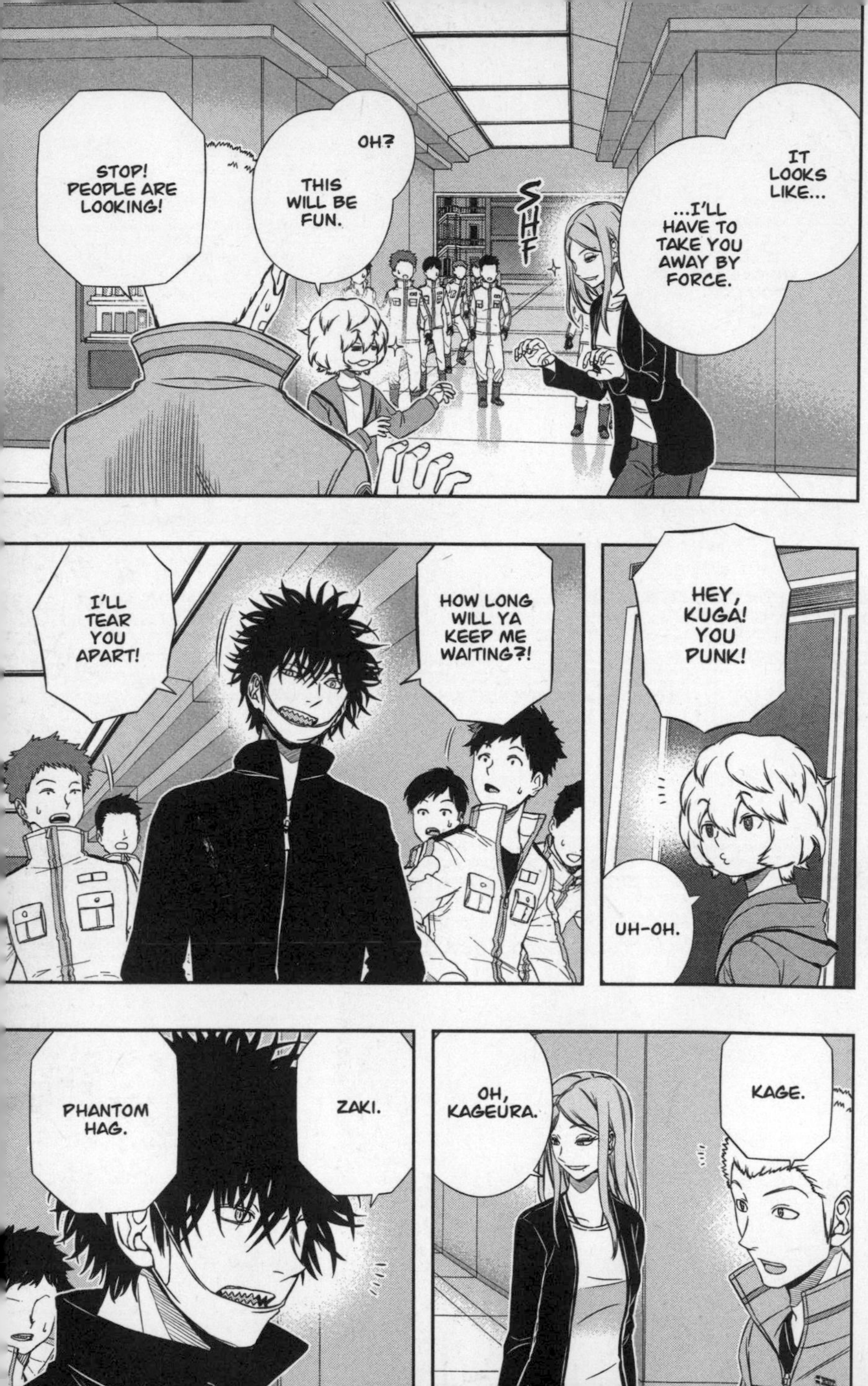
IT LOOKS LIKE...
...I'LL HAVE TO TAKE YOU AWAY BY FORCE.
SHF
OH?
THIS WILL BE FUN.
STOP! PEOPLE ARE LOOKING!
HEY, KUGA! YOU PUNK!
UH-OH.
HOW LONG WILL YA KEEP ME WAITING?!
I'LL TEAR YOU APART!
KAGE.
OH, KAGEURA.
ZAKI.
PHANTOM HAG.

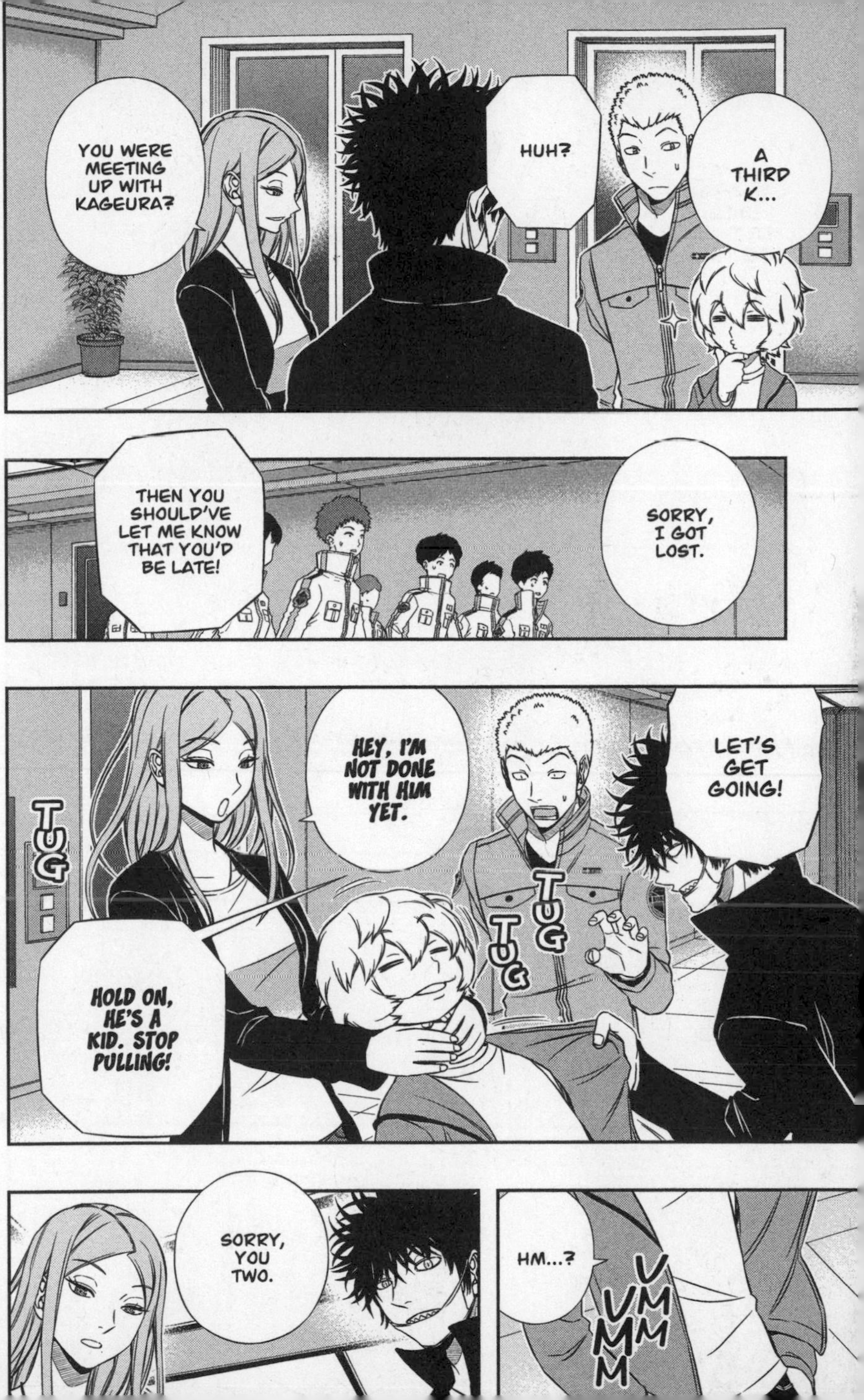
A THIRD K...
HUH?
YOU WERE MEETING UP WITH KAGEURA?
SORRY, I GOT LOST.
THEN YOU SHOULD'VE LET ME KNOW THAT YOU'D BE LATE!
LET'S GET GOING!
HEY, I'M NOT DONE WITH HIM YET.
TUG
TUG
TUG
HOLD ON, HE'S A KID. STOP PULLING!
HM...?
VUMM
VUMM
SORRY, YOU TWO.

MY LEADER'S CALLING SO I GOTTA GET BACK.

Tachikawa Squad Strategy Room

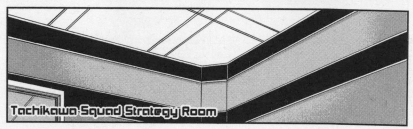

ANYTIME.

SURE THING.

CHEW

CHEW

THERE'S SOMETHING I WANT TO TRY...

AND SO...

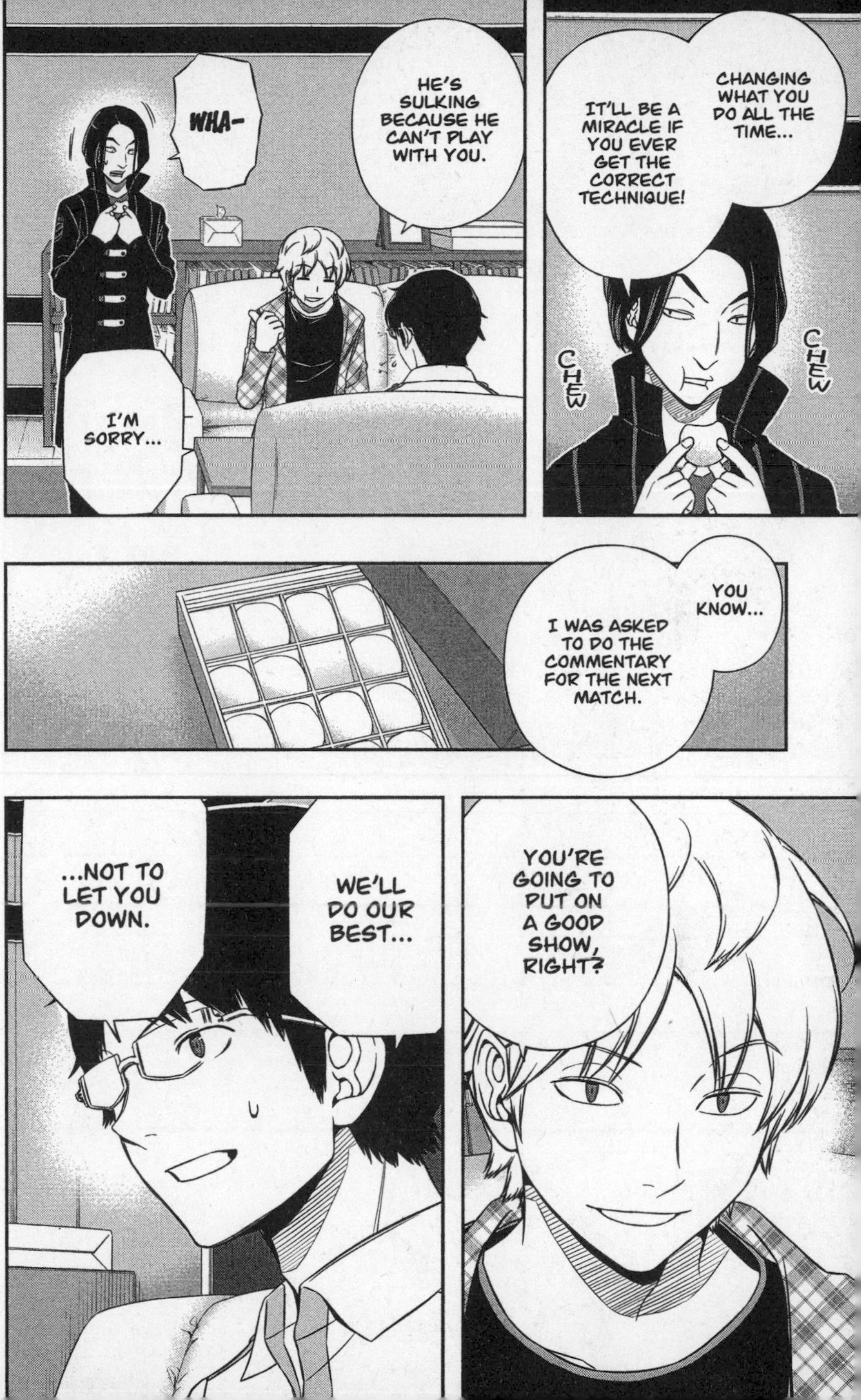
CHANGING WHAT YOU DO ALL THE TIME...
IT'LL BE A MIRACLE IF YOU EVER GET THE CORRECT TECHNIQUE!
CHEW
CHEW
HE'S SULKING BECAUSE HE CAN'T PLAY WITH YOU.
WHA-
I'M SORRY...
YOU KNOW...
I WAS ASKED TO DO THE COMMENTARY FOR THE NEXT MATCH.
YOU'RE GOING TO PUT ON A GOOD SHOW, RIGHT?
WE'LL DO OUR BEST...
...NOT TO LET YOU DOWN.

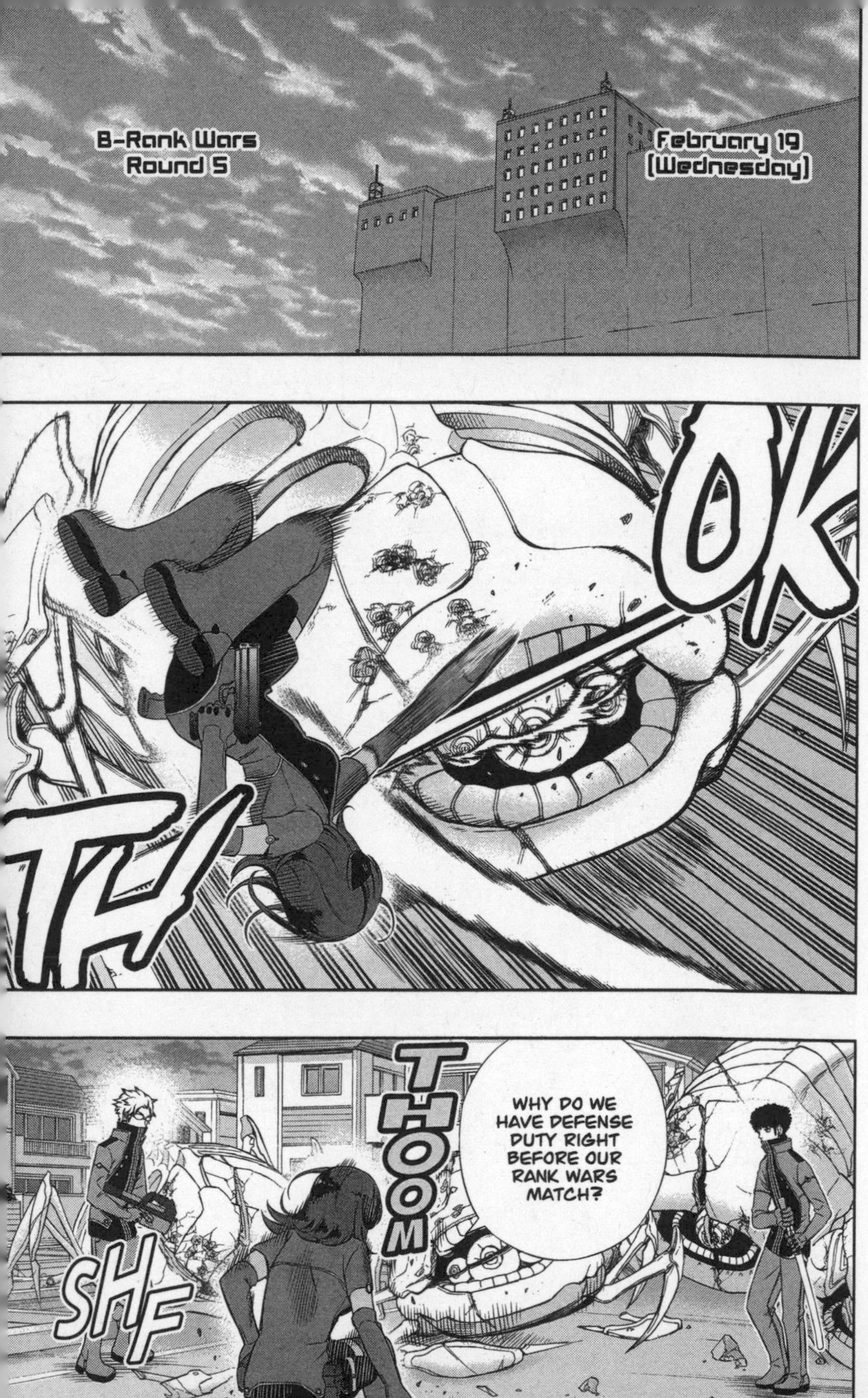
February 19 (Wednesday)
B-Rank Wars Round 5
THOK
WHY DO WE HAVE DEFENSE DUTY RIGHT BEFORE OUR RANK WARS MATCH?
THOOM
SHF

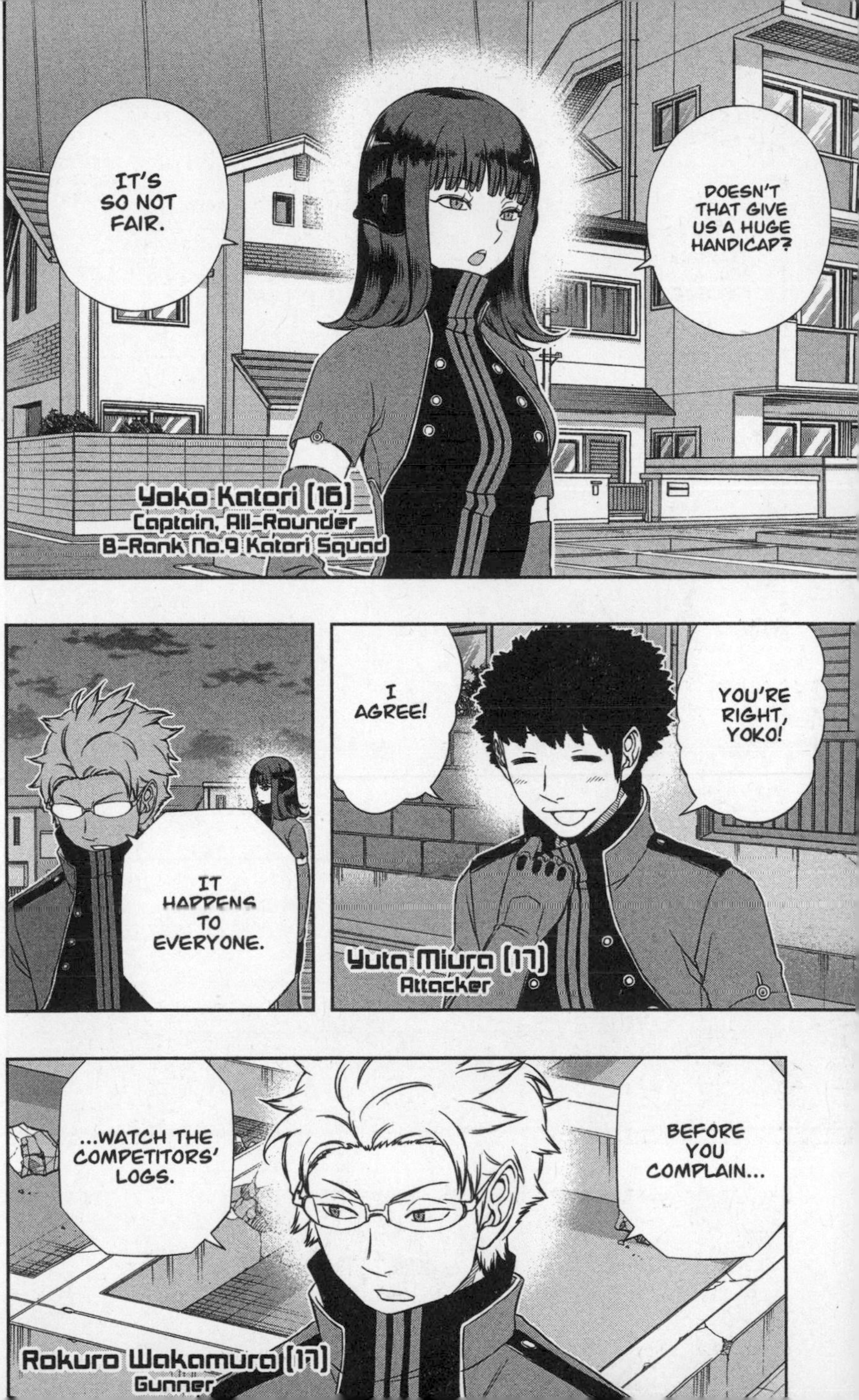
DOESN'T THAT GIVE US A HUGE HANDICAP?
IT'S SO NOT FAIR.
Yoko Katori (16)
Captain, All-Rounder
B-Rank No.9 Katori Squad
YOU'RE RIGHT, YOKO!
I AGREE!
Yuta Miura (17)
Attacker
IT HAPPENS TO EVERYONE.
BEFORE YOU COMPLAIN...
...WATCH THE COMPETITORS' LOGS.
Rokuro Wakamura (17)
Gunner

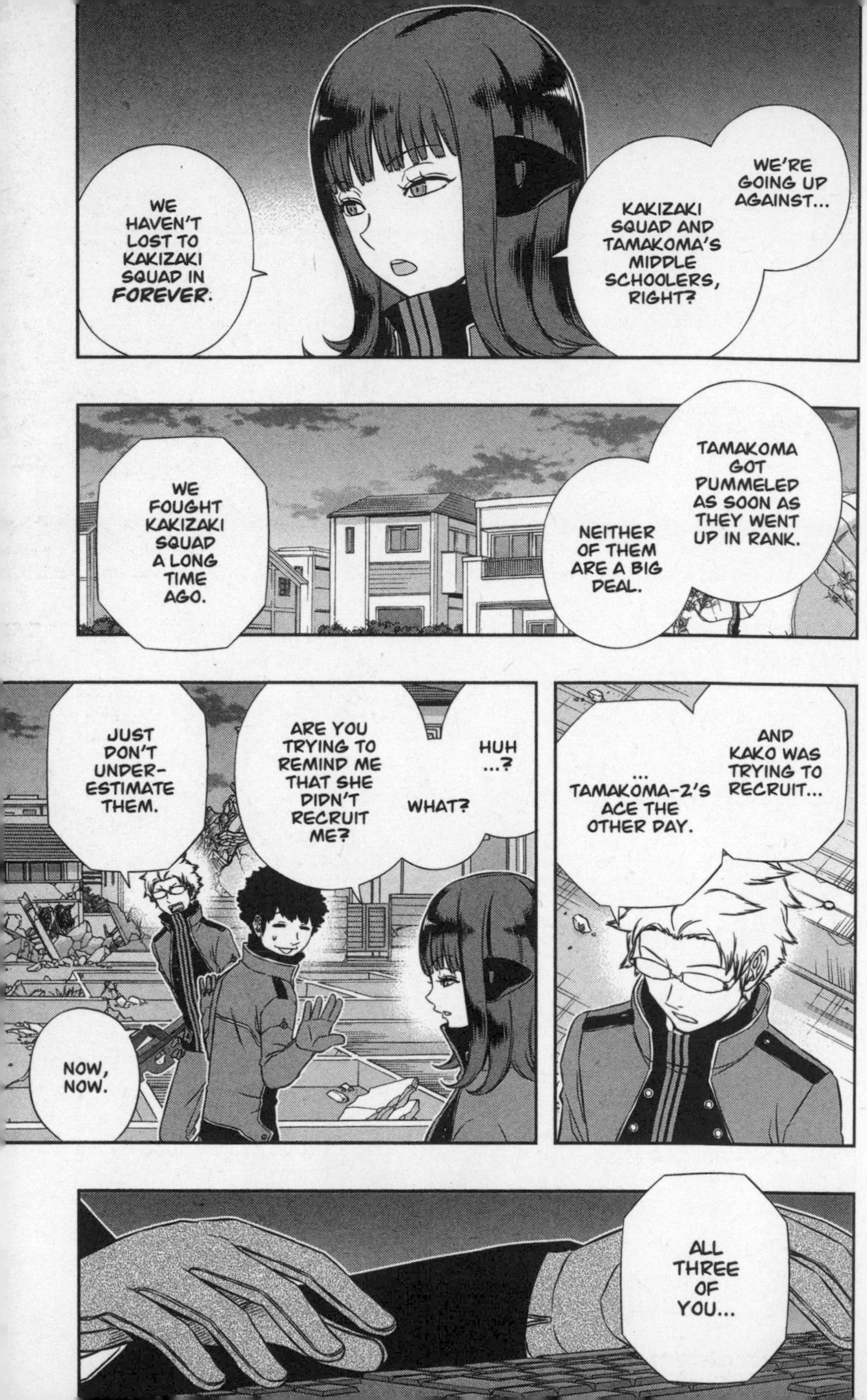
WE'RE GOING UP AGAINST...
KAKIZAKI SQUAD AND TAMAKOMA'S MIDDLE SCHOOLERS, RIGHT?
WE HAVEN'T LOST TO KAKIZAKI SQUAD IN FOREVER.
TAMAKOMA GOT PUMMELED AS SOON AS THEY WENT UP IN RANK.
NEITHER OF THEM ARE A BIG DEAL.
WE FOUGHT KAKIZAKI SQUAD A LONG TIME AGO.
AND KAKO WAS TRYING TO RECRUIT...
...TAMAKOMA-2'S ACE THE OTHER DAY.
HUH ...?
WHAT?
ARE YOU TRYING TO REMIND ME THAT SHE DIDN'T RECRUIT ME?
JUST DON'T UNDER-ESTIMATE THEM.
NOW, NOW.
ALL THREE OF YOU...

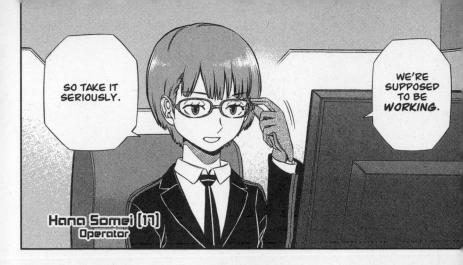

WE'RE SUPPOSED TO BE WORKING.
SO TAKE IT SERIOUSLY.
Hana Somei (17)
Operator
SEE... HANA YELLED AT US.
IT'S YOUR FAULT.
NOW, YOU TWO...
...
SLIP

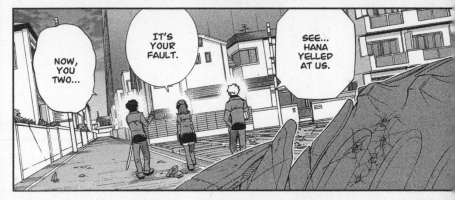

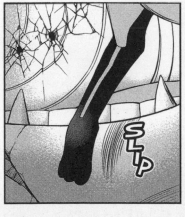

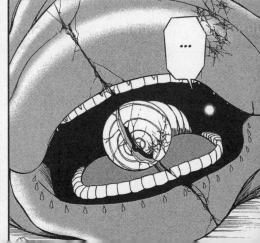

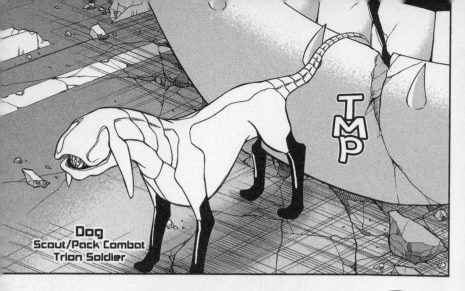

Dog
Scout/Pack Combat
Trion Soldier

TMP

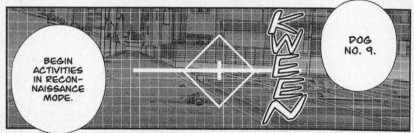

BEGIN ACTIVITIES IN RECON- NAISSANCE MODE.

KWEEN

DOG NO. 9.

...HAVE SKILL.

MEEDEN SOLDIERS...

FLIP

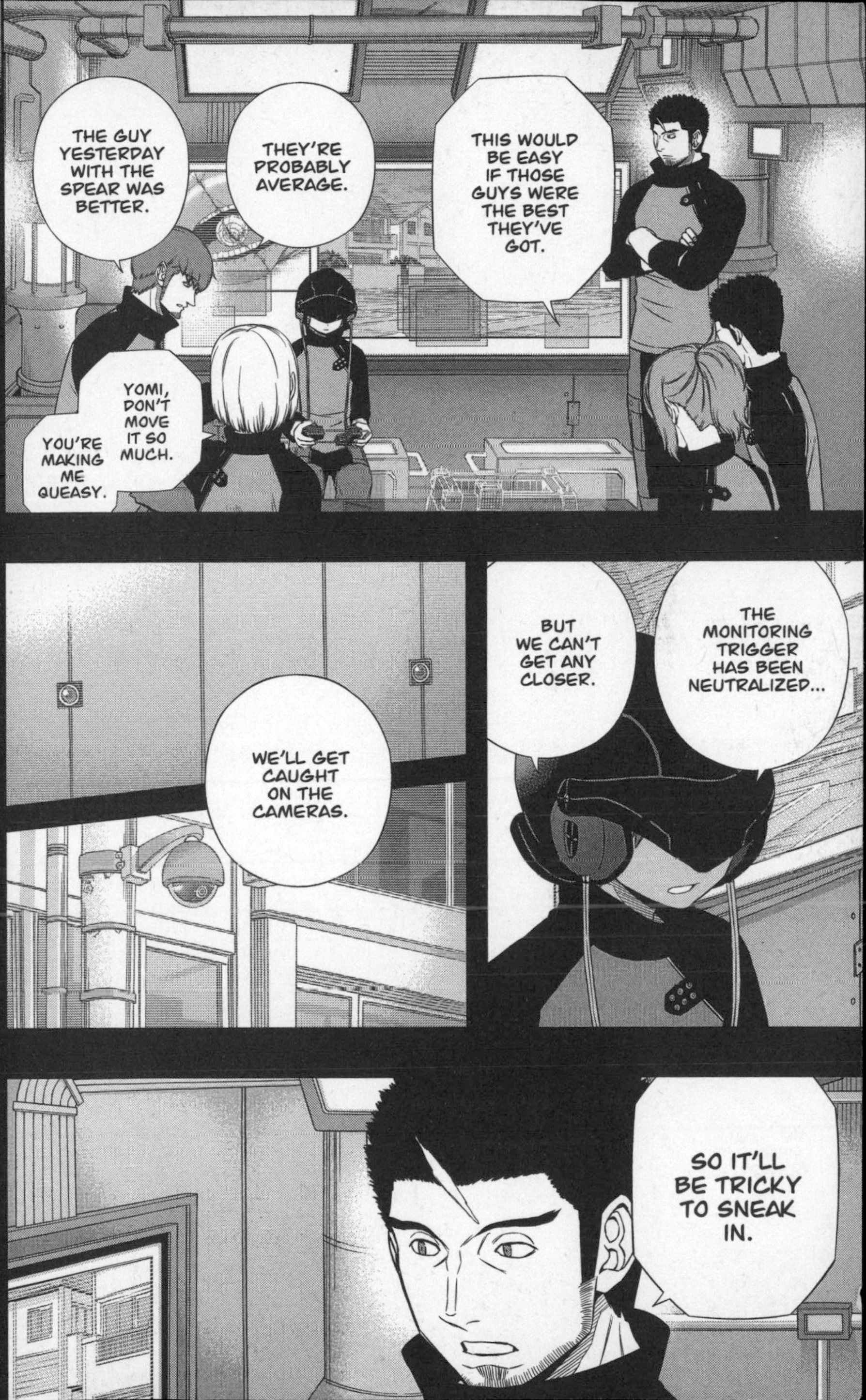
THIS WOULD BE EASY IF THOSE GUYS WERE THE BEST THEY'VE GOT.
THEY'RE PROBABLY AVERAGE.
THE GUY YESTERDAY WITH THE SPEAR WAS BETTER.
YOMI, DON'T MOVE IT SO MUCH.
YOU'RE MAKING ME QUEASY.
THE MONITORING TRIGGER HAS BEEN NEUTRALIZED...
BUT WE CAN'T GET ANY CLOSER.
WE'LL GET CAUGHT ON THE CAMERAS.
SO IT'LL BE TRICKY TO SNEAK IN.

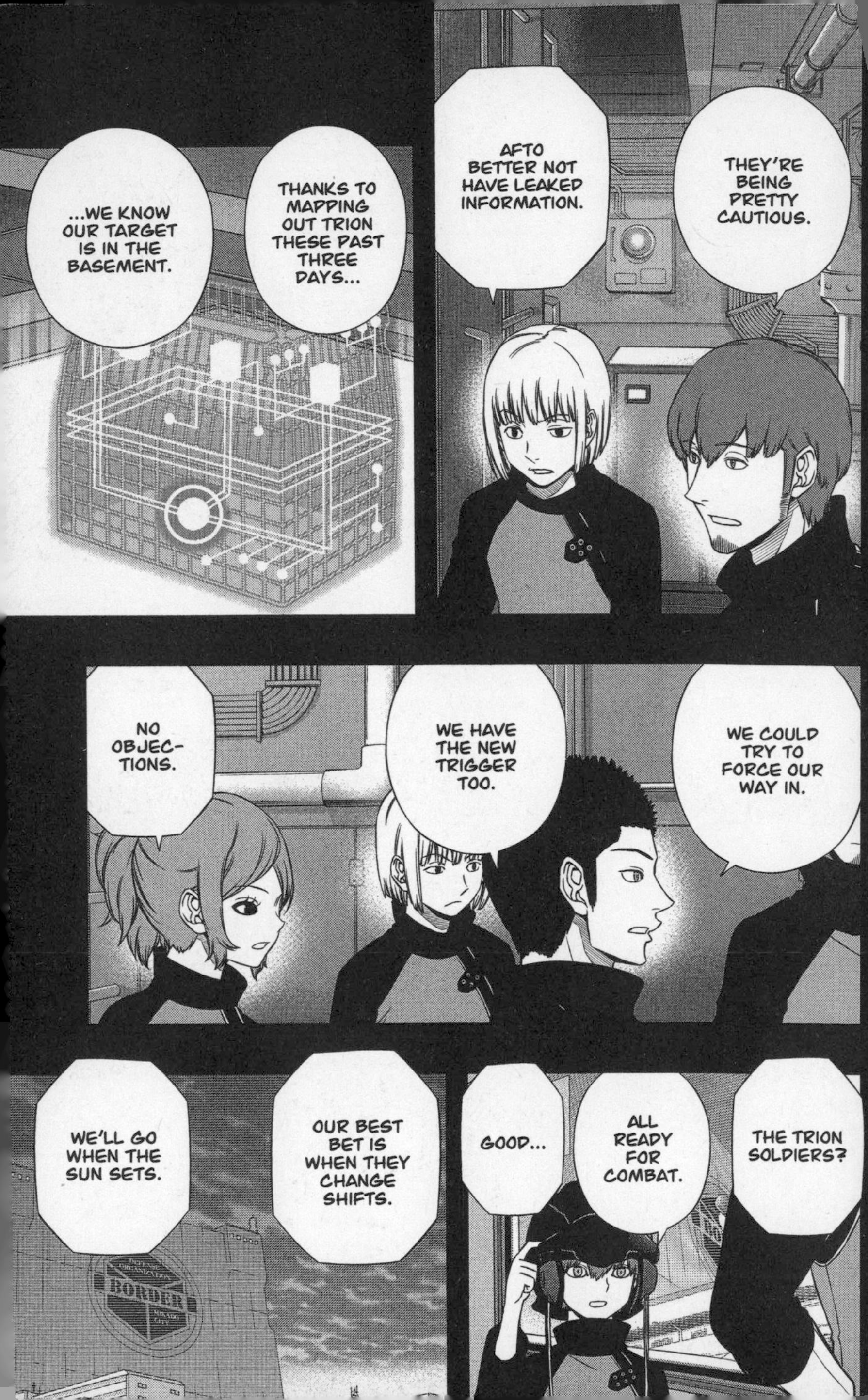
THEY'RE BEING PRETTY CAUTIOUS.
AFTO BETTER NOT HAVE LEAKED INFORMATION.
THANKS TO MAPPING OUT TRION THESE PAST THREE DAYS...
...WE KNOW OUR TARGET IS IN THE BASEMENT.
WE COULD TRY TO FORCE OUR WAY IN.
WE HAVE THE NEW TRIGGER TOO.
NO OBJEC-TIONS.
THE TRION SOLDIERS?
ALL READY FOR COMBAT.
GOOD...
OUR BEST BET IS WHEN THEY CHANGE SHIFTS.
WE'LL GO WHEN THE SUN SETS.
BORDER

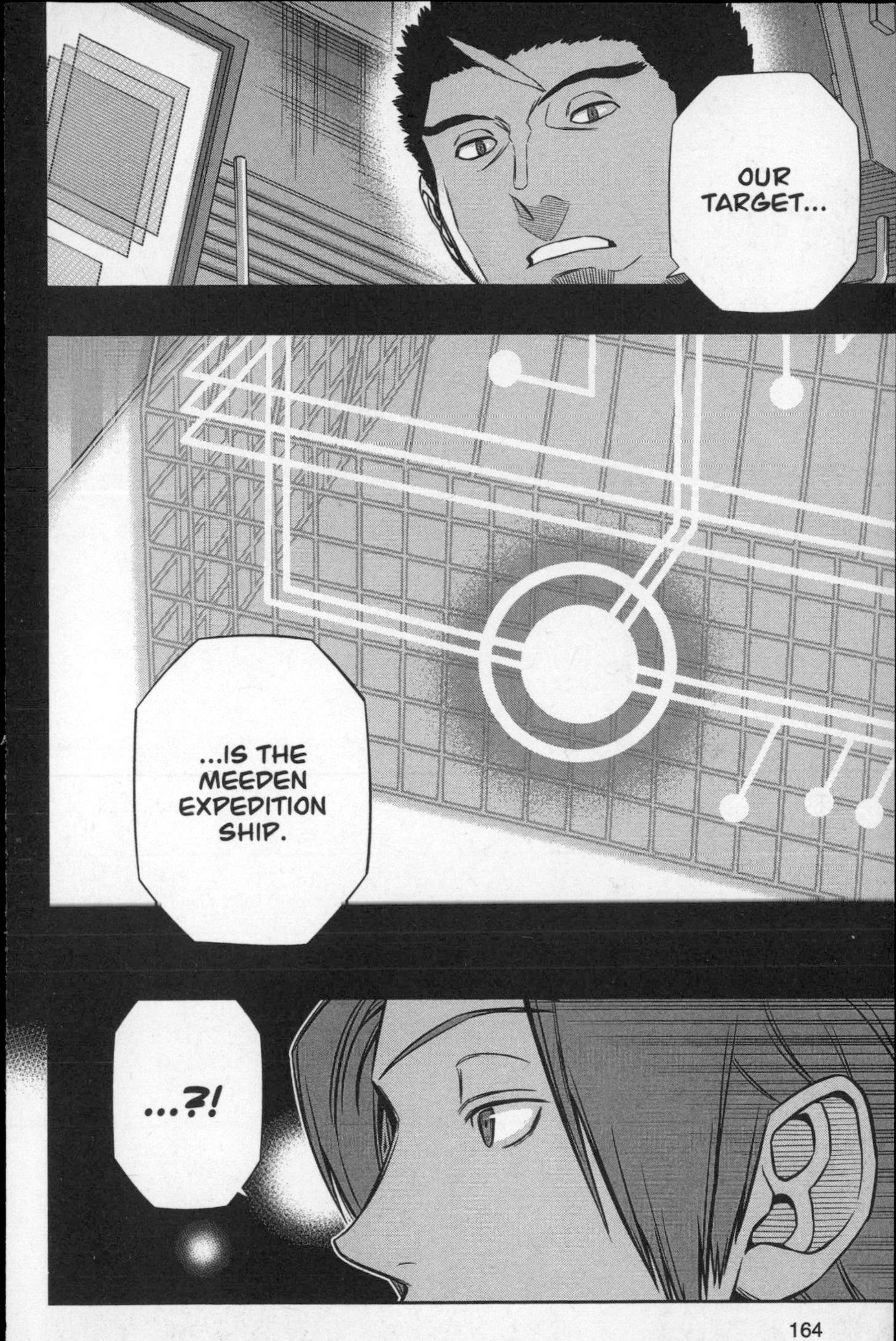
OUR TARGET...
...IS THE MEEDEN EXPEDITION SHIP.
...?!

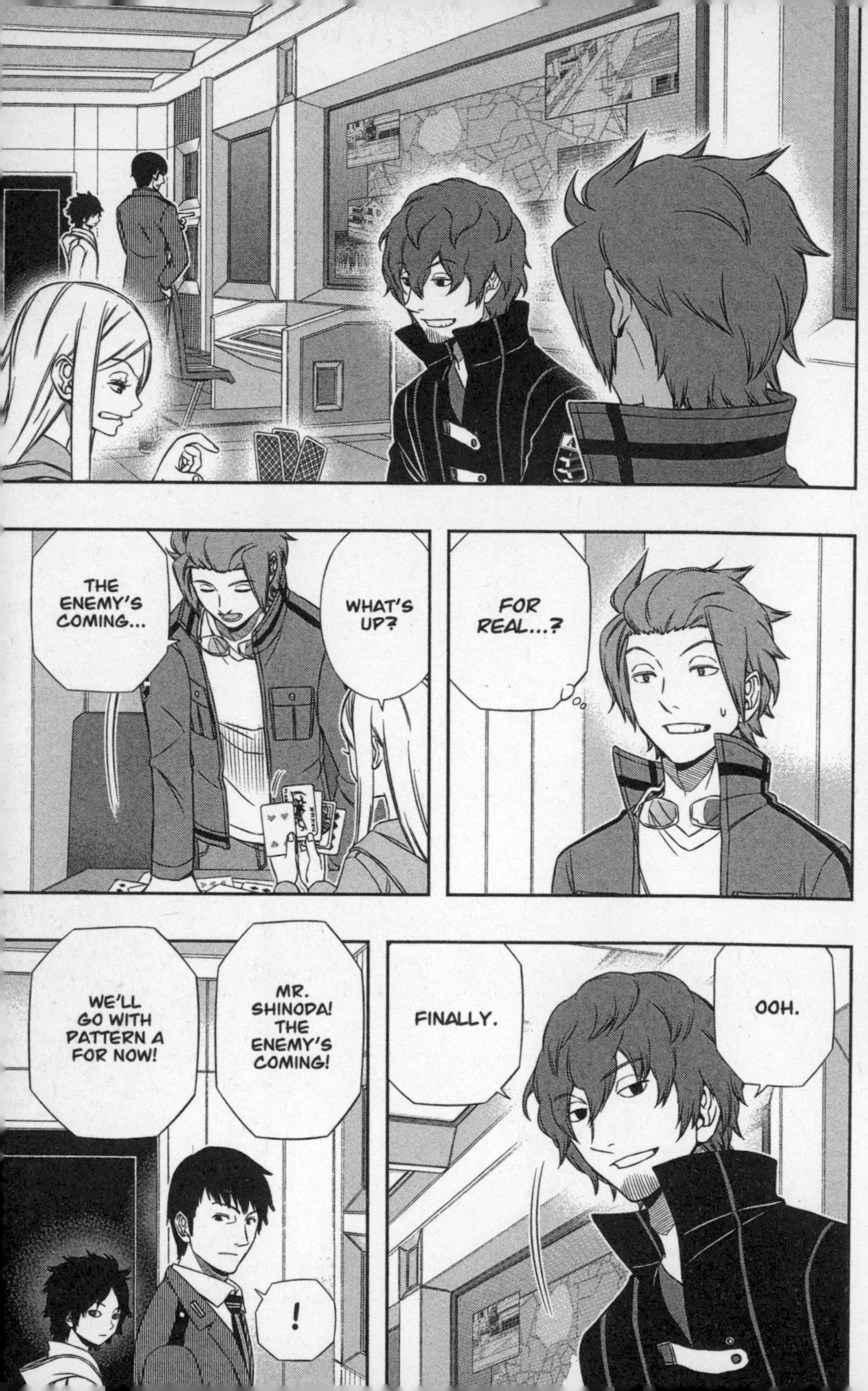
FOR REAL...?
WHAT'S UP?
THE ENEMY'S COMING...
OOH.
FINALLY.
MR. SHINODA! THE ENEMY'S COMING!
WE'LL GO WITH PATTERN A FOR NOW!
!

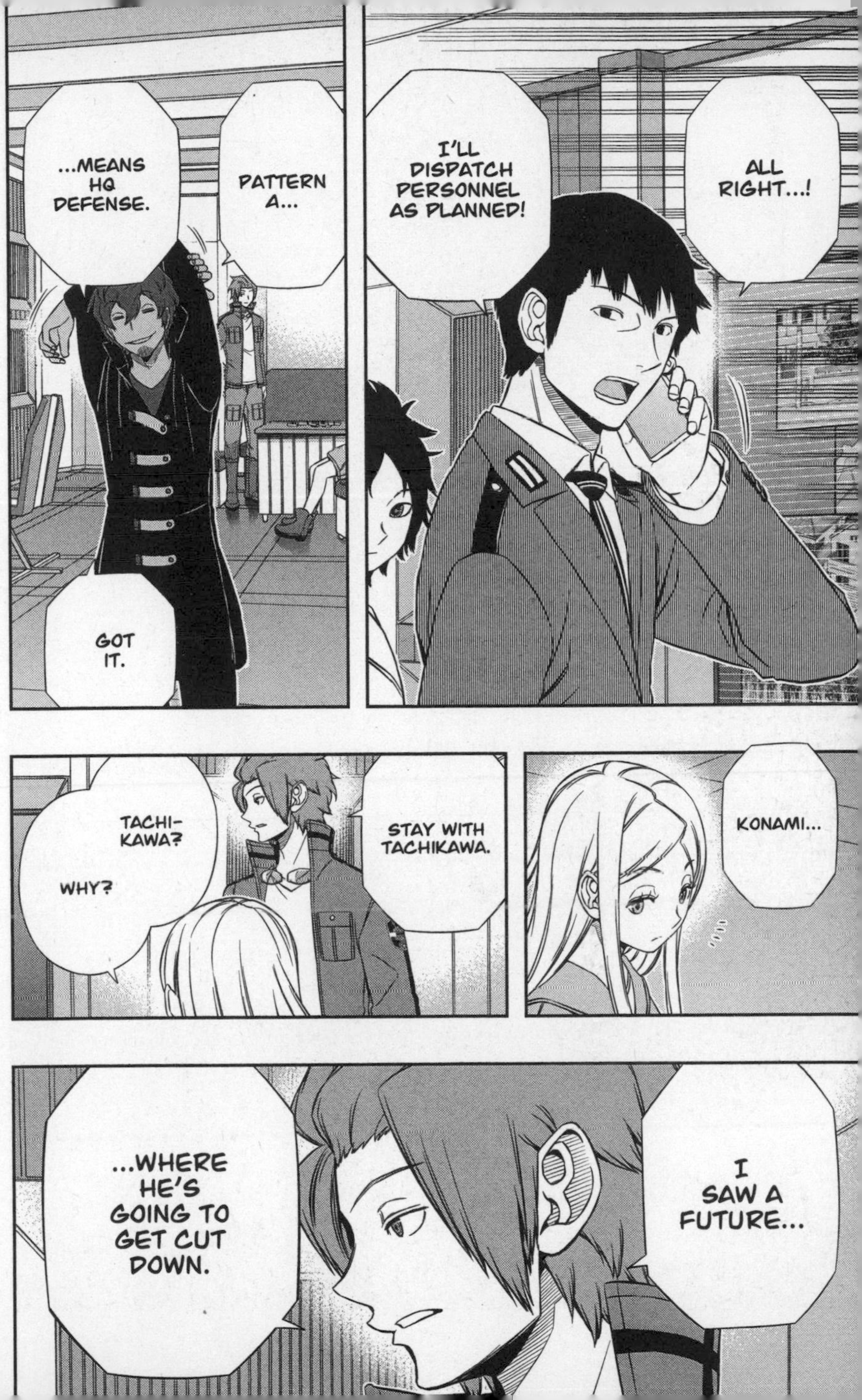
ALL RIGHT...!
I'LL DISPATCH PERSONNEL AS PLANNED!
PATTERN A...
...MEANS HQ DEFENSE.
GOT IT.
KONAMI...
STAY WITH TACHIKAWA.
TACHI-KAWA? WHY?
I SAW A FUTURE...
...WHERE HE'S GOING TO GET CUT DOWN.

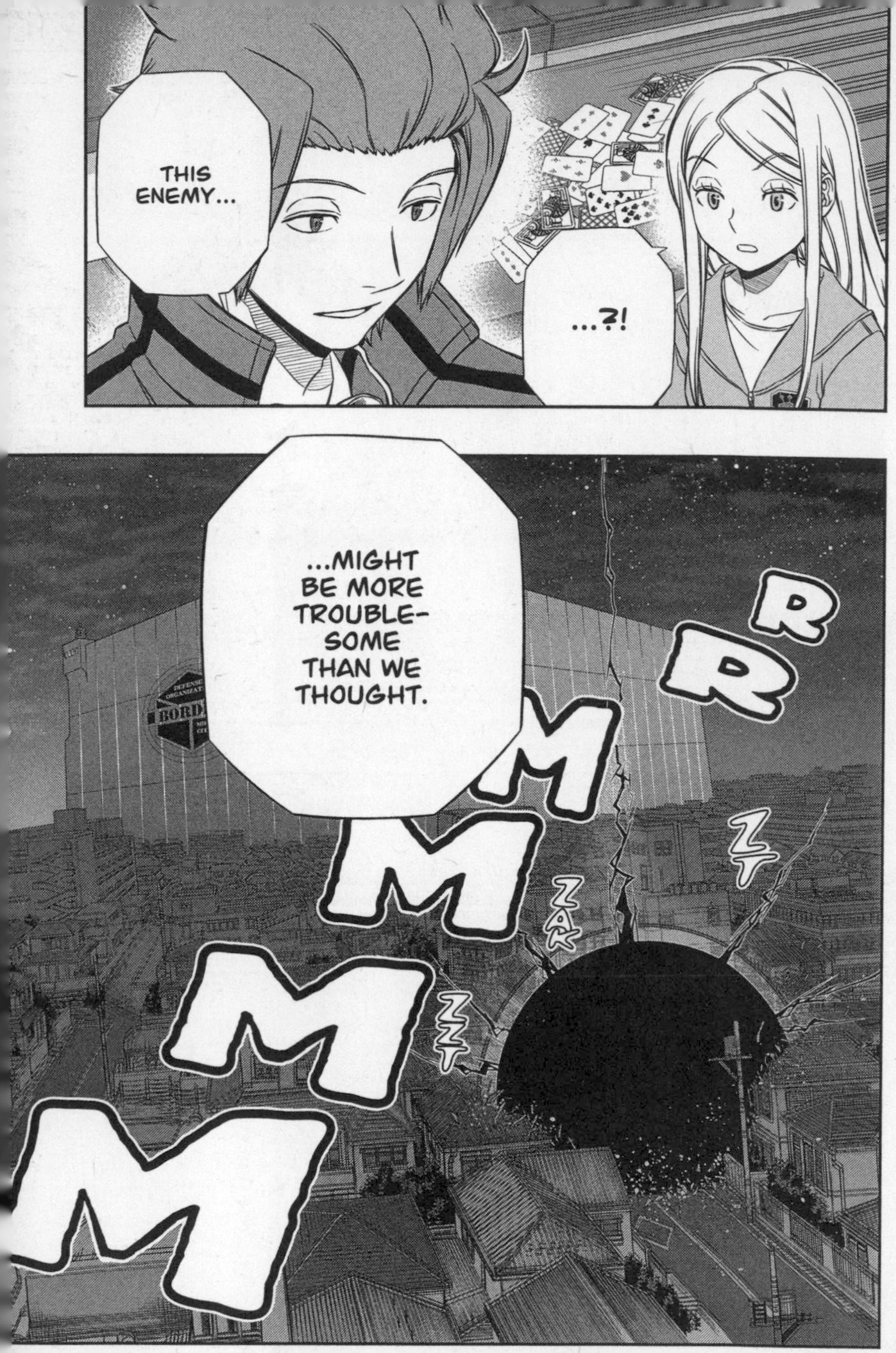
THIS ENEMY...
...?!
...MIGHT BE MORE TROUBLE-SOME THAN WE THOUGHT.
RRMMMM
ZT
ZAK
ZZZT

Mysterious Files 3

■Arashiyama Squad (Kitora)'s protector belt.

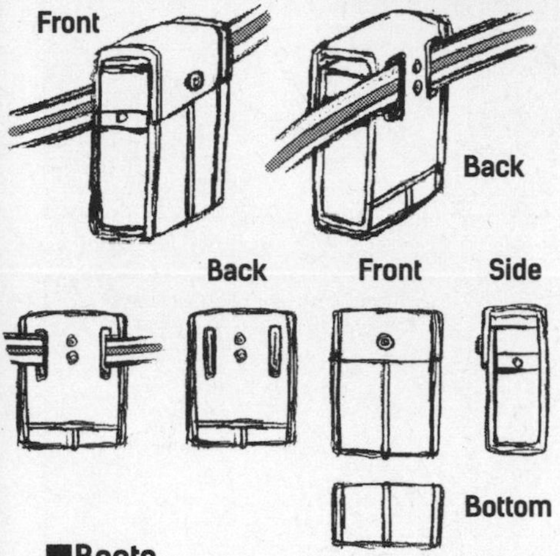
Front
Back
Back
Front
Side
Bottom

■Yuma and Kitora (Arashiyama Squad's belt.)

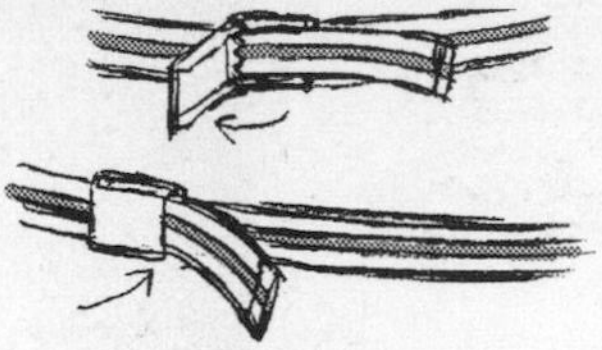

Made of cloth, held by a buckle with teeth. Yuma's belt doesn't have a stripe.

■Boots

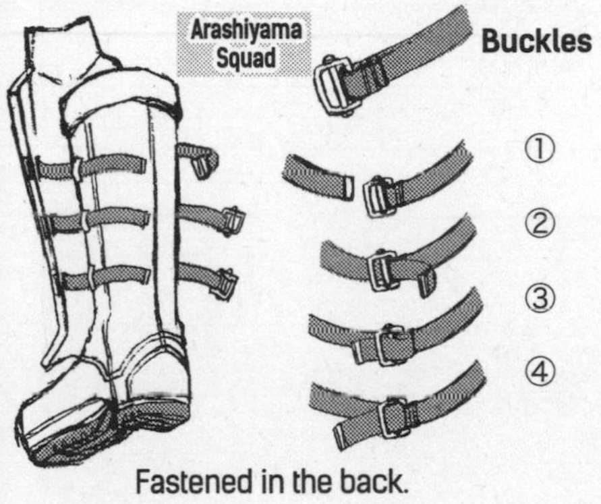
Arashiyama Squad
Buckles
①
②
③
④
Fastened in the back.

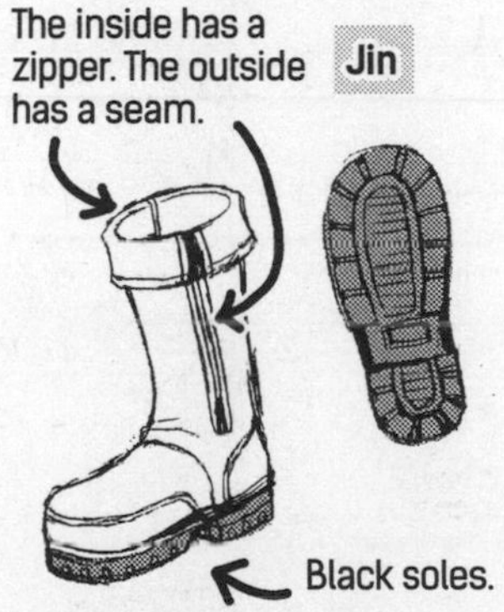
The inside has a zipper. The outside has a seam.
Jin
Black soles.

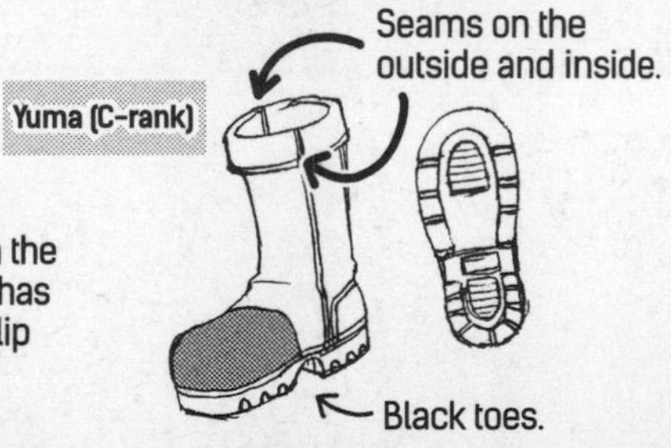
Seams on the outside and inside.
Yuma (C-rank)
Black toes.

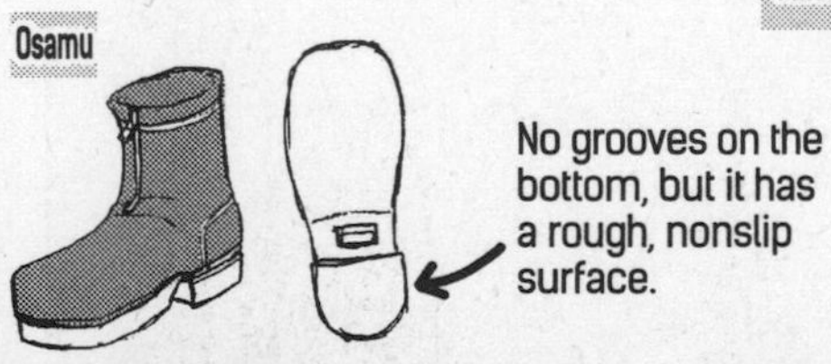
Osamu
No grooves on the bottom, but it has a rough, nonslip surface.

Chapter 124 Galopoula: Part 3

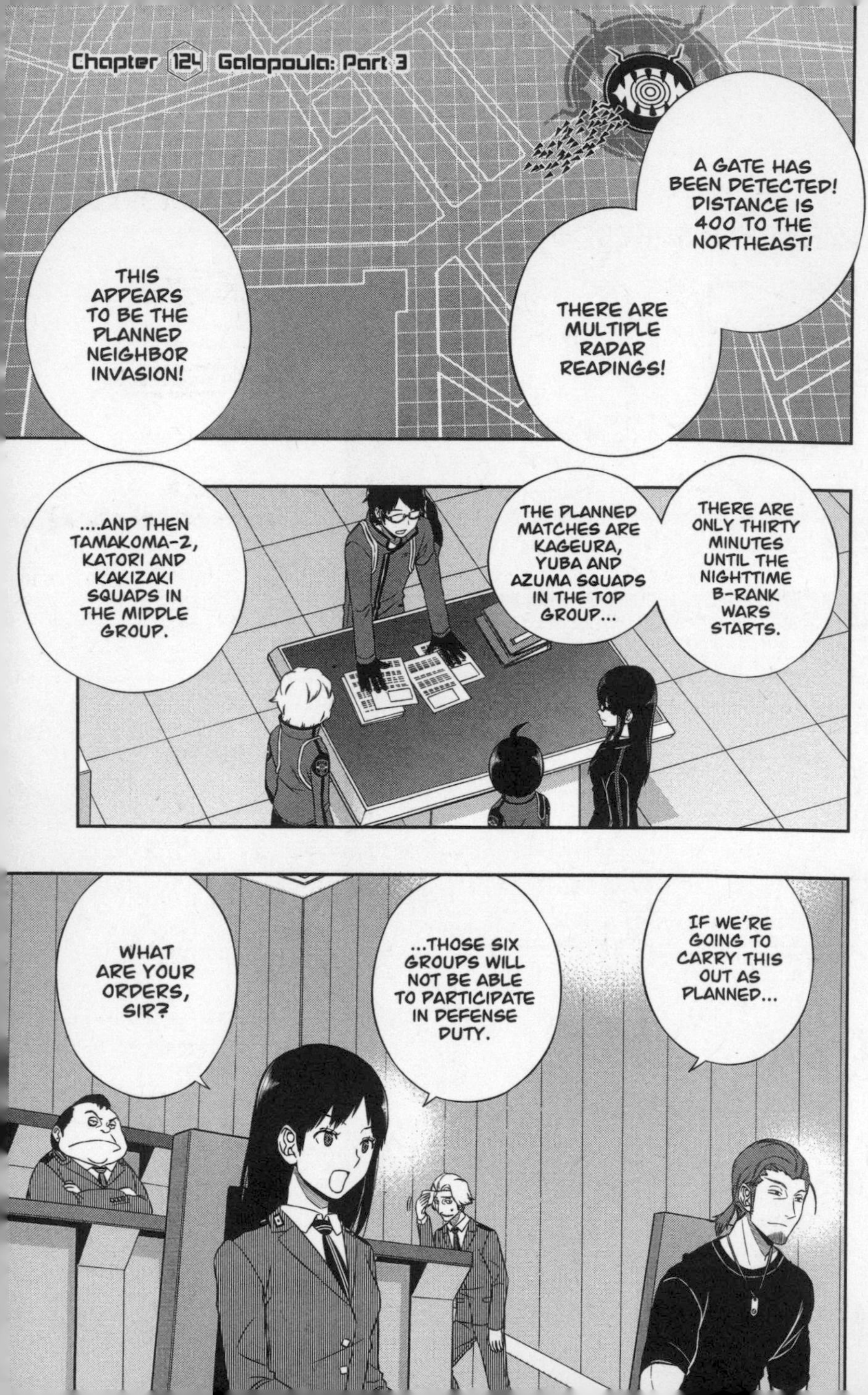
A GATE HAS BEEN DETECTED! DISTANCE IS 400 TO THE NORTHEAST!
THERE ARE MULTIPLE RADAR READINGS!
THIS APPEARS TO BE THE PLANNED NEIGHBOR INVASION!
THERE ARE ONLY THIRTY MINUTES UNTIL THE NIGHTTIME B-RANK WARS STARTS.
THE PLANNED MATCHES ARE KAGEURA, YUBA AND AZUMA SQUADS IN THE TOP GROUP...
....AND THEN TAMAKOMA-2, KATORI AND KAKIZAKI SQUADS IN THE MIDDLE GROUP.
IF WE'RE GOING TO CARRY THIS OUT AS PLANNED...
...THOSE SIX GROUPS WILL NOT BE ABLE TO PARTICIPATE IN DEFENSE DUTY.
WHAT ARE YOUR ORDERS, SIR?

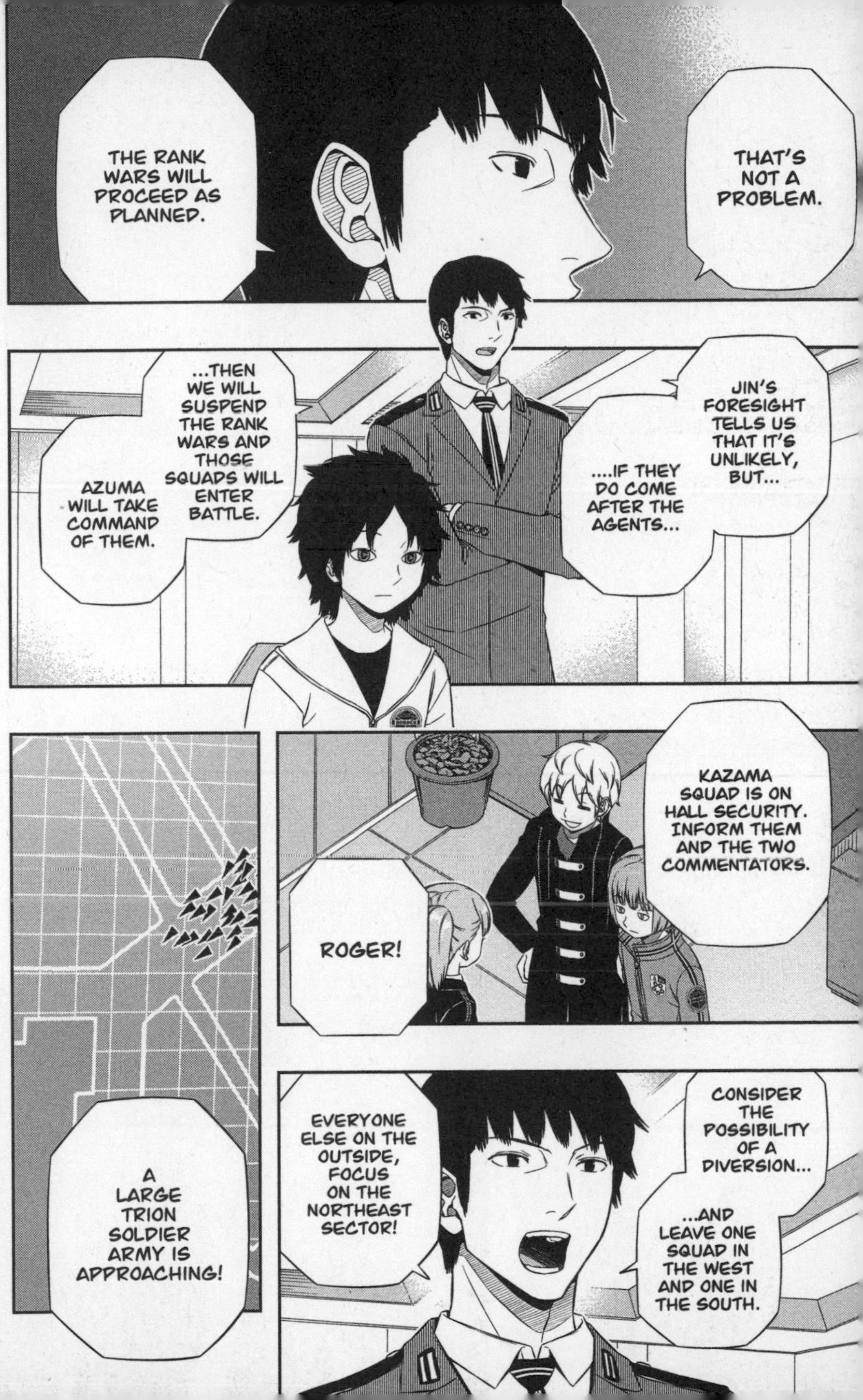
THAT'S NOT A PROBLEM.
THE RANK WARS WILL PROCEED AS PLANNED.
JIN'S FORESIGHT TELLS US THAT IT'S UNLIKELY, BUT...
....IF THEY DO COME AFTER THE AGENTS...
...THEN WE WILL SUSPEND THE RANK WARS AND THOSE SQUADS WILL ENTER BATTLE.
AZUMA WILL TAKE COMMAND OF THEM.
KAZAMA SQUAD IS ON HALL SECURITY. INFORM THEM AND THE TWO COMMENTATORS.
ROGER!
CONSIDER THE POSSIBILITY OF A DIVERSION...
...AND LEAVE ONE SQUAD IN THE WEST AND ONE IN THE SOUTH.
EVERYONE ELSE ON THE OUTSIDE, FOCUS ON THE NORTHEAST SECTOR!
A LARGE TRION SOLDIER ARMY IS APPROACHING!

Chapter 124
Galopoula: Part 3

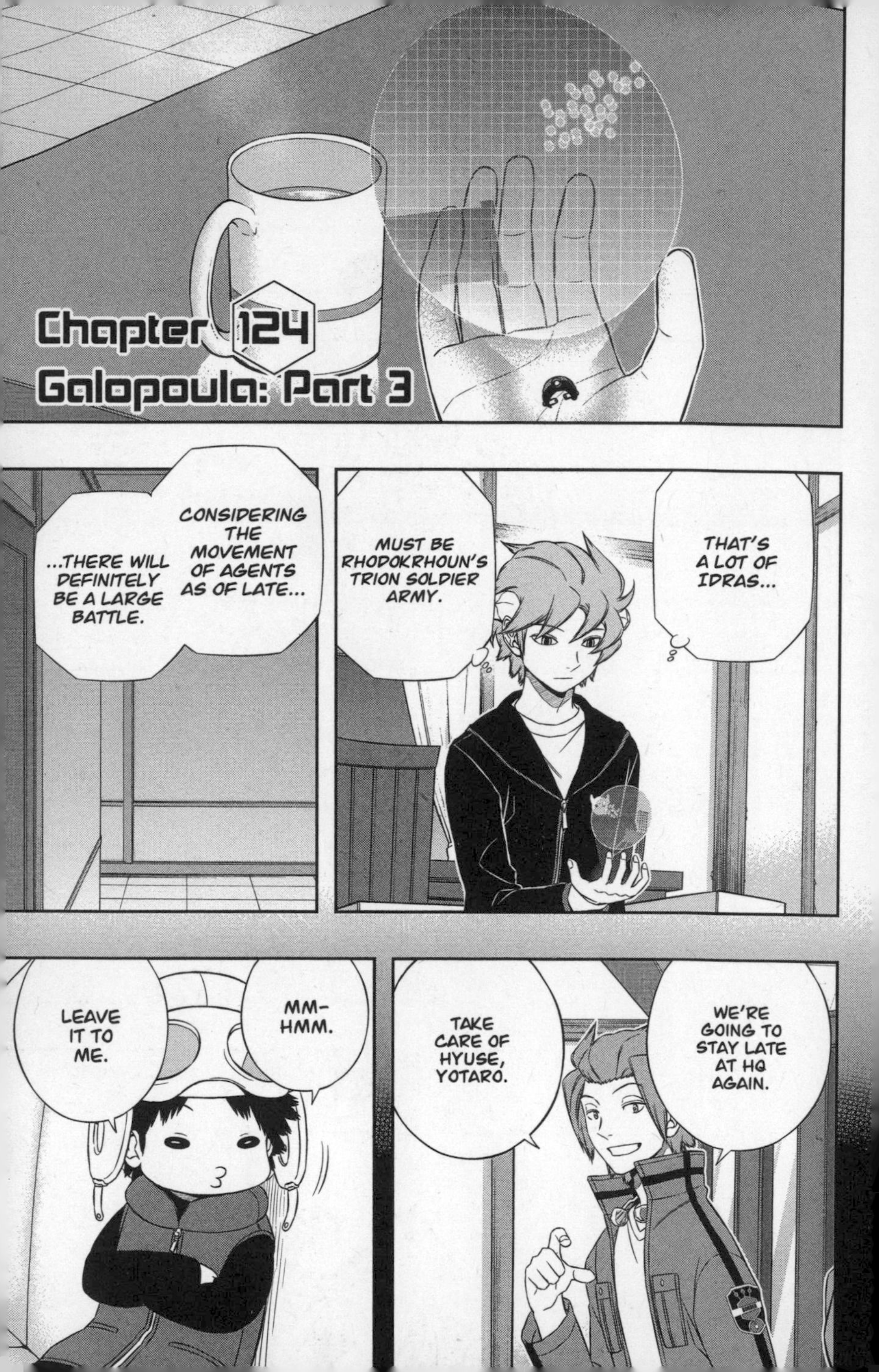
THAT'S A LOT OF IDRAS...
MUST BE RHODOKRHOUN'S TRION SOLDIER ARMY.
CONSIDERING THE MOVEMENT OF AGENTS AS OF LATE...
...THERE WILL DEFINITELY BE A LARGE BATTLE.
WE'RE GOING TO STAY LATE AT HQ AGAIN.
TAKE CARE OF HYUSE, YOTARO.
MM-HMM.
LEAVE IT TO ME.

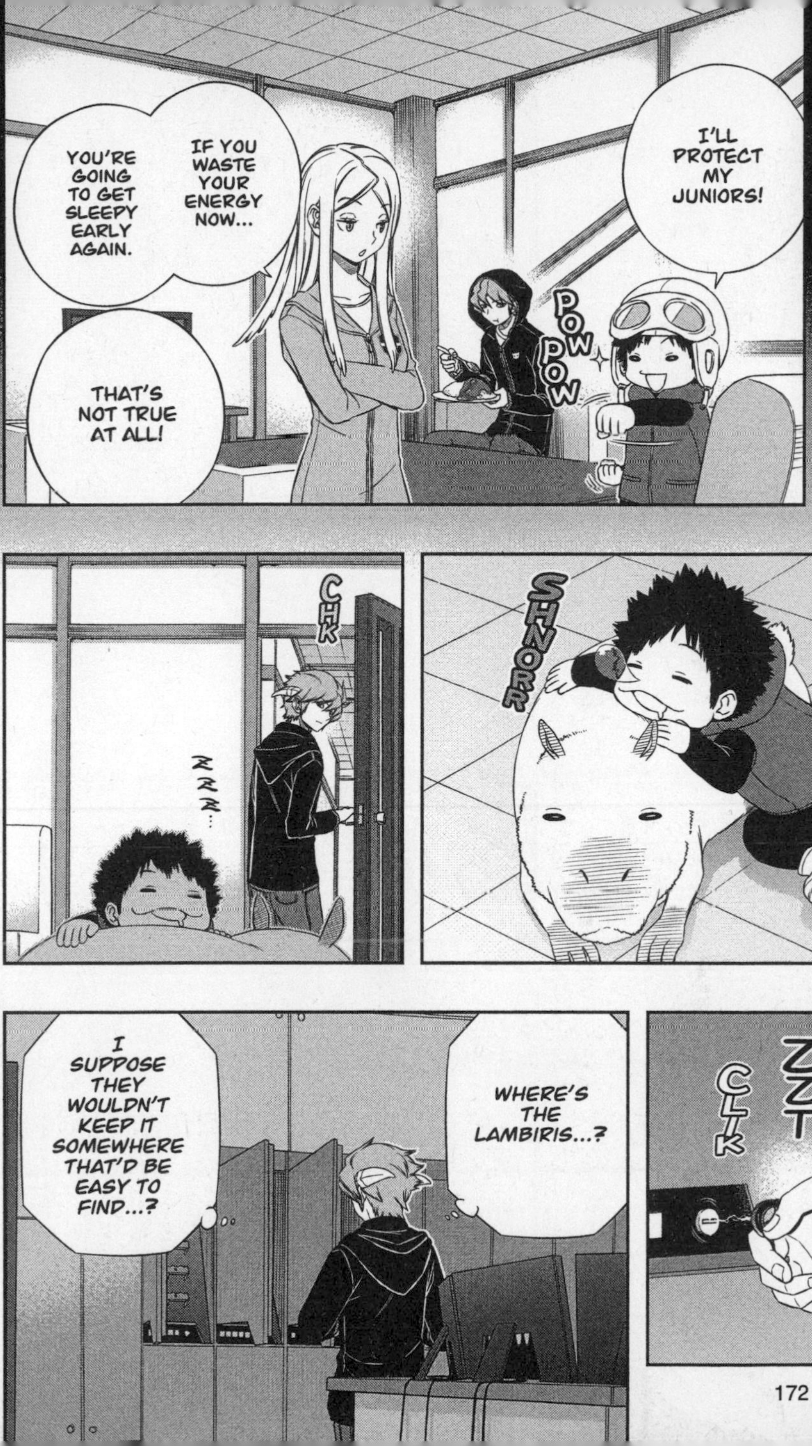
I'LL PROTECT MY JUNIORS!
POW POW POW
IF YOU WASTE YOUR ENERGY NOW...
YOU'RE GOING TO GET SLEEPY EARLY AGAIN.
THAT'S NOT TRUE AT ALL!
SHNORR
CHK
ZZZ...
ZZT
CLIK
WHERE'S THE LAMBIRIS...?
I SUPPOSE THEY WOULDN'T KEEP IT SOMEWHERE THAT'D BE EASY TO FIND...?

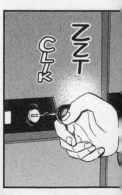

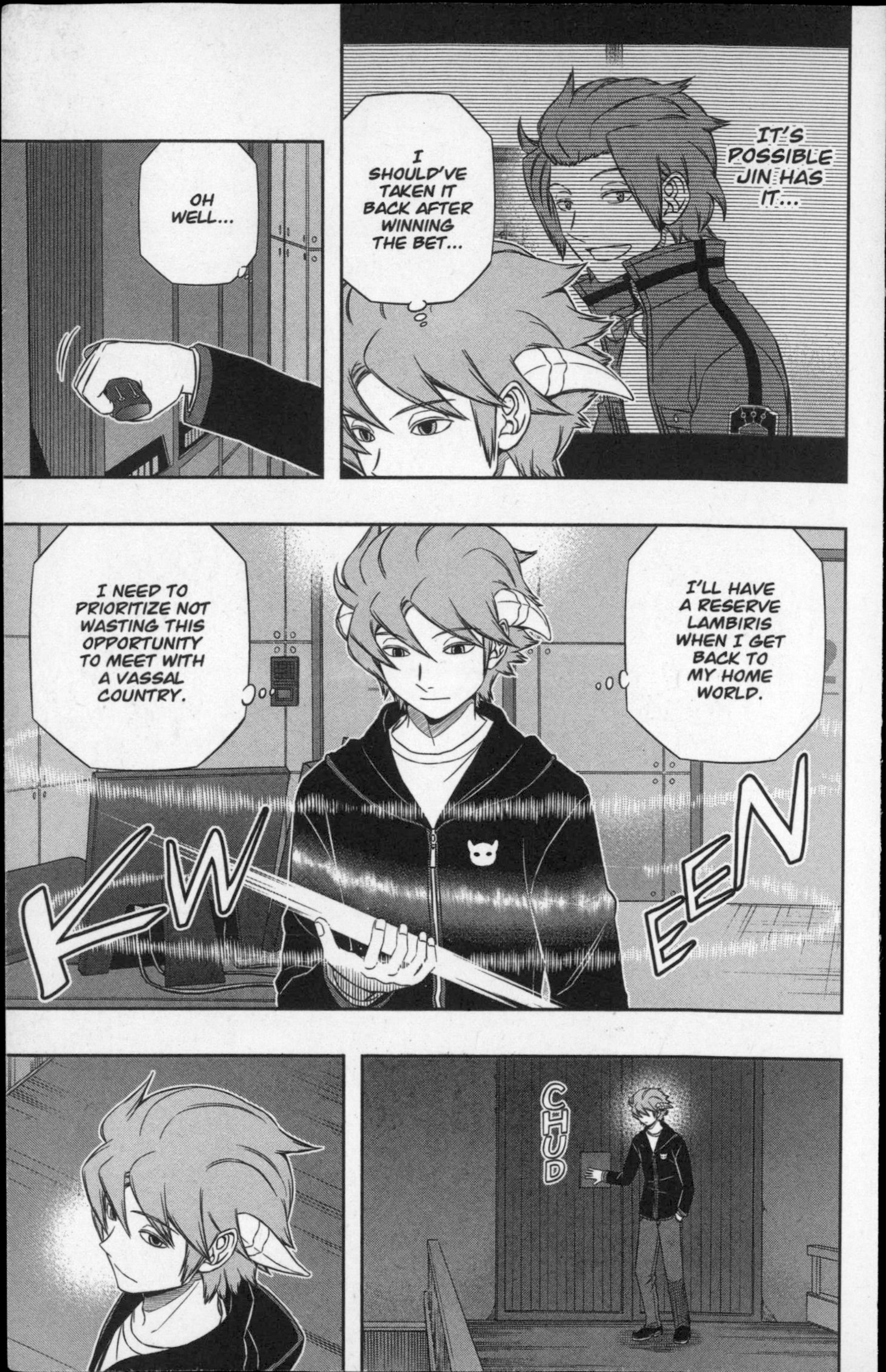
IT'S POSSIBLE JIN HAS IT...
I SHOULD'VE TAKEN IT BACK AFTER WINNING THE BET...
OH WELL...
I'LL HAVE A RESERVE LAMBIRIS WHEN I GET BACK TO MY HOME WORLD.
I NEED TO PRIORITIZE NOT WASTING THIS OPPORTUNITY TO MEET WITH A VASSAL COUNTRY.
KWEEN
CHUD

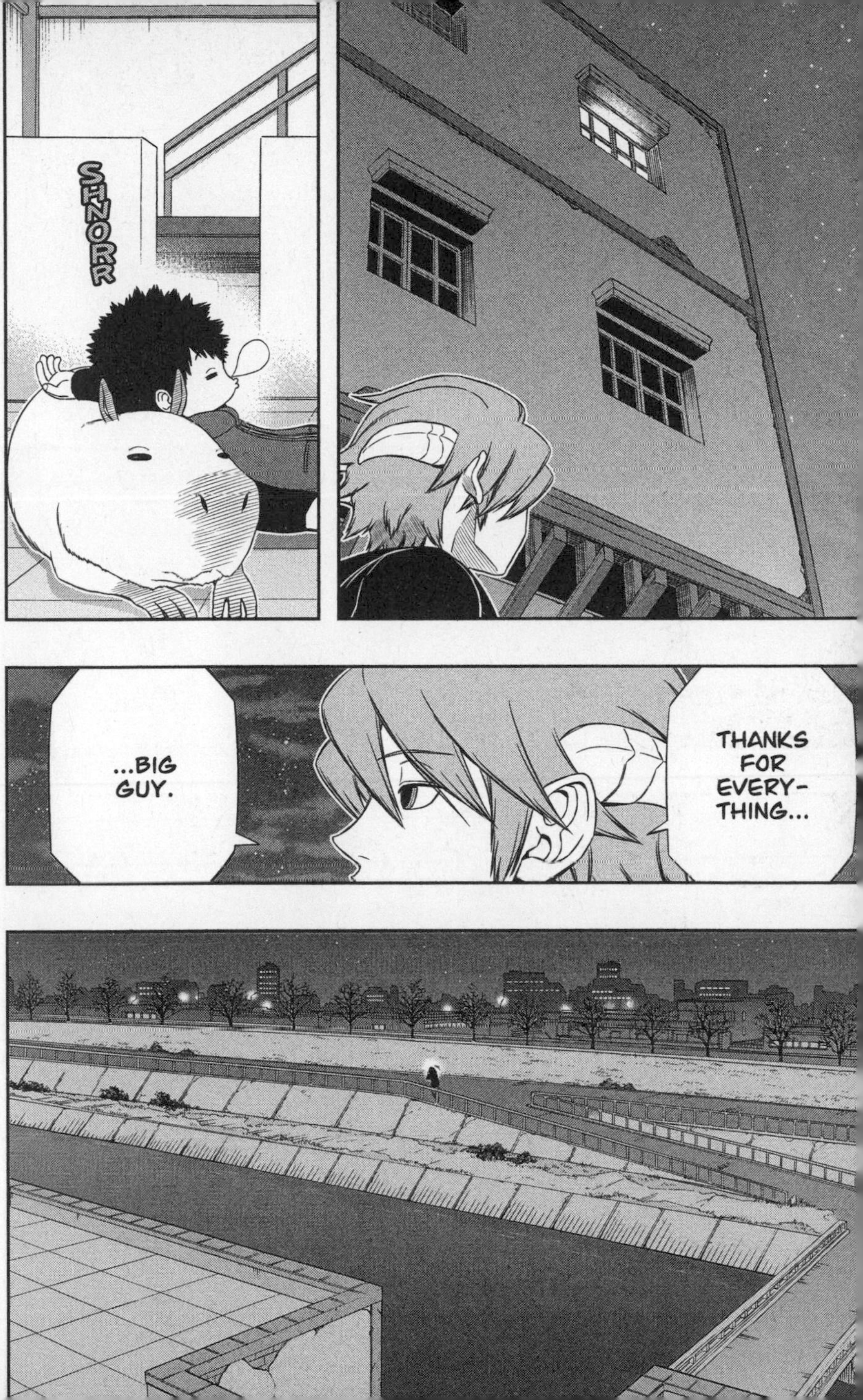
SHNORR
THANKS FOR EVERY-THING...
...BIG GUY.

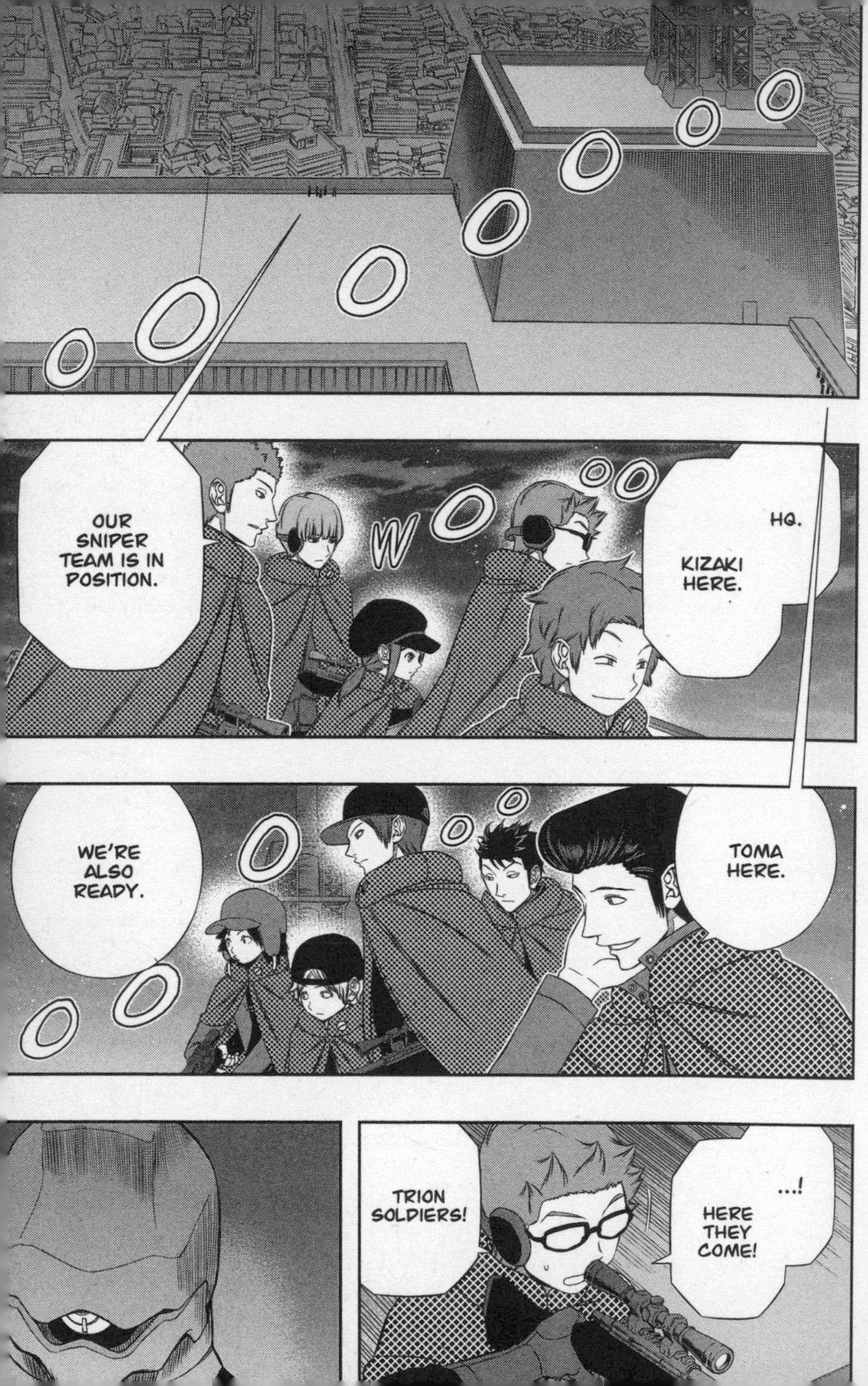
HQ.
KIZAKI HERE.
OUR SNIPER TEAM IS IN POSITION.
TOMA HERE.
WE'RE ALSO READY.
...!
HERE THEY COME!
TRION SOLDIERS!

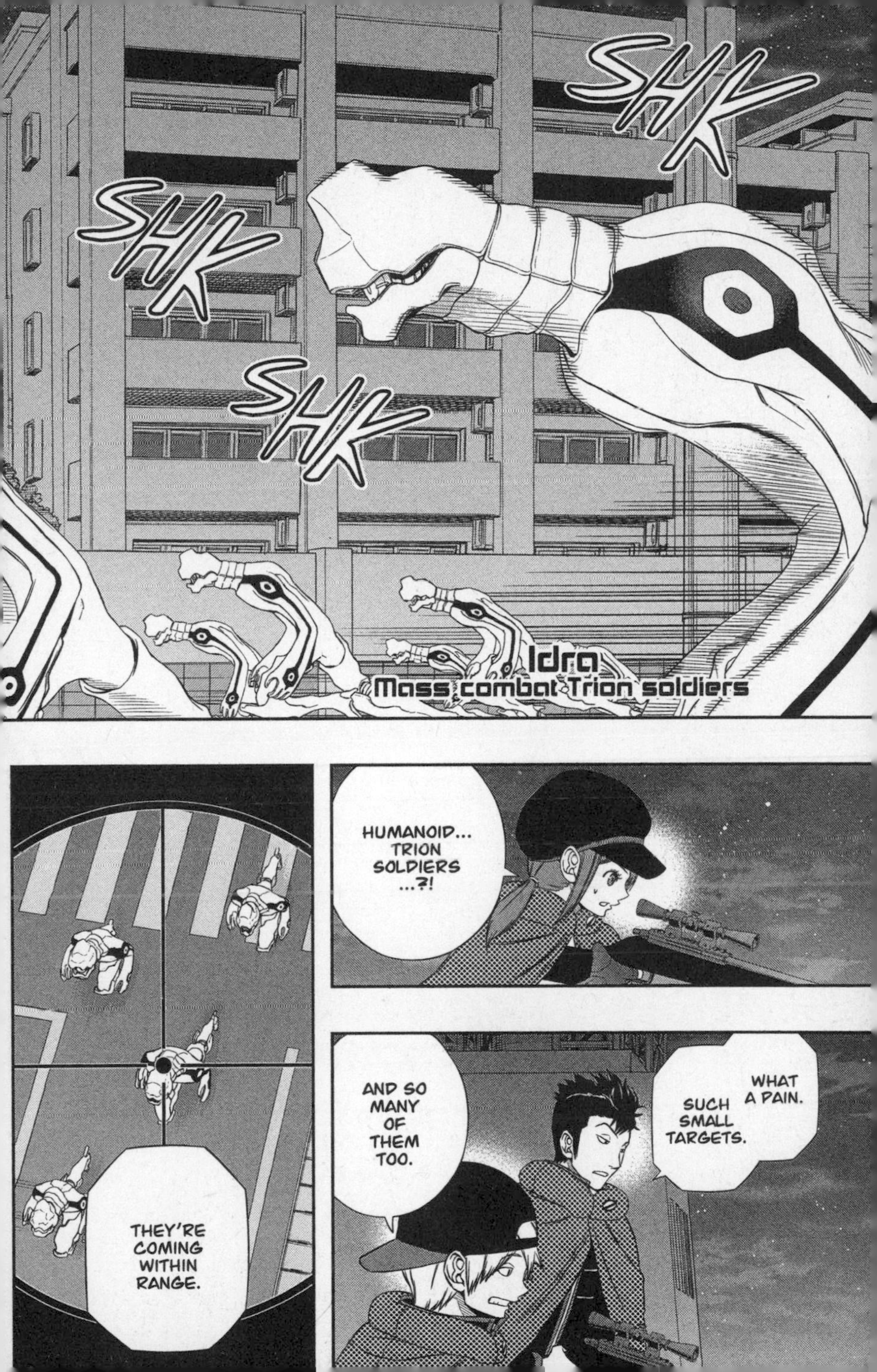
SHK
SHK
SHK
Idra
Mass combat Trion soldiers
HUMANOID... TRION SOLDIERS ...?!
WHAT A PAIN.
SUCH SMALL TARGETS.
AND SO MANY OF THEM TOO.
THEY'RE COMING WITHIN RANGE.

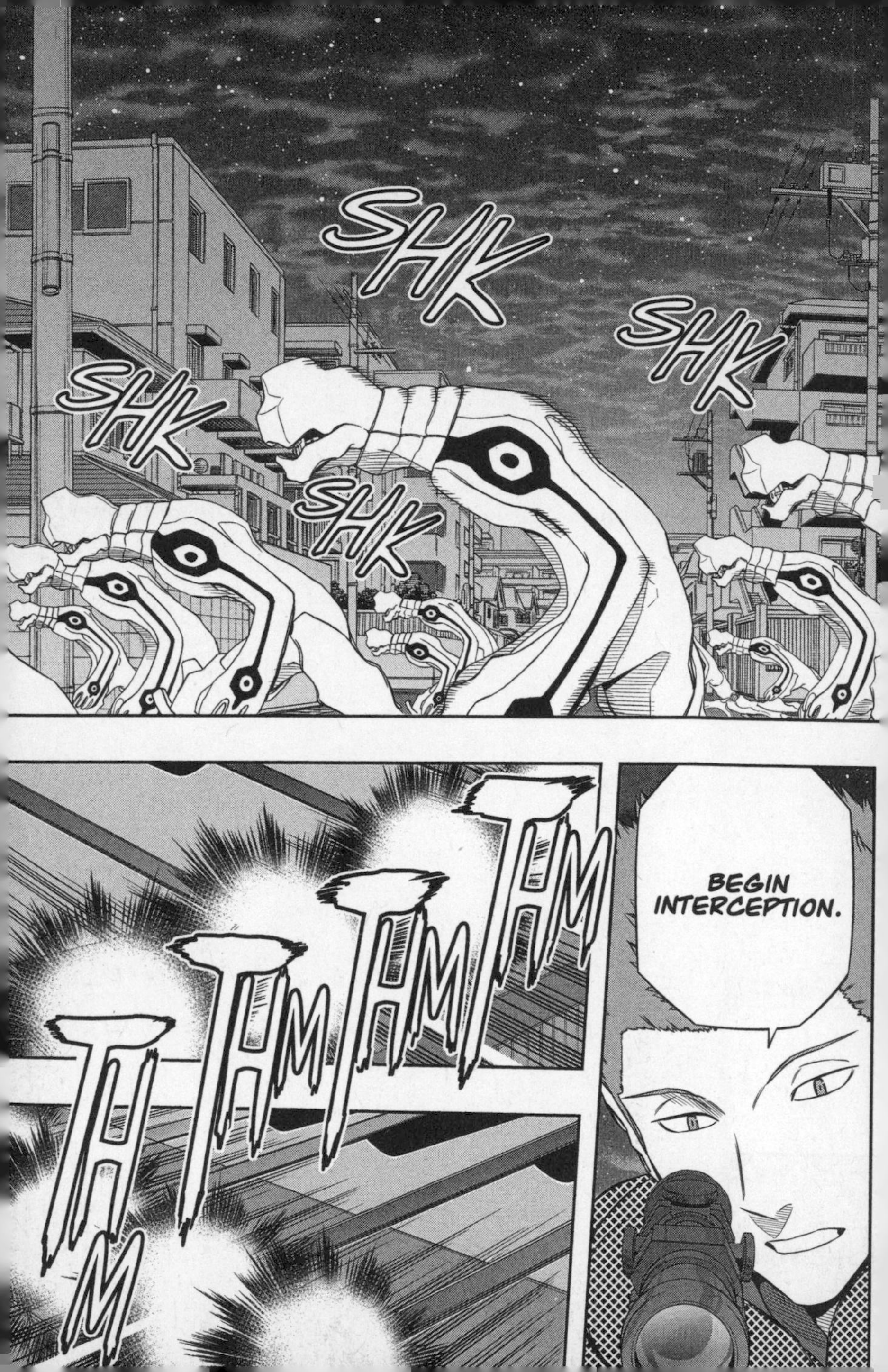
SHK
SHK
SHK
SHK
BEGIN INTERCEPTION.
THMTHMTHMTHM

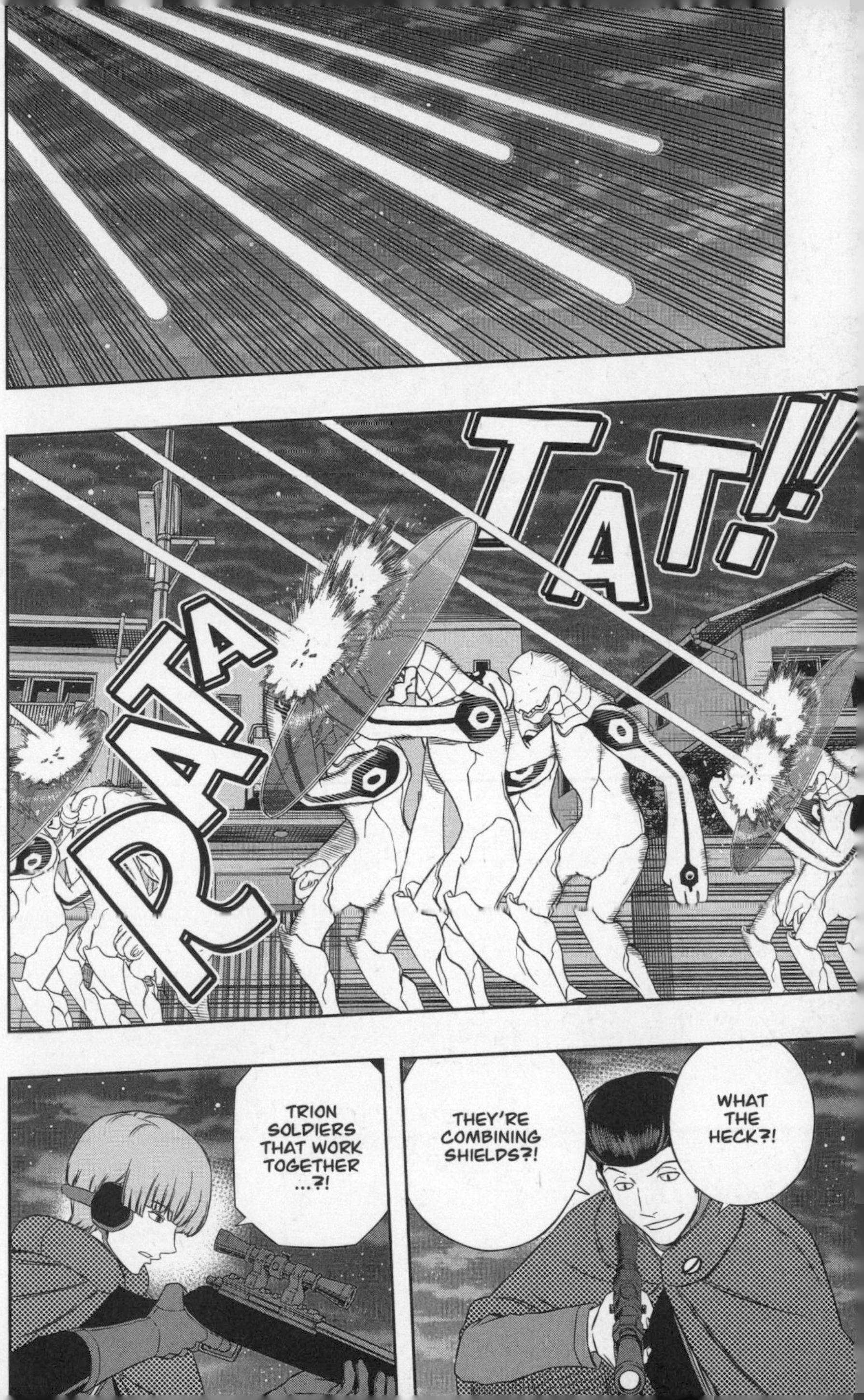
RATATAT!!
WHAT THE HECK?!
THEY'RE COMBINING SHIELDS?!
TRION SOLDIERS THAT WORK TOGETHER ...?!

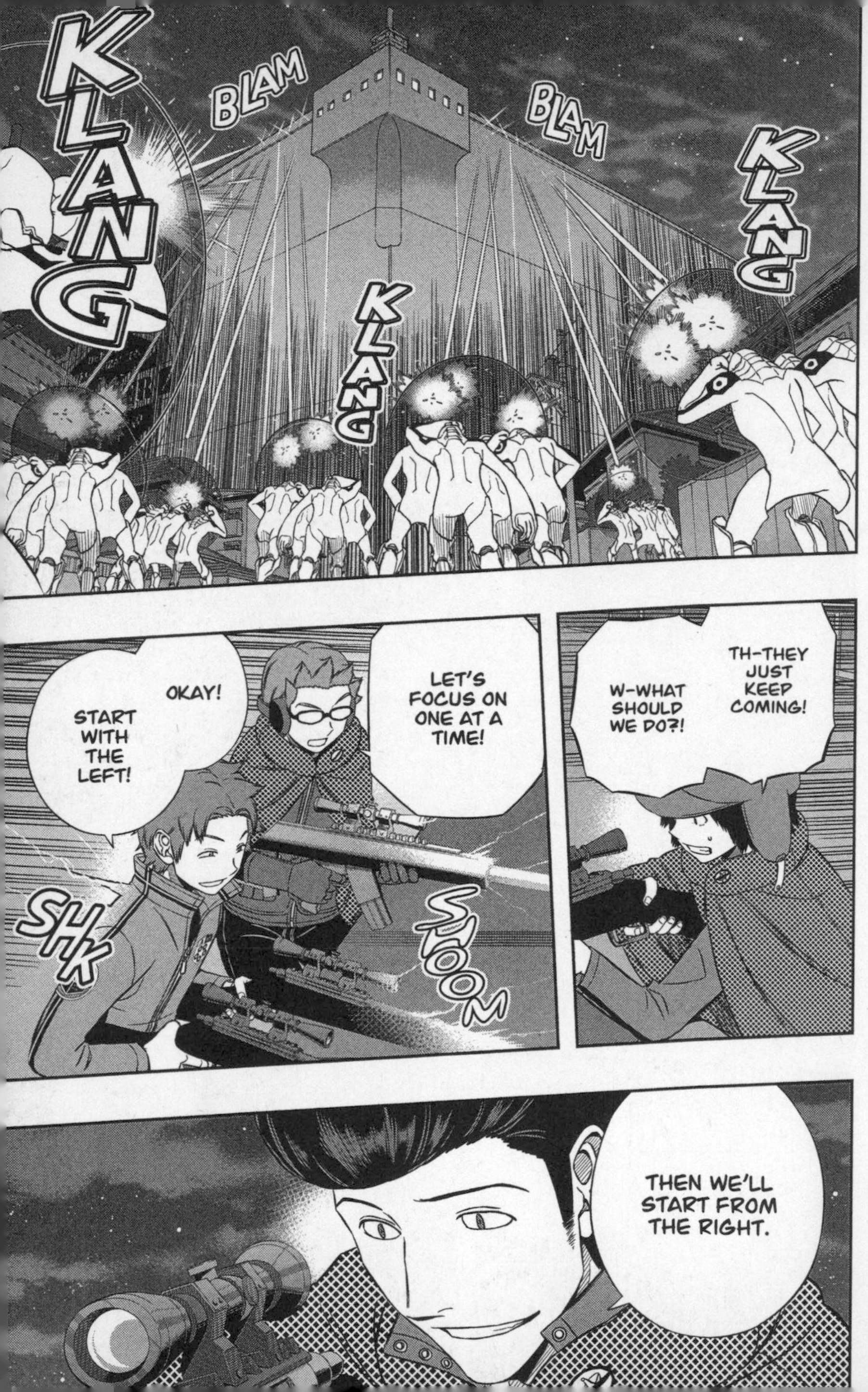
KLANG
BLAM
KLANG
BLAM
KLANG
TH-THEY JUST KEEP COMING!
W-WHAT SHOULD WE DO?!
LET'S FOCUS ON ONE AT A TIME!
OKAY!
START WITH THE LEFT!
SHOOM
SHK
THEN WE'LL START FROM THE RIGHT.

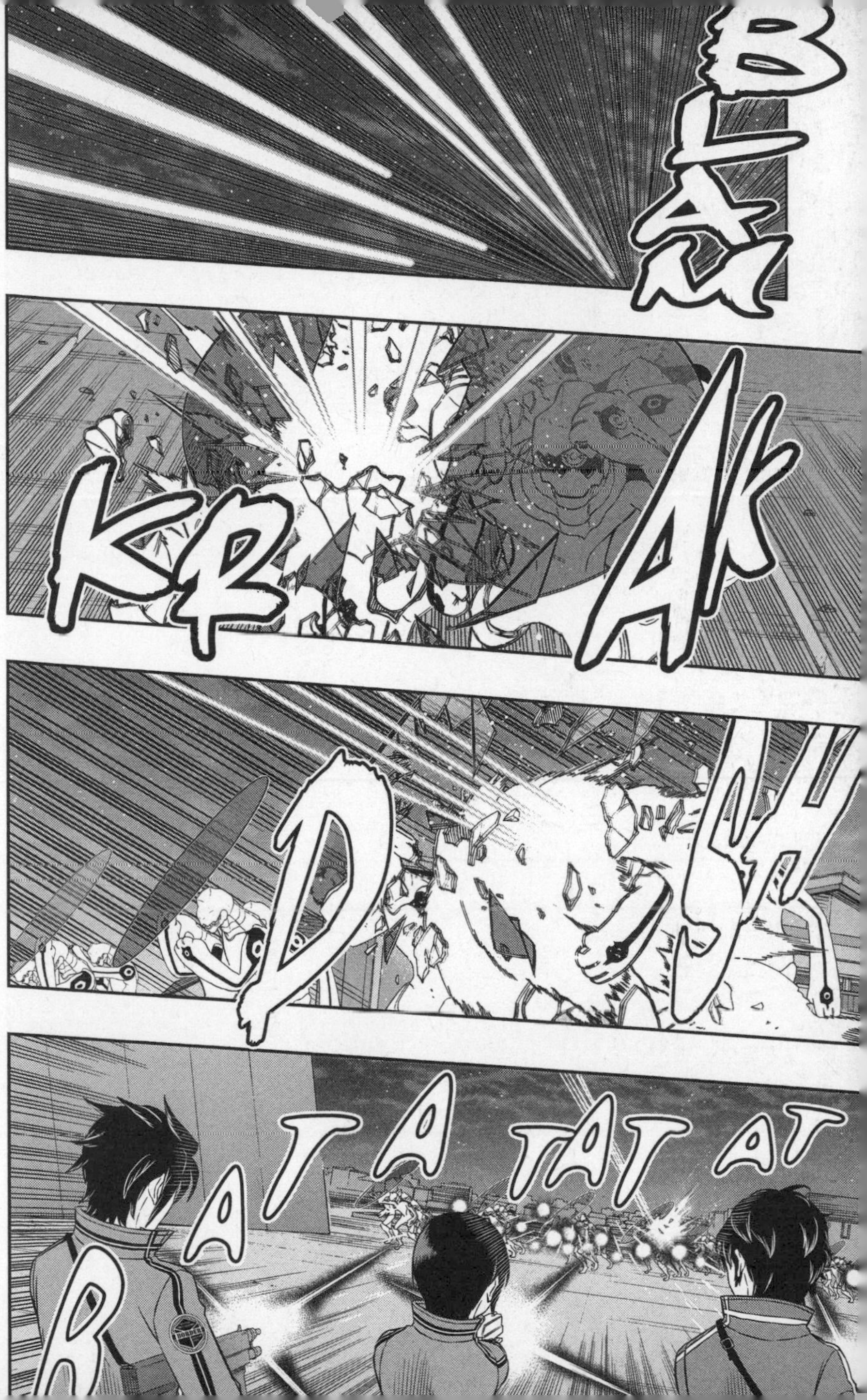
BLAM
KRAK
DASH
RATATATAT

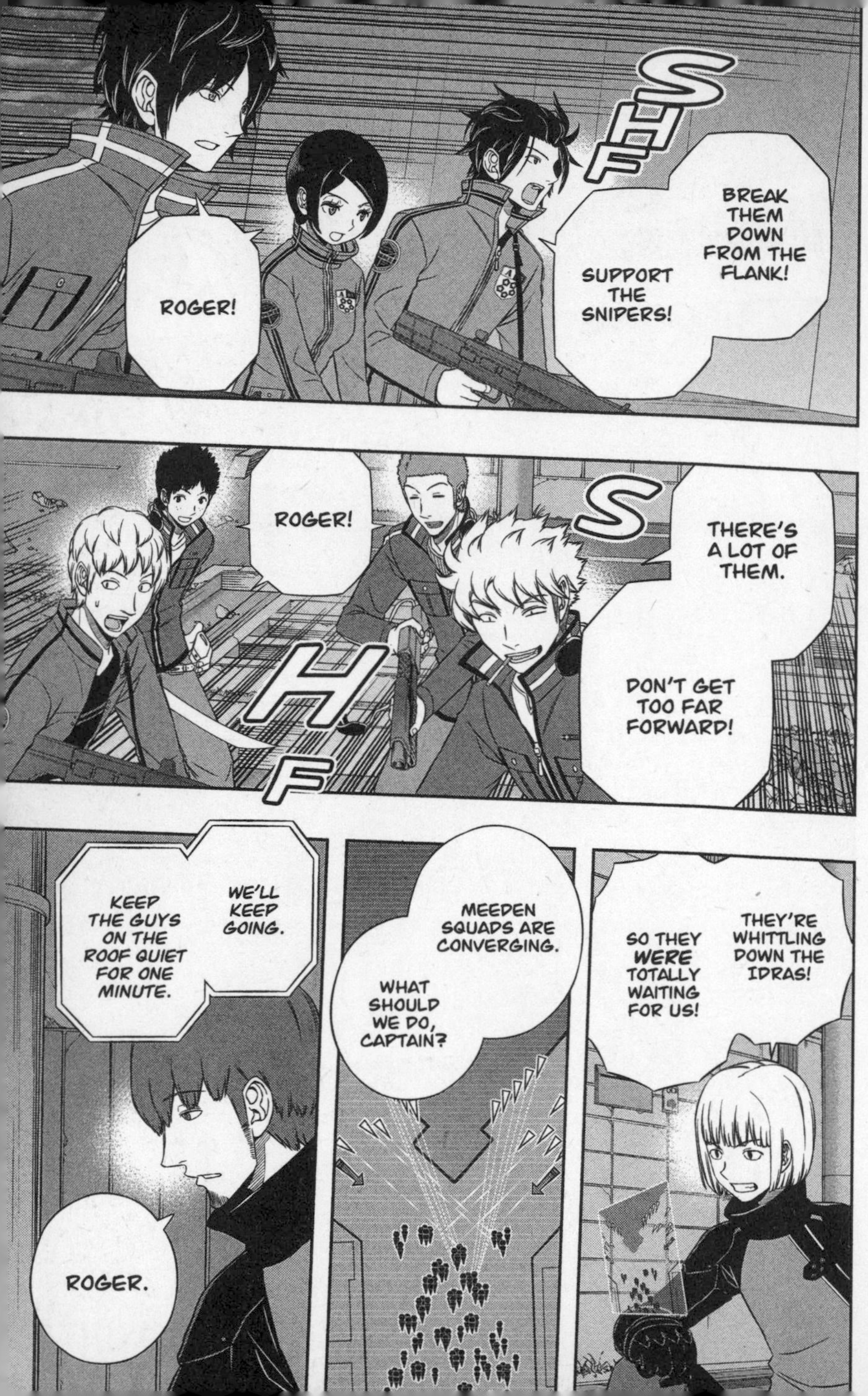
SHF
BREAK THEM DOWN FROM THE FLANK!
SUPPORT THE SNIPERS!
ROGER!
S
THERE'S A LOT OF THEM.
DON'T GET TOO FAR FORWARD!
HF
ROGER!
THEY'RE WHITTLING DOWN THE IDRAS!
SO THEY **WERE** TOTALLY WAITING FOR US!
MEEDEN SQUADS ARE CONVERGING.
WHAT SHOULD WE DO, CAPTAIN?
WE'LL KEEP GOING.
KEEP THE GUYS ON THE ROOF QUIET FOR ONE MINUTE.
ROGER.

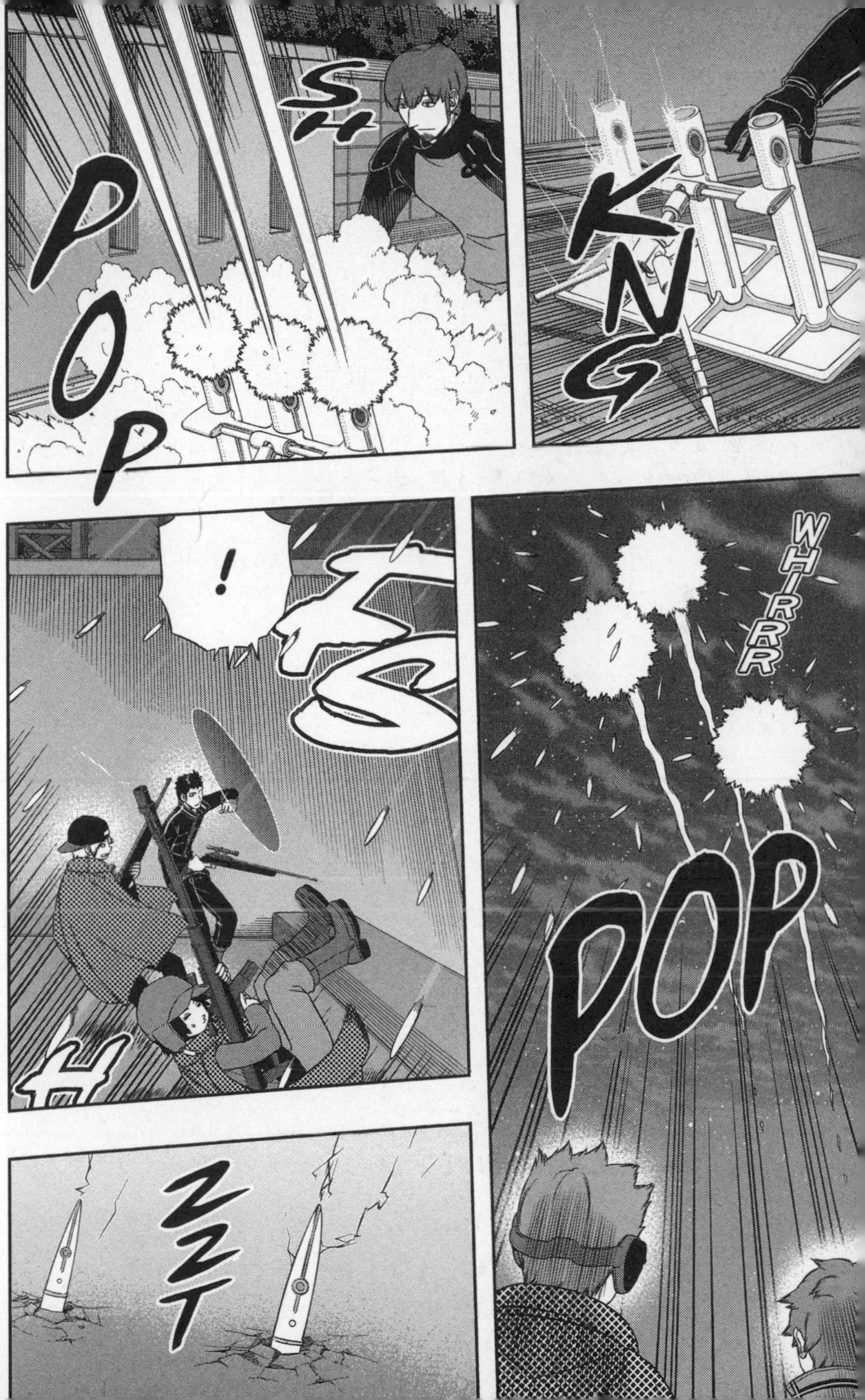
KNG
SH
POP
WHIRRR
POP
!
ZZT

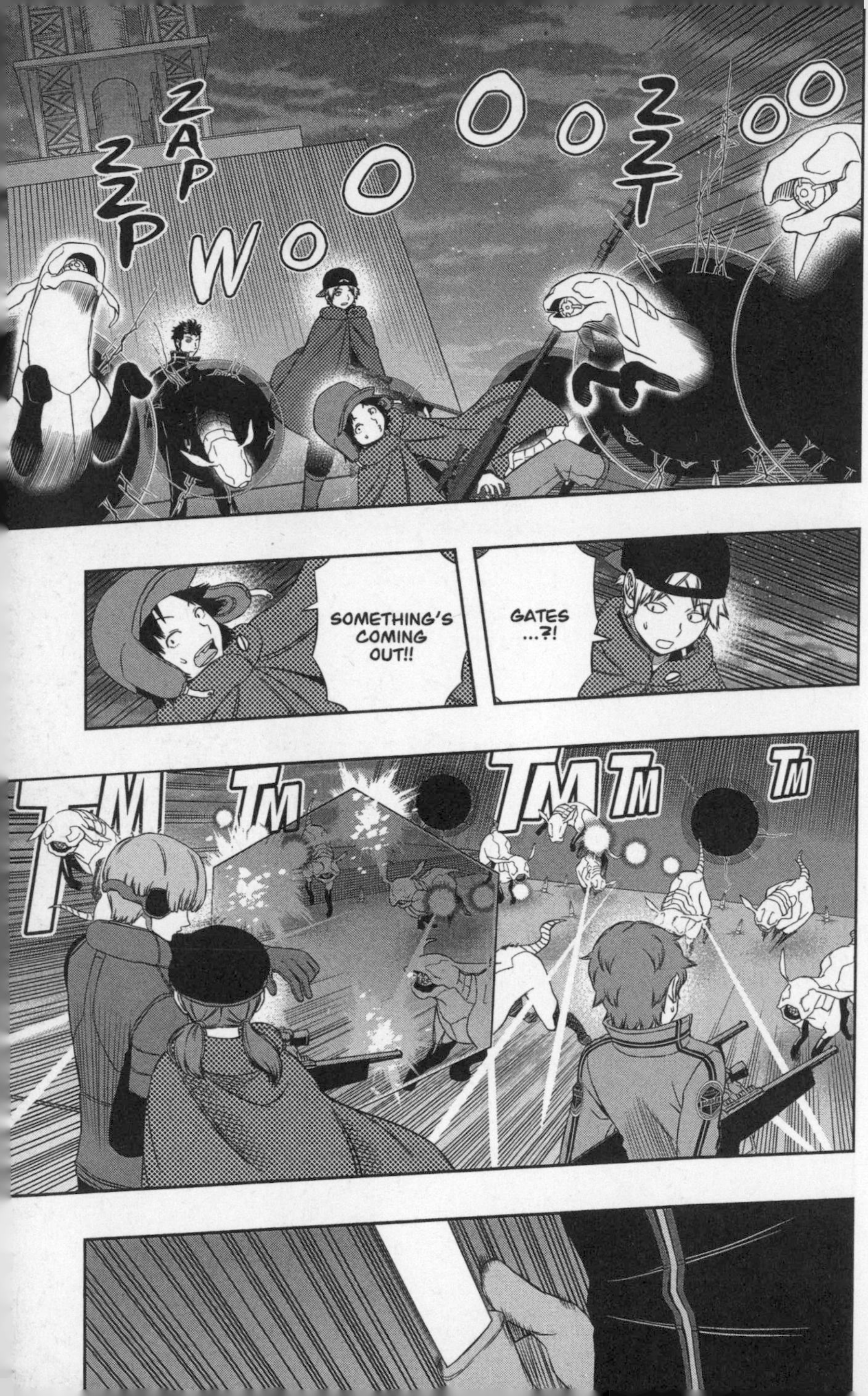
ZZZT
WOOOOOOO
ZAP
ZZP
GATES ...?!
SOMETHING'S COMING OUT!!
TM
TM
TM
TM
TM

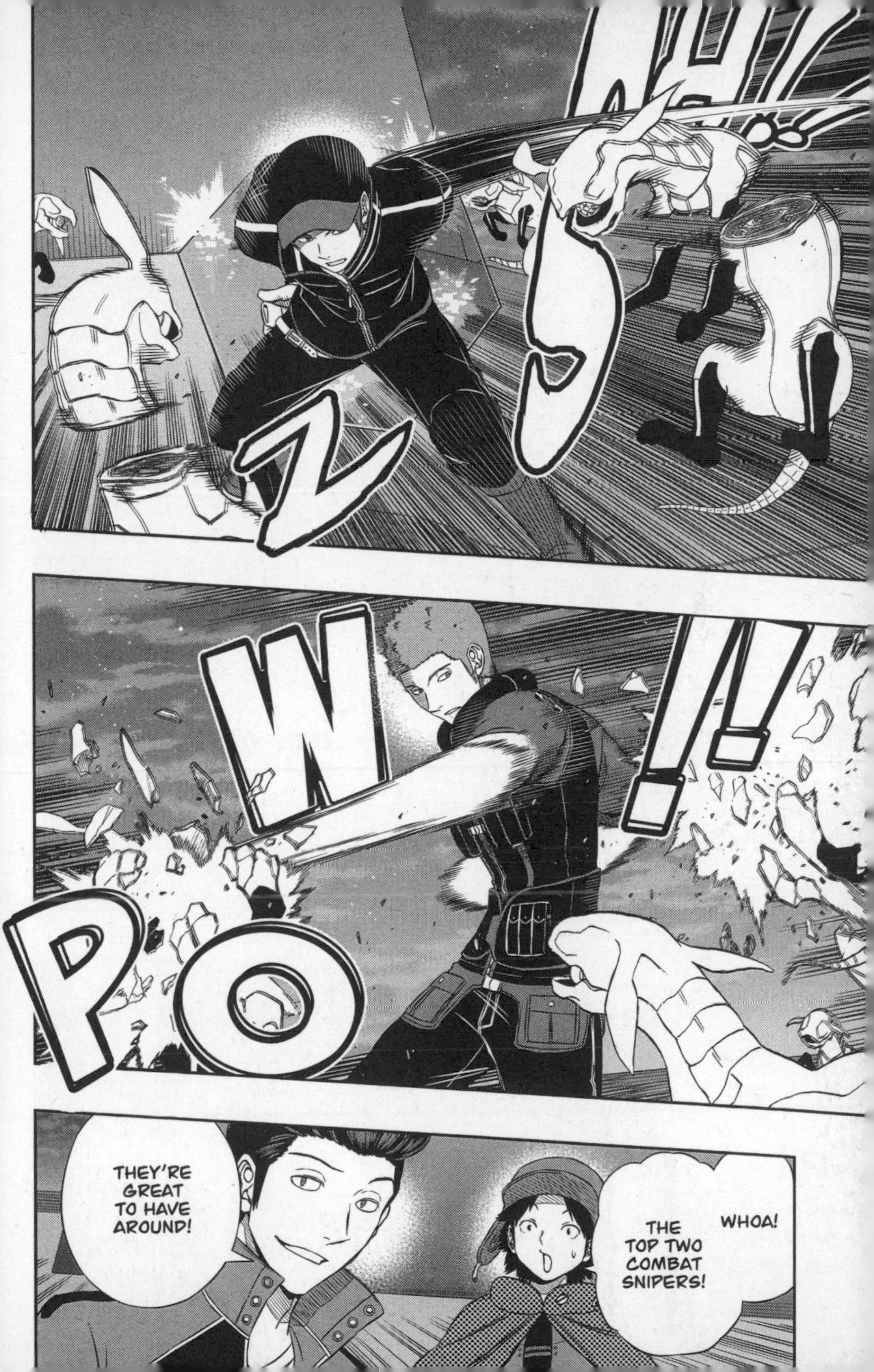
POW!!
WHOA!
THE TOP TWO COMBAT SNIPERS!
THEY'RE GREAT TO HAVE AROUND!

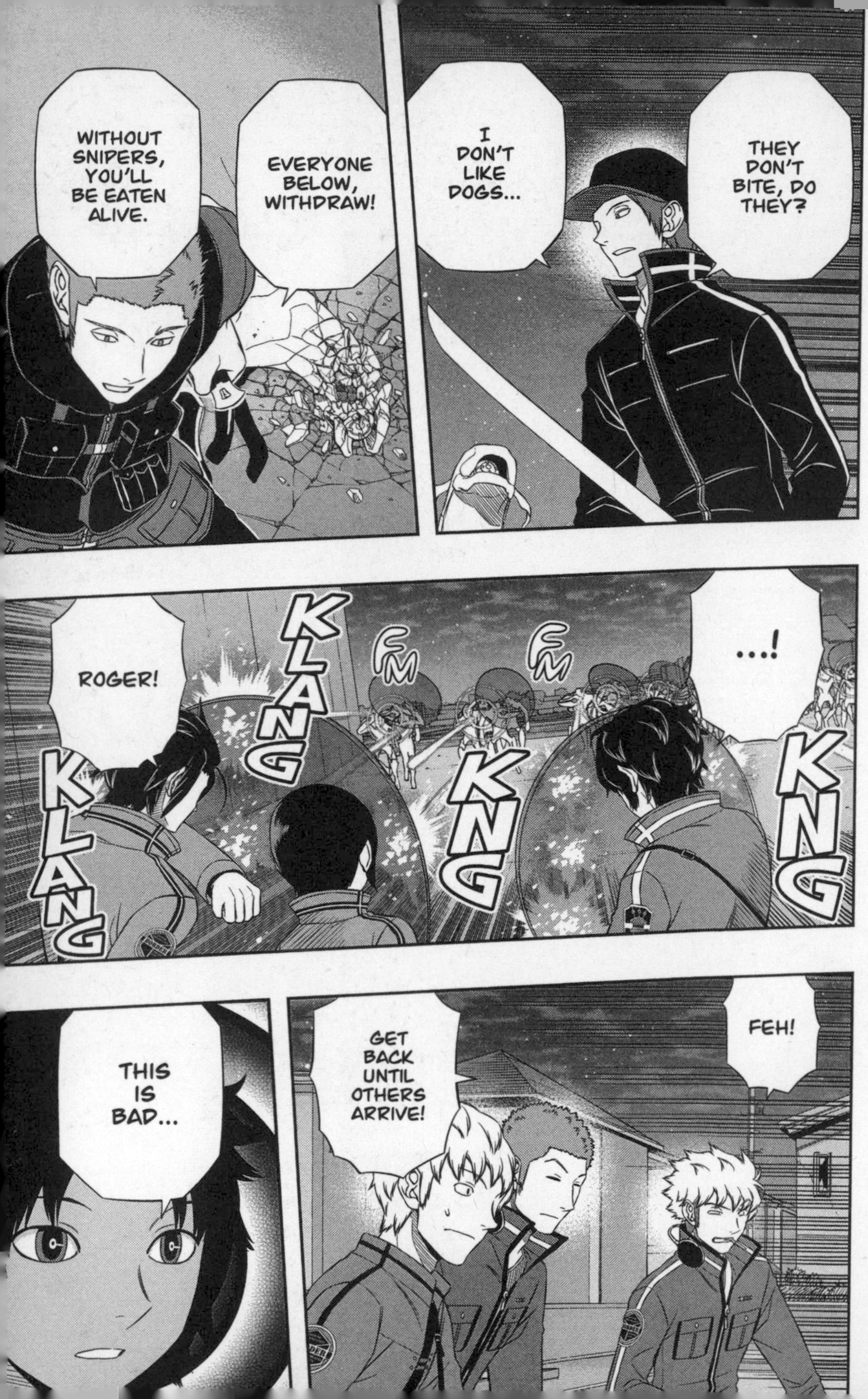
THEY DON'T BITE, DO THEY?
I DON'T LIKE DOGS...
EVERYONE BELOW, WITHDRAW!
WITHOUT SNIPERS, YOU'LL BE EATEN ALIVE.
...!
FM
FM
KLANG
ROGER!
KNG
KNG
KLANG
FEH!
GET BACK UNTIL OTHERS ARRIVE!
THIS IS BAD...

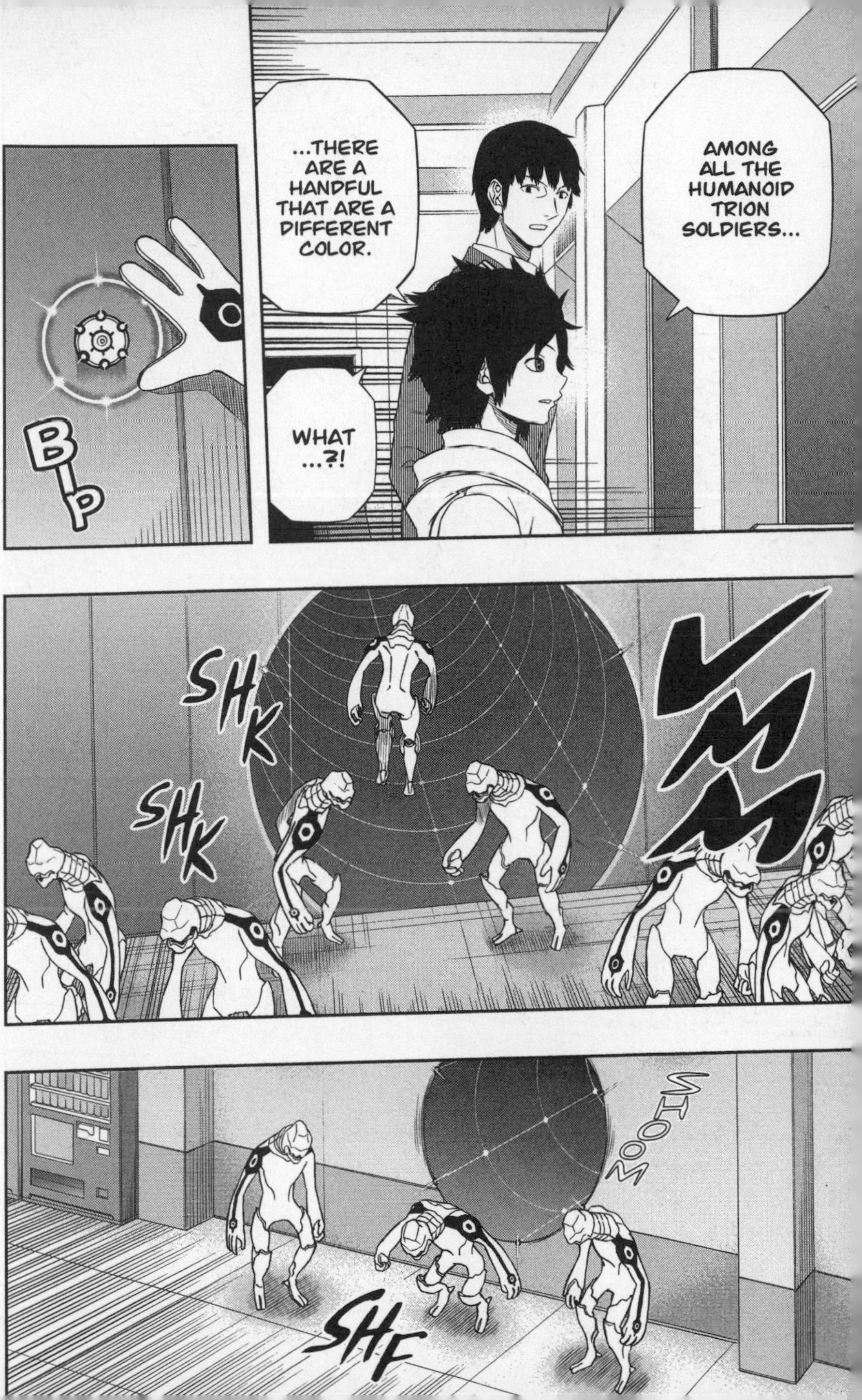
AMONG ALL THE HUMANOID TRION SOLDIERS...
...THERE ARE A HANDFUL THAT ARE A DIFFERENT COLOR.
WHAT...?!
BIP
VMM
SHK
SHK
SHOOM
SHF

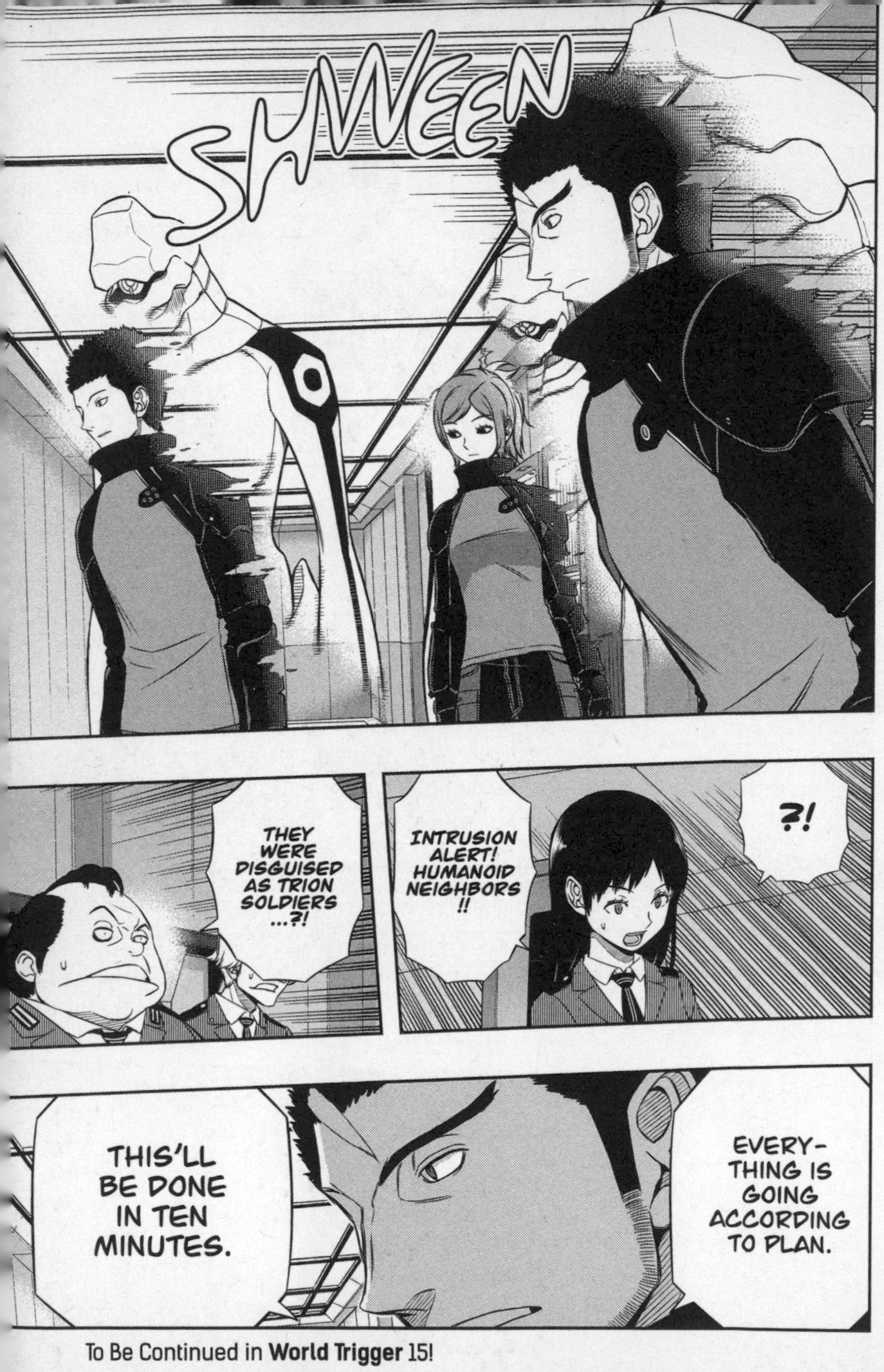
SHWEEN
?!
INTRUSION ALERT! HUMANOID NEIGHBORS!!
THEY WERE DISGUISED AS TRION SOLDIERS ...?!
EVERY-THING IS GOING ACCORDING TO PLAN.
THIS'LL BE DONE IN TEN MINUTES.

To Be Continued in **World Trigger** 15!

WORLD TRIGGER

Bonus Character Pages

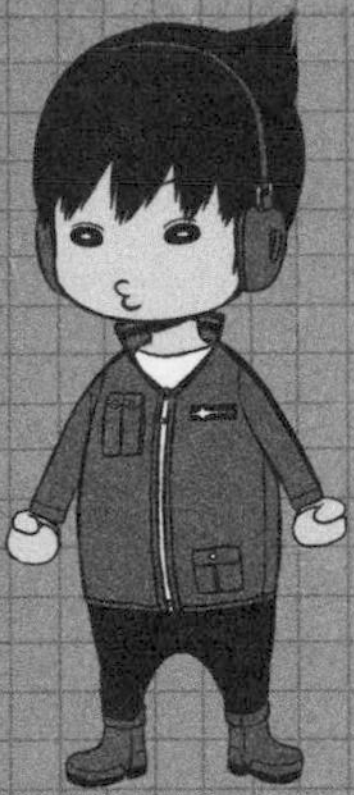

OKUDERA

Exploding with Prudence

Azuma squad's rear cowlick. A quick-learning child prodigy who has always been calm. After a Rabit took him out during the invasion, he's become even more prudent! He's school friends with Tokieda and Torimaru and has had a crush on Mako, who lived near him, ever since he was little, but not even Koarai has noticed. You can do it, Okudera! His messy hair is actually just bedhead.

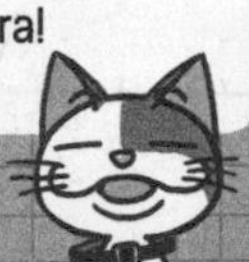

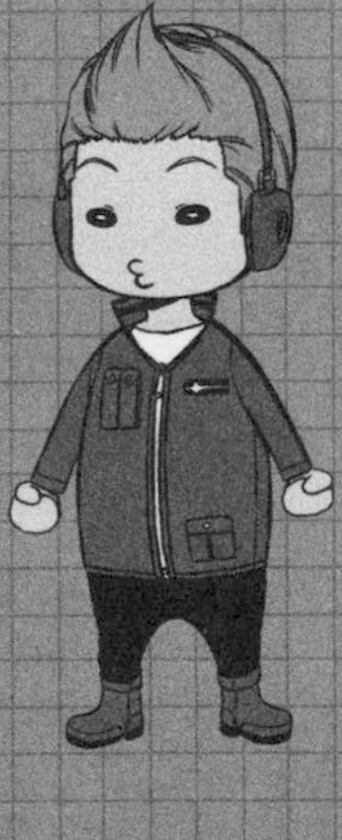

KOALA

Almost Eaten but Still Looking for Fun

Azuma Squad's forward cowlick. A child prodigy who has always been carefree. Even though a Rabit almost ate him in the invasion, he has the mental strength to move on. He's school friends with Taichi and Sato-ken. He had to cling to Azuma's leg for over an hour to let him join his squad. Calm down, Koarai the koala!! His hair is the product of careful styling.

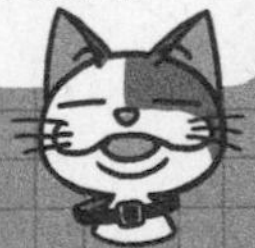

MAKO
Natural Born Big Sister

Azuma Squad's big sister. She doesn't even have younger brothers, yet this child prodigy was born with a responsible personality. She's school friends with Kagami, Kon and Zoe. Her grandfather died protecting her in the first invasion, so after thinking long and hard about what she could do with the rest of her life, she decided to join Border. Okudera and Koarai tagged along with her. Good luck, C-cup.

HYAMI
Slick

The top B-rank Operator and one of the countless Torimaru fans at HQ. She was the shy, nervous type, but Hatohara asked her, "Why be nervous around anyone who isn't Karasuma?" And then she conquered her fears in two seconds. She has the slickest hair out of all the characters, courtesy of my editor's finishing touches...he's very particular about female characters. An A-cup girl in love.

HIKARI
Sleepy Helpful Sister

She has some of the worst grades among the 17-year-olds, but she's pretty competent as an Operator. She's an all-business powerful strategist willing to sacrifice Zoe. She succeeded in placing the kotatsu in their Strategy Room by taking credit for recruiting Yuzuru to their squad. She has a younger brother at home, but since he's brilliant and doesn't need to be taken care of, she's always hungry for someone to fawn over. This B-cup hates the cold.

ENEDORAD
Ultimate Reincarnation

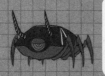

It's a combination of the top three *moe* characters in *World Trigger*, sending a soft shock through the industry! This guy's willing to hand out all sorts of secret information. Now that Replica's gone, he's aiming for the *moe* and mascot roles. When he appeared in the same panel as Mr. Kinuta, who also fulfills both roles, I wondered if I pandered to readers too much. One of my favorite characters.

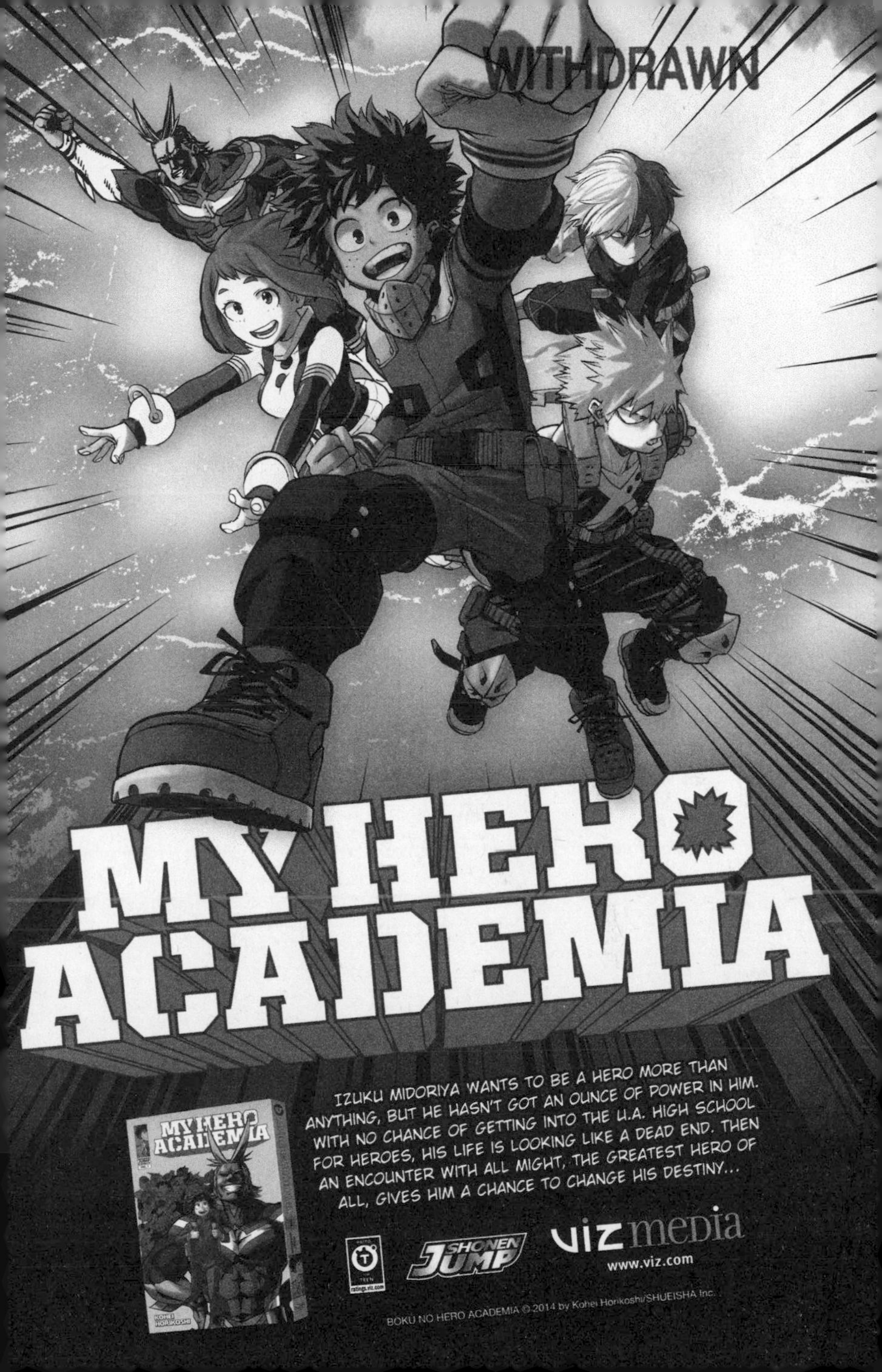
WITHDRAWN
MY HERO ACADEMIA
IZUKU MIDORIYA WANTS TO BE A HERO MORE THAN ANYTHING, BUT HE HASN'T GOT AN OUNCE OF POWER IN HIM. WITH NO CHANCE OF GETTING INTO THE U.A. HIGH SCHOOL FOR HEROES, HIS LIFE IS LOOKING LIKE A DEAD END. THEN AN ENCOUNTER WITH ALL MIGHT, THE GREATEST HERO OF ALL, GIVES HIM A CHANCE TO CHANGE HIS DESTINY...
MY HERO ACADEMIA
KOHEI HORIKOSHI
TEEN
ratings.viz.com
SHONEN JUMP
viz media
www.viz.com
BOKU NO HERO ACADEMIA © 2014 by Kohei Horikoshi/SHUEISHA Inc.

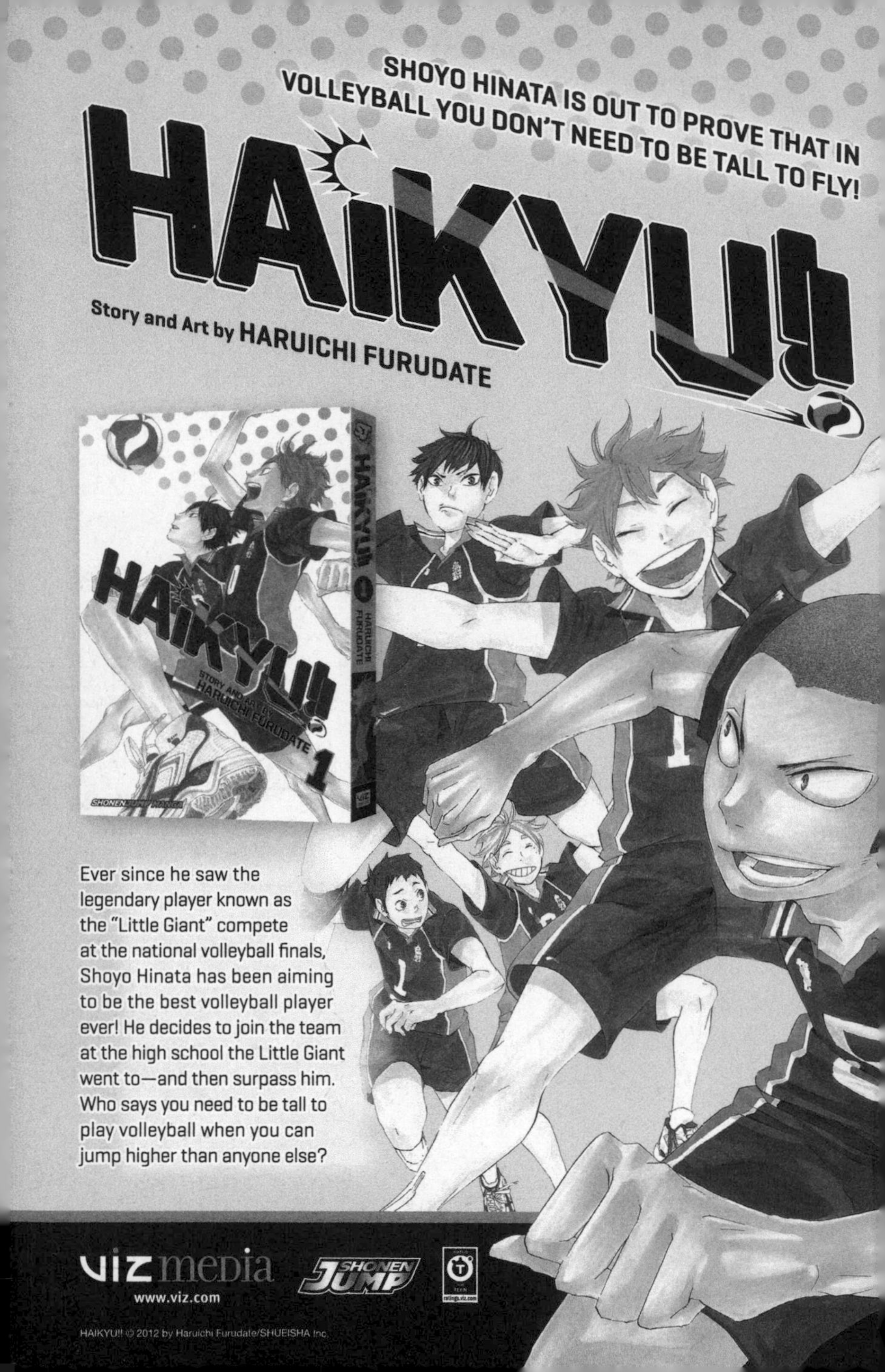

SHOYO HINATA IS OUT TO PROVE THAT IN VOLLEYBALL YOU DON'T NEED TO BE TALL TO FLY!
HAIKYU!!
Story and Art by HARUICHI FURUDATE
HAIKYU!! 1
STORY AND ART BY HARUICHI FURUDATE
SHONEN JUMP MANGA
Ever since he saw the legendary player known as the "Little Giant" compete at the national volleyball finals, Shoyo Hinata has been aiming to be the best volleyball player ever! He decides to join the team at the high school the Little Giant went to—and then surpass him. Who says you need to be tall to play volleyball when you can jump higher than anyone else?
viz media
www.viz.com
SHONEN JUMP
TEEN
ratings.viz.com
HAIKYU!! © 2012 by Haruichi Furudate/SHUEISHA Inc.

YOU'RE READING THE WRONG WAY!

World Trigger reads from right to left, starting in the upper-right corner. Japanese is read from right to left, meaning that action, sound effects, and word-balloon order are completely reversed from the English order.

142